FRENCH AND JEWISH

THE LITTMAN LIBRARY OF
JEWISH CIVILIZATION

*The Littman Library of Jewish Civilization is a registered UK charity
Registered charity no. 1000784*

FRENCH AND JEWISH

Culture and the Politics of Identity in Early Twentieth-Century France

NADIA MALINOVICH

London
The Littman Library of Jewish Civilization
in association with Liverpool University Press

The Littman Library of Jewish Civilization
Registered office: 4th floor, 7–10 Chandos Street, London WIG 9DQ

in association with Liverpool University Press
4 Cambridge Street, Liverpool L69 7ZU, UK
www.liverpooluniversitypress.co.uk/littman

Managing Editor: Connie Webber

Distributed in North America by
Oxford University Press Inc., 198 Madison Avenue,
New York, NY 10016, USA

First published in hardback 2008
First published in paperback 2012

Catalogue records for this book are available from the
British Library and the Library of Congress

ISBN 978–1–906764–25–8

Publishing co-ordinator: Janet Moth
Proofreading: Kate Clements
Index: Nadia Malinovich
Designed and typeset by Pete Russell, Faringdon, Oxon.

Printed and bound in Great Britain by
CPI Group (UK) Ltd., Croydon, CR0 4YY

For my mother,
MYRIAM MIEDZIAN

and in loving memory of my father,
STANLEY MALINOVICH

◆

Acknowledgements

THE SUPPORT and encouragement of many individuals and institutions were vital in bringing this project to fruition. I would like to begin by thanking my first mentors, Joel Doerfler and Geoffrey Blodgett, who sparked my interest in history and encouraged me early on in academic pursuits. Todd Endelman, my adviser at the University of Michigan, guided me through the process of research and writing the dissertation that this book grew out of, as did doctoral committee members Laura Lee Downs, Raymond Grew, and Anita Norich.

The Rachkam School of Graduate Studies at the University of Michigan, the Memorial Foundation for Jewish Culture, and the National Foundation for Jewish Culture provided research and writing grants. Members of the staff of the library at the Alliance Israélite Universelle in Paris, where I completed the majority of my research, were always helpful and created a friendly work environment that was very much appreciated. Both Aron Rodrigue and Paula Hyman provided direction in the early stages of the project and encouragement once it was completed. Marion Kaplan and Maud Mandel generously read the completed dissertation and gave me suggestions for revisions.

A Dorot Post-Doctoral Fellowship in the Department of Hebrew and Judaic Studies at New York University in 2001/2 provided the opportunity to begin transforming the dissertation into a book, as did the continuing encouragement and advice of Todd Endelman and Laura Lee Downs, whose support, both personal and professional, has been invaluable to me since I relocated to France in 2002.

Catherine Nicault also helped me to regain my footing in France, and I am particularly grateful to her for inviting me to co-ordinate an issue of *Archives juives* dedicated to the 'Réveil juif des années vingt' that I describe in the pages to come. The opportunity to participate in dialogue with the colleagues who contributed to this volume, including Catherine Nicault, Catherine Fhima, Dominique Jarrassé, Chantal Meyer-Plantureux, and Michel Leymarie, was extremely helpful to me as I prepared the final version of the manuscript. Thanks also to Ronald Schecter for his enthusiasm for the project and invitation to contribute to a special issue of *Historical Reflections* on the significance of French Jewish history, as well as to Evelyn Ackerman, whose glowing praise for the manuscript encouraged me immensely.

Other friends and colleagues too numerous to name provided support and encouragement at different stages. I would particularly like to thank Lisa Moses Leff, the first reader of my first chapter, and Eric Goldstein, with whom I have had many helpful conversations over the years. It has been a pleasure to work with Janet Moth, Connie Webber, and Ludo Craddock at the Littman Library. The Hanadiv Charitable Foundation (now the Rothschild Foundation Europe) helped finance the publication of the book.

I could not have completed this book without the love and support of my family. Thank you to my mother, Myriam Miedzian (who helped translate the quotes from French), my stepfather Gary Ferdman, my sister and best friend Alisa Malinovich, and my dear relation, fellow historian, and always willing reader and critic, Bonnie Anderson.

My husband Max Silberztein has seen me through from beginning to end, and I can only begin to thank him for his enthusiasm and encouragement, both professional and personal. Our wonderful children, Avram and Rosa, arrived just as I was beginning to transform the dissertation into a book, and special thanks go to Justyna Iwanicka, a niania who has made it a pleasure to be both a mother and a historian.

I only wish that I could place this book in the hands of my father, Stanley Malinovich, whose steadfast love and faith in me I will always carry in my heart.

Contents

List of Illustrations

Note on Transliteration and Conventions Used in the Text

THE transliteration of Hebrew in this book reflects consideration of the type of book it is, in terms of its content, purpose, and readership. The system adopted therefore reflects a broad approach to transcription, rather than the narrower approaches found in the *Encyclopaedia Judaica* or other systems developed for text-based or linguistic studies. The aim has been to reflect the pronunciation prescribed for modern Hebrew, rather than the spelling or Hebrew word structure, and to do so using conventions that are generally familiar to the English-speaking reader.

In accordance with this approach, no attempt is made to indicate the distinctions between *alef* and *ayin*, *tet* and *taf*, *kaf* and *kuf*, *sin* and *samekh*, since these are not relevant to pronunciation; likewise, the *dagesh* is not indicated except where it affects pronunciation. Following the principle of using conventions familiar to the majority of readers, however, transcriptions that are well established have been retained even when they are not fully consistent with the transliteration system adopted. On similar grounds, the *tsadi* is rendered by 'tz' in such familiar words as barmitzvah. Likewise, the distinction between *ḥet* and *khaf* has been retained, using *ḥ* for the former and *kh* for the latter; the associated forms are generally familiar to readers, even if the distinction is not actually borne out in pronunciation, and for the same reason the final *heh* is indicated too. As in Hebrew, no capital letters are used, except that an initial capital has been retained in transliterating titles of published works (for example, *Shulḥan arukh*).

Since no distinction is made between *alef* and *ayin*, they are indicated by an apostrophe only in intervocalic positions where a failure to do so could lead an English-speaking reader to pronounce the vowel-cluster as a diphthong—as, for example, in *ha'ir*—or otherwise mispronounce the word.

The *sheva na* is indicated by an *e*—*perikat ol*, *reshut*—except, again, when established convention dictates otherwise.

The *yod* is represented by *i* when it occurs as a vowel (*bereshit*), by *y* when it occurs as a consonant (*yesodot*), and by *yi* when it occurs as both (*yisra'el*).

Names have generally been left in their familiar forms, even when this is inconsistent with the overall system.

Unless otherwise noted, translations from French sources are by the author.

Abbreviations

AAIS   Association Amicale des Israélites Saloniciens

AJJ   Association des Jeunes Juifs

LICA   Ligue Internationale contre l'Antisémitisme

PCF   Parti Communiste Français

SFIO   Section Française de l'Internationale Ouvrière

UPJ   Université Populaire Juive

UUJJ   Union Universelle de la Jeunesse Juive

Introduction

THIS STUDY of Jewish cultural innovation and self-definition in early twentieth-century France highlights the complex and ambivalent nature of Jewish grappling with the issue of identity in the modern world. During this period a growing number of French Jews began to question how they should define Jewishness in a society where Jews enjoyed full political equality. Writers who had previously given little thought to their Jewish identity began to explore biblical themes, traditional Jewish folklore, and issues of identity and assimilation in their novels, plays, and poetry. A plethora of journals focusing on Jewish religion, history, and culture came into being in France between 1900 and 1932, when a multitude of associations that emphasized Jewish distinctiveness—literary societies, youth groups, religious organizations—also formed. This blossoming of Jewish cultural life, which contemporaries often referred to as a 'renaissance' or 'awakening', provides a particularly interesting vantage-point from which to explore the complex ways in which both 'Jewishness' and 'Frenchness' were renegotiated in the early twentieth century.

Scholars have documented the variety of responses to modernity that Jews have developed over the last two centuries. To be sure, different and opposing 'camps' have played an important role in shaping Jewish life in the modern period. As this study demonstrates, however, exploring the interface between these various groups is as important as delineating the differences between them. French Jews argued from a variety of perspectives—Orthodox versus Reform, religious versus secular, Zionist versus integrationist—and it is the dialogue that ensued from these debates that infused new energy into French Jewish identity and culture in the early twentieth century.

The expansion of Jewish cultural life that took place in France during this period was part of a larger shift in Jewish identity and community in the West. Historians of Germany and the United States in particular have documented the founding of Jewish community centres, youth groups, and sports clubs, as well as the creation of new forms of Jewish literature, art, and scholarship, as part of the transition from a religious to an ethno-cultural form of Jewish identity.[1] The trajectory of Jewish social and political integration in France has often been contrasted to the situation in both central Europe, where antisemitism strongly delineated the parameters of Jewish life, and the United States, where a more pluralistic society allowed for greater expression of Jewish cultural autonomy. In fact, French Jews were not immune to the social and cultural forces that reshaped Jewish life elsewhere during this period. The ways in which they acted on and articulated their changing sense of identity, however, were dictated by the specific French national context.

French republican social and political policy was firmly rooted in the principle of individual rights, and as a result state-supported anti-Jewish discrimination, which kept Jews out of the liberal professions and government positions elsewhere in Europe, did not exist in France. As Pierre Birnbaum has shown, the majority of Jews active in politics during the Third Republic maintained open ties with the Jewish community: unlike their counterparts in central Europe, they felt little pressure to practise radical forms of assimilation such as conversion or name-changing.[2] At the same time, however, the centralizing thrust of French social and political policy, with its ideological commitment to encouraging cultural assimilation at the expense of regional, religious, or other group identities, created a set of challenges particular to French Jewry.

From the time of the revolution the French nation has been conceived of as a universal political entity that stands above any particular group interest. While in reality, of course, this concept of citizenship has always been strongly linked to adaptation to French social and cultural norms, the power of the universalist paradigm has shaped the ways in which groups expressing particularisms of any kind—whether rooted in class, religion, ethnicity, or region—have worked out their own sense of difference. This holds true for Jews as well, who, above all, sought to cast a positive light on Jewish particularism by reconciling notions of cultural difference with French values and identity.

In his study of Jewish culture in Weimar Germany, Michael Brenner describes the creation of a distinct German Jewish cultural sphere, similar to other 'subcultures' such as those of workers and Catholics, which played an

---

[1] In Germany this intensification of Jewish cultural life and move towards a self-consciously ethnic sense of Jewish identity followed a similar time-line as in France, as Michael Brenner has shown in *The Renaissance of Jewish Culture in Weimar Germany*. In the United States, scholars have described a Jewish cultural revival beginning as early as the 1880s. See e.g. Sarna, *JPS: The Americanization of Jewish Culture, 1888–1988*, and *A Great Awakening*; Schwartz, *The Emergence of Jewish Scholarship in America*; and Kaufman, *Shul with a Pool*.

[2] Birnbaum, *The Jews of the Republic*.

important role in German society and political life in the early twentieth century.[3] I have found, however, that, unlike their German counterparts, French Jews did not create a distinctive subculture. Their associations and publications were characterized by a high degree of non-Jewish interest and participation, blurring the boundaries between 'Jewish' and 'French' culture. Furthermore, in France—where antisemitism was generally thought to be declining in the years following the First World War—the creation of new forms of Jewish associational and cultural life was less motivated by a sense of alienation from the mainstream than in either Germany or the United States. French Jews who created new forms of Jewish cultural life in the 1920s did not reject the nineteenth-century ideal of Jewish integration and acculturation. Rather, they attempted to work out a new kind of French–Jewish synthesis in step with the changing cultural and social realities of the day.

Both the arrival of east European immigrants and the birth of the Zionist movement opened up new avenues for discussion of the nature of Judaism and the place of Jews in French society. The 1880s marked the beginning of the immigration of east European Jews to France, which became much more important after 1905. These immigrants, who had not experienced a century of integration and acculturation, provided native French Jews with a living model of a public, visible brand of Jewishness openly defined in ethno-cultural terms. Similarly, the birth of the Zionist movement in 1897, based on the idea that the Jews comprised a 'nation' rather than a religious group, introduced an ethno-cultural schema for thinking about Jewish identity. Shifts in the broader French cultural landscape also played an important role in this process. In the aftermath of the French Revolution, progressive republican thought was strongly wedded to a universalist paradigm of citizenship. From the late nineteenth century, however, an ethnically rooted 'blood and soil' understanding of what it meant to be French became more pervasive. By the early 1930s, one scholar of the period concludes, there was no longer a debate as to whether one could distinguish between the legally defined, politically constituted *pays légal* and the historical, cultural *pays réel*. People across the political spectrum took for granted the existence of the latter, and debate focused on what values and cultural heritage constituted this true, essential France.[4]

---

[3] Brenner, *The Renaissance of Jewish Culture in Weimar Germany*.

[4] Lebovics, *True France*. On the increasing pervasiveness of a racial/ethnic understanding of Frenchness in the early 20th century, see also Brubaker, *Citizenship and Nationhood in France and Germany*, and Ezra, *The Colonial Unconscious*.

This shift posed a particular set of problems for Jews, who were at once the most enduring minority group within French society and among the most ardent defenders of a universal model of republicanism. From the early twentieth century a growing number of French Jews, like their non-Jewish compatriots, became entranced by a romantic, essentialist sense of connection to their heritage. As the primary 'other' against which the antisemitic movement posited its ethno-cultural understanding of national identity, however, these same Jews knew that they could not be French in a France defined in anything other than universalist political terms. Though they might criticize some of the tenets of nineteenth-century liberalism—in particular its devaluing of group difference—they were not free to reject the universalist values of 1789. Rather, they faced the challenge of creating a politics of identity that would both legitimate Jewish particularism and affirm universalist principles of citizenship.

Historians have tended to understand Franco-Judaism—the synthesis between Jewish and French values that Jewish communal and religious leaders worked out in the aftermath of the French Revolution—as a relatively stable set of ideological principles framing French Jewish identity from the revolution until the collapse of the Third Republic in 1940. In fact, this ideology underwent important transformations in the early decades of the twentieth century. For the most part, nineteenth-century French Jews operated from the assumption that they could only legitimately assert their place in the French nation as members of a religious minority. By the early 1930s, in contrast, the idea that Jews formed a distinct ethnic or cultural group had become widely accepted, both among Jews and within French society as a whole.[5] This shift, in turn, entailed a rethinking of the synthesis between 'Frenchness' and 'Jewishness' characteristic of nineteenth-century Franco-Judaism. French Jews in the 1920s challenged a previously assumed dichotomy between universalism and particularism. Rather than trying to legitimate Jewish particularism by demonstrating Judaism's universal value, they argued that French 'universalism' and Jewish 'particularism' were com-

[5] Most discussions of Franco-Judaism focus on its evolution over the course of the 19th century. Graetz, *The Jews in Nineteenth-Century France*, and Jay Berkowitz, *The Shaping of Jewish Identity in Nineteenth-Century France*, describe the fashioning of a modern Jewish identity on the part of French Jewish intellectuals and communal leaders in the first half of the 19th century. Albert's classic study, *The Modernization of French Jewry*, shows the ways in which this ideology played itself out on an institutional level, and Simon-Nahum, *La Cité investie*, analyses the ways in which 19th-century Jewish intellectuals understood Judaism itself. These scholars have generally looked ahead to the inter-war years only to show the extent to which French Jews took their solid attachment to the republican state for granted by the early 20th century. One of Birnbaum's primary objectives in *The Jews of the Republic*, for example, is to show similarities in ideology and behaviour of French Jews in public office from the birth of the Third Republic in 1871 to its fall in 1940.

plementary, and, in turn, that French Jewish identity should be based on a synthesis between them.

Discussion of Jews in Weimar Germany, Michael Brenner notes, has tended to focus on prominent figures who played a critical role in the broader Weimar cultural and political life of the day. As his study demonstrates, however, the Weimar years also saw the creation of a distinctive German Jewish culture, from the Lehrhaus movement for the study of Jewish classics to modern forms of Jewish literature, music, and art. In a similar vein, the prominence of figures such as Emile Durkheim, Marcel Proust, and Léon Blum in French cultural and political life in the early twentieth century—figures who are often hailed as signs of the strongly assimilationist bent of French Jewish culture—has masked the fact that during this same period a significant number of French Jews, like their German counterparts, were actively engaged in creating new forms of Jewish cultural life and adapting their Jewish identity to the contemporary world.

These Jews identified themselves as French and wrote in French. A sizeable Yiddish-speaking community was also an important element in French Jewish life in the 1920s. Its concerns and perspectives differed greatly from those of Francophone Jews, and it is for this reason that I have not included a discussion of the Yiddish press or the immigrant associational structure in the present study. People active in the Yiddish-speaking Parisian Jewish world in the 1920s were almost exclusively foreign-born Jews who had arrived in France as adults, and their publications and organizational structure addressed their own needs and concerns.[6] The world that I describe here, by contrast, is one where people of immigrant and native backgrounds mingled—and in some instances, to be sure, came into conflict—propelled by a shared interest in Jewish history, culture, and religion, and a desire to question the meaning of Jewish identity in the modern world.

This world has been largely eclipsed by historians' emphasis on the rift between integrated, middle-class 'natives' and the culturally distinct immigrants from eastern Europe whom they were desperately trying to assimilate.[7] Important tensions did exist between these two groups. Many French Jews of long standing were made uncomfortable by the newcomers' numbers and poverty, as well as by the 'visibility' of their Jewishness in the public sphere, and sought to remake the immigrants in their own image as quickly as possible. Jews from an immigrant background, for their part, were often

[6] On the Yiddish press in France in the inter-war years, see Benain and Kicheleweski, 'Parizer Haynt et Naïe Presse'.

[7] This is a prominent theme both in the works of specialist students of French Jewry and in more general literature on European Jewry in the 20th century, from Hyman's classic *From Dreyfus to Vichy* to Gartner's more recent survey, *History of the Jews in Modern Times*.

resentful of the condescending attitude of 'natives' and their refusal to share power within communal institutions.[8]

This study, however, suggests that, important as these tensions and conflicts were, they represent only one aspect of the interaction between native and immigrant French Jews in the 1920s. Many of the new journals, associations, and clubs whose activities and discussions I focus on here provided a meeting-place between natives and immigrants. They also met the needs of a new generation of French Jews who had immigrated as children or were the sons and daughters of immigrants, and who thus did not fit neatly into the category of either 'immigrants' or 'natives'.

The activities and ideas that I describe were not those of the majority of French Jews, but rather of a vocal and influential minority. In this era, many loosened the ties to their Jewish heritage in favour of an uncomplicated integration into French society and culture. But those Jews who created new paradigms of French Jewish identity had a powerful voice in both the Jewish community and French society as a whole. They created Jewish youth groups and cultural associations, and wrote articles and books that brought the issues of Jewish identity and assimilation into French public discourse. Some of the people involved with this expansion of Jewish cultural life and self-reflection, in particular rabbis and other religious leaders, were voices that remained primarily within the Jewish community. Others were prominent French intellectuals and political figures, both Jews and non-Jews, whose ruminations influenced the way in which French people in general understood the nature of Jewish identity and the relationship of the Jews to French society as a whole.

I explore this development on two levels. First, I describe the emergence of new forms of Jewish associational life created between the time of the Dreyfus affair and the early 1930s, identifying the principal actors and the relations among them. Second, I develop a typology of themes in the Jewish press and literature of the period. My objective is first and foremost to describe a phenomenon—a self-proclaimed Jewish cultural renaissance or awakening—rather than the ideas of a particular group of individuals or organizations.[9] In so doing, I hope to provide a panoramic view of the ways

---

[8] Power struggles, discussions, and debates within Jewish communal institutions and the concerns raised by leaders of the immigrant and native communities have been well documented, in particular by Paula Hyman in *From Dreyfus to Vichy*.

[9] Several scholars have touched on aspects of this renewed interest in Jewish identity and culture in the early 20th century in a variety of different contexts. In *Les Deux Terres promises*, Abitbol discusses the blossoming of the French Jewish press and youth movement in the 1920s as one component of French Zionism. Hyman devotes a chapter to Jewish youth movements in *From Dreyfus to Vichy*, and the Jewish scouting movement is the subject of Michel's study, *Juifs, Français et Scouts*. Poujol's biography of one of the central figures in the Jewish ren-

in which a wide variety of people discussed and debated the question of Jewish identity—and the concept of a Jewish awakening itself—in early twentieth-century France.

The years between the Dreyfus affair and the rise of Nazi Germany were relatively free of crisis for French Jewry. Jews felt confident enough about their place in French society to formulate new ways of talking about being Jewish without worrying unduly about whether their statements would exacerbate antisemitism. Although many of the cultural developments that began in the years around the First World War continued to flourish in the 1930s, the political and social crises of those years necessarily created a new set of priorities. The rise of Nazi Germany and the influx of German Jewish refugees, as well as the resurgence of antisemitism in France in the mid-1930s, belied the assumption—dominant in France in the post-war years—that antisemitism was atavistic and in the process of disappearing with the progress of democracy. The kind of speculation about the nature of Jewish identity in the modern world and Jewish particularism in France that had dominated communal discourse in the 1920s gave way to a new emphasis on combating antisemitism, and many of the organizations and press organs that were at the centre of the Jewish cultural renaissance of the 1920s

aissance of the 1920s, Aimé Pallière (1868–1949): Itinéraire d'un chrétien dans le judaïsme, provides information on the origins and development of the French Reform, inter-faith, and youth movements, and the second volume of her doctoral dissertation of the same title includes additional information on the Union Universelle de la Jeunesse Juive. On Jewish youth movements in the inter-war years, see Danielle Delmaire's synthetic overview, 'Mouvements de jeunesse juifs en France, 1919–1939'. Pougatch's biography of the founder of the Jewish Scouts, Un bâtisseur: Robert Gamzon, and Hammel's biography of Claude Gutman, the founder of the Jeunesse Libérale Israélite, Souviens-toi d'Amalek, focus primarily on their founders' activities and fate during the Second World War. In his classic study, Anatomie du judaïsme français, Wladimir Rabinovitch (who adopted the pen name Rabi after the Second World War) provides a synthetic discussion of Jewish literature in the 1920s as well as some biographical information on particular authors. On French Jewish writers in the inter-war years, see also Feigelson, Ecrivains juifs de langue française, and Rodrigue, 'Rearticulations of French Jewish Identities after the Dreyfus Affair'. Catherine Fhima, who is writing a thesis entitled 'Un milieu d'écrivains juifs français: Identités terminables et interminables (1890–1930)' at the Ecole des Hautes Etudes en Sciences Sociales, has published several articles on Jewish writers in the 1920s. See 'Aux sources d'un renouveau identitaire juif en France'; 'Les Ecrivains juifs français et le sionisme'; 'Jean-Richard Bloch et la renaissance culturelle juive'; and Fhima and Nicault, 'Victor Basch et la judéité'. See also Archives juives, 36/1 (2003), which is devoted to the Jewish press in France in the inter-war years, and the issue entitled 'La Renaissance juive en France des années vingt', which I co-ordinated for Archives juives, 39/1 (2006). (Readers should note that there are occasional discrepancies in the titles of articles in Archives juives, between the journal's cover, table of contents, and the actual article headings; throughout I have given the titles as they appear in the table of contents.) See also my articles '"Orientalism" and the Construction of Jewish Identity'; 'Une expression du "Réveil juif" des années vingt: La Revue Menorah'; 'Race and the Construction of Jewish Identity'; and 'Between Universalism and Particularism'.

curtailed their activities or became much more politically oriented.[10] Recent scholarship on French Jewry suggests that, despite the trauma of the Holocaust, it did not mark a point of ultimate rupture for the basic ideological orientation of the French Jewish community's commitment to France.[11] Changes in French Jewish discourses of identity that took place during this period, however, set the stage for the period after the Second World War, when French Jews once again started to build on the changes in self-understanding and self-perception that had their origin in the early years of the twentieth century.

◆

Chapter 1 provides background on Jewish social and cultural history in the nineteenth century, and describes the complex impact of the Dreyfus affair on French Jewry. Whereas the first generations of post-revolutionary Jewish intellectuals and communal leaders had been primarily concerned with promoting Jewish integration and acculturation, the emergence of ethnic nationalism and the modern antisemitic movement forced French Jews to negotiate between a commitment to universalist Enlightenment principles and the racialized, essentialized discourses of identity that were becoming normative by the end of the nineteenth century. It was the explosion of the Dreyfus affair that forced certain among them to openly question the Franco-Judaism of their parents' and grandparents' generations and confront the complexity of Jewish identity in the modern world head-on. As well as being a high-water mark for antisemitism in France, the affair prompted a more sympathetic attitude towards Jews in French leftist circles that made them a welcome home for Jews grappling with issues of antisemitism and identity. A troubled engagement with the romantic, essentialist brand of nationalism that was coming into vogue in intellectual circles during this period also played a role in the 'return' to Judaism of a number of young Jewish intellectuals of this generation. Importantly, however, these young French Jews did not feel free, as did their non-Jewish colleagues, to reject the universalist ideals of 1789. As they were well aware, the Jews could not be French in a France defined in anything other than universalist political terms. As a result, they were faced with the challenge of carving out a place for themselves in the French nation that would allow them to express their

---

[10] In her synthetic history *The Jews of Modern France* Paula Hyman notes that, in contrast to the 1930s, 'antisemitism [played] virtually no political role in the France of the 1920s' (p. 145). While scholars differ in their assessment of the influence of antisemitism in French society, there is a consensus that it had increased markedly by the mid-1930s, well before the arrival of Vichy. See *Jews of Modern France*, 145–59.   [11] Mandel, *In the Aftermath of Genocide*.

particularism fully while simultaneously holding on to the values of republican universalism.

Chapter 2 explores this tension between universalism and particularism as expressed in the pre-war poetry, novels, and essays of André Spire, Edmond Fleg, Henri Franck, and Jean-Richard Bloch. By examining the question of Jewish identity in the modern world through a new lens, these writers paved the way for the much more widespread phenomenon of Jewish self-questioning that took place in the post-war years. André Spire's groundbreaking *Poèmes juifs* and *Quelques Juifs* offered a scathing critique of both Jewish assimilation and French antisemitism. Rather than breaking definitively with nineteenth-century Franco-Judaism, however, Spire remained torn between his new-found Jewish particularism and his continuing commitment to the ideals of Enlightenment universalism. Henri Franck's prose poem *La Danse devant l'arche*, which describes a young man's quest for the meaning of life, reveals a similar tension between affirming the specificity of his Jewish roots and embracing a larger French cultural heritage. Jean-Richard Bloch's epic saga of an Alsatian Jewish family, . . . *et Cie*, explores the issue of individual freedom and, more specifically, whether Jews should preserve their heritage or break free from tradition. Edmond Fleg's *Ecoute Israël*, which presents biblical and midrashic themes in a language accessible to a modern French audience, explores the tension between suffering and chosenness in Jewish history, and reflects Fleg's own struggle to understand what place his Jewish origins should have in his life. Ultimately, these 'firstwave' French Jewish writers were unsure as to how they should reconcile their deeply felt sense of belonging to France with the new importance that they had come to ascribe to their Jewish heritage. It was not a retreat into particularism that characterized their writing, but rather an obsession with dualism.

Chapter 3 focuses on the beginnings of the Zionist movement and Reform Judaism in France. A close study of the activities and publications of the Fédération Sioniste de France, created at the turn of the century, reveals an amalgam of French and east European cultural and political sensibilities, and suggests that, even before the First World War, Zionism may have had a broader influence on the outlook of French Jews than historians have previously assumed. Religious ferment also breathed new life into the French Jewish community in the pre-war years. The 1905 separation of church and state paved the way for the founding of the first Reform congregation in France in 1907. By modernizing the Jewish liturgy and Jewish religious practice along the lines of the German and English Reform movements, the founders of the Union Libérale Israélite hoped to make Judaism more relevant to the younger generation, which they feared was fast being lost to secularization and, to a lesser extent, conversion to Christianity. The birth of the Reform movement, in turn, inspired a group of young rabbis to articulate a defence of traditional Judaism centred around the journal *Foi et réveil*, founded in 1913. Although Zionist, Reform, and traditionalist Jews differed in their tactics and ideologies, they shared a sense of dissatisfaction with the status quo and an assumption that the nature of Jewish identity must be reconceptualized in modern terms to guarantee its survival in the twentieth century. Most importantly, these groups and publications created new social networks and an intellectual climate that encouraged questioning and debate on the issue of Jewish identity in the modern world.

Chapter 4 describes the impact of the First World War and the changes in French Jewish society that paved the way for the expansion of Jewish associational and cultural life in the 1920s. The war marked an important moment at which antisemitism subsided and Jewish belonging to the French nation was confirmed. At the same time, however, Jewish participation in the war helped to popularize the notion that Jews were no less French for proudly affirming their unique spiritual and cultural heritage. The link between issues of Jewish identity and national minority rights at the 1919 Peace Conference, the growth of the Zionist movement, and an increase in Jewish immigration from eastern Europe encouraged the expansion of Jewish associational life and self-questioning in the post-war years. While historians have tended to emphasize the gap between acculturated, French-speaking 'natives' and impoverished, Yiddish-speaking 'immigrants', the present study highlights both the diversity within these groups and the overlap between them. Even as the primary concern of the Consistory and Alliance Israélite Universelle was to assimilate the newcomers as quickly as possible, others within the French Jewish community joined forces with immigrants—many of whom were fluent in French and hailed from a middle-class background—to create new organizations and publications and debate issues of Jewish identity and culture. The line between the 'immigrant' and 'native' communities was also blurred by the coming of age of second-generation French Jews, as well as those who had immigrated to France as children. Many of these young men and women, looking for a 'middle ground' between French and east European Jewish cultures, participated with natives in new forms of Jewish associational life and culture in the years following the war.

Chapter 5 describes the expansion of Jewish associational life over the course of the 1920s. The growth of a whole variety of youth movements created unprecedented opportunities for young Jews to educate themselves about Jewish history and culture, debate the meaning of Jewish identity in the modern world, and, most importantly, socialize with one another. The first national youth movement, the religiously oriented Chema Israël, aimed to provide an institutional structure of educational and recreational activities that, its founders believed, were essential to transmit Judaism to future generations. The Union Universelle de la Jeunesse Juive (UUJJ), which reached the height of its popularity and influence in the mid-1920s, hoped to appeal to as wide a range of Jewish youth as possible and to build bridges between different communities. It was the Jewish scouting movement (the Eclaireurs Israélites de France), however, that was ultimately most successful in bringing together young Jews from different walks of life—religious, Zionist, secular, native, and immigrant. At least twenty smaller youth groups of varying religious, ideological, and social orientation, as well as a myriad of other organizations and activities—Hebrew classes, Zionist clubs, literary societies, debating clubs—were also created over the course of the decade. Whether they defined Judaism as a religion, a culture, a race, or a historical community, these groups shared the conviction that it was only by creating new spaces for Jewish sociability that French Jewry would survive into the next generation.

Chapter 6 focuses on the expansion of the Jewish press, the development of a lively Jewish art and music scene, and the strengthening of the interfaith movement. The creation of a wide variety of journals of differing Zionist, literary, and religious orientations marked an important change in contemporary French Jewish life. These journals served as a vehicle to discuss new developments in the Jewish associational and cultural life of the day and provided a forum to discuss diverse aspects of Jewish culture and history. The prominence of Jewish artists in the international Ecole de Paris was another important development in Jewish cultural life during the 1920s. The Jewish press reported regularly on these artists' shows, and on several occasions associations such as the UUJJ organized special exhibitions featuring their work. It was also during this period that French Jews began to form musical societies and choruses to perform Jewish music, from traditional religious compositions to Yiddish folk songs, in public settings. Hebrew classes, Zionist clubs, literary societies, and debating clubs also enlivened the Jewish public sphere. Many of these new associations and publications actively sought the participation of non-Jews. While they did this in part to bolster their legitimacy, they were also reacting to a new openness towards Judaism within liberal Christian circles. As encouraging conversion fell out of favour, Jews and Christians began to engage in inter-faith dialogue, seeking to educate themselves about each other's beliefs and establish a basis for mutual understanding.

Much of the discussion within these new press organs and associations focused on the question of identity itself: how Jewishness should be defined and expressed in contemporary French society. By the mid-1920s a number of critics had begun to voice concerns about this emphasis on self-definition. Many feared that these kinds of discussions—which often ended with more questions than answers—would ultimately do little to perpetuate new forms of Jewish culture or to encourage long-term community-building.

We see a similar set of concerns surrounding the emergence of a modern Jewish literature in the French language, the focus of Chapter 7. What had been the novelty of a few maverick intellectuals in the pre-war years became a recognized genre of writing in the 1920s, as Jewish writers began to publish novels, plays, poems, collections of folklore, and short stories exploring different aspects of Jewish life and the issues of assimilation and acculturation in modern society. Jewish literature in translation comprised one important component of this literary renaissance. French readers were also introduced to the world of east European and North African Jewry through novels and short stories written in French by writers who had migrated to France, often as children or young adults. It was also during this period that French Jews began to address a whole host of themes—generational conflict, assimilation, intermarriage—centred around the question of Jewish identity in contemporary France. Intellectuals who experienced a Jewish 'awakening' in the years before the First World War had struggled consciously with both a 'racial' sense of themselves as Jews and a commitment to an individualist model of identity. By the mid-1920s, an essentialized understanding of Jewishness had become much more widely acceptable both among Jews themselves and in French society as a whole, a development that provoked mixed feelings among Jewish writers. While some characters in this genre of fiction describe rediscovering their difference in a positive light, others experience their Jewishness as an all-encompassing primal force over which they have little control. While the Jewish press enthusiastically publicized this new wave of Jewish-themed literature, we also find concern that the emphasis on Jewish difference that had become fashionable in literary circles in the 1920s could easily dovetail with antisemitic perspectives.

Chapter 8 provides a typology of themes in the Jewish press of the day. Perhaps the most important influence on French Jewish discourse in the 1920s came from Zionism. In the Zionist-oriented press, Zionism and/or Jewishness were often equated with values held in high esteem in French society, such as justice, morality, fraternity, and universal humanism. The idea of the Jew as a 'link' between East and West provided a way for Jews to express their difference while simultaneously reinforcing the idea that they formed a vital and necessary element in Western culture. While some Zionist advocates in France remained committed to the idea of Zionism as a secular 'replacement' for a religiously based Jewish identity, a much more common discourse emphasized the spiritual and religious aspects of Zionist ideology, and by extension the idea that these two visions of Judaism should not be posed in oppositional terms. Similarly, many religious leaders sought to mesh the Zionists' ethno-cultural model of Jewishness with their continuing commitment to religion. Jewish religious discourse of the day reveals two central concerns: first, balancing a rationalist image of Judaism with an emphasis on the mystical, emotional aspect of the Jewish religion, and second, developing a theology that posed the universalist and particularist aspects of Judaism as complementary.

CHAPTER 1

Setting the Stage: Jewish Identity in the Nineteenth Century and the Impact of the Dreyfus Affair

IN THE AFTERMATH of the French Revolution, the Jews of France were officially transformed from a corporation tolerated by the king into individual members of a new nation based on the principle of citizenship. The Consistory was created by Napoleon in 1808 as a state-sanctioned Jewish governing council, giving the Jewish religion a legal status parallel to that of Protestantism and Catholicism, the other two officially recognized religions of France.[1] The French state charged this organization with the mission of transforming French Jews, who numbered approximately 40,000 at the beginning of the nineteenth century, from an autonomous community with a system of self-government and collective legal status into citizens of a modern nation for whom Judaism would be simply a set of religious beliefs. Inevitably, however, the issues raised by the Jews' particular history as a minority with a distinctive religion, history, and culture proved much more complicated to resolve than their legal status.[2] Even as French Jews became 'Israélites',[3] shedding many of their distinctive traits over the course of the nineteenth century, neither the wider society's understanding of them as a distinct group nor their own sense of particularism vanished. Rather, both they and their non-Jewish compatriots were faced with the very modern problem of negotiating a new political reality with age-old emotions, assumptions, and prejudices.

[1] For a comprehensive study of the Consistory, see Albert, *The Modernization of French Jewry*. For an interesting recent analysis of the Consistory arguing that it in fact perpetuated Jewish group distinctiveness in the post-revolutionary era, see Shurkin, 'Consistories and Contradictions'. On continuities between Jewish culture and community life in old- and new-regime France see also Jay Berkowitz, 'Ritual and Emancipation'.

[2] For an excellent recent analysis of French debates surrounding Jews and Judaism in the years preceding and immediately following the revolution see Schecter, *Obstinate Hebrews*.

[3] This term, intended to hark back to the Jews' biblical past and dissociate contemporary Jews from negative stereotypes of the medieval era, became the standard one by which Jews referred to themselves, and were referred to, in the 19th century. In the early 20th century the term began to be used, often pejoratively, to refer to 'assimilated' French Jews of long standing who insisted that Judaism was a purely religious identity that should be relegated to the private sphere.

The purely confessional understanding of Judaism as defined by the Consistory, contemporary scholars agree, never corresponded to the social reality of Jewish life in France. From the early nineteenth century on, French Jews founded charities, schools, and self-help organizations, and maintained a high degree of inter-group social relations, all activities that betrayed a strong sense of ethnic identity. As Phyllis Cohen Albert has pointed out, the generation of Jews born between 1820 and 1840 had in theory the choice of abandoning all forms of communal cohesion save synagogue attendance. In fact, however, this was the generation that created a Jewish press—the *Archives israélites* in 1840, followed by *L'Univers israélite* in 1844—as well as forming independent Jewish mutual aid societies, often in the face of consistorial opposition. These activities, Albert argues, show that Jewish integration into French society and culture did not erode a sense of attachment to Jewishness, but rather created the need for new forms of Jewish community and identity.[4]

The creation of the Alliance Israélite Universelle is perhaps the most salient example of the strong sense of ethnic solidarity that existed among French Jews in the nineteenth century. The Alliance was founded by a group of young French Jews who wanted to take a more active role in fighting anti-semitism and providing material support to the international Jewish community than the Consistory's ties to the French government would allow.[5] While the Alliance's leaders used the language of religious solidarity to gain support for their organization, they were clearly driven by a sense of community with Jews in other countries that had little to do with religion in the traditional sense.[6] As Jay Berkowitz has noted in his study of French Jewish identity in the nineteenth century, 'Although communities continued to be organized principally for the facilitation of religious services, Judaism as a religion had lost its attraction for many. Nevertheless, no formal ideology

---

[4] Albert, 'Ethnicity and Jewish Solidarity in Nineteenth-Century France', 261. This article was the first to point to a gap between 19th-century French Jews' ethnic behaviour and their religious self-definition. On the maintenance of French Jews' ethnic ties in the 19th century see also Albert, 'Israelite and Jew: How Did Nineteenth-Century French Jews Understand Assimilation?'; Birnbaum, *The Jews of the Republic*; and id. (ed.), *Histoire politique des Juifs en France*. This body of literature was responding to an earlier generation of scholars who tended to understand 19th-century Jewish history in western Europe from the linear perspective of 'assimilation', or the progressive loss of Jewish identity. For France, this line of argument is exemplified by Marrus's classic study, *The Politics of Assimilation*, in which he argues that French Jews identified with the Republic to the point of being blind to the persistence of anti-semitism.

[5] Albert makes this point in 'Ethnicity and Jewish Solidarity'. On the creation of the Alliance, see Chouraqui, *Cent ans d'histoire*, and Graetz, *The Jews in Nineteenth-Century France*.

[6] On the intellectual origins of the Alliance and modern Jewish internationalism, see Leff, *Sacred Bonds*.

was substituted in its place.'[7] While the social reality of their lives indicated otherwise, religion remained the only possible frame of reference for discussions of Jewish identity.

Throughout most of the nineteenth century French communal leaders and publicists did not openly debate this gap between ideology and practice because their priority was promoting and defending Jewish integration. Despite their changed legal status, in the first decades of the nineteenth century French Jews remained a highly distinct, culturally isolated minority. Alsatian Jews, who formed the vast majority of French Jewry during this period, continued to live in isolated communities and to engage in the same professions that they had followed before the revolution. The process of 'becoming Frenchmen', Paula Hyman emphasizes, was slow and a product of constant negotiation between the world of Jewish tradition and that of French society and culture.[8] As a result, the primary concern of Jewish intellectuals and publicists in the decades after emancipation was to 'regenerate' the Jewish masses in order to transform them into Frenchmen culturally as well as legally.[9] Jewish communal leaders and intellectuals were equally concerned with proving to the broader French society that the Jews were in fact fully capable of acculturation, a concern dictated by French Jewry's still tenuous social and political standing throughout much of the nineteenth century. While Jews retained the fundamental rights of citizenship that they had been granted during the revolution, they were still subject to discriminatory laws and restrictions in the tumultuous years that preceded the founding of the Third Republic in 1871.

Napoleon's 'infamous decree' of 1808, which instituted a ten-year series of economic restrictions on Alsatian Jews intended to counter usury, sent shock waves through the Jewish community. Under both the Bourbon Restoration, which gave back a great deal of power to the Catholic Church, and then again under the Second Empire, Jewish occupational possibilities were restricted. Though Judaism was recognized as a state religion by Napoleon, it was only after 1831 that rabbis' salaries, like those of priests and ministers, were paid by the government. A special Jewish oath, the More Judaico, was abolished by the High Court only in 1846, and as late as the 1860s Alsatian Jews were subject to a special tax intended to repay communal debts from the pre-revolutionary period.[10] While the central government remained committed to equality in principle, it often caved in to

---

[7] Berkowitz, *The Shaping of Jewish Identity*, 249.
[8] See Hyman, *The Emancipation of the Jews of Alsace*.
[9] On the ideology of regeneration, see Berkowitz, *The Shaping of Jewish Identity*.
[10] See Albert, *The Modernization of French Jewry*, 152.

local demands that Jews be removed from positions of public power and influence, in particular in teaching and law.

French Jewish communal leaders and intellectuals in the early nineteenth century were thus faced with a number of challenges. They needed to convince their fellow Jews that it was possible to integrate into the French nation while preserving their group distinctiveness, while at the same time convincing the French population at large that the Jews were truly worthy of the emancipation that they had been granted.[11] In order to promote these objectives, French Jews began to formulate new ways to talk about Judaism and the place of the Jews in the modern world. This ideology, which contemporary scholars have come to refer to as Franco-Judaism, was rooted in a synthesis of traditional Jewish religious concepts, such as messianism and the idea of the Jews as a 'light unto the nations', with French republican and nationalist ideals.

The intellectual origins of Franco-Judaism can be found in two main ideological currents of nineteenth-century Jewish historical scholarship. The first was the French version of Wissenschaft des Judentums, a school of German Jewish scholarship dedicated to the 'scientific study of Judaism'. In Germany the Wissenschaft school, which was founded at the beginning of the nineteenth century, was directly associated with the Jewish struggle for political equality. By showing that Judaism was in essence a rational religion perfectly compatible with belonging to a modern nation-state, German Jewish intellectuals wanted to prove that Jews should be granted full citizenship. While this political agenda did not exist to the same extent in France, the French Wissenschaft scholars, most importantly Salomon Munk, Joseph Derenbourg, and Adolphe Franck, all of whom were educated in Germany, shared the same basic ideological programme as their German counterparts: to define and defend the basic precepts of Judaism to both their fellow Jews and the surrounding non-Jewish society.[12]

Also important in the creation of Franco-Judaism were a number of 'peripheral' scholars and intellectuals who were often distanced from both the mainstream Jewish community and normative Judaism itself. As Michael Graetz shows in his study of the ideological origins of the Alliance Israélite Universelle, the ideas of scholars such as Joseph Salvador, the son of a Jewish father and a Catholic mother, or Léon Halévy, who was part of the Saint-Simonian movement, came to exercise an important influence on French Jewish intellectual life in the early nineteenth century, and ultimately played a key role in the creation of the Alliance in 1860.

[11] On protracted debates concerning French Jewish patriotism, see Berkowitz, *The Shaping of Jewish Identity*, ch. 2.

[12] On Wissenschaft scholarship in France, see Simon-Nahum, *La Cité investie*.

Despite their differences, these scholars shared a deeply progressive, universalist world vision that shaped their understanding of both Judaism and the nature of Jewish identity in the modern world. Informed by Hegelian and Saint-Simonian ideas, these scholars read Jewish history through a positivist lens. Responding to both Christian and Enlightenment thinking, which portrayed Judaism as a stagnant religion that had become irrelevant with the advent of Christianity, they wanted to show that Judaism was in fact constantly in the process of evolution towards a more universalist ideal. An important objective of both Salomon Munk's and Joseph Salvador's scholarship was to draw a parallel between the political life of ancient Israel and modern republican ideology.[13] From this perspective, ancient Israel was a proto-republic, organized around the same basic ideological principles as those that guided the French revolutionaries of 1789. This ideological perspective achieved two important goals: it enabled Jewish scholars to simultaneously defend Judaism and to express their commitment to the ideal of republican France during the years of the Restoration and the Second Empire. The revolutionary year 1848, Michael Graetz notes, was an important moment in the development of this discourse of French Jewish synthesis. Jews such as the writer Alexandre Weill, and Eugene Manuel and Isidore Cahen, both of whom would later become active in the founding of the Alliance Israélite Universelle, called upon their fellow Jews to leave their particularism behind and join in the universal struggle for human freedom: 'the faith in universal harmony and in reconciliation between religions and races banned every sign of Jewish particularism. Universal optimism dominated.'[14]

As Graetz has aptly argued, the creation of a universalist basis for Jewish identity posed a certain paradox: this new spiritualized Judaism, intended to remove all obstacles to integration, gave rise to a new concept of Jewish peoplehood: 'by emphasizing [Jewish] specificity, a specificity that lay, not only in the monotheistic idea or in a moral rule, but that was also a law, a way of life, a particular historical past, and a sociopolitical future—far from reducing their distance from the surrounding society, they were engaged in widening it'.[15] In other words, the Franco-Judaism that developed in the decades after emancipation was never as firmly rooted in an individualist,

---

[13] On Joseph Salvador, see Hyman, 'Joseph Salvador: Proto-Zionist or Apologist for Assimilation?   [14] Graetz, *The Jews in Nineteenth-Century France*, 200.

[15] Ibid. 239. Unfortunately, Graetz's perceptive analysis of this early French Jewish scholarship is somewhat marred by his conclusion that this ideology should be considered proto-Zionist, a contention that most scholars have dismissed as anachronistic and inaccurate. For a critique of Graetz's position, see Caron, 'French Jewish Assimilation Reassessed: A Review of the Recent Literature'.

'religious' model of Jewish identity as it pretended. It involved the retelling of the story of the Jewish people in terms consistent with the liberal values of the day, such as progress, liberty, and fraternity, and the surrounding political climate influenced what values and ideals were highlighted at any particular moment.[16]

For example, while most French Jewish intellectuals and communal leaders were hostile to the creation of the political Zionist movement at the start of the twentieth century, the first stirrings of modern Jewish nationalism in the 1860s met with widespread interest and enthusiasm among French Jews. This discrepancy, Phyllis Cohen Albert suggests, can be attributed at least in part to the weakness of centralizing Jacobin values and enthusiasm for emerging European nationalist movements during the Second Empire, both of which made French Jews of this generation less concerned than those who came before or after them that giving voice to the nationalist aspect of Jewish identity would compromise their French patriotism.[17]

French Jews overwhelmingly hailed the Third Republic as the final victory of the universalist principles of 1789 and a conception of citizenship based on the principle of legal equality: to be French meant to be born on French soil, irrespective of one's family origins. The establishment of these values as the guiding ideology of the French state gave Jews new confidence in belonging to the French nation and unprecedented opportunities for professional advancement. By the turn of the nineteenth century native French Jewry was overwhelmingly middle-class. While the majority of Jews continued to work in finance and commerce, they also played an important role in the political life of the Third Republic and were represented in the civil service in proportions far beyond their numbers in the wider society.[18] According to Pierre Birnbaum's calculations, 171 Jews attained high administrative positions within the French government under the Third Republic as prefects, generals, and state advisers, as well as in elected offices as ministers and senators.[19] As the last vestiges of state-sponsored discrimination fell

---

[16] Leff makes a similar point in her article 'Self-Definition and Self-Defense', which demonstrates that French Jewish intellectuals of the early 19th century, writing at a time when the word 'race' was used primarily to describe different historical and regional groups within France, developed the idea that the Jews—like the Gauls, Celts, and Franks—had their own distinctive racial traits that contributed to the strength of the French nation. By the late 19th century, however, the advent of modern racial 'science', with its emphasis on racial hierarchy rather than racial mixing, made the notion of a Jewish race much more loaded and problematic. On this shift, see my own article, 'Race and the Construction of Jewish Identity'.

[17] See Albert, 'Les Juifs de France et l'idée de restauration nationale'.

[18] This process had already begun during the Second Empire, as David Cohen has shown in *La Promotion des Juifs en France*. On Jewish professional distribution in the late 19th century, see Hyman, *From Dreyfus to Vichy*, ch. 2.   [19] Birnbaum *The Jews of the Republic*, 8.

away, Jews also began entering the liberal professions and the arts in large numbers.[20]

The fact that anti-clericalism—a campaign to reduce the power of the Catholic Church in state and society—was one of the central projects of the founders of the Third Republic facilitated Jewish integration. Those who entered French institutions of higher learning to prepare for careers in these fields did so at a time when the French education system had become firmly identified with republicanism and *laïcité*, a principle that encompasses a commitment to both the separation of church and state and a secular public sphere. A compulsory system of secular schools for children between the ages of 6 and 13 was voted into law in 1882. Positivism, a philosophical system based on the idea that human society can be explained through the application of scientific, rationalist principles, became the dominant philosophy in universities, and French educators were imbued with the mission of inculcating republican ideology in the first generation to be educated in republican schools. It was during this period that the modern French university system came into existence, and a new community of full-time liberal arts students was created in Paris.[21]

The entrenchment of the republican tradition, however, was accompanied by a counter-tradition: the birth of a new kind of nationalism rooted in the idea of group difference. Rather than grounding itself in the ideals of universal human rights and equality, the new nationalism saw shared history and ethnic origin as the glue that binds groups of people together. These kinds of ideas were intertwined with the rise of modern antisemitism, as the Jew became the primary 'other' against which new, racialized concepts of European nationhood were defined. The Jew represented the quintessential outsider who, despite his intellectual allegiance to the state, could never truly belong because of his foreign blood and spirit. These ideas spread throughout western Europe in the 1880s and 1890s as a new industry of antisemitic political tracts, newspapers, and political parties came into existence. In France, antisemitism gained popularity under the influence of Edouard Drumont. His famous newspaper, *La Libre Parole*, founded in 1892, blamed an international Jewish banking conspiracy for financial scandals such as the crash of the Union Générale bank in 1882 and the Panama crisis in 1892, and he published his antisemitic classic, *La France juive*, in 1886.

---

[20] See Hyman, *From Dreyfus to Vichy*, chs 1 and 2.

[21] Traditionally the student community primarily comprised law and medical students. It was only in 1877 that scholarships were established in the sciences and humanities, and the number of students in these domains quadrupled between 1875 and 1908. See Ory and Sirinelli, *Les Intellectuels en France*, 54.

The Dreyfus affair, of course, was the source of an avalanche of anti-semitic propaganda and publications. Most of the antisemitic ideas that gained currency among the anti-Dreyfusards—the association of Jews with capitalism and power, the belief that a Jewish syndicate controlled the French press, the idea that a Jew, no matter what his outward behaviour, could never truly be a member of the French nation—had already been formulated by the time that the affair exploded in 1897, but they now gained a much wider audience and a central place within French public discourse.[22]

This challenge to the ideology of universalism, however, was not limited to antisemitic groups, but rather was part of a broader cultural shift in French society across the political spectrum. A number of factors helped to create a more ethnic understanding of French identity, beginning in the 1880s. The sympathetic interest of left-wing French intellectuals in national movements of the late nineteenth century helped to normalize the idea of a state conceived in ethno-cultural terms. France's weakened status after its 1870 defeat in the Franco-Prussian war also encouraged a more particularist French patriotism. For early nineteenth-century French intellectuals such as Augustin and Amadée Thierry, Ernest Renan, and Hippolyte Tayne, 'race' was linked more to class than nation: they distinguished the French aristocracy, for example, from the rest of the Gallic population by its German descent. Thinking about race in this era was also associated with a discourse—typified in Jules Michelet's classic *Histoire de France*—that placed positive value on the idea that the French nation drew its strength from the wide variety of 'races'—Celts, Gauls, Franks—from which it had been forged. After 1870, by contrast, a new generation of intellectuals began to talk about a French 'race' that stood in contrast to its Anglo-Saxon or Teutonic rivals.[23]

This was a period of both massive urbanization and the popularization of culture—the birth of the modern press, avant-garde artistic movements, and the popular novel. While some hailed these developments as signs of the success of republican ideals in transforming French society, cultural innovation and progress also brought with them an obsession with degeneracy and decadence. New academic disciplines of the era—anthropology, sociology, psychology—revealed a rising scepticism about the ability of positivism to either explain the mystery of existence or create human happiness. While their founders used the language of science, many of the phenomena with

---

[22] On antisemitism in modern France, see Poliakov, *Histoire de l'antisémitisme*, vol. iv, and Stephen Wilson, *Ideology and Experience*.

[23] On this shift, see Balibar, 'Racism and Nationalism'; Brubaker, *Citizenship and Nationhood in France and Germany*, 99–102; and Lebovics, *True France*.

which they were concerned—Charcot's studies of madness and hypnosis, Gustave le Bon's studies of crowd psychology and criminology—were those that the rationalist approach of the previous generation had failed to explain.[24] Henri Bergson's philosophy, which gained immense popularity in France in the decade prior to the First World War, was based on the idea that intuition and spirituality are central to understanding human nature.[25] These kinds of ideas were not necessarily attached to conservative political agendas. Studies of human races and genotypes, for example, were the basis of the emerging field of anthropology, many of whose founders (such as Sylvain Lévi and Claude Lévi-Strauss) were Jews.

These shifts in how people understood human society and history exercised an important influence on Jewish intellectuals and publicists in the late nineteenth century. The primary goal of the second generation of Wissenschaft scholarship was not to universalize Judaism so much as to prove that the Jews had played a significant and positive role in shaping European—and in particular French—civilization.[26] Jewish intellectuals such as James Darmesteter, Théodore and Salomon Reinach, and Joseph Halévy were caught between defining Judaism in religious terms and defending the history of the Jewish people. All of these men had obtained important positions within the French academic world by the early 1880s and were among the founders of the Société des Etudes Juives, which began publishing the *Revue des études juives* in 1881.[27] As Perrine Simon-Nahum shows in her analysis of the *Revue*, Jewish scholarship became increasingly oriented towards combating antisemitism in the 1880s and 1890s. Whereas early articles aimed to bring to light various aspects of ancient Jewish history and religion, the focus soon shifted to the persecution of Jews in the Middle Ages, a topic that lent itself to refuting the kind of scholarly antisemitic arguments—for example, that antisemitism was the result of Jewish exclusivity—that were becoming increasingly prevalent in both academic circles and French society at large.

[24] For an overview of the French intellectual and cultural climate in the 1880s and 1890s, see Weber, *France: Fin de siècle*, which describes the rise of 'collectivist' organizations and attitudes—nationalist and regionalist movements, trade unions, and mass political parties—as a counterweight to liberalism.

[25] On Bergson's influence and popularity, see Grogin, *The Bergsonian Controversy*.

[26] Simon-Nahum, *La Cité investie*, 197.

[27] James Darmesteter was a philologist and professor at the Ecole des Hautes Etudes specializing in Hindi and Indian civilization. He began publishing scholarly work on Judaism in the early 1880s, including, most importantly, *Les Prophètes d'Israël*. Théodore Reinach was also a professor at the Ecole, where he taught the history of religion. Reinach's principal work of Jewish scholarship was his *Histoire des Israélites*. Joseph Halévy was born in Turkey in 1827 and began teaching Ethiopic at the Ecole in 1879. He was also a prominent Hebraist and frequent contributor to the *Revue des études juives*.

On the one hand, these scholars responded directly to negative portrayals of the role of the Jewish people throughout history that permeated French intellectual culture. While the eminent philologist Ernest Renan, for example, attributed Jewish historical separateness to the Jews' wilful desire to remain a people apart, Darmesteter and Reinach sought to prove that Jewish historical exclusiveness was a product of antisemitism, something externally imposed rather than intrinsic to the Jewish religion.[28] This line of argument, of course, was embedded in a discourse that assumed the existence of a Jewish people (not only a Jewish religion) that has played an active and positive role throughout history. In a world where nationalist narratives were becoming the dominant mode of history writing, these scholars wanted to prove that the Jewish people had a history as rich and influential as any other. Still caught within the contradictory framework of the discourse of emancipation, however, another central goal of Darmesteter, Reinach, and others of their generation was to defend the idea that Jews were distinct from other Frenchmen only in religious belief, an argument that they put forth as a counterweight to the essentialized characterizations of Jewish difference that were gaining ground during this period.

Jewish scholars in the second half of the nineteenth century, like the generation before them, emphasized the importance of the prophets as the bearers of a universal morality. Later scholars, however, put much more emphasis on the prophets as exponents of a 'personal' religion. For example, both James Darmesteter's *Les Prophètes d'Israël* and Théodore Reinach's *Histoire des Israélites* equated the 'essence of Judaism' with the words of the prophets, in which they located the origins of values such as universalism and humanism that were most often associated with Christianity. They intended this link to show that Judaism, like Christianity, was a spiritual tradition in no way contradictory to French nationalism. We see a similar trend in the writing of the Alsatian-born writer and journalist Alexandre Weill. Weill began writing on Jewish themes after his disillusionment with the failure of the surrounding society to fully integrate the Jews after the revolutions of 1848. While he had once been entirely committed to universalist ideals, he increasingly began to idealize the world of his Alsatian

---

[28] One of the central themes of European intellectual thought in the second half of the 19th century was the divide between 'Aryans' and 'Semites'. From this perspective, European civilization is directly descended from the Aryan tribes of India, who represent the highest level of human moral, social, and cultural development. The Semitic peoples of the Middle East by contrast are considered to have played a negligible or, even worse, negative role in the development of European civilization. For Renan, one of the foremost philologists of the day, for example, the very progress of European civilization was dependent on its distancing itself from 'the Semitic spirit'.

village and to search for a way to synthesize his French and Jewish identities.[29]

The generation of Jewish intellectuals of the 1880s and 1890s was thus caught between two visions and conceptions of Jewish identity. Its members were forced to negotiate between a commitment to the universalist principles of the Enlightenment and the French Revolution and the racialized, essentialized discourses of identity that were becoming normative at the turn of the century. At the same time that they were compelled to defend the 'Jewish people' against its detractors, their defence was essentially to evoke the principles of 1789. It was the generation of French Jews who came of age in the aftermath of the Dreyfus affair who were the first to break out of this paradigm and confront the complexities of Jewish identity in the modern world head on.

Breaking the Mould: The Dreyfus Affair and the Beginnings of a Jewish Cultural Renaissance

In a 1913 article for the *Revue de Paris*, the then literary and theatre critic Léon Blum heralded the birth of a new literary and intellectual generation in France. Each generation of intellectuals has its defining philosophy, Blum wrote, and for the generation that came of age around the turn of the century it was the rejection of a scientific, rational world-view that characterized its break with the past. 'A new energy has been released, freed of the mechanical universe where science reigns supreme. [This new spirit] feels itself to be in communion with other forces, ill defined but spiritual in nature, and bathed in a world filled with mystery.'[30] Interestingly, the figure that Blum chose to elaborate on as the embodiment of this generation was Henri Franck, an obscure Jewish poet who died at the age of 22, the year before Blum published his article. Franck's principal publication was *La Danse devant l'arche*, a book-length poem best described as a philosophical chronicle of a young man's quest for the meaning of life. Like others poets of his generation, Franck in his writings communicates a sense of searching for roots—a tangible, physical belonging to a particular place and history that he felt was missing from his life as an urbanized intellectual. Significantly, however, Franck did not simply describe the metaphysical yearnings of a young Frenchman, but rather invented a personal spiritual lineage that placed him in the historical trajectory of the Jewish people. For the historian Hans Kohn,

---

[29] On Weill, see Richard Cohen, 'Nostalgia and "Return to the Ghetto"', and Albert, 'Les Juifs de France et l'idée de restauration nationale', 30–2.

[30] Blum, 'La Prochaine Génération littéraire', repr. in id., *Œuvres*, ii. 429.

Franck was exemplary of 'the Jewish poets of western Europe' who came of age at the beginning of the twentieth century. It is in this generation, he noted, that there had been 'an intriguing renaissance of racial awareness among Jewish youth in the Western world'.[31]

Whereas the challenge of previous generations had been to synthesize their French and Jewish identities in order to provide an ideological basis to the process of Jewish integration, for Franck and his contemporaries integration was already a fait accompli. Born into highly acculturated, middle-class families, sent to French public schools, and immersed in a French cultural milieu, a certain number of French Jews now began to call into question the Franco-Judaism of their parents' generation. This phenomenon posed a certain paradox. This was the first generation to grow up within the political stability of the Third Republic, to be educated in republican schools, and to mix with non-Jews on a social level from a young age—in other words, to grow up more as 'Frenchmen' than as Jews. Why then, would Jews in this generation, having fulfilled their parents' and grandparents' dream of full integration, begin to question the very ideology that appeared to have made their success possible?

This new kind of Jewish self-questioning grew out of a confluence of social and cultural forces that came together at the turn of the century. The rise of political antisemitism, the irrationalist intellectual mood of the *fin de siècle*, the birth of the Zionist movement, and the influx of east European Jewish immigrants were all important changes in the landscape of French Jewish life that posed a challenge to Franco-Judaism. It was the explosion of the Dreyfus affair, however, that, by bringing 'the Jewish question' to the centre of French public discourse and creating new networks of social and cultural interaction, provided the necessary spark to produce the beginnings of a Jewish cultural awakening. As we shall see, however, the 'return' to Judaism in this generation took place through the conduit of its immersion in French republican culture. Jews of this era created a new way of being Jewish that was fully modern, and a product of their French, republican, identity rather than a rejection of it.

The Dreyfus Affair

The explosion of the Dreyfus affair brought 'the Jewish question' to the centre of French public discourse and created networks of social and cultural inter-

---

[31] Kohn, *L'Humanisme juif*, 82. Hans Kohn (1891–1971), a Czech-born historian best known for his landmark studies of nationalism published after the Second World War, lived in Paris, London, and Germany, as well as in Palestine in the 1920s, where he played an active role in the Zionist movement. He immigrated to the United States in 1933.

action that helped spark off a new kind of Jewish self-questioning in France. While Alfred Dreyfus was arrested and convicted for treason in 1894, it was not until 1898 that the affair came to the centre of the political arena. It was at this point that Emile Zola, convinced by evidence gathered by the Dreyfus family and first put forward by the fiery Jewish anarchist, writer, and journalist Bernard Lazare,[32] published *J'accuse*, which charged the army command with framing Dreyfus and covering up the identity of the true traitor. Thus the Dreyfus case was transformed into the Dreyfus affair, from a trial to determine the innocence or guilt of one man to an ideological battle over the values and ideals on which the French Republic was founded. Under mounting public pressure, Dreyfus was given a retrial in 1899 in which he was once again found guilty by the military judges, but pardoned by the president of the Republic. The case did not come to a full close until July 1906, however, when the Appeal Court reversed the conviction and reinstated Dreyfus in the French army.[33]

Narratives of modern Jewish history often locate the importance of the Dreyfus affair in the crisis of antisemitism that it revealed. It was the cries of 'death to the Jews' that accompanied Dreyfus's degradation ceremony, according to Jewish popular mythology, that prompted Theodor Herzl to launch the Zionist movement and forced increasing numbers of European Jews to question the ideology of assimilation. This narrative, however, was not relevant to the vast majority of French Jews, for whom the final outcome of the affair in favour of Dreyfus bolstered their confidence in the Republic. 'The felicitous, if long-delayed conclusion of the affair', Paula Hyman concludes in her classic study of the period, 'confirmed in French Jewry its love of and confidence in its native land.'[34] For many Jews who would become active in the Jewish press and associational life in the 1920s, however, the affair marked a critical reference point in the development of their Jewish identity. This was not simply a response to antisemitism. Rather, the importance of the Dreyfus affair for French Jews must be understood in the broader context of the new networks and social spaces that it created.[35]

[32] On Bernard Lazare, whose involvement in the Dreyfusard struggle led him to reject an almost self-hating endorsement of total assimilation and to embrace Zionism, see Nelly Wilson, *Bernard Lazare: Antisemitism in France and the Problem of Jewish Identity*; Bredin, *Bernard Lazare: De l'anarchiste au prophète*; Oriol (ed.), *Bernard Lazare: Anarchiste et nationaliste juif*; and Oriol, *Bernard Lazare*.

[33] A vast literature exists on the Dreyfus affair. The best recent accounts include Bredin, *The Affair*, and Burns, *Dreyfus*. In *More Than a Trial*, Robert Hoffman provides a succinct account of the wider social issues that the affair raised. See also *Archives juives*, 27/1 (1994): the issue is entitled 'Les Juifs et l'affaire Dreyfus'.   [34] Hyman, *From Dreyfus to Vichy*, 34.

[35] For a balanced discussion of the affair as both a 'moral upheaval' for French Jews and a moment during which the classic French–Jewish synthesis was strengthened, see Nicault, 'L'Israélitisme au tournant du siècle'.

While the affair gave impetus to the antisemitic movement, in the political sphere it marked the victory of the republican left over its right-wing challengers. The conservative government responsible for the army's cover-up of Dreyfus's innocence was forced to resign, and the radical-socialist coalition that had spearheaded the revisionist campaign came to power in 1901. It was the Dreyfusard/anti-Dreyfusard divide that created the basic division between right and left in France, a division that would endure for the remainder of the Third Republic. On a cultural level, the affair gave birth to the 'intellectual' as a distinct social category in France,[36] and marked the entry into left-wing politics of many in the literary, artistic, and university worlds. The affair forged an alliance between these intellectual circles and the French socialist movement, helping to bring French socialism within the bosom of republicanism. The drama of the Dreyfus affair was played out through the press, giving new importance to newspapers and magazines as conduits of politics and ideas. In addition, Dreyfusard activism gave rise to a whole series of new magazines and journals that represented the meeting-place of literary, political, and university groups.[37] Finally, by sparking interest in both the problem of antisemitism and issues of Jewish identity and culture more broadly, the Dreyfus affair gave Jews a new kind of visibility in French public culture.

Politicization through the Left

The affair prompted important changes in French leftist circles that would make them a welcome home for Jews grappling with issues of antisemitism and identity. Firmly committed to the principles of class struggle and internationalism and divided into five warring factions, French socialists in the 1880s and 1890s existed on the fringe of the political sphere. Involvement in the Dreyfusard struggle brought about the conditions for the creation of a unified socialist party, the SFIO (Section Française de l'Internationale Ouvrière), and marked the ascendancy of Jean Jaurès as its leader.[38] Jaurès's brand of socialism, which was as firmly wedded to a commitment to human

---

[36] It was in the early heated exchanges between Dreyfusards and anti-Dreyfusards that the term first came into use to describe the group of people who signed Zola's *J'accuse*. See Ory and Sirinelli, *Les Intellectuels en France*, ch. 1.

[37] Ory and Sirinelli (ibid.) locate three principal networks that grew out of Dreyfusard activism: the university, the press, and the artistic and literary world.

[38] French socialists were initially slow to come to Dreyfus's defence because of his bourgeois status: the innocence or guilt of an elite military officer, they argued, should not be of concern to the working classes. This position gave way to support for the Dreyfusard cause after the explosion of Zola's *J'accuse*, largely due to the influence of Jean Jaurès, who had come to recognize the importance of the cause as a humanitarian issue. See the chapter entitled 'French Socialism and the Dreyfus Affair' in Wistrich, *Between Redemption and Perdition*.

rights as it was to a class-based analysis of society, came to dominate the movement in the years before his assassination in 1914. Integral to this position was a new appreciation of antisemitism as a force to be fought, irrespective of the specific class issues involved, as part of the larger socialist struggle for justice and equality. With the exception of certain fringe circles,[39] antisemitism became the bastion of the political right in the aftermath of the Dreyfus affair, and leftist groups of varying persuasions no longer saw their interests as being allied with anti-Jewish politics and rhetoric.[40]

The Dreyfus affair also marked the affiliation of a number of young intellectuals with the socialist movement.[41] While many of those active in the literary and artistic avant-garde of the 1890s were already intellectually committed to socialism by the end of the century, the political crisis created by the affair gave them the opportunity to act on their convictions. Many intellectual and literary figures described the electric atmosphere of the period, as their political action in favour of Dreyfus grew into a much larger project of social justice and political involvement. One of the most important meeting-places for left-wing intellectuals of the day was the Librairie Bellais. This bookstore, founded by Charles Péguy in May 1898, was quickly transformed into a centre of Dreyfusard activism. In his memoirs, the historian Jules Isaac, an advocate of the reform of Catholic teaching on Jews, and of interfaith dialogue, in the years following the Second World War, fondly recalled the Librairie Bellais as 'the meeting-place of Péguy and his entourage, a centre for socialist and Dreyfusard activity, a battleground'.[42] Many of these activists, including Péguy, Isaac, and Edmond Fleg, were affiliated with the Ecole Normale, which had the highest proportion of pro-Dreyfusard students and faculty of any French university.[43] It was not, however, a concern with antisemitism that initially propelled Jews active in left-wing circles towards support of Dreyfus. Rather, increased sensitivity to antisemitism and Jewish particularism was, for Spire, Blum, and others in their circle, part of a larger process of politicization.

Many Jews in this milieu were initially slow to come to Dreyfus's defence. Jules Isaac, for example, recalls that his 'conversion' to socialism while a

[39] Certain radical anti-establishment figures within the syndicalist movement continued to engage in the kind of 'anti-capitalist antisemitism' that had been common on the French left in the 19th century. See Sternhell, 'The Roots of Popular Antisemitism in the Third Republic'.

[40] On this shift, see Wistrich, 'French Socialism and the Dreyfus Affair', in *Between Redemption and Perdition*.

[41] For a discussion of French intellectuals and socialism at the beginning of the century see Prochasson, *Les Intellectuels, le socialisme et la guerre*, and Ory and Sirinelli, *Les Intellectuels en France*, ch. 1.

[42] Isaac, *Expériences de ma vie*, 134. On Isaac, see Landeau, 'Jules Isaac', and Wigoder, *Dictionary of Jewish Biography*, 222–3.   [43] Ory and Sirinelli, *Les Intellectuels en France*, 29.

student at the Ecole Normale was much less problematic than his 'conversion' to Dreyfusism. While the Ecole had become a centre of Dreyfusard activism by early 1898, Isaac was at first reluctant to join the battle. His scepticism stemmed, he recalled ironically, in part from the fact that he was Jewish: like many of his Jewish contemporaries, Isaac hesitated to take the Dreyfusard side as a sort of counter-reaction to Jewish solidarity.[44] In a similar vein, Léon Blum recalls in his memoirs that when Lucien Herr, the librarian at the Ecole and a passionate Dreyfusard, brought up the issue of Dreyfus's innocence with him in autumn 1897, Blum was reluctant to take a pro-Dreyfus stand. The middle-class Jewish milieu that he frequented, Blum reminds his readers, was not in the least predisposed towards Dreyfusism. Like others in his circle, he was ultimately drawn to the Dreyfusard movement because of his commitment to individual human rights, antimilitarism, and social justice rather than by a concern about antisemitism in and of itself.[45] For most Jews who did become active Dreyfusards, their political activism and opposition to antisemitism remained wedded to universalism: Jews, for example, were active in forming the Ligue des Droits de l'Homme, which played a central role in defending Dreyfus.[46] For some, however, engagement with socialism and left-wing activism opened the door to both a greater sensitivity to antisemitism and an interest in issues of Jewish identity and culture. A new sensitivity among those on the French left to the plight of east European Jews also played an important role in this process.

The 1880s and 1890s were a time of increasing oppression and poverty for Jews in the Russian empire, as pogroms and expulsions became routine. While Russian antisemitism had been criticized to some extent in French left-wing circles throughout this period, the new sensitivity to antisemitism sparked by the Dreyfus affair helped bring the issue centre stage. Even more than an awareness of the Jewish plight in eastern Europe, however, the 'discovery' of a Jewish proletariat in France sparked a reassessment of Jewish identity in progressive circles. Between 1881 and 1914, 40,000 east Euro-

---

[44] Isaac, *Expériences de ma vie*, 122.   [45] Blum, *Souvenirs sur l'affaire*, 42–6.

[46] Marrus's characterization of French Jews in *The Politics of Assimilation* as 'passive' during the affair has been considerably revised in recent years. As Pierre Birnbaum, Philippe Landau, and others have pointed out, Jews did respond to the Dreyfus affair, but they did so primarily by invoking the language of universal human rights rather than by making the case into a 'cause célèbre' in the fight against antisemitism. Contemporary critics agree that both Blum and Péguy, in his memoir *Notre jeunesse*, first published in 1910, exaggerated Jewish passivity during the affair for polemical purposes. Rabinovitch notes that many Jewish intellectuals, including Marcel Proust, Julien Benda, and René Schwob, privately admitted to supporting Dreyfus before they took a public stand. For Jewish responses to the Dreyfus affair, see Birnbaum, 'La Citoyenneté en péril'; Stephen Wilson, *Ideology and Experience*, ch. 19; and Landau, *L'Opinion juive et l'affaire Dreyfus*.

pean Jewish immigrants settled in Paris. This influx meant that the Parisian Jewish community, acculturated and almost entirely middle-class at mid-century, had acquired an important working-class component by the time of the First World War. For acculturated middle-class Jews, the poverty and cultural distinctiveness of the immigrants were often an embarrassment, and many feared that their presence would bolster the growing antisemitic movement.[47] For certain Jewish intellectuals in the process of 'rediscovering' their Jewishness, however, east European Jews came to represent a kind of Jewish authenticity that offered a welcome contrast to the seemingly sterile Jewish world into which they had been born.

The experience of André Spire, who, like Isaac and Blum, initially became active in the Dreyfusard movement more for 'humanitarian' than for 'Jewish' reasons, is instructive. Spire was born in 1868 into a well-to-do, highly acculturated, non-observant Lorraine Jewish family. While he was a socialist sympathizer by the late 1890s, his writings from this period reveal disdain for his own bourgeois Jewish milieu, as well as repugnance for the Jewish immigrants from eastern Europe arriving in Paris.[48] In the aftermath of the affair, he threw himself into various left-wing organizations and activities focused on helping the working classes. The most successful of these was the creation of a network of *universités populaires* (adult education centres), which aimed to provide both vocational training and a taste of higher education to the working classes.[49] These activities consumed Spire until 1904, at which point his interests began to turn more specifically to the plight of the Jewish proletariat. Interestingly, he first encountered working-class Jews in London, which had a much larger and more distinct Jewish immigrant neighbourhood than Paris.[50] Sent by the French government in 1902 to report on the 'sweating system', Aron Rodrigue notes, 'Spire saw the social question and the Jewish question merged into one in the slums and back alleys of Whitechapel ... These were the "real" Jews, the centerpiece of a new discourse of authenticity that he, like many other nationalists, would develop in the process of identity formation.'[51] From that point on, Spire

---

[47] For a discussion of native Jews' reactions to immigrants, see Marrus, *The Politics of Assimilation*, and Hyman, *From Dreyfus to Vichy*.

[48] See Spire, *Souvenirs à bâtons rompus*, and Rodrigue, 'Rearticulations of French Jewish Identities after the Dreyfus Affair', for a discussion of Spire's activities during the affair.

[49] See Cacérès, *Histoire de l'éducation populaire*, and Mercer, *Les Universités populaires*.

[50] In contrast to both England and the United States, where Jewish immigration peaked in the 1880s and 1890s, in France immigrants began to arrive in large numbers only after 1905. In addition, there was much less of a distinct immigrant neighbourhood in Paris than in either London or New York. Immigrant Jewish housing patterns are discussed in greater detail in Chapter 4 below.

[51] Rodrigue, 'Rearticulations of French Jewish Identities after the Dreyfus Affair', 8.

focused his writing and social activity almost entirely on fighting both anti-semitism and assimilation, and on bringing the culture of east European Jewry to life for middle-class French Jews.

While the Dreyfus affair is often remembered for the boost it gave to the antisemitic press, Dreyfusard activism also gave rise to a whole series of political and literary journals oriented towards issues of social justice.[52] These journals, which functioned as political and social associations,[53] were critical in creating the networks of left-wing intellectuals, both Jews and non-Jews, who would emerge as key figures in Jewish associational and press culture in the 1920s. They marked the meeting-point of French intellectuals and left-wing political action, and represent one of the first forums in which we see a new emphasis on Jewish particularism from a sympathetic perspective. It was in this constellation of Dreyfusard reviews that Jewish writers such as André Spire and Edmond Fleg made their literary debuts, where Yiddish literature was first translated into French, and where Zionism was debated outside purely Jewish circles.[54]

More than any other publication that emerged in the immediate aftermath of the Dreyfus affair, it was the *Cahiers de la Quinzaine* that brought antisemitism and issues of Jewish identity to the centre of progressive French intellectual culture. The *Cahiers*, the first issue of which appeared in January 1900, was founded by the maverick socialist Charles Péguy. Péguy himself was committed to an eclectic kind of philosemitism, and saw the promotion of Jewish culture as a central project of his journal.[55] He became a

[52] On the left-wing press in the aftermath of the Dreyfus affair, see Prochasson, *Les Intellectuels, le socialisme et la guerre*, chs 1 and 2.

[53] In describing the left-wing literary and political journals that emerged between 1900 and 1938, Prochasson (ibid. 44) insists on the need to study them not only as collections of articles, but as 'espaces de vie' that became the social centre of a new generation of socialist activism.

[54] Articles on contemporary antisemitism first began to appear regularly in *La Revue blanche*, a beaux-arts review that became political in orientation with the explosion of the Dreyfus affair (see Barrot and Ory, *La Revue blanche*), and *Le Mouvement socialiste*, which was founded in 1899 by Jean Jaurès and his coterie. *La Phalange* (founded in 1906) and *L'Effort libre* (founded in 1910) published the writings of André Spire and other French Jews who were in the process of 'rediscovering' their Jewishness, as well as introducing Yiddish literature and poetry to the French reading public. A translation and discussion of the poetry of the Russian Jewish 'worker poet' Morris Rosenfeld, for example, appeared in *La Phalange* in February 1913.

[55] While Péguy was part of the Dreyfusard circle grouped around the Ecole Normale and the Librairie Bellais, he soon grew disillusioned with what he saw as the politicization of the Dreyfusards into doctrinaire socialists. Whereas Lucien Herr, Léon Blum, Jean Jaurès, and others became politically affiliated socialists, for Péguy socialism remained an ideology rather than a doctrine, a perspective that should inform rather than determine one's political and ideological perspectives. Péguy's ideas about Jews and Judaism are developed most fully in *Notre jeunesse*. In this memoir, written after his 1908 conversion to Catholicism, he develops the idea that the Jews are a prophetic people with a mission to spread justice throughout the world. On Péguy and the Jews see Prajs, *Péguy et Israël*.

cult figure among French intellectuals. As we have seen, the Librairie Bellais, where the *Cahiers* was published, was an important centre of Dreyfusard activism and meeting-place for his circle of friends and collaborators,
many of whom were Jewish. Péguy's own fascination with issues of Jewish
identity and culture played an important role in encouraging Jewish intellectuals in his circle to explore their own particularism from a positive perspective.[56] The 1904 publication of the English writer Israel Zangwill's
short story 'Chad-gad-ya' played a particularly important role in sparking a
reassessment of Jewish identity for many in Péguy's circle.[57]

'Chad-gad-ya' is the story of a young Italian Jew who has moved away
from the ghetto of Venice and the spiritual world of traditional Judaism in
which he was raised. He returns home for a visit on Passover night to find his
father leading a seder. Suddenly re-immersed into the world of his youth, the
son begins to feel the emptiness of his life as an assimilated Jew and the
sterility of his search for abstract universals to imbue his life with meaning.
As the evening wears on, he increasingly feels the warmth of the Judaism
that he has abandoned and the bonds of 'race' that tie him to his fellow Jews.
He feels himself to be too alienated from this world to re-enter it, however,
and as the seder ends he slips out and drowns himself in a canal, uttering
'Hear O Israel, the eternal our God, the eternal is one', the traditional last
words of a dying Jew. For Spire, the reading of 'Chad-gad-ya' was a moment
of 'conversion', the final step in a process of reaffirmation of Jewish identity
that began during the Dreyfus affair. This was not an individual phenomenon, he later recalled—'Chad-gad-ya' played a pivotal role in prompting
many Jews of his generation towards an affirmation of Jewish identity:
'Young French Jews who had lost all contact with Jewish life, who were
almost completely ignorant of all Jewish history, began to study it with fervour.'[58] Importantly, however, the 'return' to Judaism that Spire and others of

---

[56] The influential role that Péguy's journal played in the intellectual culture of his day, and
in particular for Jewish writers, was noted by many of his contemporaries. Kohn remarks on
the critical role that the *Cahiers* played for the circle of Jewish intellectuals that he discusses in
L'Humanisme juif. See Isaac, *Expériences de ma vie*: 'Péguy', as well as Lunel, 'André Spire et
notre génération'.

[57] 'Chad-gad-ya', trans. Mathilde Solomon, *Les Cahiers de la Quinzaine*, 6/3 (1904). The
story originally appeared as part of Zangwill's *Dreamers of the Ghetto*. In the first four years of its
existence the *Cahiers* also dedicated several volumes to antisemitism and Jewish life in eastern
Europe. See e.g. Bernard Lazare, 'L'Oppression des Juifs dans l'Europe orientale: Les Juifs en
Roumanie', 3/8 (1902); Henre Dagan, 'L'Oppression des Juifs dans l'Europe orientale: Les
Massacres de Kishineff et la situation des prolétaires juifs en Russie', 5/1 (1903); and Elie Eberlin and Georges Delahache, 'Juifs russes: Le Bund et le sionisme, un voyage d'études', 6/6
(1904).

[58] Spire, 'Les Problèmes juifs dans la littérature', III. Spire wrote on numerous other occasions about the impact that 'Chad-gad-ya' had on him, including in the introductions to

his generation experienced at the time of the Dreyfus affair did not stem only from contact with an increasingly sympathetic French left, but also from their troubled engagement with right-wing nationalism.

Jewish Intellectuals and Right-Wing Nationalism: A Troubled Encounter

During the Dreyfus affair French Jews faced an unprecedented level of antisemitic agitation: an outpouring of antisemitic press articles, anti-Jewish riots, and social ostracism.[59] Even more important than the actual amount of antisemitic agitation, however, was the change in its locus: it is during this period that we see the birth of an antisemitic intellectual milieu. In particular, the antisemitic turn of the writer Maurice Barrès and others in his circle gave the movement new importance to Jews in the academic and literary worlds. Barrès was part of a circle of intellectuals grouped around the prestigious Ecole Normale,[60] which was at the centre of the Parisian intellectual and artistic avant-garde in the 1890s. It was during this period that poetry, novels, and memoirs that celebrated and romanticized 'enracinement' came into vogue. A regionalist literary revival spread throughout the French provinces. Young writers began exploring local history and folklore, writing in their native dialects, and creating new journals and regional associations, all of which sought to preserve local identities in the face of the centralizing tendencies of the Third Republic.[61] During this period, Barrès's intellectual orientation shifted from the celebration of individualism, as expressed in his 1892 trilogy, _La Culte du moi: Examen de trois idéologies,_ to an ideology linking identity to one's native soil and ancestors. He now focused his literary efforts on writing the history and ethnology of his own native Lorraine.

Quelques Juifs and the 1959 edition of _Poèmes juifs._ He also referred to the emotional impact the poem had on his 'Jewish soul in the process of dissolving' in a letter written to Marc Jarblum in 1963 (this letter is in the file on Spire in Jarblum's papers at the Central Zionist Archives in Jerusalem). Writer and communal activist Wladimir Rabinovitch similarly recalled that 'Only those who were part of this era are able to remember the inner reverberations that the _Cahiers_ caused for many Jews . . . Suddenly, we understood that the history of this de-Judaized Jew, whether brutally or insidiously rejected by a society that only reluctantly accepted him, was their own story, and exposed the tragedy of their own condition' (Rabi, 'André Spire', 25).

[59] On French Jews' experience of antisemitism during the Dreyfus affair, see Stephen Wilson, _Ideology and Experience._

[60] It was here that students prepared for the _agrégation_ in literature, philosophy, and history, an exam that qualified them to teach these subjects at both lycée and university level.

[61] The Fédération Régionaliste Française was created in 1900. On the regionalist cultural revival see Thiesse, 'Le Mouvement littéraire régionaliste'; Pasquini, 'Le Félibrige et ses traditions'; Bandone, 'Ethnicity, Folklore and Local Identity in Rural Brittany'; Reece, _Bretons against France_; Ford, _Creating the Nation in Provincial France_; and Lebovics, _True France_, ch. 4.

Initially, Barrès's ideology spoke as strongly to young Jews in his circle as to other French intellectuals of his day.[62] Writing in 1903, Léon Blum analysed the seductive aspect of Barrès's philosophy for his generation: 'to a society quite positive, quite coldly sceptical, that Taine and Renan had turned toward either the tranquil research of facts or the slightly detached manipulation of ideas, Barrès has just brought a thinking dry in appearance, but dry as the hand of one suffering from a fever, a thinking all charged with metaphysics and poetry'.[63] To the shock of many of his Jewish protégés, however, Barrès came out as an anti-Dreyfusard, and his ideology took a decidedly antisemitic turn in the heat of the affair. 'The Jews do not have a country in the sense that we understand it', Barrès wrote in *Scènes et doctrines du nationalisme* in 1902. 'For us, *la patrie* is our soil and our ancestors, the land of the dead. For them, it is the place where their self-interest is best pursued.'[64] Barrès's embrace of antisemitism marked a moment of crisis for many of his Jewish protégés, and forced them to engage directly with the implications of ethnic nationalism for themselves as Jews. While Drumont and his colleagues could be dismissed as political buffoons with little weight among serious thinkers in the 1880s and 1890s, antisemitism now had to be taken more seriously on both a political and an intellectual level.

Political lines were starkly drawn during the affair, with the right attacking Jews as dangerous outsiders and the left defending them in the name of republican universalism. On one side stood conservative anti-democratic forces, for whom the issue of Dreyfus's innocence or guilt was largely irrelevant: no matter what the evidence, his conviction must be upheld in order to maintain the honour of the army. On the other stood the Dreyfusards, for whom the battle to free Dreyfus became a battle for the France of the revolution, for the principles of individual human rights and justice: 'Two tragic choruses insulting each other', a contemporary wrote of the affair, 'with each side convinced that it alone was France.'[65]

The split between Léon Blum and Maurice Barrès perhaps most poignantly exemplifies this political parting of the ways and is one of the most famous incidents in the intellectual history of the affair. Blum, as he recounts in his memoirs, went confidently to gain Barrès's signature on his petition supporting Zola. Barrès, however, did not sign; instead he wrote Blum a letter explaining that he had chosen the 'national instinct' over

---

[62] For a discussion of Barrès's following and his status as a cult figure for the Ecole Normale circle of the 1890s, see Sternhell, *Maurice Barrès et le nationalisme français*.

[63] Quoted in Stock, 'Students versus the University in Pre-World War I Paris', 96.

[64] Quoted in Hyman, *From Dreyfus to Vichy*, 14. Barrès's interest in nationalism was first signalled by the publication of *Les Déracinés* (1897).

[65] Quoted in Mayeur and Rebérioux, *The Third Republic*, 193.

the possibility that an individual's human rights had been violated. Blum described this encounter as the ultimate break with the artistic and literary world of his young adulthood, a critical moment in which intellectual ruminations and politics became inextricably linked, and his commitment to socialism and the principles of universal human rights affirmed.[66]

As Ilan Greilsammer demonstrates in his biography of Léon Blum, however, this moment of political cleavage, 'the mythic and inevitable rupture between the left, humanism, the Jew, on one side, and the right and antisemitism on the other', was not as black and white as Blum's account suggests. Rather, he argues, Blum's critical stance towards Barrès's views pre-dated the affair, and his friendship and admiration for his work survived it. Greilsammer's research shows that Blum and Barrès maintained a friendly, if strained, correspondence throughout the affair, and Blum's later writings testify to the respect that he continued to hold for Barrès's writings in its aftermath. While he distanced himself from Barrès's politics, the challenge posed by his 'mystical' approach to questions of national identity and the relationship between an individual and his heritage posed an ongoing challenge to Blum throughout his life.[67]

The affair similarly marked the political parting of the ways for Edmond Fleg and Lucien Moreau, friends at the Ecole Normale in the 1890s. By 1899 Fleg had joined the Dreyfusard camp and Moreau had fallen under the spell of Barrès, the beginning of an intellectual and political trajectory that would lead him to support Charles Maurras and the Action Française. Despite this political split, however, Fleg and Moreau remained friends and engaged in a correspondence over the next few years that illustrates the extent to which they were following parallel paths. Both rejected the nihilistic orientation of their youth and set out to find greater meaning in their lives, a path that would lead them both to reconnect with their respective 'national' origins. Moreau's new-found identification with France as the focus of his identity and values was parallel to Fleg's reconnection with his Jewish heritage: 'I have felt the need to connect myself to an exciting whole, to a past, to a tradition', Fleg wrote to Moreau; 'the past that I have discovered, sleeping really in the very depths of my being, is the past of my race.'[68]

Fleg's rearticulation of his Jewish identity in more particularistic terms could not, as did the parallel phenomenon for Maurras and Barrès, lead to an abandonment of the universalist principles of 1789. As he was well aware, as members of a distinct cultural and religious minority Jews could not be

---

[66] Blum, _Souvenirs sur l'affaire_, 83–6.　　　[67] Greilsammer, _Blum_, 122–30.
[68] _Correspondance d'Edmond Fleg_, ed. Elbaz, 96–7, trans. in Rodrigue, 'Rearticulations of French Jewish Identities after the Dreyfus Affair', 11.

French in a France defined in ethno-cultural rather than legal terms.[69] And yet, during this period, certain French Jews—Fleg and Blum among them—struggled to carve out a place for themselves within the French nation that would allow them to fully express their particularism while simultaneously holding on to the values of republican universalism.

[69] In contrast to Germany, conservative nationalism in France was rooted as much in culture and history as in 'race'. While racialized ideas about human difference were not without influence in France in the late 19th and early 20th centuries, they never achieved the kind of widespread acceptance that they did in Germany. See Brubaker, *Citizenship and Nationhood in France and Germany*, 102. Nonetheless, for Barrès and others in his camp—though they might have defined Jewish 'otherness' in historical-cultural rather than in racial terms—the Jews remained the quintessential outsiders to the French nation.

CHAPTER 2

The Beginnings of a French Jewish Literature

IN THE AFTERMATH of the Dreyfus affair a handful of Jewish writers including, most importantly, André Spire, Henri Franck, Jean-Richard Bloch, and Edmond Fleg, delved into previously untouched (and controversial) issues such as antisemitism, assimilation, and intermarriage. As a close look at these authors' writings from the pre-war years reveals, it was not a retreat into particularism that characterized this first wave of literature on French Jewish themes, but rather an obsession with dualism. The interest of these Jewish intellectuals in exploring the nature of Jewish particularism stemmed from their immersion in a cultural climate that increasingly valued group difference. At the same time, however, they were wary of exoticizing their Jewishness or presenting it as rendering them fundamentally different from their non-Jewish compatriots. These perspectives were too close to the antisemitic movement, which they all recognized as a threat. For Spire, Franck, Bloch, and Fleg, who were immersed in a French rather than a Jewish cultural landscape, reconnecting with their Jewish identity was an alienating as well as an empowering experience. At the same time that 'becoming' Jewish gave them the sense of historical connection and rootedness that they were seeking, it also forced them to recognize the limitations of the universalist values that formed the core of their identity.

André Spire

The 1908 publication of André Spire's controversial *Poèmes juifs*, contemporaries agreed, marked the birth of a modern Jewish literature in the French language.[1] The poems, Spire explains in his preface, were written as

---

[1] These poems were first published by the Société du Mercure de France in 1908 together with two previous collections of Spire's poetry, under the title *Versets; Et vous riez; Poèmes juifs*. A second, enlarged, edition was published in 1919, and a definitive edition came out in 1959. In the preface to the 1959 edition, Spire provides an overview of the press reaction to *Poèmes juifs* at the time of their original publication. All quotes are taken from this edition. On the impact that these poems made when they were first published, see Kohn, *L'Humanisme juif*; Rabi, 'André Spire'; and Crémieux, 'La Littérature juive française'.

a militant response to those Jewish literary and intellectual figures of the day who wanted to 'excuse their origins' and in doing so stifle 'what is the deepest and perhaps the best in them, leaving only the French patina that is the legacy of a few years of classical education and sophisticated Parisian prattle'.[2] While *L'Univers israélite* and the *Archives israélites* ignored the publication of the *Poèmes*, no doubt because of Spire's critical stance regarding the Jewish establishment,[3] Spire's book inspired lively discussion and debate in left-wing literary circles. Reviewers for *L'Art moderne* and *Le Mouvement socialiste* praised Spire for refusing to succumb, 'like the majority of his co-religionists, to the spirit of the race they live among', and 'cast[ing] his lot with those who live, fight, and die for the resurrection of Jewish dignity'.[4] Daniel Halévy, one of the main contributors to the *Cahiers de la Quinzaine* and a friend of Spire's from his early activist days, took a more critical stance.[5] While Halévy—the son of the noted Jewish composer Ludovic Halévy, who had converted to Christianity before Daniel's birth—admired Spire's boldness in taking on the Jewish establishment, he was wary of the work's 'physiological and essentialist aspects, the racial instinct'.[6] It is not surprising that the publication of the *Poèmes* provoked anxiety in someone of Jewish origin who did not identify as a Jew. For Spire, Jewishness was a matter of blood and history rather than religious belief, and by stating this in no uncertain terms his *Poèmes juifs* made a clear break with the traditional parameters of Franco-Judaism.

Spire's *Poèmes* painted a tragic portrait of the Jewish bourgeoisie of his day, which he criticized for attempting to eradicate their difference in hopes of eliminating antisemitism. As Spire saw it, the Jewish attempt to 'be like everyone else' was a charade, which, ultimately, only accentuated Jewish difference and made the Jews appear ridiculous. This is the theme of 'Tu es

---

[2] Spire, *Poèmes juifs*, 11.

[3] While we do not have any direct evidence as to negative responses to the *Poèmes juifs* among the French Jewish establishment, the silence of both *L'Univers israélite* and *Archives israélites* clearly speaks of their lack of approval. This sentiment was perhaps shared by Charles Péguy, who had originally promised to publish the poems as a sequel to *Et vous riez*, which first appeared in the *Cahiers* in 1905. For reasons that he never fully explained, however, Péguy rejected *Poèmes juifs*. Spire himself attributed Péguy's change of heart to his fear of promoting antisemitism and alienating certain segments of Jewish society that were sympathetic to (and financially supportive of) him. See Spire's 1959 preface to *Poèmes juifs* (pp. 13–14).

[4] Francis de Miomandre, in *L'Art moderne* (3 May 1908), quoted in *Poèmes juifs*, 19; Georges Sorel, in *Le Mouvement socialiste* (15 Apr. 1908), quoted in *Poèmes juifs*, 20.

[5] On this early period, see Halévy, 'Voici quelques quarante ans'.

[6] *Pages libres* (7 Nov. 1907), quoted in *Poèmes juifs*, 19. The Halévy family counted numerous prominent members in the French literary and artistic world in the 19th century, including the playwright and historian Léon Halévy and Geneviève Bizet-Strauss (née Halévy). On the Halévy family, see Loyrette (ed.), *La Famille Halévy*, and Silvera, *Daniel Halévy and his Times*.

content' ('You are contented'), which mocks Jewish self-effacement: 'You are pleased! You are pleased! Your nose is almost straight, yes indeed! And then again, so many Christians have their noses a little curved!'[7] Spire's scathing critique of Jewish behaviour is matched by his indictment of the hypocrisy of the surrounding society, as in 'Tu as raison' ('You are right'), which mocks 'civilized' Christians' fear of letting Jews into the intimate spaces of their lives: 'Christian, you think I am your friend . . . You take me in, you seat me next to your wife, and your daughter smiles at me. Christian, you are not at ease. Your eyes never leave mine, and on your lips I read the old insult.'[8] For Spire, French culture, and Western culture in general, represented a frustrating temptation for the Jew, tantalized by its marvels but never really allowed to gain full access. Assimilation, the tactic of the previous generation, had failed because no matter how perfectly the Jew adapted himself to the values and mores of the surrounding society he was still identified as Jewish. It was only through the positive affirmation of Jewish identity that Jews would become proud members of French society as opposed to stepchildren, forever trying to please their motherland and losing all respect for themselves in the process.

Another theme that Spire developed in the collection was Jewish suffering in eastern Europe. The penultimate poem, 'Pogromes', presents Russian Jews as both victims and the incarnation of Jewish authenticity, and chastises readers for their ignorance of the plight of their brethren, offered as a model of Jewish pride.[9] In the last poem of the collection, 'Exode', Spire expressed his support for the nascent Zionist movement, calling upon the people of Israel to 'flee all these false homelands' and invoking the promise of a new land. The placement of 'Pogromes' and 'Exode' side by side was hardly arbitrary. While Spire embraced Jewish nationalism as part of his 'conversion' to Jewishness, the political Zionist movement was, and for him remained, a viable option primarily for east European Jews. Significantly, he called upon his fellow Jews to 'March towards Odessa, Hamburg or Bremen' in preparation for their journey, rather than to Le Havre or Marseilles.

As both contemporaries and later critics have noted, Spire's poems do not recommend any specific course of action. They are clearly the work of someone who has recently embarked on a journey. Spire threw out the problem of the persistence of both Jewish identity and antisemitism and challenged his fellow Jews to create some kind of positive Jewish culture in response. What that culture should consist of, however, remained vague.[10]

[7] *Poèmes juifs*, 14.   [8] Ibid. 44.   [9] Ibid. 55.

[10] Both Crémieux and Rodrigue make this point. See Crémieux, 'La Littérature juive française', 196, and Rodrigue, 'Rearticulations of French Jewish Identities after the Dreyfus Affair', 16.

Henri Franck, in a review of the *Poèmes*, remarked on the note on which they end: 'It is a marvellous exodus to which Spire beckons his people. In the end, the last hope in which he takes refuge is not a port, but a journey.'[11] If 'Exode' is a literal call for departure aimed at east European Jews, it could also be read as a spiritual call for departure to his fellow French Jews.

With the 1913 publication of *Quelques Juifs*, a collection of three essays each focusing on a different Jewish figure, Spire further developed these themes. If the *Poèmes juifs* were the fruit of his emotional 'conversion', in *Quelques Juifs* Spire plotted the intellectual leg of the journey.[12] The first essay, 'Israel Zangwill', was first published in the *Cahiers de la Quinzaine* in 1909 as a response to Péguy's lengthy introduction to 'Chad-gad-ya'.[13] Though entitled 'Zangwill', Péguy's article addressed the universal problem of identity in the modern world rather than Zangwill as an individual. Spire's essay, by contrast, provided his readers with a history of Zangwill's life and a thematic overview of his literature. Spire addressed the lack of Jewish content in Péguy's essay in his introduction to *Quelques Juifs*. It was not the universal Zangwill who interested Spire, but rather the Jewish Zangwill, the son of immigrants, whose stories embodied the 'authentic' Jew. He dedicated the essay to a Jewish acquaintance, Gustave Sittenheim, who, like himself, was thrust into an emotional reconnection with his Jewish heritage through his reading of 'Chad-gad-ya'. Both men regretted, however, that they knew nothing at all about the author. 'In the ninety pages that he placed in front of Chad-gad-ya', Spire remarked, Péguy cited 'Taine, Renan, La Fontaine, Hugo ... but taught us nothing about Zangwill.'[14] Spire promised to find out more about Zangwill, but after he had completed his research he returned to find that Sittenheim was too busy to see him and had all but forgotten his reading of the poem. A promised letter to set a date to discuss the story never materialized, and thus, Spire wrote, 'It is I who am obliged to write to him, to remind him of that feverish moment when he remembered that he was a Jew.'[15] Spire's essay on Zangwill is both a tribute to the short story that led him to affirm his Jewish identity and a chronicle of the activities on which

[11] This review, originally published in the *Nouvelle revue française*, reappeared in essay form in Franck, *La Danse devant l'arche*, 177.

[12] The book, originally published by the Société du Mercure de France in 1913, was reissued in 1928 as the first volume of *Quelques Juifs et Demi-Juifs*. All quotes are taken from this edition. The second volume includes essays on Marcel Proust, Henri Franck, the Czech poet Otokar Fischer, and Gabriel Marcel, a French Jewish playwright, as well as the writers Armand Lunel and Jacques de Lacretelle, whose writings are discussed in Chapter 7 below.

[13] The other two essays in the collection, 'Otto Weininger' and 'James Darmesteter', were also published in essay form in the *Mercure de France* before being re-edited for *Quelques Juifs*. The piece on Darmesteter was also published in *L'Effort libre*, and both essays appeared in *L'Echo sioniste*. [14] *Quelques Juifs*, 14. [15] Ibid. 16.

he embarked in reconnecting with the Jewish people. The two principal purposes of the essay are to familiarize his readers with Zangwill's Jews—the poor east European immigrants of London's East End—and to contrast their way of being Jewish with that of the western Jews with whom Spire was familiar. By painting a positive picture of the 'Jewish Jews' of the ghetto, Spire dared his reader to draw inspiration from them. This act of identification, he hoped, would help counter Jewish self-hatred: rather than priding themselves on their ability to blend in, he wanted Jews to celebrate their difference.

Jewish self-hatred is the central theme of the next essay, on the Viennese Jew Otto Weininger who, after he became convinced of the biological inferiority of the Jews, committed suicide at the age of 23.[16] Rather than focusing on Jewish behaviour, this essay criticizes antisemitism and hypocrisy in Christian society, which Spire ultimately blamed for Weininger's suicide. A classical European education, Spire argued, taught Jewish children to be ashamed of their heritage; they learn that the Jews killed Christ, and the contribution of Semitic peoples to Western civilization is belittled. Spire also criticized the 'false universalism' of emancipation. The Jews were tricked into believing that if they gave up their particularism they would be fully accepted as equals. But once everything had been sacrificed, the non-Jews said: 'You are not quite finished: uncurl your hair, change your accent and your face.'[17] For Spire, Weininger's suicide was the extreme but logical outcome of assimilation and antisemitism. As even the act of conversion was not able to 'cure' Weininger of being perceived, both by himself and by others, as Jewish, his only choice was to take his own life.

In his next essay Spire focused on the great prophet of Franco-Judaism, James Darmesteter, both familiarizing his reader with the dominant influences on Darmesteter's thinking and offering a critique of it. Darmesteter, Spire reminded his readers, was part of a generation that believed in the idea of progress. Like Weininger, he grew up in the shadow of Christian civilization, and it was the message of universal humanism that shaped his world vision. As part of this universalism, Spire argued, Darmesteter envisioned not so much the disappearance of Judaism as its fusion with French and European culture. This ideology, Spire suggested, was naive in its blindness to the persistence of anti-Jewish sentiment in Christian society, and ignorant of the rise of the modern antisemitic movement. As Darmesteter elaborated his vision of a world where Judaism and

---

[16] Weininger's pathological self-hatred and its implications have interested a number of cultural historians in recent years. Sander Gilman was among the first to discuss his case in his now classic study, *Jewish Self-Hatred*.   [17] *Quelques Juifs*, 199.

Christianity would fuse to create a new religion of universal brotherhood, Drumont began publishing *La Libre Parole*: 'the more that [Darmesteter] talked of reconciliation, the harder the blows fell upon him. And he had no weapons with which to fight but ideology and gentleness.'[18]

Quelques Juifs, like *Poèmes juifs*, was read in French literary circles as a bold challenge to both Jews and antisemites: 'I do not believe that even the most hardened antisemite could read this essay without shame', we read in *La Phalange*: 'Spire, as if it were necessary, has given the Jewish people its letters of nobility.'[19] And yet, while they criticize what he understood to be the stagnant, assimilationist tradition of Franco-Judaism, Spire's essays do not represent a break with universalist values. Rather, he was constantly walking the line between the twin poles of universalism and particularism. If the essay on Otto Weininger was intended to show the need for Jews to define their identity within the specificity of their Jewish heritage, it was also an indictment of a society that privileged one historical narrative, that of the 'Aryan', to the exclusion of all else. In his essay on Darmesteter, Spire criticized his views not so much because he found them objectionable in and of themselves, but because he recognized that they were hopelessly out of step with the reality of the surrounding society. Given the rise of modern antisemitism, Jews were left with no choice but to arm themselves for the struggle. Spire's solution, however, was not for Jews to retreat into their own cultural exclusivity but rather to affirm their Jewishness as an attempt to bring a truly universal society into being.

At the same time that he advocated a reconnection with the specificity of Jewish history on the part of western Jews, however, Spire forcefully rejected a biologically based understanding of ethnic identity. His understanding of Jewishness, like Barrès's sense of connection to Lorraine, was rooted in an emotional connection with his history and ancestors. While the line between biology and culture as the source of these emotions was fluid for Barrès,[20] for Spire it was vital to distinguish between them. This concern, which was shared by other like-minded Jewish intellectuals of the day, stemmed from a keen awareness of the dangers of an essentialist, biological definition of Jewish identity. This danger came not only from the use of such characterizations of Jewishness on the part of the antisemitic movement, but also from the ambiguous attitudes towards Jews of many 'sympathetic' French literary figures of the day.

---

[18] Ibid. 257   [19] *La Phalange* (20 Oct. 1913), 345–6.

[20] French conservatives, Rogers Brubaker notes, tended to use the categories of race and culture more inconsistently than their German counterparts. See *Citizenship and Nationhood in France and Germany*, 102.

Just as the Dreyfus affair gave impetus to a strong pro-Jewish sentiment in French politics, so too did it spark an interest in Jews and Judaism on the part of non-Jewish French writers. In their novels and short stories both Emile Zola and Anatole France, for example, criticized the antisemitic current in French society that the affair revealed and defended Jewish integration as part of their broader commitment to the ideal of universal humanism.[21] It was also during this era, however, that a number of French authors began to represent the persistence of Jewish difference in positive terms. For writers such as Charles Péguy and Romain Rolland, it was their distinctiveness that gave the Jews their value in French society. For Rolland, as for Péguy, it was the Jews who were responsible for the promotion of justice throughout the world, and it was only by maintaining their status as a stateless people that they would be able to fulfil this mission.[22]

The line between sympathy and hostility in this kind of essentialist characterization of Jews and Jewishness, which literary scholar Bryan Cheyette has coined the term 'semitism' to describe, was a very fine one.[23] At one point in *Jean Christophe*, for example, Rolland wrote, 'for the time being, [Jews] occupy a position out of all proportion to their true merit. The Jews are like women: admirable when they are reined in; but with the Jews as with women their use of mastery is an abomination.'[24] In a similar vein, André Gide, who admired the work of many Jewish writers of his day, nonetheless saw the over-representation of Jews in French literature as exercising a distorting influence on 'genuine' French culture. As he saw it, literature written by Jews was imbued with a particular sensibility, even when it was devoid of any explicitly Jewish content.[25]

A wariness of this kind of semitic discourse comes across very strongly in *Quelques Juifs*. In his essay on Zangwill, for example, Spire proposed that the

[21] See Charles Lehrmann's discussion of Zola's novel *La Vérité*, France's short story 'Crainquebille', and the novels *L'Anneau d'améthyste* and *L'Ile des pingouins*, in *The Jewish Element in French Literature*, 190–5.

[22] Lehrmann, *The Jewish Element in French Literature*, 208, 245.

[23] Cheyette uses this term to describe essentialized discourses about Jewish difference, whether positively, negatively, or neutrally construed. As he points out in *The Construction of the 'Jew' in English Literature and Society*, 12–15, there was often a very fine line between antisemitism and philosemitism in this kind of writing.

[24] Quoted in Hyman, *From Dreyfus to Vichy*, 18. Hyman points to both the similarities between sympathetic and hostile characterizations of the nature of Jewish difference among non-Jewish French writers during this period and the ambiguous attitudes of figures such as Rolland and Péguy (pp. 19–23).

[25] See Marc Jarblum's unpublished article on Gide in Jarblum's papers in the Central Zionist Archives in Jerusalem. Jarblum was a Russian Jew who immigrated to France at the turn of the century and became a leading figure in both the Socialist Party and the labour Zionist group, Poalei Tsion. His papers contain many unpublished articles on, and interviews with, both Jewish and non-Jewish French intellectuals of his day.

sensitivity and admiration with which Zangwill writes about Christianity should serve as a foil to Barrès's contention that Jews, by virtue of their ethnic heritage, are not capable of truly understanding the mysteries of the Christian soul. He went on to criticize Barrès's comment that if one seeks to understand the Hebrew prophets, by contrast, 'no one can understand them better than James Darmesteter'.[26] For Spire, the idea that a Jew is inherently better able to understand biblical texts than a Christian was as ridiculous as the supposition that only a Christian can understand Pascal.[27] 'Nationalism, this demagogy, this weakness', he lamented, 'has it successfully closed your eyes to the truth? Do you truly believe that a Jew whose ancestors have sung these psalms, psalms that have been theirs for much longer than they have been your own, cannot understand Pascal, whose God is our God?'[28] Clearly, for Spire the notion that a person's 'race' inevitably determines his or her talents and world-view was as repugnant as the false universalism that, he believed, had forced French Jews to negate the value of their particularism.

Henri Franck

Henri Franck, the young Jewish poet whom Blum referred to in the *Revue de Paris*, echoed Spire in wavering between asserting Jewish difference and affirming Jewish belonging to French culture. Franck, who was too young to have been politically active at the time of the Dreyfus affair, came of age in the political and cultural upheaval of its aftermath. Born in 1888 to a wealthy, highly acculturated Jewish family, he was the grandson of Arnaud Aron, the chief rabbi of Strasbourg, but by the time of his birth the family had abandoned traditional religious practice and moved in mostly non-Jewish circles.[29] Franck studied philosophy at the Ecole Normale and was beginning his career as a professor and writer when he died of tuberculosis at the age of 23. His most important publication was a prose poem entitled *La Danse devant l'arche*. First published in *La Phalange*, the poem appeared in book format in 1912, along with a collection of Franck's articles and an introduction by the poet Anna de Noailles.[30] It caused a stir in French intellectual circles, in part, no doubt, because of Franck's premature death. He gained a posthumous reputation as one of the great philosophical minds of his gener-

---

[26] *Quelques Juifs*, 125.

[27] This is a reference to a book by Barrès entitled *L'Angoisse de Pascal*.

[28] *Quelques Juifs*, 126.

[29] See Spire's article, 'Henri Franck', *Europe* (15 Feb. 1925), 129–38, as well as his essay on Franck in *Quelques Juifs et Demi-Juifs*.

[30] See 'La Danse devant l'arche', pts 1 and 2, in *La Phalange* (20 Sept. 1911 and 20 Nov. 1912). André Spire edited and wrote a preface for a posthumous collection of Franck's letters in 1926, entitled *Lettres à quelques amis*.

ation: 'Henri Franck is known by the entire intellectual elite of France', André Spire wrote thirteen years after Franck died: 'His oeuvre occupies an important place in the literature of the early twentieth century, because it is a typical example of the effects of French culture on a Jew from a comfortable family, established for many years on French soil.'[31]

Like Spire's writings, *La Danse devant l'arche* reflects an obsession with dualism. Franck did not try to resolve the divergent pulls on his identity, but rather laid them out for the reader to ponder. The poem is best described as the philosophical quest of a young man for the meaning of life. It begins with the prayer of a young Levite in the holy temple as he declares his pride in fulfilling his duty of service to God. It is here that Franck expressed his own pride in his Jewish heritage and the privilege he felt in being part of an ancient tradition: 'I am proud to participate in your ceremonies, God of my chosen people, my lord. I am happy that my childhood has been nourished in your sacred temple, by your sacred law.'[32] His sense of cohesion and desire to further his understanding of the divine word in the tradition of the Hebrew prophets, however, is shattered with the destruction of Jerusalem and the dispersion of the Jewish people.[33] With the God of Israel apparently vanquished, the poet is thrust into a world devoid of meaning. He turns his gaze towards the West, where he sees civilization rising up again, and begins afresh his search for the God that he has lost. In the pages that follow, Franck's roaming poet finds God in many different places: in the youth of his generation, with whom he feels a great kinship and spirit of unity, but who go off in their own directions in search of their individual destinies in France, the spiritual heir of Israel, the country that has given birth to the God of human freedom in the form of the French Revolution. Here Franck expresses his profound love of and attachment to France, as well as his chagrin at finding it divided, without soul, and no longer believing in itself. Having searched for God everywhere and found him nowhere, the poet decides that he must place himself at the crossroads of humanity, at the intersection of all these influences, in order to feel his presence.[34] While the poet's journey does not lead him to any absolute truth, he does not despair because it is the journey itself that counts. 'If the ark is empty where you thought you would find the law', he concludes, you should remember that 'Nothing is real but your dance.'[35]

Critics have debated the nature of Franck's connection to his Jewish heritage. For some, the poem conveyed nineteenth-century Franco-Judaic faith par excellence. 'The title of his poem', Benjamin Crémieux commented in

---

[31] Franck, *Lettres à quelques amis*, ed. Spire, 130   [32] *La Danse devant l'arche*, 36.
[33] Ibid. 38.   [34] Ibid. 106.   [35] Ibid. 115.

1937, 'fools no one.' While Franck's poet takes his Jewish heritage as his starting point, Crémieux argues, he ultimately leaves its specificity in his search for spiritual and philosophical wholeness.[36] In an essay written in 1931, Hans Kohn analysed Franck's poem from another perspective. Kohn located an important turning-point in Franck's poetry in the way that he made sense of the dual pulls of his French and Jewish identities. Rather than submerging the former in the latter, Kohn argues, Franck attempted to bridge his Jewish heritage with his present reality and that of his generation: 'unlike the naivety of Alexandre Weill or Darmesteter, who sought to place the two sources of their existence on the same footing, [Franck], sensing his otherness, felt himself to be different, and he draws on the treasure of his inner soul'.[37] Franck was read by many of his contemporaries in a similar light.

The poem was discussed extensively in the Jewish press. Tributes to Franck appeared in both *L'Echo sioniste* and *L'Union scolaire*, a journal published by an association of Jewish graduates of Parisian secondary schools,[38] shortly after his death. 'Henri Franck, O my brother—in the gardens of Israel, you are the most beautiful flower', wrote Raymond Geiger in *L'Echo sioniste*. 'We love you and we cry because your soul was so profound, and in your quest to understand yourself, you found the ancient Jewish people.'[39] Geiger's comment reflects the new vogue for exploring the particularities of 'the Jewish soul' among French intellectuals during this period, a number of whom, like Geiger, were sympathetic to the emerging Zionist movement. Many of Franck's critics, both Jews and non-Jews, wrote about his Jewishness by invoking the prophetic quality of the poem, which they identified as growing out of his particularly Jewish sensibility. Anna de Noailles, for example, located its originality and beauty in Franck's concrete sense of connection with biblical history, which she saw as very different from that of a Christian:

[36] Crémieux, 'La Littérature juive française', 197.

[37] Kohn, *L'Humanisme juif*, 72. Rabinovitch offered a critique of the poem similar to that of Crémieux, in which he compared *La Danse devant l'arche* to the writings of both Darmesteter and Joseph Salvador. See Rabi, *Anatomie du judaïsme français*, 88.

[38] This association, which was also called L'Union Scolaire, is discussed in greater detail in Chapter 5.

[39] Geiger, 'La Danse devant l'arche', pt 1, *L'Echo sioniste* (10 July 1912), 141–3; pt 2 *L'Echo sioniste* (10 Aug. 1912), 157–9. See also André Spire, 'Henri Franck', *L'Echo sioniste* (10 Mar. 1912), 55, and Pierre Geismar, 'Henri Franck', *L'Union scolaire* (May/June 1912), 3–4. Franck's poem did not receive any attention in either the *Archives israélites* or *L'Univers israélite*, where we find only routine notices of his death. The lack of interest in Franck in these periodicals is not surprising given the fact that his family maintained no institutional connection with the Jewish community, and even less so given the maverick religious sensibility of his poems.

While the mysterious terrain of the holy scriptures filled our childhoods with fear-ful wonder, Henri Franck was able to contemplate its burning blue sky with filial confidence, to recognize the paths of Mount Lebanon, the valley of Jordan, the Dead Sea . . . that is the great contribution of those who, born in France, partake through study and meditation in their sense of origins, and deliver the fruits of their particularism.[40]

This sense of being different and the mystical, philosophical orientation that went along with it was for Franck, as for Spire, a source of great ambivalence. Like others of his generation, Franck was influenced by the philosophy of Henri Bergson, for whom intuition and spirituality rather than scientific rationalism were central to understanding human nature.[41] For Franck, however, the new anti-positivist philosophy did not necessitate a rejection of the Enlightenment tradition of universalism and rationality, but rather posed the challenge of synthesis. Franck was also very engaged with Barrès, who was the subject of several of his scholarly essays and ruminations in his personal correspondence.[42] For Franck, Barrès's genius came from the very fact that he devoted his life to the search for a meaningful set of values. He admired the beauty and the passion of his prose. But if Franck respec-ted Barrès's journey, like Spire he vehemently rejected his final destination. Barrès's Lorraine, Franck contended, was nothing but a figment of his imag-ination, created to satisfy his own spiritual needs but unrelated to any kind of exterior reality: 'It is not Lorraine that has created Maurice Barrès, but rather he who has created Lorraine.'[43]

Like Barrès, Franck yearned to give his history spiritual roots. Liberated from the rationalist constraints of the previous generation, he felt free to let his sense of himself as a Jew come out in his writing. The new questioning of the master narrative of the forward march of rationality and progress meant that Franck was not forced to see himself as part of a story that began with the

[40] Franck, *La Danse devant l'arche*, 16. Léon Blum, in his article 'La Prochaine Génération lit-téraire', *Revue de Paris* (1913), repr. in id., *Œuvres*, ii. 247, questioned Anna de Noailles's attribu-tion of the prophetic tone of the poem to Franck's Jewish heritage: 'It is also possible', he suggested, 'that an entire generation shared these symptoms.' Blum did not offer a resolution to this question, but rather left it for his reader to ponder.

[41] Bergson reached the height of his influence in the decade before the First World War. Unlike Barrès, Bergson, whose father was Jewish, did not attach any particular political agenda to his philosophy. While his ideas appealed to right-wing nationalists, Charles Péguy, taken with his mystical Catholicism, was one of his greatest devotees. His ideas were an inspiration to secular humanists at the same time as they played a key role in sparking the conversion to Catholicism of a number of French intellectuals in the pre-war years. On Bergson and his fol-lowing, see Grogin, *The Bergsonian Controversy.*

[42] See *Lettres à quelques amis*, as well as Franck's essays 'Maurice Barrès en Auvergne' and 'Sur la morale et la pédagogie de Maurice Barrès', which were published in the same volume as 'La Danse devant l'arche'.   [43] Franck, *La Danse devant l'arche*, 202.

French Revolution but rather could connect with something more ancient and unabashedly particularistic. Yet as a Jew, he recognized the dangers of this new philosophical orientation and thus saw no choice but to articulate his new-found particularism in the language of the universalist values of 1789.

In an essay on Franck written in 1928, André Spire discussed the tension in his writings between the anti-rationalist, romantic philosophies of Bergson and Barrès and the republican tradition of universal humanism:

La Danse devant l'arche is the song of a young bourgeois Jew, obligated by nationalist exclusion to look towards his origins, towards the 'royal race' to which humanity owes some of its highest aspirations. And in the end, in the name of this race that one so easily insults, honour required him to display his heritage like a banner.[44]

Spire's comment betrays the ambivalence that surrounded both his own and other intellectuals' emphasis on the specificity of their Jewish heritage. As much as Franck's praise of his 'royal race' grew out of an autonomous sense of connection with his roots, Spire suggested, this invocation of Jewish particularism was the only possible response he could give in an intellectual climate in which a pure attachment to universalism was no longer seen as a valid basis for identity.

In an interview with the Zionist labour leader Marc Jarblum, Spire recalled that it was not so much the overt, brutal antisemitism of the era that caused him to reject an assimilationist stance, but rather his shock on reading the work of several unnamed 'supposed opponents of antisemitism' who portrayed the Jews as exotic and particularistic in a way that was 'foreign to the French spirit'.[45] While both Franck and Spire were, to some degree, products of the same cultural mood that prompted non-Jewish writers such as the Tharaud brothers and Romain Rolland to praise the originality of the Jewish soul, as Jews they were aware of the danger of being classified as 'different' whether from a hostile or an overtly sympathetic perspective. This issue, as we shall see, would continue to plague Jewish writers and critics throughout the 1920s.

Jean-Richard Bloch

Like Henri Franck, Jean-Richard Bloch was born too late to participate personally in the political battle of the Dreyfus affair, but he grew up under the

[44] Spire, *Quelques Juifs*, 160.
[45] This reference is from an undated but clearly post-Second World War interview with Spire entitled 'Fifty Years with André Spire', now found in Marc Jarblum's papers at the Central Zionist Archives, Jerusalem.

shadow of its impact. Bloch was born in Paris in 1884 into a bourgeois Jewish family of Alsatian origins. With his brothers he was subjected to antisemitic attacks at their lycée at the height of the affair, an experience that had a great impact on the development of his Jewish identity.[46] Bloch received his *agrégation* in history and geography from the Sorbonne in 1907, and became active in the socialist movement.[47]

Bloch's first full-length novel, ...*et Cie*, written between 1911 and 1914, explored two central themes: the specificity of the Jewish experience in France and the weight of tradition versus the opportunity for an individual to create his or her own destiny.[48] The novel is the chronicle of three generations of the Simler family, Alsatian Jews who opt for France after the Franco-Prussian war. The story begins as Guillaume and Joseph, the sons of the family patriarch Hippolyte, set out in search of a new factory in which to re-locate the family business after the defeat of 1870. They find an appropriate setting in Vandeuve, an imaginary town in 'the West'. The first section of the novel is focused on the family's painful transplantation into this alien environment, made difficult by both the antisemitism of their new neighbours and their own clannish tendencies. The Simlers are excluded from the Vandeuve 'Cercle de Commerce', whose members invoke their foreignness both as Alsatians—referring to them derogatively as Prussians—and as Jews as the basis for their exclusion. 'What French virtues do the Simlers bring to us?'[49] one of the members exclaims in response to the Simlers' sole defender, M. Le Pleynier. What could Vandeuve be for 'those people' adds another, 'but a mere stop on the road'?[50]

If the community is less than welcoming, however, the Simlers themselves, in particular the older generation, are staunchly traditional and little interested in social mixing. 'A nice *goy* has nothing more in common with us than a hostile *goy*',[51] Myrtil Simler reminds his nephew, Joseph, reprimanding him for spending an entire afternoon in the company of the Pleynier family. Soon enough, however, Joseph begins to free himself from this dichotomy and falls in love with Le Pleynier's beautiful, intelligent, and cultured daughter Hélène. His dreams of marrying her and living the life of a gentleman farmer, however, are cut short by the weight of tradition and

[46] See Abraham, *Les Trois Frères*, and Albertini, 'Jean-Richard Bloch: De l'affaire Dreyfus à la *Nuit kurde*'.

[47] Bloch remained an active member of the SFIO throughout the pre-war years, and opted for the communists after the party's split at the Tours convention in 1920.

[48] The book was in press when publication was halted by the onset of the war, as Bloch explained in a brief preface to the first edition, published in 1918. All quotes are taken from the 19th edition, published in 1947; translations are my own.

[49] ...*et Cie*, 99.

[50] Ibid. 100.

[51] Ibid. 144.

family obligation. 'A *goy* in our home? You know that's impossible', his brother responds to Joseph's naive insistence that 'I will marry Mademoiselle Le Pleynier and I will not separate myself from you'.[52] There is no middle ground, Joseph is made to realize. Marrying a Christian woman would mean a complete break with the Simler clan, and he cannot bring himself to take this route.

In the third section of the novel we find Joseph married to Elisa Stern, the wealthy but repugnant daughter of another Alsatian Jewish manufacturer, a match that has enabled the merging of the two family firms and thus the creation of Simler & Co. The family business continues to prosper and grow, and the Simlers become respected members of the Vandeuve business establishment. When Hippolyte dies in 1880, all Vandeuve attends his funeral. It is also at this point that the next generation of the Simler clan is faced with the choice of staying within the bosom of the family or creating an independent life. For Justin, Joseph's nephew, it is not marriage that threatens to remove him from the weight of tradition, but academic success: having finished first in his class at the lycée, he is offered a place at the prestigious Ecole Normale to prepare for an academic career. Though this offer has great appeal for the young Simler, like his uncle Justin he opts for family tradition and the prosperous, secure life that awaits him in joining the family firm. 'You are right, Justin', his uncle Joseph reassures him. 'You are a brave boy, and you have chosen the best path. Stay with us, and we will give you the position you deserve.'[53]

The last section of the novel is an epilogue, set in 1889. Benjamin, a renegade Simler son who left for the United States in 1870, returns to Vandeuve a multi-millionaire and takes Joseph and Elisa's son, Louis, aside for a tête-à-tête. In the ten pages that follow, Benjamin explains his philosophy of life to the young Simler. The main purpose of Benjamin's speech is to encourage Louis to create his own future rather than following in his father's and uncle's footsteps. Simler and Company of Vandeuve has been reduced in spirit, Benjamin says to Louis, to '...et Cie', an amoral capitalist enterprise that threatens to swallow up all who come under its influence. Justin, we learn, has become a lazy, arrogant dandy, completely insensitive to the factory workers, interested only in the pursuit of pleasure. 'What happened to the Simlers is what happens to all those who found businesses, the business swallows the man, ...et Cie swallows Simler, and if you're not careful, soon there will be nothing left', Benjamin warns his nephew.[54]

...*et Cie* is, above all else, a study of the problem of individual freedom. To what extent should an individual preserve his heritage and follow in the foot-

[52] Ibid. 292.   [53] Ibid. 357.   [54] Ibid. 396.

steps of his ancestors, and to what extent should he break free of tradition and define himself independently? What makes ...*et Cie* both a fascinating and a frustrating novel, however, is Bloch's refusal to give a clear answer. Wladimir Rabinovitch, writing almost forty years after the novel was first published, noted that it is the complexity of Bloch's characters, none of whom is wholly likeable or wholly repugnant, that gives the novel its rich-ness.[55] At the same time that Hippolyte is presented as a tyrannical patri-arch, suspicious of social mixing with his non-Jewish neighbours, he reveals himself as an honest and generous man, helping his competitor when a fire breaks out at his factory. Joseph Simler appears as weak in his decision to marry the vulgar, rich Elisa in order to further the family business instead of the refined, intelligent Hélène Le Pleynier in whom he has found a soul-mate. Nonetheless, Guillaume's appeal to tradition, to the intangible 'thing' that has held the family together—'we have always been one heart and one spirit, and *chez les nôtres*, this is always the way it is'[56]—is not without appeal to the reader. What is the desire of one month when compared to the weight of thirty centuries, Bloch asks rhetorically, and at the end of the novel we are not really sure of the answer.

Bloch's ambivalence towards Jewish tradition comes across most strongly in his epilogue. On the one hand, Benjamin appears as the prophet of individual freedom. Given the sequence of events— Joseph's and then Justin's sacrifice of individual freedom in favour of family obligation—Ben-jamin's advice appears, at first glance, to be a rejection of the whole of the oppressive tradition of the Simler family. But although he criticizes the pres-ent '...et Cie', Uncle Benjamin sings the praises of the old Simlers of Alsace, bonded together by history and tradition rather than money. Hippolyte, he tells Justin, while he might have appeared to have lived only in the material world, 'did not really live in the world of everyday events, but first trans-formed them into a world of ideas . . . He manufactured cloth like a kabbalist, not a weaver.'[57] Benjamin's speech ultimately leaves the young Simler con-fused as to what he should do with his life, what his attitude should be towards his family and his heritage. 'My mission', Louis asks his uncle, 'is it to destroy or to preserve? Is it the boss's side or the workers' side?' 'The side of justice', Benjamin replies ambiguously.[58]

'Jean-Richard Bloch exemplifies the constant dualism that sways us', Rabinovitch wrote, 'from the particular to the general, from the Jewish people to the universality of the human race.'[59] For Bloch, a commitment to

---

[55] Rabi, 'Jean-Richard Bloch', *La Terre retrouvée* (30 Apr. 1947), 2. (As noted in the Introduc-tion, Rabinovitch used the pseudonym Rabi after the Second World War.)   [56] ...*et Cie*, 292.
[57] Ibid. 395.   [58] Ibid. 401.   [59] Rabi, 'Jean-Richard Bloch', 2.

socialism clearly played a critical role in shaping this dualism. Capitalist exploitation was an important secondary theme in the novel, and Bloch's critique of capitalism and interrogation of Jewish identity clearly come together in the epilogue. Ultimately it is not so much his Jewish identity that Benjamin encourages Louis to leave behind as his identity as a bourgeois Jew. For Bloch, it is above all the embourgeoisement of the Simler family that has led to its moral downfall, and it is this path that he wants the young Louis to avoid. 'French and bourgeois, okay. French and Jewish, I see less difficulty in that combination than in any other',[60] Benjamin tells his nephew. But bourgeois and Jew, by contrast, are not two identities that mesh acceptably.

It is here that Bloch's brand of Jewish messianism first comes across. While Bloch, like Spire and Franck, was left alienated and confused by his engagement with issues of Jewish identity and culture, his commitment to socialism enabled him to transcend this alienation in a way that was impossible for the other two authors.[61] For Bloch, the only way to synthesize his attachment to Jewish particularism and his adherence to socialist universalism was to attribute to the Jews a particular historical mission, which consisted, as expressed in Benjamin's prophetic advice to Louis, in the pursuit of justice. This idea, which was to permeate Bloch's later writings, became a central theme in French Zionist writing in the 1920s.[62] The messianic quality of Bloch's writings is echoed in the writings of Edmond Fleg, who made his Jewish literary debut with the publication of the first volume of *Ecoute Israël* in the *Cahiers de la Quinzaine* in 1913.

---

[60] *...et Cie*, 394.

[61] While André Spire was active in left-wing politics throughout his life, he was not a politically committed socialist in the same way as Bloch. Spire was part of Péguy's circle, many of whom became disillusioned with socialist politics soon after the heat of the Dreyfus affair died down. For Spire, the decision to devote his life to Jewish causes represented the embrace of a new cause that replaced his former devotion to socialism. For a discussion of the progression of Spire's socialist and Jewish identities in this early period, see Rodrigue, 'Rearticulations of French Jewish Identities after the Dreyfus Affair', and Fhima, 'Aux sources d'un renouveau identitaire juif en France'.

[62] Bloch's critics generally agree that *Lévy* and *...et Cie* were Bloch's two most successful literary efforts. His fiction in the 1920s consists mostly of escapist, romantic stories set in the Middle East. Wladimir Rabinovitch attributes the lack of literary genius in Bloch's later works to his adherence to the Communist Party. This intellectual commitment to universalism, Rabinovitch argues in 'Jean-Richard Bloch', did not permit him to further explore the vagaries of French Jewish identity from the same critical and 'unresolved' perspective as he did in his two earliest works of fiction. Fhima explores Bloch's ambivalence with regard to the world of the Jewish cultural renaissance of the 1920s in 'Jean-Richard Bloch et la renaissance culturelle juive'.

Edmond Fleg

Much more than any of the other pre-war Jewish authors, Fleg's writing was imbued with a religious sensibility. Edmond Flegenheimer, who adopted the literary pseudonym Fleg in 1921, was born in Geneva in 1874 into a family of Alsatian Jewish origin. In his memoir, *Pourquoi je suis Juif* (1928), Fleg described his family as religiously observant, but not strictly so. They kept kosher at home and 'to have entered a tram-car on Saturday would have seemed as venturesome as to ascend to the moon'.[63] Nonetheless, he was permitted to eat non-kosher food outside the home, and his father went to his office on Saturday after synagogue services. By the time that he arrived in Paris to study at the Ecole Normale in 1892, Fleg had abandoned all religious practice and initially saw little reason to remain attached to his Jewish heritage. As the decade wore on, however, he began to feel growing irritation towards the antisemitic movement, which was exacerbated by the turn towards antisemitism of his friend and fellow Normalien Lucien Moreau,[64] which came to a head with the explosion of the affair. Through his growing identification with Dreyfus's plight, Fleg recalled, came his reconnection with the Jewish people: 'when Dreyfus was recalled from the island by his judges at Rennes and condemned for the second time my life stood still. I could take no food. I felt myself banished from the brotherhood of man. And I asked myself "Jew, what is your place in the world?".'[65] For Fleg, this sense of banishment eventually led him to dedicate his life to studying and transmitting Jewish knowledge and culture.[66] While he never returned to the more Orthodox lifestyle of his childhood, much more than Spire, Franck, and Bloch, Fleg sought to transcend the sense of alienation prompted by his Jewish 'return' through a reconnection with Judaism itself. After the birth of his first son in 1908 he abandoned all secular pursuits for three years and immersed himself in traditional Jewish learning.[67] The product of this period of religious immersion was *Ecoute Israël*, a series of poems that present biblical and midrashic themes in a language accessible to a modern French audience.[68]

[63] Fleg, *Why I Am a Jew*, 2; all references are to the English translation published in 1929.

[64] In this account, Fleg refers to Moreau—who was eventually to become a leading intellectual in the Action Française—only as 'my Logician'. In reading Fleg's correspondence with Moreau during the Dreyfus affair, however, it becomes clear that Moreau is the logician.

[65] *Why I Am a Jew*, 37.

[66] For other first-hand Jewish accounts of antisemitism during the affair, see Spire, *Souvenirs à bâtons rompus*; Arnold Mandel, *Les Temps incertains*; and Abraham, *Les Trois Frères*. Pierre Abraham was the pen name of Pierre Bloch, Jean-Richard Bloch's brother. See also Leroy (ed.), *Les Ecrivains et l'affaire Dreyfus*.   [67] *Why I Am a Jew*, 52.

[68] These poems originally appeared in *Les Cahiers de la Quinzaine* in 1913. The seven-

The poems are, to a certain extent, a reflection of Fleg's own struggle to understand what place his Jewish origins should have in his present life. Their central themes are the fidelity of the Jewish people to God in the face of the trials of history and Jewish persistence through the ages. One of Fleg's primary purposes was to explore the tension between suffering and chosenness in Jewish history. The first volume is divided into three sections—'Les Pères du monde' ('The Patriarchs'), 'La Maison d'esclavage' ('The House of Bondage'), and 'La Terre promise' ('The Promised Land')—which correspond to the books of Genesis and Exodus. Like Bloch, Fleg saw the Jewish people as imbued with a mission. Whereas Bloch understood Jewish messianism through the lens of socialism, however, Fleg remained much closer to traditional religious belief. His poetry, in a sense, was meant to remind his readers of the age-old idea that Israel's apparent wretchedness is in fact a sign of her chosenness.

In the poem 'La Vision d'Isaac', Isaac has a vision of the sad fate which awaits his people, 'dispersed and bruised, in space and time'. What good was my sacrifice on Mount Moriah, he cries to God, if after I am gone my people must endure such suffering? God replies that he can remove this burden, but in this case another people will gain immortality by spreading the word of God throughout the world. 'Elohim! Elohim! do not change their fate!', Isaac responds, 'Let them live, if necessary condemned to servitude. Let them wander sobbing through places and ages, but let them see your face!'[69]

In 'Moïse et Bithia',[70] Fleg conveyed Moses' bittersweet choice of accepting Jewish identity and suffering as his own. 'What is your pleasure today, my child?' Moses' Egyptian mother asks him. 'To ride an elephant, to dance? . . . to be adored like a God?' To which her son replies, 'I want to suffer, like my brothers.'[71] In the next poem, God explains to Moses that it will be his fate to lead his people to freedom, but not to set foot himself in the promised land: 'Because your impure flesh doubted my force and my creation . . . you will bring my people from the land of distress and help them find the promised land . . . But you will rest at its threshold.' Moses, his head hanging, accepts his destiny: 'I will be your prophet, I will be your victim, Elohim . . . I will lead your children towards you, out of Mitsraim.'[72]

Fleg's poetry was very well received by both the rabbinate and the Zionist community. Poems from the volume were published in *L'Echo sioniste* as well

volume series was published between 1913 and 1948. The completed work was issued in one volume in 1954. All quotations, unless otherwise noted, are taken from this edition.

[69] *Ecoute Israël*, 17–18; trans. in Rodrigue, 'Rearticulations of French Jewish Identities after the Dreyfus Affair', 17.

[70] This poem also appeared in *L'Univers israélite* (24 Dec. 1915), 397–8.

[71] *Ecoute Israël*, 39.   [72] Ibid. 42.

as *L'Univers israélite* shortly after appearing in the *Cahiers*. Announcing a reading of the poems at the Société des Etudes Juives, *L'Univers israélite* remarked of Fleg, 'All his poetry is marked by an ardent love of Judaism . . . a poet of our very own has been born.'[73] Unlike Spire's writings, Fleg's poetry could not be read as an attack on the Jewish establishment, but rather evoked a traditional religious sensibility that was very appealing within this milieu. At the same time, however, his poems could be read by Zionists as a call for solidarity and the expression of a culturally based Jewish identity: 'The love that Judaism inspires within him—Judaism as a people, as a vibrant community—is profound', wrote Baruch Hagani, the editor of *L'Echo sioniste*.[74] Fleg was to remain closely linked to both the Jewish establishment and the Zionist movement throughout his life.

◆

André Spire, Henri Franck, Jean-Richard Bloch, and Edmond Fleg were united by their self-conscious struggle with the dual pull of their French and Jewish heritage. Like others of their generation, these Jewish intellectuals expressed a deep emotional connection to their ethno-cultural roots. Unlike many of their non-Jewish compatriots, however, they continued to feel a strong sense of attachment to the universal, humanist values of republican France that, they were well aware, had made their own integration into French society possible. Ultimately, these 'first-wave' Jewish writers were ambivalent as to how they should reconcile their deeply felt sense of belonging to France with the new importance that they had come to ascribe to their Jewish heritage. By opening up a new kind of dialogue about what it means to be Jewish in the modern world, however, they paved the way for a much wider-reaching phenomenon of Jewish self-questioning that took place in the 1920s. Reassessments of Jewish identity during this period were also related to the birth of the Zionist movement and Reform Judaism in the years between 1900 and 1914. It is to these strands of the Jewish cultural awakening that I will now turn.

[73] *L'Univers israélite* (11 Apr. 1913), 106.   [74] *L'Echo sioniste* (10 May 1913), 105.

CHAPTER 3

Between Religion and Ethnicity: Zionism and Reform Judaism before the First World War

THE BIRTH of both the Zionist movement and Reform Judaism opened up new avenues of debate and interaction among French Jews in the years between the Dreyfus affair and the First World War. Zionists, Reformers, and traditionalist Jews[1] often disagreed with each others' politics and varied in their vision of how one should live as a Jew in the modern world. This period also saw the creation of Jewish youth groups of varying social, political, and cultural orientations, paving the way for a much more widespread upsurge of activity in the post-war years. Despite the differences between them, however, these new movements and organizations shared a dissatisfaction with the status quo and a sense of being part of a new generation, charged with breathing new life into a stagnant French Jewry. While their methods differed, their goals were essentially the same: to create a vibrant, modern Jewish culture that would sustain French Judaism for generations to come. These groups were not isolated from one another. They read and responded to each other's publications and engaged in debates that were more often friendly than hostile. This contact helped to bring together Jews from different backgrounds—native and immigrant, Zionist and religious—and create networks in which Jewish cultural life would flourish in the 1920s.

French Jews and Zionism: An Uneasy Encounter

Pointing to the foreign origins of French Zionist leaders, low membership figures, and a general hostility towards Zionism among French Jews,

---

[1] This is the term that mainstream religious leaders, most of whom sought some kind of compromise between the exigencies of modern life and Jewish law, commonly used to describe themselves. Traditionalists contrast themselves with both Reformers, who sought to actively change Jewish liturgy and ritual, and Orthodox Jews, most often immigrants from eastern Europe, who allowed for no adaptation of traditional religious law.

historians have emphasized the movement's relative lack of impact in France, especially in the years before the First World War.[2] As I will suggest, however, Zionist ideology, even during these early years, may have had a broader influence on the outlook of French Jews than we have previously assumed. A close study of the activities and publications of the east European leaders of the pre-war French Zionist movement demonstrates that their brand of Zionism represented an amalgam of French and east European cultural and political sensibilities rather than simply being a foreign import. Contact with this Zionist milieu gave intellectuals such as André Spire and Edmond Fleg a framework in which to place their growing dissatisfaction with the Franco-Judaism of their parents' generation, and, in so doing, played a critical role in sparking the beginnings of a Jewish cultural renaissance.

It was Theodor Herzl's 1897 publication of *Der Judenstaat* that launched Zionism as a political movement with the specific goal of an autonomous Jewish state in Palestine. In 1901 the World Zionist Organization, created at the first Zionist conference in Basle in 1897, organized the Fédération Sioniste de France. This group drew almost exclusively on immigrant Jews, mostly small merchants, intellectuals, and professionals, for support.[3] The birth of the political Zionist movement was, by and large, greeted with scepticism among French Jews.[4] Its basic premise—that the grand project of the Enlightenment and the French Revolution, to liberate Jews from the constraints of a separate existence and enable them to become equal citizens of their countries of residence, had failed—was contrary to the ideological basis of nineteenth-century Franco-Judaism. At the core of this ideology, which was central to the Alliance Israélite Universelle and the Consistory, was the belief that the French Revolution had transformed France into a spiritual Jerusalem, rendering the old dream of a physical return to the Land of Israel irrelevant.[5] On a political level, the birth of political antisemitism and the explosion of the Dreyfus affair militated against sympathy for Zionism. For Jews who had to respond to the charge that they were not truly French, the Zionist thesis was not a welcome addition. Early articles on Zionism in

[2] The two most important scholarly works on pre-Second World War Zionism in France are Nicault, *La France et le sionisme*, and Abitbol, *Les Deux Terres promises*.

[3] See Hyman, *From Dreyfus to Vichy*, 154. On the French delegates to the 1897 Zionist Congress in Basle see Jean-Marie Delmaire, 'La France à Bâle'.

[4] The hostility of the French Jewish establishment to the nascent Zionist movement has been well documented by historians of the period. See Nicault, *La France et le sionisme*, Abitbol, *Les Deux Terres promises*, and Hyman, *From Dreyfus to Vichy*.

[5] On the Alliance's response to the Zionist movement, see Benbassa, 'L'Alliance Israélite Universelle et le sionisme'.

L'Univers israélite and the *Archives israélites* pointed to similarities between Zionist arguments and those of French antisemites, most importantly Edouard Drumont. The antisemitic press was the first to praise Zionism, one Jewish critic noted: though the Zionists' intentions might be honourable, he remarked, they had in fact provided antisemites with some of their most powerful weapons.[6]

Despite the hostility of the Consistory, the Alliance, and the Jewish press, the movement did gain sympathizers within the Jewish establishment during these early years. In a 1949 interview Myriam Schach, a veteran activist,[7] spoke of the diversity of support for the Fédération Sioniste de France publication *L'Echo sioniste* between 1900 and 1905.[8] Chief Rabbi Israël Lévi, Schach recalled, was among the first subscribers when the paper was founded in 1899. While he was not always in agreement with the group's politics or its ideological perspective, she recalled the importance of his moral support: 'he often expressed his solidarity with us, and the positions he took often went against his better judgement'.[9] Another chief rabbi, Zadoc Kahn, maintained a similarly distant yet sympathetic relationship. Kahn had been an active supporter of the Baron Edmond de Rothschild's colonies in the 1880s and took part in organizing a conference of Palestino-phile societies in Paris in 1894.[10] While he never endorsed Herzlian Zionism, Kahn maintained cordial relations with Herzl and was one of the few west European rabbis to send him a message of congratulations at the first Zionist congress in Basle.

Michel Abitbol describes Zadoc Kahn's attitude as characteristic of a romantic Zionism that attracted many French Jews who remained officially unaffiliated or even opposed to political Zionism. In particular, he notes, Kahn was supportive of aspects of the Zionist movement that related to the promotion of Jewish cultural life, both in Palestine and in France.[11]

---

[6] Cited in Abitbol, *Les Deux Terres promises*, 33. For other examples of anti-Zionist articles in *L'Univers israélite* and *Archives israélites*, see Abitbol, *Les Deux Terres promises*, ch. 1, and Hyman, *From Dreyfus to Vichy*, ch. 6.

[7] Myriam Schach was the sister of Fabius Schach, a prominent figure in the German Zionist movement. The interview was published in two parts, in February and March 1949.

[8] This journal was originally founded by Myriam Schach, Alexander Marmorek, and David Jacobson in 1899, and became the voice of the Fédération Sioniste de France in 1901. It ceased publication in 1905 as result of disagreement over Britain's offer of Uganda as a Jewish homeland. It was subsequently revived in 1912 under the leadership of Baruch Hagani.

[9] Schach, interview in *La Terre retrouvée* (1 Mar. 1949), 10.

[10] This early Jewish colonization movement was generally greeted sympathetically by French Jews as a form of philanthropy for their less fortunate brethren in eastern Europe. At this point Zionism was understood simply as an attempt to resettle Russian Jews, whose social and political situation had worsened rapidly after the accession of Alexander III in 1881.

[11] Abitbol, *Les Deux Terres promises*, 38–9.

Interestingly, Myriam Schach also recalled that *L'Echo sioniste*'s readership included a number of people who declared themselves firmly opposed to the movement. In particular, she gave the example of a certain 'Greek scholar, who was an avowed anti-Zionist and a multi-millionaire' (undoubtedly Salomon Reinach), who wrote: 'although I am not among your subscribers, please note my new address'. For Schach, this was 'proof that we were being read in ultra-assimilated circles that took great pains not to enrich our organization by subscribing'.[12] She also recalled that it was during these early years that the future president of the League of the Rights of Man, Victor Basch, and writer and activist Henry Marx, both of whom would become active in the communist and Zionist movements in the 1920s, first attended functions sponsored by the Fédération.[13]

As Paula Hyman has argued persuasively in her classic study *From Dreyfus to Vichy*, focusing on public opposition to Zionism and the failure of Zionist organizing campaigns can obscure the indirect influence that the movement exercised over French Jewry.[14] The birth of Jewish nationalism in western Europe represented the first coherent intellectual challenge to the ideology of assimilation. As a result, the questions that Zionist publicists raised about antisemitism, assimilation, and the course of Jewish history inevitably shaped the discourse on Jewish identity in France as a whole. For its adherents, sympathizers, and opponents alike, the Zionist movement played an important role in pushing questions of Jewish identity and assimilation to the fore in French public discourse.

Jewish Intellectuals and Zionism on the French Left

As we have seen, the Dreyfus affair prompted changes in French leftist circles that made them a sympathetic home to Jews grappling with issues of antisemitism and identity. For Basch, Spire, Fleg, and others in their circle, the initial encounter with Zionism took place within this milieu and was often intimately linked to their engagement with socialism and sense of solidarity with the Jewish working classes. By focusing on the Jewish proletariat, they found a way to make the socialist struggle more concrete.

[12] Interview in *La Terre retrouvée* (1 Mar. 1949), 10.

[13] According to Schach, Basch was present at the celebration of the first anniversary of the founding of *L'Echo sioniste* in 1901. He did not actually declare his support for Zionism until 1911, however, at which point the widely publicized ritual murder trial of Mendel Beilis convinced him that a Jewish state was the only viable response to the persistence of antisemitism in eastern Europe. On the evolution of Basch's position, see Fhima and Nicault, 'Victor Basch et la judéité'. Henry Marx was a maverick writer and social activist; he is discussed in more detail in subsequent chapters.   [14] *From Dreyfus to Vichy*, 153.

Spire's decision to turn his efforts towards the Jewish proletariat was linked to a sense of disillusionment with two organizations that he had helped to found, the Société des Visiteurs and the Université Populaire, both of which sought to go beyond charity to provide workers with education and job training. Spire increasingly felt that his efforts on behalf of the workers, who remained apolitical and interested primarily in the 'traditional distractions of dance, music and entertainment', were in vain.[15] Zionism, by contrast, provided him with a concrete channel for his commitment to social justice, as comes across very clearly in his dedication of *Poèmes juifs* to both 'the only proletariat in which I can still believe' and Zionist leaders Israel Zangwill, Theodor Herzl, Max Nordau, and Bernard Lazare.

For intellectual and social activist Victor Basch, who served as president of the League of the Rights of Man from 1926 to 1940, Zionism was also a logical extension of a commitment to socialism and a new sensitivity to antisemitism in the wake of the Dreyfus affair. Basch, who was born into a bourgeois Jewish milieu in Hungary, immigrated to France at a young age and became a professor, first of German language and literature and then of aesthetics, at the Sorbonne.[16] Married to an equally secular Jewish woman, Basch recalled that he maintained no Jewish affiliations as an adult: 'I had practically forgotten that I was a Jew.' Shocked by the antisemitic comments of one of his colleagues during the affair, however, Basch suddenly felt linked to past generations of Jews by a long chain of persecutions. Eventually, this sense of solidarity led him to support Zionism. 'When my noble friends Max Nordau and Alexander Marmorek brought the Zionist movement to my attention', Basch recalled in 1924, 'I entered it with all my heart. I entered with the great hope that those Jews who do not have a country will find one, that the eternal wanderers will finally be able to settle down in a homeland that no one will be able to take away from them.'[17] For men like Spire and Basch, who were devoid of religious sentiment and detached from the Jewish mainstream, Zionism provided a coherent intellectual system to legitimate their new-found but still amorphous sense of Jewish kinship and solidarity.[18]

[15] Cited in Rodrigue, 'Rearticulations of French Jewish Identities after the Dreyfus Affair', 7.

[16] Gruson, 'La Carrière universitaire de Victor Basch', 43.

[17] Basch, 'Mon Judaïsme', *Connaître*, 1 (Aug. 1924), 5. Active in the French Resistance during the Second World War, Basch was captured and executed by the Gestapo in 1944. See his granddaughter Françoise Basch's biography, *Victor Basch: De l'affaire Dreyfus au crime de la Milice* and her *Victor Basch: Un intellectuel cosmopolite*.

[18] As Nicault points out, however, while Spire and Fleg embraced Zionism first and foremost as a way to resolve their own identity issues, Basch's interest in the movement remained primarily 'humanitarian or philanthropic'. See Nicault, 'L'Acculturation des Israélites français au sionisme', 2.

Zionism also provided a Jewish historical narrative similar to that of the new nationalist movements that so influenced Jewish intellectuals of the day. As much as Zionism was a concrete plan for resettling Jews in Palestine, it was also a new way of understanding Jewish history that—like other ethnic nationalisms at the turn of the century—emphasized the bonds of history and blood as the basis for group pride. It was this aspect of Zionism that Edmond Fleg blended into his own version of the ethnic nationalism of his friend Lucien Moreau. For Fleg, as we saw in Chapter 2, Moreau's turn towards antisemitism during the Dreyfus affair marked a moment of crisis. Convinced by many aspects of Moreau's argument but unable to embrace it because he was himself a Jew, Fleg drew from Zionism the sense that he was now on an equal footing with his friend: 'The antisemites accused the Jews of constituting a nation within the nation: but the Jews, at least those whom I met, denied this. And now, lo and behold, the Jews were declaring: We are a people as others are . . . The Zionist idea thrilled me by its loftiness . . . this fidelity to the ancestral soil that had endured two thousand years.'[19]

A 1904 article by André Spire in *Pages libres* revealed a similar logic. Spire painted a dire picture of the fate of the Jewish child growing up in western Europe. Already feeling different, the child would inevitably encounter the antisemite who would tell him to his face 'not to be a Jew: this is the fantasy of every Jewish child born in a village or a small town'. The child's fate once he had fled to one of the great capitals of Europe as an adult, however, would not be much better. He would attempt in vain to find fellow Jews, friends, 'a milieu', but it would be too late, because his unhappy youth had already damned his adulthood. Only Zionism, Spire felt, could offer rescue from this deep sense of alienation and 'render to this worthy race its ancient pride' by giving it a piece of land to call its own.[20] Here we see, as in Fleg's writings, a close link between the possession of a national soil and the security and happiness of a group of people, a link almost identical to that made by right-wing nationalists.

New Encounters: French Jews, Russian Jews, and Zionism in Paris before the First World War

Students of the early Zionist movement have portrayed its activists in France as travelling in their own tight-knit circle, largely unintegrated into the surrounding French society. This, however, is over-simplistic.[21] The French

[19] Fleg, *Why I Am a Jew*, 43.
[20] Spire, 'Irons-nous à Jérusalem?', *Pages libres* (29 Oct. 1904), 349–55.
[21] This is the portrait that both Catherine Nicault and Michel Abitbol draw of the early Zionist militants. See Nicault, *La France et le sionisme*, ch. 1, and Abitbol, *Les Deux Terres promises*, ch. 1.

Jewish press tended to portray the early Zionists as uneducated and working-class, Myriam Schach recalled in her 1949 interview. In fact, however, the movement's leaders were intellectuals and professionals, most of whom had achieved a secure standing in French society by the turn of the century.[22] Schach herself had been naturalized as a French citizen in 1897 and taught German at the Lycée Molière. Other early Zionist activists included Yehouda Tchernoff, who became a distinguished jurist after his immigration to France from Russia in 1892, and Oskar Marmorek and Vladimir Haffkine, scientists at the Institut Pasteur. Marmorek and David Jacobson, a doctor, were the presidents of the Fédération Sioniste de France. Max Nordau, who had been living in Paris since the 1880s, was also part of this circle.[23]

Michel Abitbol argues that Russian Jewish intellectuals who immigrated to France in the 1880s and 1890s came, by and large, with their political orientation already formed. The great split between socialist internationalism and Zionist nationalism that was at the centre of Jewish intellectual life in Russia, he contends, shaped their world-view. As a result, the political activity on which they embarked in France was 'more often the continuation of that which they had left behind, rather than something that had a direct relationship with their experience in Paris'.[24] Abitbol's portrait of these early Zionists as unshaped by their French environment is overdrawn. France always held a very particular place in the east European Jewish imagination as the birthplace of republicanism and the first country to grant Jews civic equality.[25] This association was very much alive for Zionist émigrés, and in many cases played an important role in shaping their political and ideological perspective.

In his memoirs, Yehouda Tchernoff placed great importance on the French environment in his political development. He came from a highly Russified family and was among those Russian Jewish intellectuals who moved towards Jewish nationalism after the pogroms of the 1880s and 1890s. He came to France as a student of modern French history, drawn by 'an instinctive impulse towards Paris and French culture'.[26] He described his embrace of Zionism as a melding of different political and ethical traditions 'dictated by my biblical culture and reinforced by my study and reflection in Paris'.[27] His study of republican organizations between 1814

---

[22] Schach, interview in *La Terre retrouvée* (15 Feb. 1949), 10.

[23] On the early French Zionist movement in Paris, see Hagani, 'Les Débuts du sionisme à Paris (souvenirs d'enfance)', *La Terre retrouvée* (20 Mar. 1929); Levigne-Nicault, 'Le Mouvement sioniste en France'; and Abitbol, *Les Deux Terres promises*, ch. 1.

[24] Abitbol, *Les Deux Terres promises*, 21.

[25] Nancy Green talks about Russian Jews' idealization of France as the country of liberty and civilization in *The Pletzl of Paris*, 25–9.

[26] Tchernoff, *Dans le creuset des civilisations*, i. 84.   [27] Ibid.

and 1870 led him to the belief that the ideals of universal humanism could be realized most effectively through national groupings, an idea he then translated into support for Jewish nationalism. Tchernoff also talked about the role his participation in Dreyfusard political activism played in expanding his social circle beyond the east European immigrant community. He moved into the larger French and Jewish intellectual world at the turn of the century, developing close friendships with the philosopher Frédéric Ruah and the Orientalist scholar Sylvain Lévi. It was at weekly soirées at Lévi's home, he recalled, that he met many prominent French intellectuals, including Marcel Mauss and Jean-Richard Bloch.[28] Tchernoff also recalled that early Zionist efforts to gain the backing of prominent French politicians and other public figures had borne fruit by the time of the First World War. Léon Bourgeois, Georges Clemenceau, Anatole de Monzie, Paul Boncour, and Justin Godart, he noted, had all expressed their support for Zionism by the time the Balfour Declaration was issued in 1917.[29]

The support of important scholars, professors, and young university-affiliated intellectuals between 1910 and 1914, Tchernoff recalled, breathed new life into the French Zionist movement in the years immediately prior to the First World War. *L'Echo sioniste*, defunct since 1905,[30] was revived under new leadership. André Spire,[31] Edmond Fleg, Victor Basch, Henry Marx, and Charles-Edouard Lévy, an Alsatian-born doctor active in the Jewish youth group the Union Scolaire (see Chapter 5), all began contributing. This was also the moment that the Zionist leadership shifted to a new generation: whereas immigrants had originally dominated the movement, now their children's generation took charge.[32] Representative of this group was Baruch Hagani (born as Baumgarten) who became the editor of *L'Echo sioniste* in 1912. Hagani himself was born in France, but his parents were

[28] Other people mentioned by Tchernoff as regular guests at Lévi's home include Paul Painlevé (who would later become a government minister) and the noted physicist Paul Langevin, both of whom became active in the Zionist movement in the 1920s, Paul Boyer, the future administrator of the Ecole des Langues Orientales, Isidore Lévi, and Antoine Meillet (Tchernoff, *Dans le creuset des civilisations*, i. 6).

[29] Ibid. 79. Léon Bourgeois was already an enthusiastic supporter of Zionism by 1899, when *L'Echo sioniste* first came out. See the first issue of *L'Echo sioniste* (5 Sept. 1899), where Bourgeois is quoted at length. Justin Godart was introduced to the cause in 1915 by Joseph and Louis Asscher, Dutch Jewish diamond merchants, philanthropists, and Zionist activists who were living in Paris at the time. See Boukara, 'Justin Godart et le sionisme', 199.

[30] See n. 8 above. The movement, which had been at a low point since the federation's disagreement over the Uganda crisis, experienced a boom after 1910. See Levigne-Nicault, 'Le Mouvement sioniste en France', 143.

[31] Hagani remarked that Spire's contribution at this point could only be literary because he was politically committed to Zangwill's territorialist movement. See 'André Spire et l'action juive', 100.   [32] Levigne-Nicault, 'Le Mouvement sioniste en France', 142.

Lithuanian immigrants who were active in the pre-Herzlian Zionist movement in the 1880s.[33] Remarking on the difference between Hagani's generation and that of his parents, Tchernoff remarked: 'The first generation of Zionists, whose faces reflected the dream, whose preoccupations were with the future, was succeeded by a new generation—younger, more optimistic, and, perhaps, more realistic.'[34] Part of this 'realism' was a recognition that French Jews could be won over only if the movement became associated primarily with the affirmation of Jewish cultural life in the diaspora.

Under Hagani's editorship, the cultural programme of *L'Echo sioniste*, now subtitled 'Revue de la vie juive et sioniste', became much more pronounced. As Zionism was more than a mere political party, the journal's editors announced, they had decided to transform *L'Echo sioniste* accordingly so as to link Zionism directly with fighting assimilation in the diaspora: 'To prevent the descent into assimilation, to reconnect our French-speaking fellow Jews to Jewish traditions and culture, seems to us at the present time to be our overarching duty. And it is on this long-term goal that we would like before all else to focus our activity.'[35] They hoped to achieve this goal by giving more space to events in the Jewish community in France. A combative stance towards winning over 'assimilated' Jews now gave way to a more pragmatic approach. In a 1912 article announcing Victor Basch's 'profession of Zionist faith', for example, Hagani impressed upon his readers that Basch's Zionism was based on his conviction that one could be a good Frenchman and a good Zionist. Though often criticized because it smacked of philanthropy, Hagani asserted, the legitimacy of Basch's brand of Zionism, current among western European Jews, must be acknowledged.[36] A man of two cultures, Hagani appears to have been somewhat uncomfortable with Basch's unashamedly diasporic Zionism. At the same time, however, he recognized the sincerity of his commitment and the necessity of embracing it in order to win French Jews over to the cause.

L'Echo sioniste published several debates between Zionist sympathizers and opponents that brought the issue of Jewish identity to the fore. In June 1912, for example, it invited the writer Henry Marx, who had published a few poems during the journal's early years, to reflect on his 'sentiment de Juif français'.[37] While Marx would later become a Zionist, at this point he was

[33] See Hagani, 'Les Débuts du sionisme à Paris' (Michel Abitbol writes that Hagani was born in Vilna, but Hagani himself says he was born in Paris).

[34] Tchernoff, *Dans le creuset des civilisations*, i. 74.

[35] 'Notre programme', *L'Echo sioniste* (10 Jan. 1912), 1.

[36] Baruch Hagani, 'Une conversion', *L'Echo sioniste* (10 Jan. 1912), 7–9.

[37] Marx's 1913 collection of poetry, *La Gloire intérieure*, which has a messianic flavour reminiscent of the poetry of Henri Franck, included several poems on Jewish themes.

Septième Année   10 Janvier 1912 (*20 Tébeth 5672*)   N° 1

L'ÉCHO SIONISTE

Revue de la Vie Juive et Sioniste
PARAISSANT LE 10 DE CHAQUE MOIS

Rédacteur en Chef : **BARUCH HAGANI**

Le Sionisme a pour but la création
pour le peuple juif en Palestine d'un
asile garanti par le droit public.
(*Programme de Bâle.*)

S. Roukhomovsky

RÉDACTION: 26, rue François-Miron (4ᵉ). — ADMINISTRATION : 21, rue de La Tour-d'Auvergne (9ᵉ).

ABONNEMENTS :

France et Colonies : un an, **5** fr.; six mois, **3** fr. — Étranger : un an, **6** fr.; six mois, **4** fr.

Vente au numéro à la Librairie SOFER, 5, rue Cadet, Paris.

Prix du Numéro : **50** Centimes

PARIS
IMPRIMERIE POLYGLOTTE A. REIFF. — HEYMANN
3, RUE DU FOUR, 3

FIGURE I The first issue of the revamped *Echo sioniste*, 10 January 1912,
which editor Baruch Hagani billed as a 'magazine of Jewish and Zionist life'
Reproduced by permission of the library of the Alliance Israélite Universelle

critical of the movement. Affirming his identity as both a Frenchman and a world citizen, he called upon his fellow Jews, 'rather than organizing a province of freedom, to prepare for the freedom of all the Jews in the world, so that each one can become a free citizen of his chosen country'. Maurice Liber, a young rabbi, criticized Marx's position for promoting a Judaism devoid of any real Jewish content and linked too exclusively with standing up to antisemitism. Rather than affirming himself as a Jew only when attacked for being one, Liber suggested, Marx should learn more about Jewish religion, history, and culture and make Judaism an integral part of his life: 'Is M. Marx's heart', he asked rhetorically, 'which is large enough to accept Sully and Napoleon, too narrow for Abraham and Moses?'[38]

As the decade progressed, rabbis, communal leaders, and intellectuals who were not necessarily in agreement with political Zionism increasingly praised the movement for promoting a renewed sense of Jewish solidarity and the expansion of French Jewish cultural life.[39] An article by a young rabbi and professor at the Ecole Rabbinique de Paris, Maurice Vexler, exemplified this enthusiasm. Writing on the occasion of the eleventh Zionist congress in 1913, Vexler praised the new direction that the Zionist movement had taken under the direction of Baruch Hagani, and aimed to convince his fellow French Jews that the goals of the Zionists were in fact similar to those of religious Jews. He noted approvingly that Zionism had played an important role in bringing Jewish intellectuals back to Judaism by providing an alternative model of Jewishness for those who were distant from synagogue practice. The emphasis here was on a shared interest in the future of the Jewish people: 'Let us unite together, my Zionist brothers, in order to return to and encourage others to return to Judaism. As for the return to Judea', he concluded, 'we shall have to see . . .'.[40]

---

[38] See Marx, 'Le Sentiment d'un Juif français', *L'Echo sioniste* (10 June 1912), 120–1, and Liber's response in the next issue (10 July 1912, p. 138) published under the pseudonym 'M'.

[39] In their reading of *L'Univers israélite* and *Archives israélites* between 1897 and 1914, both Abitbol and Hyman agree that the French Jewish establishment became less hostile to the Zionist movement: see Abitbol, *Les Deux Terres promises*, 41–4, and Hyman, *From Dreyfus to Vichy*, 155–6. They also attribute this shift in attitude to the failure of the Zionist movement to gain either widespread popular support or political allies in western Europe in the decade and a half after the first Zionist congress. This lack of success made the movement less threatening than when it first emerged, and thus not worthy of extensive rebuttals. In addition, the continuing deterioration of the situation of Jews in eastern Europe—the Kishinev pogroms, the Mendel Beilis ritual murder trial, and the general continuation of organized anti-Jewish violence in both the Russian empire and Romania—made the Zionist solution of resettling east European Jews in Palestine appear in an increasingly favourable light. French Jewish writers and publicists, Abitbol points out, often took pains to distinguish between their antipathy towards the political Zionist movement and their attachment to the Land of Israel, which they saw as a potential homeland for persecuted east European Jews. See *Les Deux Terres promises*, 6.

[40] Maurice Vexler, 'Le Sionisme en France', *L'Univers israélite* (13 Sept. 1913), 632. Vexler

The Separation of Church and State and the Religious Revival of the Belle Epoque

The period between the Dreyfus affair and the First World War was also a time of religious innovation within French Jewry. Reform Judaism emerged for the first time on French soil with the establishment of the Union Libérale Israélite as an independent congregation in 1907. Its appearance prompted a group of young rabbis to create *Foi et réveil*, a journal committed to promoting traditional Judaism. In order to understand the intellectual and social context in which these developments took place, we must first turn to broader changes in French religious life during this period, in particular, the 1905 separation of church and state and the religious revival of the belle époque.

The separation of church and state, which was voted into law in December 1905, marked a major turning-point in the history of the Third Republic and the relationship of religion to the French state. In the aftermath of Napoleon's 1801 Concordat with the Pope, Catholicism, Protestantism, and Judaism became state religions, each with a central governing body that retained the right to approve or veto the creation of independent religious groups within its jurisdiction. Objection to this link between church and state became a central feature of the political life of the Third Republic. A first wave of anti-clericalism, which succeeded in establishing a compulsory system of secular schools for all French children in 1882, sought primarily to reduce the influence of the Catholic Church in the public sphere. The 1902 election victory of the radical bloc rekindled the flame of anti-clericalism in a much more radical form, as Emile Combès initiated a series of measures intended to weaken the power of the Catholic Church, which had come to embody the anti-Dreyfusard reaction. The culmination of these measures was the separation of church and state, which removed all government funding of and control over French religious institutions.

This separation, and the extreme measures that the government used to carry it out—including, for example, forcing priests to open their tabernacles so that state officials could take inventories of ecclesiastical property—sparked widespread protest and initially deepened the divisions between secular and religious elements in French society. Once the embers of the radical anti-clerical campaign had died down, however, the separation helped to

specifically contrasted Zionism in France with Zionism in Germany. Whereas in Germany Zionists and anti-Zionists tended to be polarized and attacked each other vociferously, in France, he asserted, the Jews' superior civil and social status had enabled the community at large to appreciate the cultural benefits that Zionism had brought to French Jewish life.

reduce the stigma of religion in republican circles. The separation of church and state was also the separation of religion and politics. Whereas before religion had been connected with reactionary, anti-republican forces, as a noted historian of the period concluded, it 'cleared the way and funded the adaptation of the church to the modern world, when the debate about clericalism would no longer occupy the foreground'.[41] Religion was now a private matter, and affirming one's faith as a Catholic, Calvinist, or Jew was no longer tied to a particular government-sanctioned and -funded institution.

While the separation of church and state led to a decline in the power and influence of organized religion in France, the decade before the First World War was characterized by an atmosphere of religious revival. The emergence of progressive religious movements combining a democratic, pro-republican political agenda with Catholic faith marked this period, as did a general rise of interest in religion among intellectuals and the educated classes.[42] A number of prominent intellectuals of the day—including the writers Paul Claudel and Charles Péguy, the Orientalist Louis Massignon, and Ernest Psichari, Renan's grandson—converted to Catholicism.[43] This new religious vogue among the educated stemmed in part from the same dissatisfaction with positivism and a scientific world-view that led intellectuals such as Maurice Barrès and Charles Maurras to embrace a conservative, racially based brand of nationalism. No longer satisfied with the rationalist philosophical world-view of their parents and teachers, the promise of a deeper level of spirituality and a connection to a particular historical and cultural tradition drew young intellectuals towards Catholicism. Deeply influenced by Henri Bergson's mystical, anti-rationalist philosophy, which achieved widespread popularity in the years before the First World War, this turn towards religion was associated less with an embrace of the Catholic Church than with a quest for individual spirituality.[44]

The founders of both the Union Libérale Israélite and *Foi et réveil* saw themselves as very much part of this larger movement of religious renewal,

---

[41] Mayeur and Rebérioux, *The Third Republic*, 232.   [42] Ibid. 299–301, 310–11.

[43] On this wave of conversions, see Psichari, *Les Convertis de la belle époque*, and Gugelot, *La Conversion des intellectuels au catholicisme en France*. A famous survey of university youth was conducted in 1913 by Agathon (Henri Massis and Alfred de Tarde), the authors of *L'Esprit de la nouvelle Sorbonne*. Their study, *Les Jeunes Gens d'aujourd'hui*, showed that both nationalism and religious sentiment were on the rise among young people at university. While the authors' bias made the study less than scientific, its conclusions nonetheless captured the revolt against positivism that was increasingly prevalent among intellectuals in the pre-war years. See Ory and Sirinelli, *Les Intellectuels en France*, 57–9, and Stock, 'Students versus the University in Pre-World War I Paris', for a discussion of the survey and its implications.

[44] See Mayeur and Rebérioux, *The Third Republic*, 288. On the popularity and influence of Bergson on French intellectual life in the pre-war years, see Grogin, *The Bergsonian Controversy*, and Psichari, *Les Convertis de la belle époque*.

which sought to reconcile religion with modernity and bring spirituality back to contemporary life. While these two groups had very different religious philosophies, their goals were not that different. They saw themselves as responding to a spiritual crisis in the Jewish community and wanted to turn the tide of secularization and assimilation by showing their fellow Jews, in particular the younger generation, that Judaism had a rich spiritual heritage that should not be abandoned in the name of modernity and progress.

The Birth of Reform Judaism in France

The Reform movement, which sought to adapt Jewish religious belief and practice to the Jews' new status as citizens of their country of residence, made deep inroads in Germany and the United States over the course of the nineteenth century.[45] The failure of Reform to make inroads in France was rooted in both the centralizing force exercised by the Consistory and French Jews' equal legal status. In Germany, a desire to prove that Jews were fully modern and thus deserved legal equality fuelled Reform's major innovations, including most importantly the elimination of liturgical references to the coming of the messiah and the return to Jerusalem, the translation of prayers into the vernacular, the mixing of the sexes in the synagogue, and the relaxation of dietary laws and laws of sabbath rest.[46] Because French Jews already enjoyed the status of full-fledged citizens they did not feel this same pressure to radically alter their liturgy and ritual. Furthermore, the Consistory had brought in a number of superficial changes in the early nineteenth century, including the use of organs and choirs, the modernization of rabbis' clothing, and the introduction of sermons in French, that rendered the maintenance of traditional Jewish religious ritual acceptably 'Western' for most acculturated French Jews.[47]

The anti-clerical movement of the late nineteenth century also hindered the development of French Reform Judaism. Because France was strongly divided along religious and secular lines, progressive-minded people—Jews, Protestants, and Catholics alike—often disdained religion altogether. As a result, those Jews who no longer felt comfortable within the confines of Con-

[45] For a comprehensive history of Reform Judaism, see Meyer, *Response to Modernity*.

[46] Whereas historians once attributed the success of Reform in the United States—where (unlike Germany) Jews enjoyed full legal equality—to the theological orientation of German immigrants, it is now understood to be more a product of the American tradition of religious sectarianism and decentralization. See e.g. Jick, *The Americanization of the Synagogue*, and Silverstein, *Alternatives to Assimilation*.

[47] On the reforms introduced by the Consistory in the 19th century see Albert, *The Modernization of French Jewry*.

sistory Judaism were more likely to abandon religious practice than to seek to reform it. By the start of the twentieth century more fertile ground was developing for the birth of a French Reform movement. It was the separation of church and state, however, that provided the immediate context for the creation of a Reform congregation in France.

The Creation of the Union Libérale Israélite

The first stirrings of a French Reform movement can be traced back to 1895, when a small group of Parisian Jews centred in the fashionable sixteenth arrondissement began to discuss the idea of reinvigorating Jewish practice by focusing more attention on internal spirituality and prayer, as well as on the religious education of their children.[48] The creation of this group coincided with the decision of the chief rabbi of France, Zadoc Kahn, to publish an anonymous article in L'Univers israélite proposing the institution of additional Sunday 'sabbath' services in consistorial synagogues. Giving Jews who worked on Saturday mornings the opportunity to worship on the French day of rest, Kahn suggested, was a necessary measure to help stem the current tide of defection from synagogue attendance.[49] The proposals were met with hostility by other members of the Consistory as well as by Archives israélites editor Hippolyte Prague, and rumours that Kahn was in fact the author of the article forced the chief rabbi to divulge his identity several weeks later.[50] It was at this point that the newly formed liberal circle approached Kahn for support, and he agreed to let them use a room in the Synagogue de la Victoire. Henceforth, the liberals began meeting regularly on Sunday mornings for a 'conférence' mixed with some liturgical elements. By 1900, however, certain members of this circle began to feel that this was insufficient, and circulated a pamphlet requesting space within one of the consistorial temples to conduct full-fledged Sunday services.[51] It was signed at this point by only three people: Alfred Peyrera, a merchant and president of the Union Philanthropique Israélite, Salvadore Lévi, also a businessman, and Gaston Bach, a notary. While most members of the Jewish religious establishment were no more sympathetic to the liberals' request in 1900 than they had been in 1895, Kahn supported the group and protected the liberal congregation until his death in 1905. Pressure from conservative rabbis and laity to expel the liberals from the Synagogue de la Victoire began to mount in 1906, however, and Kahn's successor, Alfred Lévy, forced the group out in 1907.[52]

---

[48] Poujol, Aimé Pallière, 158.

[49] 'Une création urgente', L'Univers israélite (3 Jan. 1896), 460–5.

[50] 'Une création urgente: Lettre de Monsieur le grand rabbin Zadok Kahn', L'Univers israélite (31 Jan. 1896), 559–63. On this incident, see Poujol, Aimé Pallière, 158–61.

[51] Poujol, Aimé Pallière, 160–1.   [52] Ibid. 162–3.

Fortunately for the Union Libérale, however, Kahn's death coincided with the voting into law of the separation of church and state, which marked a major change in the Consistory's legal and social status. No longer funded by the state, it now became one 'religious association' among many and lost the legal authority to block the creation of independent Jewish religious organizations.[53] Hence, when the Consistory vetoed the liberals' inclusion in the newly formed Union des Associations Cultuelles Israélites de France et d'Algérie, the group began to plan the creation of an independent synagogue, and enlisted the support of Théodore Reinach, who agreed to join the congregation. It was hoped that Reinach's charismatic personality and renown, both among Jews and in French society more generally, would help the movement to recruit new members.[54] In 1906 a circular almost identical to the one published in 1900 counted thirty-eight signatures, including Reinach's, and in December 1907 the Synagogue Libérale de la rue Copernic opened its doors for the first time.[55] At its helm was Louis-Germain Lévy, a young rabbi from Dijon first recruited by Zadoc Kahn in 1900 to help build up the congregation.[56] Lévy, who had graduated from rabbinical school in 1893 and who also held a doctorate in philosophy, had been a regular contributor to *L'Univers israélite* in the 1890s. He wrote on a variety of subjects, including politics and Jewish history, but most prolifically on religious topics. He was also a specialist in German language and literature, an orientation that undoubtedly played a role in his interest in the Reform movement.[57] The congregation, which consisted of approximately a hundred families, was drawn mostly from the upper ranks of Parisian Jewish circles and included merchants, doctors, lawyers, and other professionals.

[53] The influx of east European immigrants after 1881 had already put a strain on the Consistory's monopoly on Jewish religious life as early as the 1890s, at which point it began to authorize independent immigrant congregations. The separation of church and state greatly accelerated the creation of these independent congregations, however, which no longer had to seek the Consistory's approval. See Green, *The Pletzl of Paris*, 80–7.　　　[54] Ibid. 163.

[55] See 'L'Appel de "L'Union Libérale"', *Archives israélites* (19 Apr. 1906), 123–4.

[56] Poujol, *Aimé Pallière*, 160.

[57] Lévy was the regular reviewer for German-language publications. He visited a Reform congregation in Germany in 1902, which he wrote about in *L'Univers israélite*. Interestingly, at this point he was critical of certain changes made by the Germans, in particular holding sabbath services on Sunday rather than Saturday and eliminating certain ceremonies 'that have great symbolic meaning and the cachet of ancient poetry; religion cannot rid itself of them without losing its hold on people's souls'. See *L'Univers israélite* (26 Dec. 1902), 427–30. From the beginning, however, the content of Lévy's religious essays reflected a philosophical slant very much in keeping with the perspective of Reform ideology. He focused his discussions of Jewish holidays, for example, primarily on the universal human morality that they embody. See his lecture on Shavuot, described as a 'festival of morality': 'La Pentecôte', *L'Univers israélite* (15 May 1896), 197–200.

A Jewish Universalism: The Ideology and Intellectual Heritage of the Union Libérale

While the Union Libérale modelled itself to a certain extent on existing Reform congregations in Germany, England, and the United States, its ideology and primary frame of reference were French. Perhaps the greatest ideological influence on the French Reformers was James Darmesteter.[58] In his writings, Darmesteter developed two principal ideas: that the essence of Judaism lay in the universalist ideals of the ancient Hebrew prophets rather than the Talmud, and, by extension, that Judaism represented a rational religion par excellence. Louis-Germain Lévy cited Darmesteter at length to support his thesis that, because Judaism was based on reason, it provided its followers with basic ethical guidelines rather than dictating a particular belief system.[59] For Lévy, as for Darmesteter, Judaism was the only truly universal religion because it favoured the development of positive human qualities and was in perfect harmony with the will of God.

French Reform Judaism was also shaped by its founders' contact with liberal Christian movements of the day. Aimé Pallière, an eclectic figure of Catholic origins[60] who would play a major role in Jewish communal life in the 1920s, first became involved with the Union Libérale in its formative years. Pallière provided a bridge between the Jewish Reformers and the Ecole de Lyon, a French branch of the modernist movement that sought to reconcile science and religion and stressed the similarities among different religious faiths.[61] Père Hyacinthe, a maverick Catholic priest who questioned the divinity of Jesus and preached reconciliation between Christian and Jew, was part of this group. He published numerous articles in *L'Univers israélite* in the 1890s and served as an adviser to the nascent Jewish Reform

---

[58] It was Darmesteter who most eloquently developed the idea that the essence of Judaism was in fact equivalent to the ideals of the French Revolution. Both Marrus and Meyer note the influence of Darmesteter's ideas on the French Reform movement. See Marrus, *The Politics of Assimilation*, and Meyer, *Response to Modernity*, 221–3. Poujol also points to Joseph Salvador as an ideological inspiration for the Union Libérale; *Aimé Pallière*, 152–4.

[59] Lévy, *Une religion rationnelle et laïque*, 64.

[60] Aimé Pallière, who was raised a devout Catholic, wandered into a synagogue in his native Lyons on the eve of Yom Kippur at the age of 17. He began to study Jewish religious doctrine and eventually became convinced of the essential truth of Judaism rather than Christianity. Pallière never underwent a full-fledged conversion, however, choosing instead to identify as a 'Noahide'—someone who believes in the basic precepts of Judaism and observes the Ten Commandments, but who as a non-Jew is not bound by the obligations that Jews must fulfil according to talmudic law. This decision, as well as Pallière's ideas and influence, are discussed in greater detail in later chapters. For a succinct discussion of Pallière and his near-conversion to Judaism, see Poujol, 'Autour du "cas" Pallière'.   [61] See Poujol, *Aimé Pallière*, 105–90.

movement,[62] as did the Protestant minister Charles Wagner, who called upon his fellow Christians to embrace the Jews as prophets.[63]

Both *L'Univers israélite* and the *Archives israélites* took a strong stand against the Reform movement, which from their perspective was a symptom of assimilation and the degeneration of French Jewry.[64] Hippolyte Prague was an especially vociferous critic of the nascent movement. In an article published in 1906, after the liberals' circular first appeared, he referred condescendingly to Reform as a form of 'neo-Judaism', inspired by women and young rabbis who were more philosophers than serious religious thinkers.[65] By changing age-old Jewish religious customs, he argued, they were destroying Judaism from the core. The liberals' close relationship with various Christian groups also provoked criticism from Prague and other members of the Jewish establishment: if the Reformers continued along their present path, Prague remarked sarcastically, they would wake up one day and find themselves Protestants.[66] In fact, however, the Union Libérale's universalist theology and emphasis on the similarities between Judaism and other faiths went hand in hand with a strong desire to promote Jewish distinctiveness in real social terms. In order to understand the goals and ideology of the French Reform movement and the controversy that it sparked, we must return briefly to debates about secularism and assimilation within the Jewish community in the last three decades of the nineteenth century.

Towards the Creation of a Reform Movement: Secularism and Assimilation in the Early Third Republic

The new opportunities for social and economic success that Jews experienced during the Third Republic tended to go hand in hand with the process of secularization. In an atmosphere in which progressive-minded people associated support for the Republic with secularism, it is no surprise that Jews, whose identity and social status were so tied to the republican state, often abandoned religious practice as part of their integration into French

---

[62] Pallière, *Le Sanctuaire inconnu*, 193. The excommunication of the liberal priest Alfred Loisy in 1907 brought modernists into the French public eye. See Mayeur and Rebérioux, *The Third Republic*, 310–11. On Hyacinthe's influence on and involvement with the Union Libérale, see also Poujol, *Aimé Pallière*, 145–72.   [63] Meyer, *Response to Modernity*, 222.

[64] Interestingly, the *Archives israélites* did publish an article in the mid-1890s (before the Reformers had organized in France), praising Reform in the United States for keeping young people within the Jewish fold. See 'Une innovation', *Archives israélites* (11 July 1895), 220.

[65] 'Le Féminisme dans la communauté', *Archives israélites* (23 Aug. 1906), 266. Women, Prague asserted in keeping with the more reactionary wisdom of the day, should not be allowed to exercise undue power in society, since they were prone to fancy and sentiment.

[66] Prague, 'Judaïsme pour les gens du monde', *Archives israélites* (30 Aug. 1900), 881–4.

republican culture.[67] This tendency towards religious disaffiliation created increasing anxiety on the part of the Consistory and the French rabbinate. Concern about the dwindling numbers of Jews attending religious services, lack of religious observance, and general disaffiliation from the Jewish community began to appear as a theme in the French Jewish press in the late 1870s and continued to grow stronger over the next two decades.[68]

As Pierre Birnbaum has shown, the leaders of the French Jewish community during the early years of the Third Republic expressed a great deal of ambivalence about the secularization of French society. On the one hand, both the rabbinate and the Consistory were firmly wedded to the Republic and the principle of *laïcité*. As members of a religious minority, it was in their interest to lessen the influence of the Catholic Church. On the other hand, as religious leaders, they often expressed concern about the effects of *laïcité* on both their own community and French society at large.[69] Prague, for example, was ambivalent about the Ferry Laws of 1882, which made primary education free, compulsory, and secular. While he saw the school laws as necessary for the protection of individual liberty, Prague nonetheless expressed concern that the elimination of religion from the school programme threatened to leave French youth without any moral and spiritual education.[70]

French rabbis and consistorial leaders proposed various measures to counter secularization, including more conferences and lectures aimed at young people and the reform of the existing system of Jewish religious education.[71] 'It is not sufficient to lament in flowery language and whine pathetically about the misfortunes of our age', Prague commented in the late 1890s about the mood of pessimism concerning dwindling Jewish religious affiliation. 'Rather, having looked the beast in the face, we must fight courageously to pluck away his victims.'[72] The decision to create a Reform congregation represented a radical solution to this perceived spiritual crisis.

[67] As recent scholarship has emphasized, integration and secularization were not necessarily synonymous with assimilation. In particular, Birnbaum, *The Jews of the Republic*, shows that many Jews active in French politics during the Third Republic who had abandoned religious practice and socialized in Christian circles continued to identify as Jews and took a strong stand against antisemitism.

[68] See Jeffrey Haus, 'The Practical Dimensions of Ideology'.

[69] See Birnbaum, *The Jews of the Republic*, 123.

[70] Haus, 'The Practical Dimensions of Ideology', 345.

[71] See e.g. Zadoc Kahn's article in the *Archives israélites* proposing the creation of Jewish literary societies throughout France, published just seven months before his proposal for Sunday services. 'Un projet de souscription', *Archives israélites* (11 July 1895), 221–2. For more on Kahn and his proposed reforms, see Haus, 'The Practical Dimensions of Ideology', ch. 9, and Julien Weill, *Zadoc Kahn*.

[72] Prague, 'De l'instruction religieuse', *Archives israélites* (2 Dec. 1897), 377–9.

While the liberals were at odds with the mainstream religious community over doctrinal issues, as we shall see, their primary concern, like the leaders of the Consistory, was to keep young Jews within the Jewish fold. As the liberals saw it, the reforms that they proposed were a solution to assimilation rather than a symptom of it.

Ideology and Practice: Reform Judaism as a Response to Assimilation

In describing the evolution of James Darmesteter's ideas, Michael Marrus argues that his theory of 'prophetic Judaism' was prompted by his desire to save something of a tradition to which he felt fundamentally attached, but had rejected in its Orthodox form. Over the course of his life, Marrus shows, Darmesteter's radical universalism evolved into a position that gave more validity to the idea of the maintenance of Jewish distinctiveness. Initially he ascribed to Judaism a relatively passive role in history as a critic of injustice, and imagined that it would dissolve into a 'catholic union' to be established in a utopian future.[73] His later writings, by contrast, assigned Judaism a more active role in the development of humanity, as a universal religion capable of resolving humanity's spiritual crises.[74] Nonetheless, the primary goal of Darmesteter's ideology was to show the compatibility of Judaism with the ideals of the French Revolution and the Third Republic. His philosophy represented the culmination of the central project of nineteenth-century Jewish intellectuals and publicists: to prove the Jews' worth as French citizens. The French Reform movement, by contrast, was created with the goal of fighting assimilation and preserving Jewish group distinctiveness. The very idea of reforming the Jewish religion, of creating a new synagogue in which Jewish religious rituals could be practised in a modernized form, set the movement apart from Darmesteter by proposing a new way to be Jewish in real social terms. Whereas Darmesteter's philosophy does not give a clear picture of whether he believed that the Jews should continue to exist as a distinct group, for the founders of the Union Libérale a desire for the survival of Jewish distinctiveness was paramount.

The leaders of the Union Libérale justified their proposed changes to liturgy and practice by pointing to the dwindling number of Jews attending religious services or participating in Jewish communal life. Reforming the religious education system was at the heart of the group's agenda. By de-

---

[73] These were the views expressed in *Coup d'œil sur l'histoire du peuple juif* (1880) and *Joseph Salvador* (1881). See Marrus, *The Politics of Assimilation*, 122–33.

[74] Marrus (ibid.) attributes this to Darmesteter's disillusionment with the economic crises of the late 1880s and the beginnings of the modern antisemitic movement.

veloping a system of religious instruction that would teach modern Jewish history as well as the Bible and transform the bar mitzvah ceremony from 'merely the accomplishment of a meaningless formula that leaves no durable impression on the child' into a spiritually fulfilling experience, they hoped to encourage adolescents to remain within the Jewish faith as adults.[75] From the perspective of the Reformers, it was only through change that Judaism would be able to maintain itself. Central to their argument was a conviction that the existing structure of French Judaism was failing miserably.[76]

This idea was central to the thinking of Marguerite Brandon-Salvadore, a prominent philanthropist who was one of the Reformers' most outspoken publicists.[77] Brandon-Salvadore, who became one of the Union's two vice-presidents, first drew the attention of Lévi, Bach, and Peyrera in 1900, when she expressed her support for their project in the *Archives israélites*.[78] She published numerous letters and articles in favour of Reform in the Jewish press, and edited an anthology of passages from the Bible, Talmud, and medieval Jewish literature in 1903 that became one of the Union's standard texts.[79] If French Judaism did not adjust to the new religious mood of the times, with its emphasis on spirituality and individual faith rather than ritual practice, Brandon-Salvadore suggested in an open letter to Chief Rabbi Emmanuel Weill, religiously inclined youth would be driven into the arms of Christianity.[80]

Louis-Germain Lévy shared a similar concern with keeping Jewish youth in the fold. A desire to build a stronger sense of Jewish community was central to his thinking well before he became the head of the Union Libérale.

---

[75] See 'Judaïsme pour les gens du monde', *Archives israélites* (30 Aug. 1900), 885, 891–2.

[76] Catherine Poujol similarly points out that, contrary to the insinuations of its detractors, the Union Libérale's programme was not permissive, but rather called for a serious return to religious practice. Poujol, *Aimé Pallière*, 162.

[77] Marguerite Brandon-Salvadore was the daughter of Gabriel Salvadore, a colonel in the French army and later a gentleman farmer. She was briefly married to Captain Brandon, who died in the Franco-Prussian War. After his death, Brandon-Salvadore devoted herself to writing and charitable work. Her obituary in *Le Rayon* describes her as one of the group's most active founders. See 'Mme Brandon-Salvadore', *Le Rayon* (Aug./Sept. 1925), 3–5.

[78] See the letter of Peyrera, Lévi, and Bach in *Archives israélites* (20 Sept. 1900), 908.

[79] Brandon-Salvadore, *A travers les moissons*.

[80] Brandon-Salvadore, 'Lettre ouverte à M. le Rabbin E. Weill', *L'Univers israélite* (11 Apr. 1902), 106–10: 110. Weill responded in the next issue (18 Apr. 1902), 140–2. Brandon-Salvadore's emphasis on personal faith was similar to that of Lily Montagu, one of the leaders of the Jewish Religious Union. This English movement for 'liberal Judaism', created at the same time as the Union Libérale, was also close to progressive Christianity and saw reforming Judaism as a way to fight assimilation. An earlier Reform movement centred around the West London Synagogue had existed in England since the 1850s. On the two waves of the English Reform movement, see Meyer, *Response to Modernity*, 171–80, 212–21.

During the antisemitic crisis of the Dreyfus affair, for example, he advocated for the creation of an association of young Jewish intellectuals. An organization aimed at educating young Jews about Judaism, he argued, would serve as an important weapon against antisemitism. For Lévy, one reason for the success of the antisemitic movement was Jewish ignorance: unequipped with accurate knowledge of Jewish religion and history, Jews were unable to respond effectively to the propaganda of Drumont and his colleagues. Jewish communal leaders had erred, he believed, in failing to create a vibrant associational life that would have served to counter the trend towards assimilation among Jewish youth.[81]

Le Rayon

The Union Libérale began publishing a monthly journal, *Le Rayon*, in 1912. Edited by Louis-Germain Lévy, it set out a two-part mission for itself: first, to familiarize its readers with Jewish religion, history, and literature and second, to bring to its readers' attention 'great thoughts and noble sentiments' of men of all lands, opinions, and eras. Each issue consisted primarily of short texts reprinted from other sources rather than original articles. In keeping with the second part of its mission, over half of the quotations and essays came from non-Jewish sources, including Christian, Buddhist, Muslim, and other religious texts, as well as contemporary philosophy and literature. The dual themes of rendering Judaism more universal and preserving Jewish distinctiveness run through the paper. An article entitled 'La Raison d'être de l'Union Libérale', for example, suggests that changes in Jewish liturgy were undertaken with the express goal of making services more universal, so that people of any religious persuasion could feel at home in the Union Libérale's synagogue.[82] Several months later, by contrast, Théodore Reinach argued against the idea that a universal religion was either possible or desirable. Rather, he suggested, the goal should be a fraternity of religions, which could only come into being if each one preserved its own unique qualities.[83]

Le Rayon reveals the extent to which the Union Libérale was part of a broader *fin-de-siècle* religious revival. Like liberal Christians, French Reformers wanted to reconcile religion and science. Many of the articles were intended to show that the 'prophetic Judaism' of the Union Libérale was in perfect harmony with a scientific world-view, an idea central to Lévy's writ-

---

[81] Louis Lévy, 'Une création qui s'impose', *L'Univers israélite* (3 Dec. 1897), 330–3.
[82] 'La Raison d'être de l'Union Libérale', *Le Rayon* (15 Jan. 1913), 3.
[83] 'Le Problème de la religion universelle', *Le Rayon* (15 Oct. 1913), 6.

ings and sermons. Equally important, however, was the journal's emphasis on the need for a return to religion as an antidote to the crass materialism of the nineteenth century. Bergson's philosophy, which placed intuition and spirituality rather than scientific rationalism at the heart of human nature, was represented very positively in the journal. Religion, it wanted to persuade its readers, was far from dead: it was undergoing a revival in an enlightened form, and Judaism must not be left behind.[84]

The Traditionalist Reaction: *Foi et réveil*

In 1913, a year after the liberals began publishing *Le Rayon*, another religiously oriented publication, *Foi et réveil*, appeared. Subtitled 'Revue trimestrielle de la doctrine et de la vie juive', it was initiated largely as a response to Reform Judaism. The principal contributors were four young rabbis who charged themselves with the mission of promoting traditional Judaism. Jules Bauer, the journal's editor and oldest of the group, served as a congregational rabbi in Avignon and then Nice, where *Foi et réveil* was initially published. The journal moved with him to Paris in 1919 when he was appointed director of the Ecole Rabbinique. A frequent contributor to the scholarly *Revue des études juives*, Bauer also wrote two books on Jewish prayer aimed at a lay audience, as well as a history of the Ecole Rabbinique.[85] Like Bauer, Julien Weill came from a native French Jewish family of long standing. The son of Emmanuel Weill, first chief rabbi of Versailles, Weill *fils* was also the son-in-law of Zadoc Kahn and brother-in-law of Israël Lévi, both chief rabbis of France. Weill inherited his father's congregation upon graduation from rabbinical school, and after a stint as a military chaplain during the First World War he obtained a position at the Synagogue de la Victoire in Paris, where he eventually succeeded Jacques Henri Dreyfuss as chief rabbi of Paris. Weill was a man of many talents. A gifted artist and musician who wrote musical scores for religious texts, he served as the editor-in-chief of the *Revue des études juives* and published two books on Judaism intended for a popular audience.[86]

The two other principal contributors to *Foi et réveil*, Maurice Liber and Maurice Vexler, were from east European immigrant backgrounds. Not unlike Baruch Hagani, these men were part of an 'in-between' generation, raised and educated in France but close to the immigrant community. Hagani, as we have seen, brought a French sensibility to *L'Echo sioniste*.

---

[84] See e.g. Louis-Germain Lévy, 'Notre programme', *Le Rayon* (15 Sept. 1912), 1.
[85] Bauer, *Prières à l'usage de l'enfance*, *Notre livre de prières*, and *L'Ecole rabbinique*.
[86] *La Foi d'Israël* and *Le Judaïsme*; these are discussed in more detail in Chapter 8 below.

Vexler and Liber, by contrast, helped to bring a more east European sensibility into native French Jewish circles. Liber was born in Warsaw in 1884 and Vexler in Romania in 1887, but both immigrated to France as children. Liber obtained a position teaching history at the Ecole Rabbinique in 1907. Like Bauer, he served as a military chaplain during the First World War, and became the director of courses in rabbinic Judaism at the Ecole des Hautes Etudes in 1921. Liber was a prolific writer, lecturer, and communal activist. He published extensively in both *L'Univers israélite* (using the pen names M. Li, Judaeus, and Ben-Ammi) and the *Revue des études juives*. He also assumed a leadership position in the inter-war youth group Chema Israël. Maurice Vexler (the pen name of Meyer Wolff), served as interim rabbi in Bordeaux and contributed prolifically to both *L'Univers israélite* and the *Revue des études juives* before his untimely death on the battlefield in 1914. Aimé Pallière, who straddled Reform and traditionalist groups in the years before the war, was also a founding member of *Foi et réveil* and contributed regularly to the journal.[87]

For the founders of the *Union Libérale*, French Jews' increasing disaffiliation was a product of the atavism of traditional Judaism. For the traditionalists, by contrast, the blame for the community's assimilation and secularization lay in the ignorance of the average French Jew about Judaism. It was not by changing Judaism, they held, but by educating Jews about it and demanding a greater degree of religious observance that Jews would be convinced of the need to preserve their heritage. Given the lack of an adequate system of Jewish education, Bauer remarked in his introductory article for *Foi et réveil*, it was not surprising that French Jews were so woefully ignorant of the Jewish origins of Western values and assumed instead that they stemmed from Christianity.[88] It was the goal of *Foi et réveil*, he asserted, to counter this ignorance and show progressive Jews that Judaism should not be abandoned in the name of progress and modernity.[89]

Traditionalists criticized the nascent Reform movement for equating Judaism and Christianity. Contributors to *Foi et réveil*, by contrast, em-

---

[87] Pallière's decision to move from his native Lyons to Nice in 1911, Catherine Poujol suggests (*Aimé Pallière*, 192), was prompted by Bauer's invitation to help him start up *Foi et réveil*. While Pallière was sympathetic to the Reformers' 'modernist' theological orientation, he disagreed with their lax attitude towards the practice of Jewish religious ritual. It was for this reason that, despite his close ties with the Reform circle, he refused their initial 1908 offer to become a Reform preacher, preferring to formally affiliate with the traditionalists. See Pallière, *Le Sanctuaire inconnu*, 195, and Poujol, *Aimé Pallière*, 171. As we shall see in Chapter 4, he did become officially affiliated with the Reform movement in 1922, and played a major role in working out a modus vivendi between the Union Libérale and the Consistory in 1924.

[88] Jules Bauer, 'Notre programme', *Foi et réveil* (May 1913), 7.

[89] Jules Bauer in the 1912 brochure announcing the creation of *Foi et réveil*, which can be consulted in the library of the Alliance Israélite Universelle in Paris.

phasized Jewish difference, in some instances taking a bold stand in favour of the superiority of Judaism. Liber, for example, suggested that Christian democrats and socially progressive Catholics should not look to the Gospels to back up their ideas, but rather to the 'Old Testament', which, in this regard, was 'much more modern than the New'.[90] In an address to 'progressive Christians' on the occasion of the Sixth International Congress on Religious Progress, Aimé Pallière also argued for the superiority of Judaism —interestingly, by turning Théodore Reinach's argument against the ideal of a universal religion on its head. It was Judaism, with its concept of God not tied to the historically specific personage of Jesus, that had this potential: 'Not only is a universal religion desirable and possible', he argued, 'it already exists... in its highest and purest form in Judaism... which embraces under its spiritual tent, infinitely larger than all other terrestrial sanctuaries, all humanity.'[91]

In a 1913 article entitled 'Nous Juifs', Maurice Vexler developed another related theme: countering the Pauline conception of Judaism as a dead religion that has been superseded by Christianity.[92] For Vexler, Jewish religious Reformers in the era following the French Revolution were partially to blame for the prevalence of this notion, perpetuated in the nineteenth century by the widely influential Ernest Renan, because they emphasized the universalist aspect of Judaism to such an extreme degree. In fact, Vexler argued, it was only by affirming their particularism that Jews would be able to fulfil their universalist mission. Vexler's east European origins perhaps influenced him to reason in this way: whereas popular wisdom in west European countries held that Judaism should be relegated to the private sphere, in eastern Europe, where Jews were not faced with the task of integration, Judaism had remained a distinctive public culture.

A discussion of declining synagogue attendance by Maurice Liber begins in much the same tone. One of the reasons why French Jews did not practise Judaism, Liber suggested, was that contemporary rabbis asked too little of their congregations. Bereft of any kind of real religious education, it was only natural that they had come to see Judaism as a series of meaningless rituals. Interestingly, however, Liber ended the article by suggesting various compromises that could be made to encourage people to attend services: if a town had a weekly market on Saturday mornings, he proposed, services should be held later than was customary. Here we see that at the same time that Liber

---

[90] Maurice Liber, 'L'Esprit social dans la Bible', *Foi et réveil* (Aug. 1913), 148–56.
[91] Loëtmol (pen name of Aimé Pallière), 'Les Tentes de Sem', *Foi et réveil* (Aug. 1913), 140–7.
[92] *Foi et réveil* (May 1913), 11–30.

took an idealistic stance in favour of Orthodoxy he realized the need to accommodate to the realities of contemporary French Jewish life.[93]

Zionists, Liberals, and Traditionalists: Dialogues and Differences

Though they varied in their political perspectives and ideological programmes, Zionists, Reformers, and traditionalist Jews were not isolated from one another. They reprinted articles from each other's publications, reported on events in each other's communities, and their respective journals occasionally shared contributors. Articles by Maurice Liber, Maurice Vexler, and Aimé Pallière appeared in *L'Echo sioniste* in 1913,[94] and *Le Rayon* reprinted several articles from *L'Echo sioniste*.[95] This atmosphere of co-operation stemmed from a sense of a shared mission. Despite their differences, more often than not these groups recognized each other's contribution towards enriching Jewish cultural life in France. Even more importantly, while they had different strategies they shared certain ideological similarities.

Zionists proposed their ideology as an alternative Jewish identity for those no longer attached to religious belief. The critique of French Jewry and proposals for change offered by both Reform and traditionalist Jews were intended to turn the tide of Jewish secularization. A close reading of the discourse of both Reformers and traditionalists, however, shows that while they put their call for revival in religious terms, their conception of Jewish identity was in fact rooted in an ethnic understanding of Jewishness not much different from that of the Zionists. As Michael Meyer has shown in his history of the Reform movement, the tendency of Reform theologians and rabbis to emphasize the universalist aspects of Judaism and the similarities between Judaism and Christianity inevitably raised the problem of justifying the maintenance of Jewish distinctiveness. After all, if Judaism and Christianity were the same in essence, why shouldn't one intermarry, or become a Theist or a Unitarian? Meyer addressed the response of the English Reformer

[93] Liber, 'De la restauration du culte public', *Foi et réveil* (May 1914), 6–24.

[94] See, in *L'Echo sioniste*: Liber, 'Zadoc Kahn et le sionisme' (10 Mar. 1913, pp. 49–52; 10 Apr. 1913, pp. 75–7; 10 May 1913, pp. 93–7); Loëtmol [Pallière], 'L'Hébreu, langue vivante' (10 July 1913, pp. 143–4); and Maurice Vexler, 'Universalisme et particularisme' (13 Aug. 1913, pp. 165–6). Pallière's and Vexler's pieces were sections of articles that originally appeared in *Foi et réveil*. The paper also reprinted the opening statement of *Le Rayon* (10 Oct. 1912, p. 208), and gave a lengthy, favourable review to Louis-Germain Lévy's 1911 book on Maimonides (10 Apr. 1912, pp. 84–5).

[95] These included a short piece on Jewish colonization in Palestine (15 Dec. 1912, pp. 29–30), and an article on the history of the Zionist movement by Max Nordau (15 Nov. 1913, pp. 25–30).

Claude Montefiore to this kind of criticism. The essence of Montefiore's argument was that Judaism served as 'religious home, a channel through which the waters of universal faith flow with greater momentum'.[96] While the ultimate goal of Jews and Christians was the same, they could only realize that goal by maintaining their group distinctiveness.

This idea is very similar to the sentiments expressed by Louis-Germain Lévy at a Protestant congress in Geneva in 1905, where he was invited by Charles Wagner to speak on Judaism. 'We are travelling down two different paths', Lévy told his Protestant colleagues, 'heading in a similar direction towards the same emotional and ideological destination . . . the goal that we want to achieve is the same, but the point of departure and the means may, and must, differ'.[97] For Lévy, differences among groups of people were expressions of the divine will, which could not be expressed in any one particular form. Montefiore, like Lévy, ostensibly rejected a definition of Judaism in anything other than religious terms. Both men defined themselves as anti-Zionists and in their sermons and religious writings often explicitly attacked the idea that the Jews constituted a people or an ethnic group rather than a religion.[98] In fact, however, the arguments that they used to legitimize the maintenance of Jewish distinctiveness were little different from those of the Zionists.

Speaking at the Geneva conference, Lévy explicitly criticized a universalist vision that did not allow for group difference. Prompted by similar needs and concerns, he suggested, those attending the conference had all come together to share each other's insights and knowledge. Nonetheless, he advised, 'let us safeguard the unique value of each community and not require the disappearance of Christian, Jewish, Muslim, and Buddhist groups; we must not demand that all this energy and spontaneity end up in some kind of amorphous grey blob'.[99] Classic Enlightenment universalism, based entirely on the idea of the rights of the individual, had been transformed into respect for the rights of human collectivities. Whereas Zionists defined these groups in national or ethnic terms, Lévy expressed a similar sentiment but spoke of different *religious* groups. Rather than rejecting the classic nineteenth-century definition of Judaism as a religion, he reformulated it to fit with a new world-view in which differences among groups of

---

[96] Meyer, *Response to Modernity*, 216.

[97] Lévy, 'Le Congrès de Genève', supplement to *L'Univers israélite* (3 Aug. 1905), 11.

[98] See e.g. Lévy's article, 'Pour et contre les Juifs', *L'Univers israélite* (11 Sept. 1896), 774–9, in which he criticizes a Christian author for referring to 'the Jewish people' because the Jews were now a confessional group. On Montefiore's opposition to Zionism and insistence on a purely religious definition of Judaism, see Meyer, *Response to Modernity*, 216.

[99] 'Le Congrès de Genève', 11.

people were increasingly respected in progressive circles. Clearly, for Lévy, a theology emphasizing Judaism's universality did not rule out a commitment to the maintenance of Jewish distinctiveness in concrete social terms. Ivan Strenski makes a similar point in his study of the relationship of Emile Durkheim's philosophy to the French Jewish culture of his day. Central aspects of Durkheimian sociology, Strenski argues, were related to the shift towards a 'societist' world-view. Whereas nineteenth-century Jewish intellectuals defined Judaism as 'hyperspiritual', he argues, by the turn of the century, 'French Jews had become more conscious of the need to embody their religion in suitable societal terms'.[100]

Théodore Reinach's commitment to Reform Judaism can perhaps be understood in a similar light. Reinach, a professor of religion at the Ecole des Hautes Etudes and the Collège de France and deputy from Savoy in the National Assembly from 1906 to 1914, was the author of *Histoire des Israélites depuis la ruine de leur indépendance nationale jusqu'à nos jours*, which was in its fifth edition by 1914. One of the main purposes of Reinach's history was to prove the central thesis of nineteenth-century Franco-Judaism: that modern Jews, as distinct from their ancestors, constituted a religious group rather than a people. Interestingly, however, Reinach's desire to give this theory a solid historical basis appeared at exactly the moment when its contradictions were becoming increasingly apparent.

As we have seen, while French Jews in the nineteenth century in fact functioned and thought of themselves on a day-to-day basis in ethnic terms, they officially defined themselves as a religious group. By the beginning of the twentieth century, however, the rise of racial antisemitism, the immigration of 'ethnically visible' Jews from eastern Europe, and the birth of the Zionist movement were making this gap between ideology and practice increasingly transparent. As a result, Reinach, Lévy, and others in their circle perhaps felt the need to reassert the ideology of integration, grounded in a confessional definition of Judaism, in unequivocal terms. For Reinach as for Lévy, however, a universalist, integrationist model of Jewish history and religion was in no way synonymous with the end of Jewish particularism. Like those religious and communal leaders who sought to preserve Jewish distinctiveness in the radically changed landscape of post-revolutionary France, Reinach's involvement with Reform Judaism stemmed from his desire to adapt Judaism in order to ensure its survival for generations to come.

Contributors to *Foi et réveil* also used the language of ethnicity. In an article published in both *Foi et réveil* and *L'Echo sioniste*, for example, Vexler argued that:

[100] Strenski, *Durkheim and the Jews of France*, 41.

Religion must necessarily take into account the traditions and the history of each people, of each group, as well as those other factors, such as its *mentalité* ... which constitute its character ... it is the divine will that different groups of people, spread out over the globe, reflect in their soul the colour of the sky above their head and the mysterious flavour of the land that has nourished them.[101]

Here we see Jewish religious difference defended in a language of blood and history similar to that of the Zionists (and ethnic nationalists more generally). *Foi et réveil*'s contributors essentially opposed Zionism because of its secularism. While accepting the Zionists' critique of the state of French Jewry, they rejected their suggestion that it was possible to treat the renaissance of the Jewish people separately from the renaissance of Judaism. As we have seen, many contributors to *Foi et réveil*, including Maurice Vexler, Maurice Liber, and Aimé Pallière, openly praised Zionism for its cultural achievements. Armand Lipman, a career military officer who contributed prolifically to the Jewish press in the inter-war years, took a more adversarial stance towards the Zionist movement.[102] Lipman headed the French branch of Agudat Israël, an anti-Zionist religious movement founded in Germany in 1912.[103] In an article for *Foi et réveil* he presented this group to his French readers as a religious alternative to Zionism. In fact, however, his criticisms of Zionism show that, like Liber and Vexler, he understood Jewish identity in ethnic terms not that different from those of the Zionists. Lipman did not deny the Zionist claim that the Jews comprised a distinct race, but rather criticized their emphasis on the national or 'racial' dimension of Judaism over its religious aspect: 'The Jewish race? No doubt it exists, but it is the daughter of the Jewish religion; a minor daughter, incapable of self-direction or even of life itself apart from her mother.'[104]

A story in *Foi et réveil* intended for children made a similar point. A teacher gives a group of Jewish children a lecture on antisemitism and the

---

[101] Vexler, 'Universalisme et particularisme', 165–6.

[102] Lipman was the son of the chief rabbi of Metz and husband of the feminist activist and writer Gabrielle Moyse. Both husband and wife penned essays and books of religious commentary. Moyse, who often published under the pen name Gemma, was a founding member of the Fédération des Femmes Radicales et Socialistes, and many of her publications such as *Le Féminisme dans la Bible hébraïque* and *Héroïnes bibliques* reflected her dual allegiance to feminism and traditional Judaism. Her 1910 play *Les Sanédrin*, a polemical drama intended to counter stereotypes about Jews and Judaism and present intermarriage in a negative light, foreshadowed the post-First World War genre of Jewish-themed literature that is discussed in Chapter 7. This play was her first publication, and the only one for which she used her married name. On Moyse, see Bitton, *Présences féminines juives en France*, 196–7.

[103] According to Lipman, the Parisian section of Agudat Israël had 200 members at the time his article was published. See A. Lipman, 'Vers la renaissance juive: L'Agoudath Israël', *Foi et réveil* (Aug. 1913), 113–33. [104] Ibid.

nature of Jewish identity in the modern world. He begins by explaining to the children that the Jews are 'a great people dispersed throughout the world'. But what does that imply, he asks rhetorically: 'Are we not French? Do we not exercise the same rights and duties as our fellow citizens?' In order to resolve this apparent contradiction, he explains that the term 'people' does not refer simply to possession of a particular corner of the globe, but rather to a shared spiritual and intellectual heritage: 'Look around you and you will hear talk of a Catholic people, a Protestant people, a people of workers . . . Why should it then be astonishing that at the same time that you are French, you are in your own way a people apart?'[105] Here we see Jewish difference defended by a reversal of the classic nineteenth-century line of argument: rather than pointing to the similarities between Jews and other Frenchmen in order to argue that the two identities were compatible, the author argued that Jewish particularism was no different from the hundreds of other particularisms that made up French society. Each of these groups, whether religious, social, or professional, contributed 'each in its own way' to the glory of France and the progress of humanity. Like Lipman, the author went on to affirm the centrality of religion, the 'sacred flame' of the Jewish people: 'without it, we have no internal flame, no tangible existence, no raison d'être'.[106] It was a renewed commitment to religious Judaism that must be at the core of a renaissance of Jewish cultural life.

For the author of this story, the similarity of Jews to other Frenchmen was a given; it was the validity of Jewish difference that needed to be explained to the younger generation. At the same time, however, the particular affinity of France and the Jews remained central to the author's thinking. Republican France, he suggested, was particularly equipped to understand the Jewish soul because of its deep commitment to the rights of minorities—whether Poles, Finns, or any other oppressed group—around the globe. It was this commitment, he asserted, that comprised 'the true nature of our national soul'.[107] This line of argument fitted well into the framework of Franco-Judaism, but it was a Franco-Judaism that had been given a new twist. Like nineteenth-century Jewish intellectuals and communal leaders, the author linked French and Jewish values and attributed special meaning to the presence of the Jews in France. Now, however, it was France's role as a protector of minorities, rather than her status as the first country to extend political rights to Jews, that was invoked as proof of the affinity between the French and Jewish peoples.

[105] 'Habib', 'Le Chagrin de Samuël', *Foi et réveil* (May 1913), 80.
[106] Ibid. 84.   [107] Ibid. 83.

The Beginnings of a Jewish Youth Movement

It was in 1897 that the Union Scolaire, created fifteen years earlier to help Jewish graduates of Parisian primary schools find employment, expanded its activities to become the first Jewish community centre in France.[108] Whereas Jewish associations had traditionally been formed with religious observance or charitable work as their primary aim, the Union Scolaire was unique in that it defined its mission primarily in social terms. Officers of the organization included two chief rabbis, Alfred Lévy and J. H. Dreyfuss, and the poet Henry Marx, who was one of the main contributors to the group's monthly publication.[109] The leadership saw the group as an alternative educational model which would complement the rigid, formal atmosphere of lycées and universities. Rather than simply 'educating' young people's minds, they hoped to encourage young Jews to socialize among themselves and discuss issues and ideas of current interest in an informal atmosphere. Towards this end, the organization provided a library and game and conference rooms for members, as well as sponsoring lectures and concerts.

Louis-Germain Lévy heralded the Union Scolaire as a welcome addition to French Jewish life and expressed his hope that it would serve as a vital weapon in the fight against assimilation. While Jews had set up a few schools for children in the aftermath of emancipation, he lamented, they had done nothing for teenagers and young adults: 'Where did we bring them together, where did we teach them Jewish history, religion, and literature? Where did we arm them psychologically to combat antisemitism?' The Union Scolaire, he hoped, would help remedy this situation by continuing Jewish education into adulthood and creating strong social bonds among young Jews.[110] Writing about the group's goals in 1910, its then president J. H. Dreyfuss linked the Union Scolaire's emphasis on sociability with the 'principle tenets' of the Jewish religion: the ancient Hebrews, Dreyfuss informed his readers, placed great value on sociability. It was only through camaraderie and friendship, he concluded, that 'a taste for joy and liberty' could flourish.[111]

[108] See the note announcing the group's creation in *L'Univers israélite* (16 July 1882), 649. An article in *Menorah* notes that originally the group was an alumnus society for one Jewish communal school (Communale Israélite de la rue des Hôpitaliers Saint-Gervais). In 1897, when it opened its community centre, it expanded membership to all graduates of Jewish primary and secondary schools. See Jules Meyer, 'L'Union Scolaire', *Menorah* (29 Apr. 1923), 275–7.

[109] The group started publishing a monthly journal, also called *L'Union scolaire*, in 1900. Only a few issues of the paper remain in the library of the Alliance Israélite Universelle.

[110] See Lévy, 'L'Union Scolaire', *L'Univers israélite* (5 Mar. 1897), 755 8. Another article L.K., 'Serrons les rangs', *L'Univers israélite* (18 Dec. 1896), 402–4 emphasized the group's value in helping young Jews respond to antisemitism.

[111] See the statements of Lévy and Dreyfuss in *L'Union scolaire* (May/June 1910), 1–2.

Within the next few years, the Union Scolaire was joined by several new Jewish educational societies and social clubs. The impetus for the creation of the Université Populaire Juive in 1902 came from within the Zionist community. This group was inspired by the larger Université Populaire movement created in the post-Dreyfus years by progressive intellectuals to provide education for the working classes. Directed by Zionists and located at the centre of the immigrant Marais neighbourhood, the Université Populaire Juive also received a great deal of support from the native Parisian Jewish community. Chief Rabbi Zadoc Kahn was one of the organization's earliest supporters, and helped secure the financial backing of both the Rothschild family and the Consistory.[112] While the organization functioned primarily as a social service agency for the immigrant population, it also served as a link between different elements of the Parisian Jewish community. 'During certain evenings', an observer noted in 1904, 'our popular university constitutes a veritable Jewish school . . . Alongside our working-class audience . . . we attract an intellectual, university-educated public eager to educate itself about things Jewish.'[113] This cultural function of the UPJ became more important with time.

Whereas the majority of the UPJ's initial conferences were on immigrant-oriented topics such as alcoholism, infant hygiene, and the naturalization of foreigners, the lecture series gradually expanded to include a diverse range of subjects, from 'Jewish Emancipation in Romania' to 'The Alliance Israélite Universelle', 'The Theatre of Henri Bernstein', and, in April 1911, a debate between Victor Basch and Max Nordau entitled 'Can Modern Judaism Survive in the Diaspora?'[114] It was this year that saw the creation of two educational societies aimed specifically at Jewish youth: the Association des Jeunes Juifs (AJJ) and Amis du Judaïsme. Like the UPJ, these groups brought Jews from different walks of life together and encouraged open debate on the meaning of Jewish identity in the modern world. Taking Jewish integration into French society as a given, their primary aim was to convince Jewish youth that an affirmative, public Jewish identity did not conflict with a sense of belonging and loyalty to France.

Comprised primarily of the sons and daughters of immigrants, the Association des Jeunes Juifs had its headquarters at the Université Populaire Juive. The group began publishing a journal called *Les Pionniers* in 1912, and had 400 members by 1913. The Amis du Judaïsme, like the Union Scolaire, drew its membership primarily from the native community. Chief Rabbi

---

[112] Université Populaire Juive, *Compte rendu annuel et statuts*, 8. [113] Ibid. 10.
[114] *L'Echo sioniste* reported on all the activities and courses offered by the UPJ, as did *L'Univers israélite*.

Israël Lévi was among its founding members, as were a number of prominent Jewish intellectuals of the day, including Victor Basch, Salomon Reinach, Jacques Hadamard, the composer Darius Milhaud, and Edmond-Maurice Lévy, the librarian of the Sorbonne.[115] The poet Gustave Kahn presided over the group, which held it meetings at the Ecole des Hautes Etudes.[116] Although both of these groups explicitly rejected being labelled as religious, Zionist, nationalist, or otherwise, the Amis du Judaïsme was less politically oriented than the AJJ. It saw its raison d'être exclusively in the cultural realm, organizing lecture series and musical and literary evenings featuring Jewish music and poetry readings, as well as a series of courses on Hebrew literature and civilization. A 1913 'Soirée de Poésie et de Musique', for example, featured discussion and reading of the poetry of André Spire, Edmond Fleg, Henri Franck, James Darmesteter, Morris Rosenfeld, Heinrich Heine, and the Hebrew poet Hayim Nahman Bialik, followed by a concert of Jewish folk songs and liturgical chants.[117]

The Union Scolaire, Université Populaire Juive, Association des Jeunes Juifs, and Amis du Judaïsme were all part of a new trend towards defining Jewish identity in ethno-cultural terms. The president of the AJJ, speaking at a 1913 conference in Germany, talked about the group as part of a larger movement throughout 'la grande France' (France and her colonies) towards emphasizing Jewish particularism: Jews everywhere, he asserted, were now affirming their '"moi" ethnique'. Many young people were abandoning Jewish religious practice, declared Dr S. Mélamet, precisely because they experienced Judaism as more than a religion. The only way to prevent this disaffiliation, he suggested, was to embrace a broader definition of Jewish identity.[118] An article by Charles-Edouard Lévy in *L'Union scolaire* in the spring of 1912 made a similar point. Addressing the issue of whether or not Jews with no religious faith could rightly be called Jews, he concluded unequivocally in the affirmative: the philosophy of Henri Bergson was as much a part of the patrimony of the Jewish people as the works of talmudic scholars. Acknowledgement of the contribution of secular Jews, Lévy went on to assert, 'has proved it to be a powerful antidote to renunciation, mixed marriage, and baptism'.[119] While, with the exception of the Union Scolaire, these groups did not survive the upheaval of the First World War, their

---

[115] Hyman, *From Dreyfus to Vichy*, 45.

[116] See the pamphlet, *Les Amis du judaïsme*, published by the group in 1914, in the library of the Alliance Israélite Universelle. No information exists as to the number of members the group had. [117] On the group's activities see its pamphlet, *Les Amis du judaïsme*.

[118] Reported in *Les Pionniers* (June/July 1913), 3.

[119] Lévy, 'L'Œuvre de l'Union Scolaire', *L'Union scolaire* (Feb./Apr. 1912), 3–4.

mission was continued on a much larger scale by a whole new network of
Jewish clubs and educational societies created in the 1920s.[120]

◆

Between the Dreyfus affair and the First World War, French Jews created new
forms of sociability and discourses of identity. Changes in the social and cultural landscape in the late nineteenth and early twentieth centuries forced
those Jews concerned about maintaining a viable community to rearticulate
the meaning of their Jewishness in modern terms. The rise of ethnic nationalism, the birth of modern antisemitism, the arrival of immigrants from
eastern Europe, the new emphasis on spirituality, irrationalism, and religious revival all made the limits of classical Franco-Judaism increasingly
apparent. For reflective Jews, an understanding of Jewish identity based
entirely on Enlightenment universalism and the concept of the individual
was no longer sufficient. While Zionist, Reform, and traditionalist Jews differed in their tactics and ideology, they shared a sense of dissatisfaction with
the status quo and an assumption that the nature of Jewish identity must be
reconceptualized in modern terms. While the Zionists openly called into
question the narrowly confessional nineteenth-century definition of Judaism, Reform and traditionalist Jews tried to adapt a religious definition of
Jewish identity to fit a changed cultural landscape in which group difference
was increasingly being taken for granted in French society as a whole. Most
importantly, these groups and their publications created new social networks and an intellectual climate that encouraged questioning and debating
of Jewish identity in all its complexity. This in turn paved the way for an
explosion of Jewish cultural activity in the 1920s, to which we will now turn.

[120] While the Union Scolaire began sponsoring monthly lectures and dances again in 1919,
it lost its community centre during the First World War and did not acquire another one until
1929. Over the course of the 1920s, the group changed its orientation to providing for the
needs of immigrant Jews. See Hyman, *From Dreyfus to Vichy*, 138–9.

CHAPTER 4

The First World War and the Shifting Landscape of French Jewry

THE REFIGURING of French Jewish identity that began in the aftermath of the Dreyfus affair developed into a much broader social and cultural phenomenon in the 1920s as new youth groups, magazines, and educational and literary societies challenged the nineteenth-century wisdom of relegating Jewishness to the private sphere. A proliferation of novels, short stories, and plays that touched on the issue of Jewish identity in the modern world also created a new kind of Jewish visibility. Finally, as an analysis of the central themes in the Jewish press of the day reveals, this was a period during which many French Jews re-evaluated the ideology of Franco-Judaism itself and suggested new ways of understanding their integration into French society. In order to make sense of this Jewish awakening—as contemporaries had come to call it by mid-decade—we must first turn to the forces that reshaped Jewish life in the 1920s, beginning with the experience of the First World War.

Strengthening the Bond, Affirming Difference

The First World War played an important role in furthering Jewish identification with and integration into French society. For young Jewish men, military service was an effective conduit to social assimilation, providing immigrant and first-generation youth in particular with an unprecedented opportunity for fraternizing and social mixing.[1] In contrast to the situation in Germany, where Jews were often bitterly disappointed by the antisemitism they encountered in military service, in France the war confirmed their sense of belonging. The French government was responsive to the particular needs of Jewish soldiers, arranging for them to celebrate Jewish holidays on the front, employing rabbis to minister to them, and ensuring that Jewish graves were marked with plain markers rather than crosses.[2] Jews

---

[1] See Landau, *Les Juifs de France et la Grande Guerre*.
[2] Hyman, *From Dreyfus to Vichy*, 51.

were invited to participate in religious services honouring the war dead, and multi-denominational services were held in synagogues as well as in churches. While antisemitism did not disappear during the war years, a general mood of national solidarity and unity militated against expressions of animosity towards Jews.[3]

This wartime atmosphere carried over into the post-war years. In contra-distinction to the situation in both the United States and Germany, in France the 1920s was a period in which antisemitism appeared to many to be on the decline.[4] While antisemitic leagues and ideologues did not disappear during this period, they remained, for the most part, marginal to French political life.[5] While the royalist Action Française, created in 1908 by Charles Maurras, continued to diffuse antisemitic propaganda in the 1920s, its divisive rhetoric was seen by most on both right and left as contrary to the spirit of national unity.[6] The Ligue des Patriotes, presided over by Maurice Barrès until his death in 1923, welcomed Jews as members, as did the majority of patriotic movements created in the 1920s.[7]

As we saw in Chapter 3, a religious revival among intellectuals became a discernible phenomenon in the France of the belle époque. Influenced by the mystical Catholicism encouraged by Henri Bergson and the abatement of the clerical/anti-clerical divide that had plagued nineteenth-century French society, increasing numbers of educated French youth were attracted by a new kind of religiosity rooted in personal spirituality and free of the conservative political tradition of the Catholic Church. It was this liberal brand of Catholicism that came to exercise a dominant influence in France after the First World War. The legacy of the Union Sacrée helped to reintegrate Catholics into the nation and mend the split between religious and secular

[3] On the decline in antisemitism in France during and in the aftermath of the First World War, see Landau, *Les Juifs de France et la Grande Guerre*; Hyman, *From Dreyfus to Vichy*; and Millman, *La Question juive entre les deux guerres*.

[4] The rise of antisemitism in Weimar Germany was of course on a different scale from antisemitism in the United States, where it was manifested primarily in immigration restriction and social exclusion. The year 1923 saw the culmination of nativists' attempts to impose immigration restrictions, and quotas for Jewish and other 'undesirable' immigrants were implemented. It was also during this period—which coincided with the coming of age of the sons and daughters of the immigrant generation, many of whom had the education and financial means to enter the mainstream of American middle-class society—that 'social' antisemitism, such as quotas on the number of Jews admitted to universities as well as housing and job discrimination, became more common.

[5] While there is some disagreement among historians as to the impact and importance of antisemitism in France in the 1930s, there is a general consensus that the 1920s was a period in which antisemitism was relatively insignificant. Hyman, *The Jews of Modern France*, 45. See also Winock, *La France et les Juifs, de 1789 à nos jours*, ch. 8.

[6] Millman, *La Question juive entre les deux guerres*, 73–4. Drumont died in 1917 and *La Libre Parole* ceased publication in 1924.　　　　　　　　　　　　　　　　　　　[7] Ibid. 40.

elements of society. A number of the measures taken against religious con-gregations by the Combès government were lifted during the war years, and conservative, anti-republican Catholicism became increasingly associated with fringe organizations like Action Française.[8] Social Catholicism, repre-sented by groups such as Action Catholique and the Christian syndicalist movement, became more influential in the 1920s, and actively voiced their opposition to antisemitism, as did the progressive Catholic press.[9] Within Christian youth groups of the inter-war years, a spirit of internationalism and tolerance that extended to Jews also dominated.[10]

The recognition and respect that Jews received as a result of their partici-pation in the war effort helped to popularize the notion that they were no less French for proudly affirming their unique spiritual and cultural heritage. Particularly striking was the shift in attitude of Maurice Barrès, as expressed in his 1917 book *Les Diverses Familles spirituelles de la France*, which first appeared as a series of articles in *L'Echo de Paris*. Here for the first time Bar-rès acknowledged French Jews as genuine Frenchmen, who alongside Catholics, Protestants, socialists, and traditionalists comprised one of the 'spiritual families' of France.[11] Barrès's reading of letters that Jewish soldiers wrote home from the front convinced him that Jews could indeed feel the sense of 'flesh-and-blood' patriotism of which he had previously believed them incapable. A special recruiting centre for immigrants at the Université Populaire Juive, he also noted with approval, had been immediately inun-dated with volunteers.[12]

Barrès did not limit himself to praise of Jewish patriotism, but rather expressed a new appreciation of Jewish particularity and an openness to accepting Jews *as Jews* as members of the French nation. As was the case for all of France's 'spiritual families', he suggested, by defending France Jews were defending their own faith as well. This comes across in particular in his discussion of Amédée Rothstein, a young immigrant Jew with Zionist sym-pathies who was inducted into the Légion d'Honneur for his bravery in 1915 and who died on the battlefield a year later. What fascinated Barrès in Roth-stein was his letters openly declaring his desire to devote his life 'to the

---

[8] Coutrot, *Les Forces religieuses dans la société française*, 38. The Papacy's condemnation of Action Française in 1926 played an important role in legitimizing the 'new Christianity' of Jacques Maritain and other liberal Catholics, who encouraged understanding of other reli-gions—whether Islam, Judaism, or non-Catholic Christianity—rather than conversion. See Le Goff and Rémond (eds), *Histoire de la France religieuse*, iv. 136.

[9] See Pierrard, *Juifs et catholiques français, 1886–1945*, 246, and Millman, *La Question juive entre les deux guerres*, 40.   [10] See Coutrot, 'Le Mouvement de jeunesse', 52.

[11] Barrès used the term 'traditionalists' to describe those who, like himself, felt a strong sense of connection with the land and the history of their ancestors.

[12] *Les Diverses Familles spirituelles de la France*, 68.

beautiful and unfortunate people of Israel whose issue I am'.[13] Rothstein and his Zionism remained somewhat of a mystery to Barrès. 'There is something sad and appealing in this young spirit', he concluded, 'who looked at the world and at life exclusively through the Jewish nation and who died in the service of those that he loved the most [the French] but chose to distinguish himself from.'[14] Although he did not know quite what to make of Rothstein's strong sense of Jewish particularism, for Barrès the fact that Rothstein gave his life for France meant that his beliefs and motivations, even if difficult for the average Frenchman to understand, were worthy of respect.

Barrès's sentiments, the evidence suggests, were indicative of a larger mood swing in French society. In the 1920s, most Jewish commentators agreed that antisemitism was on the decline, and many expressed confidence that Jews as a group had come to be respected as an integral part of the French nation. Rather than deriving their status within French society uniquely from their ability to integrate, participation in the war effort provided French Jews with a new language with which to link their particular religious heritage to their French patriotism. Writer and publicist Pierre Paraf captured this mood in a 1928 article for the *Revue littéraire juive*. Paraf, who was born into the Parisian Jewish bourgeoisie in 1893, married Mathilde Dons, the stepdaughter of Max Nordau, in 1921. A lawyer by training, he became a prominent journalist as well as a leader of both the Ligue Internationale contre l'Antisémitisme (LICA) and the Ligue des Droits de l'Homme.[15] Recalling the First World War as 'a crucible where French and Jewish souls melted together', Paraf warned his fellow Jews against turning in on themselves defensively. To the contrary, he suggested, 'we must, in the name of respect for all confessions, draw as many sympathizers towards us as possible'.[16] As Paraf's comments suggest, many French Jews in the 1920s felt free to challenge an 'assimilationist' model of identity precisely because they felt that the Jews' place in French society was secure.

The lack of a political or social crisis in France in the 1920s also helped to create a sense of confidence among French Jews, which in turn gave them the freedom to create more public, visible forms of Jewish life without undue fear of antisemitism. The 1920s were a time of relative stability in France. While we tend to speak of the 'inter-war years' as a distinct historical period,

---

[13] *Les Diverses Familles spirituelles de la France*, 72.   [14] Ibid.

[15] In addition to a book of poetry and prose entitled *Sous la terre de France* based on his experiences as a solider during the First World War, Paraf penned several literary and theatrical studies. He helped to found the journal *Notre temps*, dedicated to Franco-German reconciliation, in 1927, and served as editor of *La République* from 1930 to 1939.

[16] Paraf, 'Le Réveil du judaïsme français', *Revue littéraire juive* (July 1928), 591, 593.

the 1920s were in many ways an era unto itself. In contrast to the 1930s, which were marked by both a worldwide economic depression and the rise of fascism, the 1920s were a period of relative economic prosperity and political stability. The burning political issues of the *fin de siècle* and belle époque faded into the background, and a tendency towards centrist coalitions dominated the French political scene. The militant nationalism of the pre-war years gave way to widespread support for pacifism and internationalism. The League of Nations' attempts to avoid military conflict through negotiation and international co-operation inspired a great deal of confidence and hope across the French political spectrum.[17]

At the same time that the integrative experience of the First World War and decline in antisemitism in the 1920s gave French Jews the confidence they needed to assert their ethnic particularism, they set in motion a number of social and cultural forces that both encouraged Jewish self-reflection and created new networks of pro-Jewish activism. It is to this complex interplay of forces that I now turn.

French and East European Jewish Soldiers on the Battlefront

The encounter between eastern and western Jews during the First World War, Michael Berkowitz notes, led many American, German, and English soldiers towards a new appreciation of the different forms of Jewish identity possible in the modern world. Jewish soldiers both witnessed antisemitic violence in eastern Europe at first hand and, in some instances, struck up friendships with east European Jews sympathetic to Jewish nationalism. While only a small number became fully fledged Zionists in the wake of these encounters, Berkowitz argues, they nonetheless influenced the attitude of many soldiers: 'many were sensitized to notions of Jewish cultural nationhood', he concludes, 'which might have made them more accepting of Zionism. It led some, to be sure, to question their own identity as more complex than earlier assumed.'[18] A survey of the French Jewish press during and in the immediate aftermath of the war years suggests that these encounters raised similar issues for French Jews.

The Russian-born rabbi David Berman, who like Vexler and Liber immigrated to France as a child, expressed the new appreciation of Jewish diversity that grew out of his wartime experience as a military chaplain. While Jews may have functioned as a religious minority in France, Berman argued in a 1918 article for *L'Univers israélite*, in eastern Europe and the Ottoman

[17] Wright, *France in Modern Times*, ch. 27.   [18] Berkowitz, *The Reception of Zionism*, 16.

empire they indisputably comprised a distinct ethnic group. Rather than trying to impose these different kinds of Jewishness on one another, he suggested, Jews should rather recognize and accept their differences.[19] Berman developed this theme in several short stories in *Foi et réveil*, in which soldiers from divergent Jewish backgrounds meet and learn from each other's understanding of Judaism. In 'Entre Juifs', which is set in a small village in Turkey, for example, two native French Jews, Lucien Lévy and Adrien Blum, are indignant when a local Jewish merchant of Zionist sympathies suggests that they are not fighting for 'their' country in the same way as their non-Jewish compatriots. 'Our country is France', Lévy and Blum exclaim unequivocally: 'we know no other.' The two young men are surprised to learn, however, that Abraham Michalewsky, a fellow French soldier from a Russian immigrant family, shares the Turkish Jew's sentiments. When an inquisitive non-Jewish comrade asks him to define the Jewish people, he responds: 'simple: a people without a land'.[20] Soon thereafter the Frenchmen discover that Michalewsky's Zionism is firmly opposed by a Russian with Bundist sympathies.

To a certain extent, Berman's story reinforces the idea that it was appropriate to the particular social and cultural situation of French Jews to contend that they were 'no different from any other Frenchmen except in their form of worship'. In other instances, however, he appears to call this model into question. At several points in the story, Ottoman and east European characters explain their differences to their French comrades in a manner that does not call into question the latter's model of Jewish identity *for themselves*: while the superiority of French culture makes it natural for French Jews to desire acculturation, both the east Europeans and Ottomans suggest that this is not the case for Oriental Jews, who are surrounded by a culture inferior to their own.[21] At other points, however, Berman pushed his readers to question their own self-definition as a solely religious group. In the course of a lively conversation with his Zionist and Bundist comrades, for example, Lucien Lévy remarks that French Jews' alleged 'indifference' to Judaism should not be exaggerated: 'I'm not very observant', he reflects, 'but I like to eat gefilte fish on Friday night.'[22] The opportunity to interact with Jews who openly define their Judaism in cultural terms, this comment suggests, forces Lévy to reflect critically on his own relationship to his Jewish heritage.

---

[19] Berman, 'Les Deux Judaïsmes', *L'Univers israélite* (25 Jan. 1918), 481–4.

[20] 'Entre Juifs: Dialogue d'Orient', *Foi et réveil*, 7 (Apr./June 1918), 132. Berman's story 'Discussions juives', published the following year (*Foi et réveil*, 10 (1919), 42–55), explored the same theme. (A note on citations: after June 1918 issues of *Foi et réveil* were identified solely by number, rather than month of publication. The journal was subsequently issued three times a year, rather than monthly.)   [21] 'Entre Juifs', 133, 141.   [22] Ibid. 139.

The Nationalities Debate at the Paris Peace Conference

With the creation of new nation-states in eastern Europe, the question of Jewish self-definition became a concrete political problem rather than a theoretical topic of discussion. Whereas in France Judaism had been officially defined as a religion since the time of the French Revolution, within Romania and the Russian empire Jews were considered a distinct national group and subject to laws that kept them socially and politically separate. Some Russian Jews—for the most part those from urbanized, upper-middle-class backgrounds—envisioned an emancipation of east European Jewry similar to that which had taken place in the west a century before. By the turn of the century, however, these voices had been outnumbered by groups such as Zionists and cultural nationalists,[23] who shared a national/ethnic rather than religious understanding of Jewish identity. This difference between east and west European Jews became a critical issue at the Paris Peace Conference in 1919. It was here that Jewish delegations from around the world offered various plans regarding the place of the Jews in the successor states.

By 1919 most east European Jews had come to assume that the Jews' status in these countries would involve some kind of national autonomy. American and English Jewish delegates at the conference also accepted the nationalist definition of Judaism as a reality of the new world order; however, French representatives of the Alliance Israélite Universelle remained committed to the position that the Jews formed a religious rather than a national group.[24] Recognizing this national minority status and endorsing the Zionist goal of establishing a Jewish state in Palestine, they felt, would undermine the ideal of political emancipation and equality for Jews everywhere. This tension came to a head when, at the audience granted to the Zionist representatives at the conference, Alliance leader Sylvain Lévi expressed his disapproval of establishing a Jewish national homeland. The other participants, including André Spire and the international Zionist leaders Nahum Sokolov and Chaim Weizmann, were furious with Lévi's comments and, as Spire reports in his memoirs, refused to shake Lévi's hand at the session's close.[25]

In principle, both the Consistory and the Alliance Israélite Universelle remained committed to the idea that Jews, both in France and internationally, should define themselves as a confessional group alone. However, even those who believed in this principle were increasingly forced to accommodate the ethno-cultural brand of Jewishness that had come to the fore at

[23] This group, inspired by the ideology of Simon Dubnow, envisioned an equal, independent Jewish society and culture on Russian soil rather than a politically separate Jewish state.

[24] On this clash, see Levene, *War, Jews, and the New Europe*, ch. 14, and Spire, *Souvenirs à bâtons rompus*, ch. 6. [25] Spire, *Souvenirs à bâtons rompus*, 109.

the Paris Peace Conference. In an article written for *L'Univers israélite* in 1927, William Oualid, a law professor and member of the Consistory, stated that 'nothing is stranger and more unpleasant to French people of all confessions and beliefs than the idea of a national minority . . . of all the countries in Europe, France is the most unified and homogeneous'. Nonetheless, he argued, because the French understanding of a nation had evolved from an entity defined strictly in territorial terms to include 'language, race, religion, and sentiment' as determining factors, the phrase could 'apply temporarily to Jews wherever historical circumstances have maintained them in political and administrative isolation, and where they themselves wish to preserve this status'.[26] The use of the word 'temporarily' (*momentanément*) is significant here: while Oualid remained committed to the hope that Jews in all countries would ultimately become incorporated into the larger society and be distinguishable only by confession, he believed that the best means of encouraging this evolution was to recognize national rights in the short term.[27]

Maurice Liber made a similar point in a 1928 article for the Alliance Israélite Universelle's journal *Paix et droit*, in which he argued that the national minority status of Jews in the Soviet Union and Poland did not raise the spectre of 'dual loyalty'. Unlike France, he explained, these countries had a concept of citizenship that allowed for a person to be a legal member of both the larger nation and a particular ethnic group. Within this political universe, he thus concluded, Jews were better able to assert their rights as citizens if they were organized as a political entity.[28] Liber concluded his article, as did Oualid, by imploring his readers to respect the Judaism of their east European brethren as a legitimate expression of the Jewish will to survive, even it went against their own desires.[29]

Responding to Antisemitism in Eastern Europe

At the same time that the encounter with east Europeans on the battlefront and the nationalities debate at the Paris Peace Conference encouraged Jews

[26] 'Le Problème juif est-il un problème de minorité nationale?', *L'Univers israélite* (22 July 1927), 457.

[27] Some members of the Consistory and Alliance, of course, refused to engage with these ideas at all. In an article in *Paix et droit* in 1926, for example, Alfred Berl articulated the idea that Jews owe unequivocal loyalty to their country in exchange for civil rights, with no concessions whatsoever to the idea of national minority rights in eastern Europe. See 'Le Devoir civique des Juifs dans les états modernes', *Paix et droit* (Apr. 1926), 1–2.

[28] Liber, 'Le "Judaïsme national": Son développement, ses caractères, son avenir', *Paix et droit* (May 1928), 3–5. Liber, then a military chaplain, expressed a similar perspective in a 1916 article for the *L'Univers israélite*. See 'Intelligence mutuelle', *L'Univers israélite* (11 Feb. 1916), 578.   [29] 'Le "Judaïsme national"', 5.

to think about their identity in more ethno-cultural terms, gathering support for beleaguered Jewish communities in Russia and Poland helped to create new networks of Jewish activism in France. The Ligue pour la Défense des Juifs Opprimés was created in 1915. This group, which numbered 425 by July 1916, was created to enlist French support for the emancipation of Russian and Romanian Jews. Membership was a mix of professionals, students, and businessmen, as well as manual workers and artisans. The board of directors comprised prominent left-wing political and literary personalities, both Jewish and non-Jewish. These included the poet Gustave Kahn, Sylvain Lévi, Ferdinand Buisson, president of the Ligue des Droits de l'Homme, its vice-presidents Victor Basch and André-Ferdinand Hérold, Victor Bérard, a senator and professor at the Ecole des Hautes Etudes, and a number of other professors at the Sorbonne and the Collège de France. André Spire, Edmond Fleg, and David Berman were all members.

The opening statement of the group's publication *L'Emancipation juive*, which appeared from January to December 1916, described the Ligue as both a cultural and political endeavour. Though its objective was to work for the liberation of Russian and Romanian Jews, the editors declared, 'pure and simple information will not suffice. It is also imperative to make known the larger universe in which these oppressed Jews live and suffer.'[30] Towards this end, the journal published Russian articles in translation, as well as pieces by French publicists exploring various aspects of Russian Jewish life, antisemitism, and the political struggle for Jewish liberation. While the majority of subscribers to the journal were French, by June 1916 it also listed fifty-two foreign subscribers.[31] Contributors often expressed their support for east European Jewish liberation within a universalist framework, trying to persuade the French public that the emancipation of Jews in eastern Europe was one of the most pressing human rights issues of the day.[32] Though the Ligue was not an explicitly pro-Zionist organization—Sylvain Lévi was a member—the tone of *L'Emancipation juive* also reflects the growing influence of Zionist ideology. André Spire and Israel Zangwill, as well as Russian contributors, sought to familiarize French readers with the ethno-cultural character of east European Jewish identity and rally support for Jewish nationalism.[33]

[30] *L'Emancipation juive* (7–21 Jan. 1916), 1.

[31] They include seventeen American subscriptions, thirteen from England, and six from the island of Rhodes, as well as subscriptions from Switzerland, Denmark, Egypt, Italy, the Netherlands, Sweden, Salonica, and Argentina. See *L'Emancipation juive* (10–25 June 1916), 185.

[32] See e.g. Gaston Milhaud, 'La Question juive en Orient', *L'Emancipation juive* (25 Apr.–10 May 1916), 107–8.

[33] See e.g. Zangwill's article in favour of the recognition of Jewish national rights in the

Though the Ligue dissolved in 1917 after the success of the February Revolution, a number of other groups, including Les Volontaires Juifs, an association of foreign volunteers in the French army headed by Edmond Fleg,[34] and the Société des Secours aux Juifs Russes, continued to raise money for Jewish war victims and protest against antisemitism in eastern and central Europe.[35] Many of the non-Jewish figures who would become prominent supporters of the Zionist movement in the 1920s—including the future senator and minister of education Anatole de Monzie, art and cultural critic Elie Faure, economist Charles Gide, and labour advocate Albert Thomas[36]—signed a petition protesting the pogroms in Poland following a large meeting in Paris to rally support for this cause in July 1919.[37] The 1926 Schwartzbard affair also played an important role in galvanizing French sympathy for east European Jews and bringing native and foreign-born Jewish intellectuals together.[38] Shalom Schwartzbard, a Russian Jew living in Paris, killed the Ukrainian nationalist Simon Petlioura, who had been responsible for carrying out pogroms during the First World War. Defended by Henry Torrès, a prominent lawyer with communist sympathies who came from the Bordeaux Jewish community, Schwartzbard was ultimately acquitted of the crime after a highly publicized trial. It was in the aftermath of this trial that Torrès and his entourage—including journalist Bernard Lecache, with whom he travelled through Russia and the Ukraine on a Jewish fact-finding mission,[39] and the Argentinian-born journalist Joseph Kessel, who immigrated to Paris via Russia before the First World War—founded the Ligue Internationale contre l'Antisémitisme.[40]

successor states: 'Les Juifs après la guerre', *L'Emancipation juive* (25 Apr.–10 May 1916), 3. For a complete list of the journal's articles for 1916, see *L'Emancipation juive* (10–25 Dec. 1916), 355–60.

[34] This group was created in 1916, at which point Fleg was still a Swiss citizen. It was primarily a mutual aid society for volunteers and their families, but it also organized protests against antisemitism in eastern Europe. It began publishing a journal by the same name in 1931, and counted 435 members by 1931.

[35] On the dire situation of Russian Jewry in the waning days of the tsarist empire and during the civil war which followed the Bolshevik revolution, see Frankel, 'The Paradoxical Politics of Marginality'.

[36] Albert Thomas was a prominent figure in the French socialist and labour movement before the First World War. In 1919 he was elected director of the Bureau International du Travail in Geneva, a position that he held until his death in 1932.

[37] For a report on the protest, see *L'Univers israélite* (25 July 1919), 481. The petition, entitled Appel à l'Humanité, was signed by twenty-one non-Jews, most of whom were prominent political, literary, or academic figures. See *L'Univers israélite* (13 Sept. 1919), 645–7.

[38] Trebitsch, 'Les Intellectuels juifs en France dans les années vingt', 54.

[39] Lecache's 1927 book, *Au pays des pogromes: Quand Israël meurt*, was based on this voyage.

[40] Trebitsch, 'Les Intellectuels juifs en France dans les années vingt', 54.

The Rise of the Zionist Movement

While the international Zionist movement failed to gain large numbers of card-carrying members in France in the inter-war years, a 'pro-Zionist periphery'[41] nonetheless came to exercise an important influence over French Jewish life. As we saw in Chapter 3, a small number of French politicians and intellectuals lent their support to immigrant-run Zionist associations in the pre-war years. In the 1920s, native French Zionist sympathizers began to organize on their own. After the 1917 Balfour Declaration announcing Britain's support—albeit in rather vague terms—for the establishment of a Jewish homeland in Palestine, André Spire, in collaboration with Roger Lévy, who worked for the Centre de Documentation de l'Histoire de la Guerre, created the Ligue des Amis Français du Sionisme. This association, which sought to gain support for Zionism in left-wing circles, brought together prominent French Jewish intellectuals, pre-war Zionist leaders, and non-Jewish fellow-travellers.[42] Edmond Fleg, André Spire, Jules Isaac, Baruch Hagani, Myriam Schach, the writer Henri Hertz, and Léon Zadoc-Kahn, son of the chief rabbi Zadoc Kahn, were all members. The group was presided over by the Protestant theologian Maurice Vernes, and included a number of other prominent non-Jews, such as Albert Thomas, historian Charles Seignobos, Gabriel Séailles, and Ferdinand Brunot. The Ligue organized conferences and meetings, published pro-Zionist tracts and, from 1918, its own bulletin, *La Palestine nouvelle*. The support of André-Ferdinand Hérold, the vice-president of the Ligue des Droits de l'Homme, played an important role in popularizing Zionism among the French public. Immigrant Zionist leaders such as Marc Jarblum and the Romanian-born Zionist activist Enric Braunstein helped to enlist the support of several prominent socialist politicians, including Anatole de Monzie, Marius Moutet, Jean Longuet, and Charles Gide.[43]

Ohabei Sion (Les Amis de Sion), created at the same time as the Ligue des Amis Français du Sionisme, was the brainchild of Aimé Pallière and Charles Baur, a wealthy banker, member of the Paris Consistory, and father of Union Libérale president André Baur. This group was representative of a distinctively French brand of religious Zionism that Aimé Pallière played a key role in theorizing and popularizing. It was only by regaining control of their

[41] Michel Abitbol coined this term in *Les Deux Terres promises*.

[42] See Spire, *Souvenirs à bâtons rompus*, 101.

[43] See Hyman, *From Dreyfus to Vichy*, 157. Many of these figures were initially members of the group's precursor, the Ligue Franco-Sioniste, founded in 1915 by two Romanians, Marcel Bernfeld and Enric Braunstein, to create a solid basis of support for the peace conference. See Nicault, *La France et le sionisme*, 53–4, and Hyman, *From Dreyfus to Vichy*, 156–7.

ancient homeland, Pallière convinced a number of prominent members of the French Jewish religious establishment by the end of the First World War, that the Jews would be able to accomplish their universalist mission of promoting peace among the nations.[44] Members of Ohabei Sion included Edmond Fleg, prominent non-Jewish lawyer Marcel Mirtil, rabbi Emmanuel Weill, who was Charles Baur's father-in-law, and Vidal Modiano, the president of the Association Amicale des Israélites Saloniciens (AAIS), who would become director of the Conseil Représentatif des Israélites de France after the Second World War, as well as Myriam Schach and Vladimir Haffkine. Chief Rabbi Alfred Lévy served as the group's honorary president.

While several attempts were made to unify the French Zionist movement over the course of the 1920s, they were largely unsuccessful. The Fédération Sioniste de France was reconstituted in 1919, but after two years of intense activity fell apart in 1921 after internal bickering.[45] In 1925 a Palestinian journalist living in Paris, Joseph Castel, attempted to revive the federation by creating the Union Sioniste Française, with leadership mostly drawn from the native French Jewish community. The board of directors included Alsatian-born retired general Gédéon Geismar, whose efforts on behalf of east European Jews had led him to assume a leadership position within the French Zionist movement,[46] André Baur, socialist politicians Léonce Bernheim, mayor of Pourcy in 1935, and Raymond-Raoul Lambert, who had worked in several government departments and who was director of *L'Univers israélite* after 1935.[47] Like the original federation, however, this group fell prey to factionalism. It was divided into three main camps, one led by the revisionist leader Vladimir Jabotinsky,[48] who was living in Paris at the time, a second 'general' faction that included most of the French members, and a third left-wing labour-Zionist group. Several hundred members participated in the group's 1927 election, at which point André Spire was elected president.[49] For reasons that have never been clarified, Spire declined the position, how-

[44] Nicault, 'L'Acculturation des Israélites français au sionisme', 15. On Aimé Pallière's influence on French Zionism, see Poujol, *Aimé Pallière*, 223–37.

[45] Abitbol, *Les Deux Terres promises*, 149.

[46] He was president of both the Zionist fundraising organization Keren Kayemet and the Eclaireurs Israélites de France (the Jewish Boy Scouts). For biographical information on Geismar, see his obituary, 'Le Général Geismar', in *Le Volontaire juif* (Sept./Oct. 1931), 10, and Job, 'Gédéon Geismar'.

[47] Both Bernheim and Lambert, who served as the president of the Union Générale des Israélites de France under Vichy, were murdered in the Holocaust.

[48] The revisionists, of whom Vladimir Jabotinsky was the principal spokesman, advocated the immediate mass exodus of Russian and Romanian Jews from pogrom-stricken areas to Palestine. This group was opposed by mainstream Zionists, led by Chaim Weizmann, who remained committed to the principle of negotiating with the British government in order to secure legal immigration and eventual statehood.   [49] Abitbol, *Les Deux Terres promises*, 270.

ever, and the revisionist faction subsequently rejected the candidature of Fernand Corcos, a lawyer and socialist politician.[50] As a result of these clashes, most of the French members had left by 1927 and the group ceased to exist entirely by 1929.[51] The federation did continue to publish a bimonthly journal, *La Nouvelle Aurore*, which boasted an international readership of 10,000 in 1924, until 1926.[52]

As a result of the federation's weakness, French Zionism consisted of an array of independent organizations, most of which were dominated by east European immigrants.[53] The Zionist organizations that gained the most support among French Jewry were the French branches of the international Zionist fundraising organizations, Keren Hayesod and Keren Kayemet Leyisrael, both of which were transferred to Paris from Alsace in the mid-1920s. Keren Kayemet, which drew its French membership and support from the now defunct Ohabei Sion, established offices in fifty French towns and cities by the end of the decade and enjoyed the support of a number of prominent French politicians, rabbis, and regional consistorial leaders.[54] With a subscriber base substantially higher than that of *L'Univers israélite*, its journal, *La Terre retrouvée*, was the most widely read Jewish paper in France by the late 1930s.[55] The success of the organization among French Jews was due in large part to the leadership of Joseph Fischer, who was sent from Jerusalem as a permanent delegate to the French branch of the organization in 1925. Fischer steered clear of factionalism and effectively represented the group as a 'neutral' organization whose sole purpose was to purchase land in Palestine.[56] As the fundraising organ of the World Zionist Federation, Keren Hayesod, by contrast, was necessarily a more political organization. It is for this reason, Michel Abitbol suggests, that it was not as successful as Keren Kayemet in winning the support of native French Jews. Though the group was presided over by Léon Zadoc-Kahn, and counted both Léonce Bernheim

---

[50] Ibid. 151.   [51] Ibid.

[52] See the paper's report on its subscriptions: *La Nouvelle Aurore* (15 Nov. 1924), 9. This paper was the successor to *L'Echo sioniste*, renamed *Le Peuple juif* during the First World War. The paper took back the name *L'Echo sioniste* in 1921, which it changed in 1922 to *La Nouvelle Aurore*.

[53] These groups were able to mobilize approximately three thousand 'shekel-paying' members by 1931, and sent one delegate to the seventeenth annual Zionist congress in Basle that year (Abitbol, *Les Deux Terres promises*, 152). On immigrant Zionist groups, see Hyman, *From Dreyfus to Vichy*, chs 3 and 6.

[54] Abitbol, *Les Deux Terres promises*, 155; Poujol, *Aimé Pallière*, 225. See *La Terre retrouvée* (25 Mar. 1931), 3, for a complete list of the thirty members of the group's central commission in France. Geismar and Marcel Mirtil are listed as the group's presidents.

[55] Abitbol, *Les Deux Terres promises*, 156.

[56] Ibid. 157. Poujol also points to Pallière's importance in building up the group in France (*Aimé Pallière*, 225–6).

and Fernand Corcos as members, its support was based primarily in the immigrant community. Nonetheless, thanks in part to hefty contributions from the Rothschild family, the group's fundraising efforts were roughly as successful as those of Keren Kayemet, and it began publishing a monthly paper, *L'Appui français*, in 1930.[57]

France-Palestine, created in 1925, was another important focus of Zionist activity in France. This group was created on the initiative of Victor Jacobson, an official delegate of the World Zionist Organization, and Justin Godart, then Secretary of Labour.[58] Conceived of as a successor to the Ligue des Amis Français du Judaïsme, this group was specifically set up to enlist the support of non-Jews to the Zionist cause.[59] Jacobson and Godart managed to procure the 'haut patronage' of the president of the Republic, Gaston Doumergue,[60] as well as the membership of an impressive number of prominent French politicians and intellectuals, including Charles Gide, Anatole de Monzie, and Albert Thomas. Jewish members, chosen primarily for their promin-ence in broader French intellectual, cultural, and political circles, included André Spire and Léon Blum, Roger Lévy, the editor of *L'Europe nouvelle* and cousin of both Henri Franck and Henri Bergson, Jacques Hadamard, a pro-fessor of mathematics at the Collège de France, feminist lawyer Yvonne Net-ter, Fernand Corcos, and writer Henri Hertz. France-Palestine's success in procuring such an impressive group of supporters, suggested Godart, editor of the group's journal *Palestine*, was due largely to Jacobson's keen aware-ness of the particularities of French political and cultural life and his ability to tailor the group's presentation of Zionism accordingly.[61] Its mission, stated in every issue, was to study the 'political, judicial, economic, social, and other questions raised by the creation of a Jewish national home in Palestine' and to 'interest "French Democracy" in renewing its historic role in shaping the history of the Middle East'. In order to achieve these goals, the group organized lectures in conjunction with other Zionist organizations and edited and translated Zionist tracts, brochures, and books into French.

[57] Abitbol, *Les Deux Terres promises*, 154–8. The paper's masthead lists Corcos as vice-presi-dent.

[58] On France-Palestine, see Boukara, 'Justin Godart et le sionisme', and Nicault, 'L'Accultur-ation des Israélites français au sionisme'. The appropriation of the word 'Palestine' by French Zionists in the 1920s, Nicault argues (p. 18), was a strategic choice. Grounding Zionism in the geographical reality of the Middle East, its supporters hoped, would help 'normalize' the move-ment and, in turn, break down opposition to it among French Jews.

[59] Abitbol, *Les Deux Terres promises*, 104–9.

[60] The group's honorary presidents included Louis Barthou, Aristide Briand, Jules Cam-bon, Edouard Herriot, Paul Painlevé, and Raymond Poincaré.

[61] See Godart, *France-Palestine*, 6. This is a pamphlet that can be consulted in the library of the Alliance Israélite Universelle.

Michael Berkowitz frames his study of Zionist culture in Germany, England, and the United States between 1914 and 1933 as 'the history of the institutionalization of a contradiction—of a permanent self-recreating diaspora Zionism among a Jewish polity which was unlikely ever to set foot in Zion except as tourists'.[62] Zionist leaders and publicists in western Europe and the United States, he shows, were constantly faced with the challenge of reconciling the fundamental premise of the international Zionist movement—the ingathering of the exiles in a restored Jewish homeland—with the reality of a diaspora population with little interest in emigration. In Germany, this contradiction became increasingly apparent after the German Zionist Federation's adoption of the 'Posen platform' in 1912. While this platform explicitly stated that all Zionists should make emigration to Palestine one of their life's goals, very few German Zionists actually emigrated, or even considered emigration, before 1933.[63]

Throughout the history of German Zionism, Stephen Poppel concludes, 'there was a general gap between rhetoric and reality, as well as between rhetoric and action . . . *Aliyah* was a remote ideal that very few would achieve, but toward which all might strive.'[64] Though rarely translated into action, Poppel indicates, the ideal of immigration nonetheless shaped German Zionist attitudes towards both the goals of the Zionist movement and their own place within German society. Although on a day-to-day basis these groups encouraged members to create a more vibrant Jewish community in Germany, they nonetheless remained theoretically committed to the idea that living in an autonomous Jewish state represented the ideal form of Jewish existence. Within the French pro-Zionist periphery, by contrast, no such ideal ever existed. As we shall see, Zionism played a critical role in reshaping French Jewish identity and culture in the 1920s. As was the case in the years before the First World War, however, it remained associated above all with an affirmative, non-religious sense of Jewish identity rather than an ideal of emigration to Palestine.

From Periphery to Centre: The Union Libérale

While Reform Judaism remained a minority movement in inter-war France, its presence, like that of the Zionist movement, infused a new sense of energy into French Judaism as it was integrated into the mainstream of French Jewish life in the 1920s. The active participation of Aimé Pallière after 1922 played a critical role in this development. The Union's first presi-

[62] Berkowitz, *The Reception of Zionism*, 194.
[63] Poppel, *Zionism in Germany 1897–1933*, 50.   [64] Ibid. 73–4.

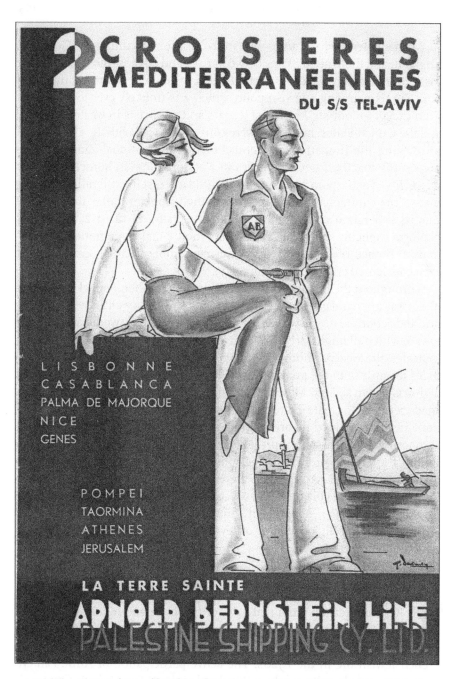

FIGURE 2 A French travel brochure from the 1920s advertising a cruise to Tel Aviv
From the personal collection of Catherine Nicault; reproduced by permission

dent, Salvadore Lévi, had asked Pallière if he would like to participate in the religious life of the synagogue in 1908, but at this point Pallière refused as he felt that the group strayed too far from Orthodox Judaism. He did, however, accept an invitation on the part of the Union's second president, René Heimann, in 1922.[65] At that point, Pallière began negotiating between liberal and conservative elements in the congregation to enable them to work out a modus vivendi with the Consistory in 1924, the same year that they completed construction of a new synagogue on the rue Copernic.[66] In exchange for eliminating those practices to which the Consistory objected most strongly, including holding sabbath services on Sundays, permitting mixed marriages, and, most importantly, authorizing conversions without circumcision,[67] the Union now held the same status as other independent Jewish religious associations, mostly small congregations created by immigrants, whose ritual varied in one way or another from that of the Consistory. As part of this agreement, rabbis from consistorial synagogues became regular guests at the Union's services and were occasionally invited to give lectures. Services were lengthened, and whereas prayers had originally been recited only in French, a cantor (*hazan*), who chanted the prayers in Hebrew, was now introduced.[68] A 1924 article in *Le Rayon* suggests that these

[65] Pallière himself never directly indicated why he accepted the offer to collaborate with the Union in 1922 when he had refused in 1908. Marcel Greilsammer suggested that the fact that Lévi made this first offer when the Union Libérale was in direct confrontation with the Consistory was in itself a factor in Pallière's reluctance to join. A newcomer to Judaism, Pallière did not want to formally associate himself with a minority faction. By the time Heimann asked him in 1922, however, Pallière was more confident about his own place within the Jewish community. See Greilsammer, 'Aimé Pallière à l'Union Libérale Israélite', one of six articles published as part of a special issue of *Revue de la pensée juive* entitled 'Hommage à Aimé Pallière' (July 1951). Poujol suggests that Pallière, who remained Orthodox at heart, made this decision in large part because he sensed that it would be an opportunity to guide the Union towards normative Judaism and reconciliation with the Consistory. See *Aimé Pallière*, 242–5.

[66] Greilsammer, 'Aimé Pallière à l'Union Libérale Israélite', 16–17.

[67] According to Poujol (*Aimé Pallière*, 248–51), this was the most controversial of the Union's practices. Other changes included using more Hebrew in services, requiring rabbis to wear the *kipah* while officiating at services (members of the congregation were still free to choose whether or not to cover their heads), and ensuring marriage ceremonies conformed to the requirements of the Consistory. See 'L'Union Libérale Israélite et le Consistoire de Paris', *Le Rayon* (15 Aug.–15 Sept. 1924), 2–5.

[68] Despite this rapprochement, the Union Libérale group continued to draw criticism from more conservative elements within the Consistory. The most persistent was Armand Lipman, who continued to criticize the group's reforms vociferously in *L'Univers israélite* and *Foi et réveil*, and at occasional lectures at Chema Israël, even after the Union ceased to be a major issue of debate within the Jewish community. Lipman's ideas were perhaps best received among Alsatian Jews, who tended to be more religiously conservative than their Parisian brethren. His attacks on the Union Libérale appeared with particular frequency in *La Tribune juive*, the Alsatian daily. See also the controversy surrounding Rabbi Giacomo A. Tedesco (who became the president of the Paris section of Chema Israël in 1928), who criticized the Consistory's deci-

changes were not undertaken simply because of pressure from the Consistory, but had support from the laity as well. The group's leadership had eliminated the cantor, the article explains, because they felt that his presence created a situation where one person prayed on behalf of rather than with the rest of the congregation. But this decision proved to be too great a break with tradition for most congregants, who felt that there was a cultural value to preserving such a 'characteristic' aspect of Judaism.[69] Pallière took charge of the group's monthly services for children, as well as education for the bar mitzvah and bat mitzvah. In 1925 Lévy began offering bi-weekly lecture courses on religion, which took place on Sunday and Thursday mornings.[70] In 1927 the group created an Association Sioniste des Dames Juives modelled on the temple sisterhoods of American Reform synagogues.[71]

Pallière also played a critical role in bringing both the leadership and individual members of the Union Libérale to support the Zionist movement. Joseph Fischer fondly recalled Pallière's role in bringing Louis-Germain Lévy, who 'became a familiar figure at Zionist meetings and demonstrations of Keren Kayemet', into the movement, and it was also thanks to his efforts that a number of female congregants, including Jenny Alfred Schwob, the mother of the convert René Schwob, became active in Keren Keyemet.[72] As we shall see, the Union Libérale's rapprochement with both the Consistory and the Zionist movement paved the way for regular contact and exchange between the Reformers and other Jewish groups of the day. Though the Union Libérale's membership consisted mainly of French Jewish families of long standing, there is some indication that the group became more diverse over the course of the decade: 'It is particularly interesting to note', we read in *Le Rayon*, 'that our Russian, Polish, and Oriental co-religionists are enlarging our congregation in increasing numbers'.[73]

The Impact of Immigrants and Second-Generation French Jews

The First World War accelerated the influx of immigrants that had begun at the turn of the century, as upheaval in both eastern Europe and the former

sion to 'allow' two of its own rabbis to give lectures to the Union Libérale's youth group. See René Haimann, 'L'Union Libérale et la communauté parisienne: Deux interviews', *L'Univers israélite* (19 Feb. 1926, p. 601; 26 Feb. 1926, pp. 629–30).

[69] See 'La Tenue dans nos offices', *Le Rayon* (15 Oct. 1924), 5–7.
[70] See *Le Rayon* (15 Oct. 1925), 2.   [71] *Le Rayon* (15 June 1927), 1.
[72] See Fischer, 'Aimé Pallière et le Keren Kayemet Leyisrael', 34. Poujol elaborates on Pallière's role in bringing the Union Libérale to support Keren Kayemet in the second volume of her thesis.   [73] *Le Rayon* (Oct. 1928), 8.

Ottoman empire sent large numbers of Jews towards the west. Restrictions on immigration to the United States in the years after the war made France the most popular destination for immigrants, the vast majority of whom settled in Paris. Between 1919 and 1939, the Jewish population of France rose from 150,000 to 300,000, an increase due almost entirely to immigration.[74] Historians of French Jewry have tended to emphasize the division between the immigrant and native communities. As Paula Hyman, Nancy Green, and others have shown, attempts to assimilate the newcomers as quickly as possible into the mainstream of French Jewish life often met with resistance on the part of the immigrants themselves, who preferred to establish their own associations and organizations. However, it is important to note that in describing immigrant and native Jews historians have tended to emphasize the extreme ends of the spectrum: discussions of 'native' Jews have generally focused on members of the Consistory and the Alliance Israélite Universelle, whereas discussions of 'immigrants' have tended to centre on the impoverished, Yiddish-speaking Jewish population. In fact, both natives and immigrants were more diverse than this dichotomous overview suggests. French Jews who created new associations and journals, many of whom were sympathetic to Zionism, were more open to and interested in contact and cultural exchange with immigrants than the leadership of the Consistory or the Alliance. Immigrants who participated in communal activities with native Jews, in turn, tended to be fluent in French and to come from a middle-class background. The line between the 'immigrant' and 'native' communities was also blurred by both the rapid pace of integration and acculturation of immigrants in France and, even more, the coming of age of second-generation French Jews.

In her study of Jewish immigrants to Paris between 1880 and 1914, Nancy Green points to the relatively high proportion of skilled labourers and professionals among the new arrivals. As we have seen, France held a special attraction for many east European Jewish intellectuals as the land of the revolution and the first European country to grant Jews citizenship.[75] While research in this area is relatively scarce, the evidence suggests that this attraction persisted through the 1920s. Polish Jews were largely urbanized

[74] The timing of Jewish immigration to France differed markedly from that to the United States and England. Between 1881 and 1914, 1,974,000 Jews immigrated to the United States and 120,000 to England. France, by contrast, attracted only 30,000. Both the failure of the Russian Revolution and immigration restrictions enacted in England in 1905 and in the United States in 1924, however, made France a much more popular destination. See Hyman, *From Dreyfus to Vichy*, 64–5.

[75] Green, *The Pletzl of Paris*, 111. Green notes that 76.8% of Jewish immigrants to France were skilled workers, compared to 64% of immigrants to the United States, and, even more strikingly, that 12.6% (compared to only 1.3% for the US) were professionals.

by the First World War, meaning that the majority of new immigrants were not arriving from shtetls but were already familiar with city life, a factor that greatly facilitated their integration into Parisian society.[76] Paris was home to a sizeable east European Jewish student population during the inter-war years, and there was a disproportionate number of prominent scientists in France of east European Jewish origin.[77] Perhaps the most prominent 'immigrant elite' during these years, however, was the group of east European Jewish artists who settled in Paris from 1910 onwards.[78]

Even the most educated and acculturated foreign-born Jews had great difficulty infiltrating the inner circle of the French Jewish establishment in the inter-war years. The right of foreign-born Jews to serve on the Consistory council remained a contested issue, and it was only in 1939 that they became eligible for full membership.[79] However, many prominent Jewish journalists, writers, and community spokesmen in the inter-war years were of foreign origin. Novelists Josué Jéhouda and Joseph Kessel were from Russia, as was Jacques Bielinky, a prominent Jewish journalist and art critic. Bielinky, who arrived in France in 1909, first worked as a correspondent for the Russian press and was active in the creation of the Yiddish newspaper *Parizer Haynt* in 1926. He was also a regular columnist for *L'Univers israélite*, where he wrote primarily on political and social issues pertaining to east European Jews, and worked as an art critic for both the Jewish paper *Menorah* and *Le Montparnasse*, a municipal journal published in the artistic centre of Paris.[80] Nina Gourfinkel, a social worker and *femme de lettres* who contributed regularly to the French-language Jewish press, was born into the Russian Jewish intelligentsia and arrived in Paris at the age of 25.[81] Léon Algazi, who was born in Bucharest in 1890, was one of the founders of Amis du Judaïsme, a youth group oriented towards native French Jews. He was active in creating Jewish youth choirs in the 1920s, wrote the music for the French version of the *Dibbouk* in 1926, and became the director of synagogue music for the Consistory in the 1930s.[82]

---

[76] Ida Benguigui makes this point in her Master's thesis, 'L'Immigration juive à Paris entre les deux guerres', which can be consulted in the library of the Alliance Israélite Universelle.

[77] Ibid. 42.   [78] These artists are discussed in greater detail in Chapter 6.

[79] On the debates over admitting foreign Jews to the Consistory, see Hyman, *From Dreyfus to Vichy*, 139–52.

[80] In her introduction to Bielinky's wartime diary, *Jacques Bielinky: Journal 1940–1942*, Renée Poznanski gives a detailed biography of Bielinky, in which she emphasizes the fluidity with which he moved in different Parisian milieus of his day. He was deported in 1942 and did not return.

[81] On Nina Gourfinkel, see Bitton, *Présences féminines juives en France*, 222–3. The second volume of Gourfinkel's memoirs, entitled *L'Autre Patrie*, focuses on her life in France from 1925 to 1945.   [82] See the biographical essay on Algazi by Tourny, in *Archives juives*, 103–5.

Another factor that played a critical role in blurring the boundaries between 'immigrants' and 'natives' during the 1920s was the coming of age of both the sons and daughters of the pre-war immigrants as well as those who had immigrated as children. Many prominent representatives of 'native' Jewry fitted into this category. Victor Basch was born in Hungary. Albert Cohen, the novelist and founder of the *La Revue juive,* and Maurice Liber both immigrated to France as small children, Cohen from Corfu and Liber from Poland. While Meyer Levyne (Meyerkey), a columnist for both *Chalom* and *Le Rayon* and a prominent figure in the Union Universelle de la Jeunesse Juive, was born in Paris in 1890, his parents were immigrants from eastern Europe.[83] Figures such as these tend to be left out of discussions of immigrant Jews, however, because they did not move in immigrant circles and often expressed viewpoints that we more readily associate with native Jews. Maurice Liber, for example, who opposed Zionism, is often cited by scholars as exemplary of the outlook of the 'native' Jewish community.[84] As I suggested in Chapter 3, however, Liber's immigrant background undoubtedly influenced his commitment to creating a more public, visible form of Judaism, something that was taken for granted among east European Jews: he was, for example, a founding member of the youth group Chema Israël, which encouraged religious practice by creating new forms of Jewish sociability. Conversely, the leader of the pre-war Zionist movement, Baruch Hagani, is generally thought of as an immigrant spokesman, even though he was born in Paris. Writing in 1926, Meyerkey suggested the problematic nature of the categories which contemporaries themselves used to distinguish between different segments of Parisian Jewish society. While people generally spoke of three groups of Jews in the capital—French, Oriental, and 'foreign' (immigrants from eastern Europe)—he noted, many of those referred to as 'foreigners' were French citizens who had achieved considerable social and economic success. Hence, they should be considered as a category distinct from new arrivals, many of whom were barely scraping by in the poorest neighbourhoods in Paris.[85]

As Meyerkey suggests, 'Oriental' Jews—Sephardi Jews from the former Ottoman empire—comprised a distinctive and often overlooked element in the inter-war Jewish population. The largest group was from the city of

[83] I am grateful to Mme Suzette Levyne, Meyerkey's daughter, for providing me with this biographical information about her father, who was murdered in the Holocaust.

[84] For example, while Paula Hyman makes numerous references to Liber in *From Dreyfus to Vichy,* at no point does she mention that he was born in Poland.

[85] Meyer Levyne, 'Flânerie à travers la capitale', *Les Flambeaux* (23 Apr. 1926), 2. In his articles for *Les Flambeaux,* of which he was one of the founding editors, Levyne did not use his pseudonym.

Salonica, which had been one of the most important centres of Jewish life in the Ottoman empire prior to the First World War.[86] There were approximately 1,700 Salonican Jews in Paris by 1926, 2,200 by 1931, and 2,600 by 1936.[87] Though relatively few in number, Salonican Jews exercised an important influence on French Jewish cultural life in the 1920s. These Jews were much more likely than their Ashkenazi counterparts to be from a middle-class background, and, having been educated for the most part in the schools of the Alliance Israélite Universelle, they were already fluent in French and familiar with French culture before their arrival.

While acculturation and adaptation to France took longer and was often more difficult for those from eastern and central European backgrounds, the strongly assimilationist thrust of French society meant that for these immigrants, and even more so for their children, the maintenance of a distinctive 'immigrant' identity was relatively short-lived. The French state was one of the most immigrant-friendly in the 1920s,[88] and its highly centralized structure and emphasis on cultural uniformity encouraged the rapid integration of immigrants and second-generation youth into French society. Jewish newcomers formed only a fraction—approximately 15 per cent—of the total number of immigrants during the inter-war years.[89] The particularities of the Jewish situation—religious distinctiveness, a history of persecution, and endogamous marriage—meant that Jewish immigrants persisted as a distinct group longer than Poles, Spaniards, or Italians, the other principal immigrant groups during this period. The evidence nonetheless suggests that they integrated into the mainstream of French life more quickly than in either England or the United States.

Commenting on the various philanthropic institutions that native Jews created for their east European brethren, Paula Hyman emphasizes the strongly paternalistic attitude of these organizations: 'The natives perceived it as their responsibility', she notes, 'to remake the immigrant Jews in their own image and to use their institutions as agents of assimilation.'[90] Immigrants, in turn, often felt the institutions and publications of native French

---

[86] The Jewish population of Salonica suffered terribly during the war. Forced population exchanges between Greece and Turkey in 1917 decimated the community, and once the city came under Greek control a government policy that aimed to impose religious and cultural uniformity created a hostile environment for the remaining Jewish population. On the Ottoman Jews in Paris in the inter-war years, see Benveniste, *Le Bosphore à la Roquette*.

[87] Ibid. 70.

[88] A law passed in 1927 that reduced the waiting period for citizenship applications from ten to three years greatly increased the number of naturalizations. It was only in 1936 that a series of restrictive laws was introduced that made both immigration and naturalization more difficult. See Hyman, *From Dreyfus to Vichy*, 66.

[89] Hyman (ibid. 68) gives this statistic for the period 1906–35.   [90] Ibid. 116.

Jewry to be 'lifeless and wanting in *Yiddishkeit*, much like the native community as whole'.[91] While this dichotomy underscores the chasm that existed
between the native French Jewish leadership and new arrivals, we should not
underestimate the strong desire for integration on the part of the immigrants themselves. Yiddish-speaking spaces created by Jewish immigrants
tended to be very transient. Even if linguistic and cultural barriers kept
immigrants within a distinct social milieu, this was rarely the case for their
children. Both the centralized French education system and lack of neighbourhood cohesion encouraged the rapid integration of children from
immigrant families into the mainstream of French life.

An important difference between France and both England and the
United States was that immigrants did not live in concentrated communities. While we can speak of Jewish neighbourhoods such as the Marais and
Montmartre in inter-war France, these areas did not form Jewish 'ghettos' on
a par with the Lower East Side in New York or the East End in London. While
both the Marais and Montmartre had a high concentration of Jewish residents, at no point did Jews form the majority of their populations.[92] This
difference in housing patterns meant that new arrivals, and even more so
their children, were much less likely to continue to speak the language
of their home country or socialize exclusively with compatriots. Many of the
associations created by the immigrants themselves focused on facilitating
rapid adaptation to French life. If groups run by immigrants had more success in attracting new arrivals than those created by native Jews, their objectives were often very similar. Beyond providing basic material aid, the
primary purpose of most immigrant associations was precisely to help their
members integrate as quickly as possible. The evidence suggests that these
efforts were largely successful. Children of Yiddish-speaking immigrants,
Paula Hyman notes, moved with ease into the general branches of the
French labour movement.[93] The Parisian-born 'native' poet and essayist
Pierre Créange who, like others of his generation, began to write on Jewish
themes in the mid-1920s,[94] remarked upon the rapid integration of the

---

[91] Ibid. 119.
[92] I am grateful to Aline Benain, who is currently completing her thesis, 'L'Espace yiddish-
ophone parisien, 1880–1939' (Paris 1), for sharing her findings on Jewish immigrant housing
patterns with me.　　　　　　　　　　　　　　　　　　[93] Hyman, *From Dreyfus to Vichy*, 114.
[94] Créange, *La Paria au manteau du soleil* and *Vers les pays qui ne sont pas*. Créange, a close
friend of the poet Gustave Kahn, was active in both socialist politics and LICA. His 1937 collection of essays, *Epîtres aux Juifs*, warned of the dangers of Nazism. He was murdered in
Auschwitz, along with his wife, in 1943. See Eladan's short essay on Créange in *Poètes juifs de la
langue française*, 171–8.

children of immigrants, pointing both to their success in commerce and their strong presence in the universities.[95]

In his memoirs Gilbert Michlin, who was born in Paris shortly after his parents immigrated from Poland in 1925, provides evidence of how immigrant Jews in the inter-war years blended their desire for integration with attachment to their Jewish heritage. Remembering his parents' 'adamant belief' in the values of secularism, universalism, and human rights, Michlin reflects on how those values shaped their relationship to Judaism. While his parents 'became good Frenchmen' and expected that he would become a 'true Frenchman' as well, he affirms, 'their desire to integrate into the national community that had welcomed them did not actually wipe out their past and their identity'.[96] The Michlins socialized with other Jews, attended performances at the Yiddish theatre, and rented a hall for the major holidays with members of their *hevrah kadishah* (burial society). While they celebrated Yom Kippur, they 'never really fasted', and favoured a universalist interpretation of Passover as symbolic of 'the deliverance from bondage'.[97] Michlin's own childhood memories—Sunday strolls down the Grands Boulevards with their lively café concerts, playing with toy boats at the Jardin des Tuileries, visits to both the Comédie-Française and the Yiddish theatre, as well as trips to the Pletzl to buy the ingredients for home-made, 'Litvak-style' gefilte fish and get-togethers with his parents' Yiddish-speaking friends—also reflect a combination of French acculturation and Jewish distinctiveness.[98]

While Michlin himself was too young to have participated in the 'réveil' of the 1920s, young adults and adolescents from immigrant backgrounds who, like Michlin's family, sought out the 'middle ground' between French and east European Jewish cultures often participated with natives in creating new forms of Jewish associational life and culture during these years. In his 1926 article for *Les Flambeaux*, Meyerkey indicated the critical role that both

[95] 'Les Juifs polonais... et les autres', in *Epîtres aux Juifs*. As Créange explained in a preface to the essay, it was written in 1925 in response to a debate sponsored by the Club du Faubourg on relations between immigrant and native Jews.

[96] Michlin, *Of No Interest to the Nation*, 20.

[97] Ibid. 20. Michlin's book unfortunately contains an inaccurate afterword by historian Zeev Sternhell, who presents the Michlin family as a paradigm of French Jews' alleged single-minded desire to 'play the game of assimilation'. See my review of the book on *H-France* (www.h-france.net).

[98] Michlin, *Of No Interest to the Nation*, 24–8. Michlin presents his Parisian childhood as a paradise lost that stands in stark contrast to the hell into which he and his parents were thrown by the German occupation and the establishment of an antisemitic French fascist state. While his youth and skill as a die- and-tool worker led him to be 'hired' by the Siemens company after his deportation to Auschwitz and thus to be spared death, both of his parents were murdered in the camps.

Sephardi immigrants and second-generation east Europeans played in the Jewish cultural renaissance of the day. It was these Jews, 'together with many of their elders in the French family', he suggested, who were currently in the process of 'regenerating our religion'.[99] As we shall see, while tensions between immigrants and natives were not absent from the wide range of Jewish youth groups, cultural associations, journals, clubs, and other activities that French Jews created in the 1920s, this flowering of activity helped to bridge the gap between them in the inter-war years.

[99]　Levyne, 'Flânerie à travers la capitale', 2.

CHAPTER 5

Enlivening the Public Sphere: Jewish Sociability in the 1920s

'BEFORE THE WAR', noted the journalist and communal activist Meyerkey in 1926, 'there was hardly any Jewish activity outside religious and mutual aid associations . . . Today, things are different. Associations of all kinds—Zionist, athletic, mutual aid, and secular—are rising up and reclaiming Judaism as their own.'[1] As Meyerkey's comments suggest, the appearance of new spaces for Jewish sociability, the expansion of Jewish popular education, and a proliferation of discussion among Jews and sympathetic non-Jews about the nature of Jewish identity and culture in the modern world constituted a major shift in French Jewish life during this period. The post-war years saw similar developments in other west European and American Jewish communities. A number of interrelated factors—the rise of the Zionist movement, the sense of spiritual vacuum created by the First World War, and a much larger population of young people remaining in school through their teenage years—all contributed to the growth of Jewish community centres, youth groups, and educational societies.

In both the United States and Germany, a rise in antisemitic politics and social exclusion of Jews was important in spurring the creation of independent Jewish social, cultural, and educational associations. As Jews realized that the opportunities for integration into the broader society were limited, they began to both question anew the issue of Jewish identity in the modern world and create organizations and cultural institutions that responded to their particular needs as a community. In France, by contrast, a general consensus that antisemitism was on the decline shaped this enlivening of the Jewish public sphere in particular ways. One of the defining characteristics of French intellectuals of Jewish origins in the 1920s, Michel Trebitsch notes, is that 'they felt profoundly integrated into French society and the diverse currents within it'.[2] As we shall see, this was equally true of the men and women who participated in various spheres of Jewish cultural life during this period. While disillusionment with the 'ideology of assimilation'—as characterized by the intellectual journey of André Spire and other pre-war

[1] Meyerkey, 'Pour l'organisation spirituelle du judaïsme parisien', *Le Rayon* (15 June 1926), 13.   [2] Trebitsch, 'Les Intellectuels juifs en France dans les années vingt', 45.

intellectuals—was a factor in reshaping Jewish identity and community, French Jews most often understood the new forms of Jewish community life and self-expression that they created to be a product of their integration into French society rather than a rejection of it.

Creating New Spaces for Sociability: Jewish Youth Movements in the 1920s

Young French Jews, influenced by many of the same factors as others of their generation—rejection of the past, commitment to political and social change, interest in organizing sporting and leisure activities in the country, and, more generally, a desire to publicly display group allegiance through insignias, uniforms, and other 'outward' signs of belonging—formed a variety of different youth groups over the course of the 1920s.[3] These groups were conceived as an antidote to the post-emancipation Jewish community's failure to encourage young Jews to socialize together, a situation, many felt, that had paved the way for total assimilation.[4] By the early 1920s, concern about the lack of a vibrant Jewish community life that had sparked the creation of the Union Scolaire, Amis du Judaïsme, and Association des Jeunes Juifs in the pre-war years became much more widespread. In an article for the Zionist-oriented journal *Menorah* in 1923, Henri Hertz commented on the Consistory's failure to meet the needs of contemporary French Jews. While the Consistory's role as a passive administrator had satisfied a homogeneous, complacent pre-war Jewish community, Hertz asserted, this was no longer the case. French Jewry, he lamented, had been transformed by the great changes of the post-war era—the rise of Jewish nationalism, religious revival, and the wave of immigration—but the Jewish establishment had done nothing to respond to these changes. For Hertz, a Zionist sympathizer who believed that French Jews should openly affirm their Jewishness in ethnic terms, the Consistory's insistence on maintaining a narrowly confessional definition of Judaism was a major part of this problem,[5] but even those people who were critical of Zionism and defended a 'religious' understanding of Jewishness had become increasingly critical of

---

[3] On the development of youth movements in France, which only began in earnest after the First World War, see Yolande Cohen, *Les Jeunes, le socialisme et la guerre*, and Cholvy (ed.), *Mouvements de jeunesse chrétiens et juifs*. In her doctoral thesis Poujol brings to light previously undocumented details about the founding and growth of the UUJJ and the power struggles within it that I outline below.

[4] For an overview of the creation of Jewish youth movements in France, see Danielle Delmaire, 'Mouvements de jeunesse juifs en France, 1919–1939', and Hyman, *From Dreyfus to Vichy*, ch. 7.   [5] Henri Hertz, 'La Situation', *Menorah* (16 Sept. 1923), 383–4.

consistorial Judaism by the early 1920s. It was this sentiment that provided the impetus behind the creation of the first national Jewish youth movement, Chema Israël, in 1919.

An important motivating force behind the creation of Chema Israël, billed as an 'organization for religious education and advocacy', was a desire on the part of the younger generation of French rabbis—the same group that created *Foi et reveil* in 1913—to counter the war's assimilating effect on Jewish soldiers. Whereas many young Catholics had come back to the church in response to the trials of their wartime experiences, Hippolyte Prague asserted in a 1919 article in the *Archives israélites*, the war had generally led to disaffiliation from the Jewish community. Young Jews who might have hesitated before marrying outside their faith in the pre-war years, he suggested 'no longer [had] any scruples about uniting with a person outside their religion'. The present challenge for Jewish religious leaders, Prague suggested, was to counter this trend by 'creating organizations and activities capable of interesting [young Jews] in Jewish life, in cultivating within them a love of religion'.[6] Maurice Liber expressed the need for the creation of Chema Israël in similar terms: 'every religion, in order to remain vibrant and endure, needs established practices and ongoing modes of public expression; in two words, appropriate *institutions*'.[7] As Liber's comments suggest, though Chema Israël was explicitly defined as a 'religious' organization, its leadership felt that it was necessary to broaden the range of activities included under that heading to accomplish this goal.[8] The group grew rapidly over the course of the decade. The Parisian section counted 500 members by 1927,[9] and sections existed in fourteen cities by the early 1930s. Chema Israël had a strong base of support in Alsace, with sections in Lunéville, Metz, Forbach, Mulhouse, and Thionville, and a particularly active section in Lyons.[10]

An important characteristic of French confessional youth movements, as distinct from an earlier genre of 'œuvres' or 'patronages' run by various religious and charitable organizations, was that the inter-war groups were

[6] Prague, 'La Marée montante des mariages mixtes', *Archives israélites* (22 May 1919), 93.

[7] Ben-Ammi, 'La Journée cultuelle du judaïsme français', *L'Univers israélite* (15 Apr. 1921), 750 (emphasis in original).

[8] Hyman makes a similar point in her discussion of the organization in *From Dreyfus to Vichy*, where she notes that, 'Following the model of the adult community, the founders of Chema Israël accepted a purely religious definition of the Jewish community in France. However, they included a wide variety of educational functions within the purview of the religious' (p. 182). However, it is important to note that, as Liber's statement suggests, even as they defined 'religion' as the basis of Jewish community, the creators of Chema Israël understood this term differently from the leadership of the Consistory.   [9] Poujol, 'Aimé Pallière', ii. 481.

[10] *L'Univers israélite* reported regularly on Chema Israël's activities throughout France. Outside Paris, activities and lectures sponsored by the Lyons section appeared most frequently.

created by young people themselves.[11] Chema Israël followed this pattern to some extent. Though created under the auspices of the rabbinate and Consistory, it was run by a committee of young people who assumed responsibility for the group's activities and programming.[12] The initiative for the creation of the two other major youth movements of the 1920s—the Union Universelle de la Jeunesse Juive (UUJJ) and the Eclaireurs Israélites (Jewish Boy Scouts)—came more decisively from outside the consistorial structure.

The UUJJ was founded in Salonica in 1921 and transferred to Paris in 1923, when its two founders, Charles Nehama and Jacques Matalon, immigrated to the French capital.[13] Created in the aftermath of the First World War, the group was originally intended as a kind of modernized Alliance Israélite Universelle, devoted to fighting antisemitism around the world and working to promote the goals of world peace and internationalism set forth at the Paris Peace Conference. Initially it functioned primarily as a social club for French-born middle-class Parisian teenagers and young adults, and was neither religious nor Zionist in orientation.[14] The World Zionist Organization, however, saw it as a potential forum for increasing support for Zionism among French youth, and played a major role in securing the unlikely election of the 58-year-old Aimé Pallière, president of Keren Kayemet, as UUJJ president. Pallière proved very successful in building the organization up internationally, and by the end of the decade the UUJJ federation counted fifty-seven sections and affiliated groups around the world.[15] He was also initially very successful at attracting new members to the original Paris section, which jumped from sixty members in 1926 to close to 600 by the end of 1927.[16]

The rapid increase in the UUJJ's membership was due primarily to Pallière's recruitment of young people from immigrant backgrounds to the organization. These young men and women, for the most part secular in orientation and more interested in fighting international antisemitism and promoting left-wing politics than in Zionism, were attracted by the UUJJ's innovative decision to abandon an exclusively religious definition of Judaism and welcome all Jews who identified as such as members. In fact, however, Pallière and his entourage saw the group as a forum for building support for Zionism and encouraging a religious revival among French

[11] Coutrot, 'Le Mouvement de jeunesse', 119.
[12] See the group's founding statement in *L'Univers israélite* (28 Nov. 1919), 222–4, which lists the members of the committee.
[13] The group, originally called L'Interjuive and conceived of as an 'exchange association for Jews around the world', changed its name with its move to Paris in 1923. See Delmaire, 'Mouvements de jeunesse juifs en France', 318.
[14] Poujol, 'Aimé Pallière', ii. 430.   [15] Ibid. 434.   [16] Poujol, 'Une exception', 30.

Jews.[17] A chasm therefore began to open between the UUJJ's leadership and the Paris section: while Pallière imposed *kashrut* on the UUJJ's community centre there, inserted a column devoted to religious life in *Chalom*, and preached the importance of Zionism to the religious renewal of the Jewish people, the Parisian members formed a close bond with LICA president Bernard Lecache, and devoted their energies to protesting against the Schwartzbard trial, *numerus clausus*, and pogroms in eastern Europe.[18] This group formed a club within the UUJJ called the Club de la Jeunesse Juive, and began publishing its own paper, *La Jeunesse juive*.[19] Tensions between the UUJJ leadership and this group of increasingly active new members culminated in their departure en masse following the UUJJ's annual conference, which was held in Strasbourg in August 1928.[20] While the UUJJ continued to publish *Chalom* and keep up appearances for the now sizeable provincial and international sections of the organization, after this defection its Paris section was in fact reduced to a core group of twenty members.[21]

Ultimately, it was the Eclaireurs Israélites de France that succeeded in accomplishing the UUJJ's mission of bridging the gap between Jews from varying social, religious, and class backgrounds.[22] The first Eclaireur troop was created in Paris in 1923 by Robert Gamzon, the 17-year-old grandson of the chief rabbi of France Albert Lévy, and son of an immigrant engineer from

---

[17] Poujol, 'Aimé Pallière', ii. 417–21.

[18] Poujol details both the increasing support for anti-religious, left-wing political organizer Lecache among new members of the UUJJ in 1926–7 and the deep antipathy of Pallière and his entourage towards Lecache and LICA: see 'Aimé Pallière', ii. 470–3, 497–504.

[19] Tellingly, Poujol notes (ibid. 472), we find only one reference to *La Jeunesse juive* (and none at all to the corresponding club) in the pages of *Chalom*. The 'Frenchness' of these young people is an interesting issue that reveals some of the problems of categorization discussed in Chapter 4. While the UUJJ leadership referred disparagingly to their east European roots as the source of these new members' predilection for left-wing politics and noisy demonstrations, they described themselves as 'all French' as well as 'the sons and daughters of immigrants'. The majority of this group probably came to France as children or young adults, and were naturalized in 1927, the year that the Poincaré government relaxed immigration laws. As André Kaspi points out, for these young people this act of naturalization was an important symbolic step, marking their decision to stake their claim as 'the Frenchmen and women of tomorrow'. Kaspi, *Les Juifs pendant l'Occupation*, 45; see also Poujol, 'Aimé Pallière', ii. 473.

[20] Poujol's account sheds new light on the history of the UUJJ. In an article written in 1951, Wladimir Rabinovitch indicated that tensions between the spiritually oriented Pallière and UUJJ members (including Rabinovitch himself) who wanted to engage in political activism had reached breaking point by 1934 (Rabi, 'Aimé Pallière et notre futile jeunesse', 30–1). As Poujol discovered in her work at the Central Zionist Archives and in Pallière's private papers, however, the departure of the 500-strong faction in 1928 in fact represented the beginning of the demise of the organization. [21] Poujol, 'Aimé Pallière', ii. 490–507.

[22] On the Jewish scouting movement see Michel, *Juifs, Français et Scouts* and 'Qu'est-ce qu'un Scout juif?'

eastern Europe. By 1924 a Jewish scouting movement had been established under the patronage of a central committee of wealthy members of the native Parisian Jewish community.[23] Gamzon originally defined the goals of the movement in terms very acceptable to the Consistory and rabbinate. Just as Catholic Scouts pledged to support 'God, the Church, and France', Jewish Scouts would pledge their allegiance to 'God, Judaism, and France'.[24] By 1926, however, the Scouts' strictly religious vision of Judaism was being called into question, largely through the influence of Edmond Fleg. Deeply moved by Fleg's *L'Enfant prophète*, the story of a young boy's search for the meaning of his Jewish heritage, Gamzon asked him to be president of the organization in 1926. While Fleg refused,[25] he did become involved with the movement, and pushed it to expand its definition of Judaism to include non-religious forms of Jewish identity.[26]

In 1927 the movement's pledge was modified to encourage Scouts to 'develop their sense of themselves as Jews', and it committed itself to admitting members from 'all the diverse tendencies' within French Judaism.[27] This redefinition opened up the possibility of collaborating with Zionists, and over the next decade 'cultural Zionist' tendencies became predominant within the movement.[28] The decision to push the group in an inclusive direction was due in large part to the collaboration between Gamzon and Aimé Pallière, who began working with Gamzon to create UUJJ-affiliated scouting troops in 1927. As it became clear to Pallière that he would be unable to make the UUJJ the meeting-place between Jews of different backgrounds and ideological orientations that he had originally hoped, Pallière wisely passed the baton to Gamzon, whose personal background and youthful energy were better suited to reaching out to young Jews across religious, ideological, and class lines. While the scouting troop arrived too late to save the Paris section of the UUJJ, the Eclaireurs' rapid climb in membership, from 150 members in 1927 to 600 in 1929, can perhaps in part be accounted for by the fact that the Scouts were able to re-enlist some of the young people

[23] Hyman, *From Dreyfus to Vichy*, 191. See also Pougatch's biography of Gamzon, *Un bâtisseur*.

[24] Michel, *Juifs, Français et Scouts*, 37.

[25] The presidency was taken over by General Geismar. Fleg's official reason for refusing was that he felt the group was too oriented towards a small, traditionalist faction of the native community for him to feel comfortable assuming a leadership position. As Gamzon recalled, however, Fleg was also hesitant to assume the responsibility of running the organization because it would take time away from his writing. However, Fleg did take on the presidency in 1935. See Gamzon, 'Edmond Fleg et les Eclaireurs Israélites de France'.

[26] Michel, *Juifs, Français et Scouts*, 43–5.   [27] Ibid. 45.

[28] The issue of a religious versus a Zionist definition was a continuing matter of debate between the Eclaireurs and the French rabbinate and Consistory. See Hyman, *From Dreyfus to Vichy*, 193–8.

who had left the UUJJ en masse in 1928.[29] It was also at this point that the Eclaireurs created a federation and began forming troops throughout Paris and the provinces, as well as Tunisia, Morocco, and Algeria. Some troops were organized by neighbourhood, others by already existing clubs with different ideological orientations. Both Chema Israël and the Union Libérale's youth wing, the Jeunesse Libérale Israélite, for example, had created their own scouting troops by the end of 1927. Lily Simon, the founder of the female scouting troops (the Eclaireuses), created a troop for disadvantaged Jewish immigrants in 1928 that had a distinctly Zionist orientation.[30] By 1931, nineteen troops existed in North Africa, seventeen in Alsace-Lorraine, and twenty-seven in the rest of France.[31]

In addition to these national movements, many smaller youth groups were created in Paris and the provinces from the early 1920s on. By 1925 Jewish youth associations existed in Bordeaux, Nice, Tours, Epinal, Besançon, Nancy, Thionville, Sarrebourg, Lille, Marseilles, and Lunéville, and by 1930 in Mulhouse, Sélestat, and Metz as well.[32] Local consistories, for the most part, provided the space for these groups. The Union Libérale's youth organization, the Jeunesse Libérale Israélite, was formed in 1924.[33] A number of groups were also created specifically for young people from immigrant backgrounds. Among the most successful of these were the Union de la Jeunesse Juive, which had 800 members by 1930,[34] and the Parisian branch of the Maccabi sports club, with a membership of 1,300 by the end of the decade.[35] In 1929 several independent immigrant youth associations merged to form the Union des Jeunesses Israélites de France.[36] While the group's activities were centred in Paris, it also established sections in several other French cities. The Union des Associations d'Etudiants Juifs en France, created in 1927 as an umbrella organization for already existing student groups in Paris, Bordeaux, Lyons, Nancy, Paris, Toulouse, Caen, Rouen, Strasbourg, Montpellier, Besançon, and Tours, counted 3,000 members by 1931.[37] Bené-

---

[29] For these points see Poujol, 'Aimé Pallière', ii. 486.

[30] Michel, *Juifs, Français et Scouts*, 49.

[31] The Eclaireurs had a total of 1,200 members by 1930 (ibid. 47).

[32] *L'Univers israélite* noted the creation of these youth groups over the course of the decade in its 'Nouvelles diverses' column.　　　　　　　[33] See *Le Rayon* (15 Nov. 1924), 5–6.

[34] *L'Univers israélite* (17 Jan. 1930), 535. This group existed as early as 1917.

[35] The Maccabi club was an international Jewish sporting organization with strong links to the Zionist movement. It became affiliated with the UUJJ in 1930.

[36] The group had 1,000 members by 1931, at which point it had begun to publish a monthly bulletin and was sponsoring weekly lectures, dances, and sporting activities. See *L'Almanach juif*, 107.

[37] See *L'Univers israélite* (12 Apr. 1929), 983–4. The groups covered included the Entr'aide Fraternelle de la Jeunesse Israélite, Le Club Familial, and Le Club de la Jeunesse Juive, the

Mizrah and La Fraternité were created by Sephardi youth in 1925 and 1930 respectively,[38] and though it did not function exclusively as a youth organization, most of the activities sponsored by the Association Amicale des Israélites Saloniciens were geared towards young people.

The primary purpose of all of these groups was to create a place for young Jews to socialize with each other. Different orientations, of course, affected programming to some degree: the religiously oriented Chema Israël and Jeunesse Libérale Israélite sponsored independent religious services[39] as well as an annual Passover seder for members who did not have a family environment in which to celebrate.[40] As a scouting movement, the Eclaireurs' activities were focused, for the most part, on various sporting and wilderness activities. Most groups held annual or semi-annual balls, as well as more informal weekly or monthly dances. The Union des Jeunesses Israélites's 1929 annual dance drew over 2,000 people, and Bené-Mizrah's 1931 Hanukah ball, presided over by Gustave Kahn, drew 900.[41] Bené-Mizrah opened an Université Populaire Juive in 1930, which sponsored sports events and parties as well as weekly lectures and debates. Speakers for 1930 and 1931 included Justin Godart, Fernand Corcos, Pierre Paraf, and Yvonne Netter, as well as the president of the Union Scolaire, Charles-Edouard Lévy. The largest range of activities was offered by Chema Israël and the UUJJ. By mid-decade, both groups had begun organizing theatre productions, group excursions, and choral singing, as well as holding annual conferences that united members from the different national and international sections. Their main activity, however, was weekly lectures and discussion groups, often followed by concerts or poetry readings.

Before the 1928 collapse of its Paris section, the UUJJ weekly Saturday night meetings for members drew on average between 100 and 150 people,[42] and the group sponsored monthly 'Grandes Conférences' that regularly

group that had split off from the UUJJ in 1928, as well as Le Club de la Jeunesse Juive de la Rive Gauche.

[38] Bené-Mizrah had 761 members by 1931 (see *L'Almanach juif*, 104). While it attracted a largely working-class membership, La Fraternité, which counted 500 members by November 1930 (see *L'Univers israélite* (28 Nov. 1930), 346), was created within a more upper-class, intellectual milieu. On the differences between these two groups, see Benveniste, *Le Bosphore à la Roquette*.

[39] Chema began sponsoring its own religious services for major holidays in 1927. See *L'Univers israélite* (14 Oct. 1927), 21. The Jeunesse Libérale Israélite held monthly services for young people.

[40] These Passover seders were an innovation of Chema Israël's, which also built its own *sukah* for the festival of Sukot (see Hyman, *From Dreyfus to Vichy*, 183). The AAIS also sponsored a Passover seder and organized its own high holy day services in accordance with Sephardi ritual.

[41] See *L'Univers israélite* (29 Nov. 1929), 280, and Bené-Mizrah's journal, also called *Bené-Mizrah* (Dec. 1930). [42] *Chalom* (Oct./Nov. 1927), 23.

FIGURE 3 A group of Jewish Scouts in the mid-1920s

Photograph from the personal collection of Alain Michel; reproduced by permission

filled the Salle Comœdia, one of the largest conference halls in the city.[43] A glance at the programme for 1925/6 gives a sense of the range of topics of interest to French Jews of the day. The season opened with a series of lectures on 'Different Aspects of Contemporary Judaism', presided over by Justin Godart. Speakers included the novelist Myriam Harry, Louis-Germain Lévy, and several non-Jewish speakers, among them Jean Izoulet, author of *Paris: Capitale des religions ou la mission d'Israël*. A debate on Jews and communists featuring Henry Marx, Henry Torrès (the lawyer who defended Shalom Schwartzbard), and an anti-communist former professor at the University of Petrograd attracted such a crowd, *Chalom* reported, that the organizers were obliged to turn people away.[44]

Jean-Richard Bloch, Aimé Pallière, and Henry Marx participated in a discussion on the future of the Hebrew University of Jerusalem, and a debate on two novels on Jewish themes, Bernard Lecache's *Jacob* and Edmond Fleg's *Le Juif du Pape*, was followed by a series of lectures on different aspects of the Jewish religion. Aimé Pallière spoke on traditional Judaism, Sacha Krinsky on Reform Judaism, and Léon Berman on 'Liberal Conservativism'. Other sessions included a lecture on Zionism by Vladimir Jabotinksy, two Catholic speakers, Paul Vulliaud and Marie-André Dieux, on Jewish symbolic poetry and Judaism and science respectively, and the (non-Jewish) novelist Lucie Delarue-Mardus on her recent trip to Palestine. André Spire's lecture on Henri Franck was followed by a debate on the merits of establishing Jewish settlements in the Crimea. The season closed with a debate on the significance and implications of the 'mode juive' itself.[45]

Many youth groups sponsored sporting events, teams, and physical education classes and, like their non-Jewish counterparts, organized day excursions to the country.[46] A survey of French Jewish youth groups' publications and lecture topics does not reveal the kind of concern with creating a 'muscular Jewry' that was so important to the more Zionist-oriented German groups. This difference was undoubtedly related to differences between German and French youth culture and the position of the Jewish community in France and Germany more broadly. While French youth groups, like their German counterparts, exhibited certain militaristic tendencies (such as the wearing of uniforms or marching in the country), they were almost exclusively inspired by a pacifist and internationalist ideology and for the most part discouraged antisemitism. Generally speaking, Jewish youth groups in France saw themselves as part of this wider community committed to international peace and understanding. The brand of Zionism that inspired these

---

[43] W. Rabinovitch, 'Rapport sur le travail de la section de Paris', *Chalom* (Aug. 1927), 6.
[44] 'Nos conférences à Paris', *Chalom* (Mar. 1926), 16.
[45] Ibid.   [46] Coutrot, 'Le Mouvement de jeunesse', 115.

groups (and French Zionism more broadly, as we will see in Chapter 8) was associated with a desire to develop Jewish particularism within a broadly universalist, humanitarian framework. While German Zionists shared many of these beliefs, a more hostile surrounding environment—and in particular the growing strength of the fascist youth movement after the mid-1920s—inevitably made self-defence and the Zionist idea of building a physically strong, independent Jewish community more of a concern in Germany than in France.

Differences and divisions among these various Jewish youth groups reflected some of the central tensions within French Jewry during this period. As we have seen, the UUJJ's rank and file did not automatically follow the leadership's decision to make the organization an organ of religious renewal and Zionist propaganda. The Zionist orientation of the group also put it at odds with more conservative elements within the rabbinate and the Consistory,[47] which sought to prevent collaboration with Chema Israël.[48] Nonetheless, members of Chema did not remain untouched by the brand of religious Zionism that Aimé Pallière played such an important role in disseminating during this era, and may have been more open to collaboration with the UUJJ than their leaders, especially after 1928. At the UUJJ's Strasbourg conference, for example, Maurice Liber objected vigorously to the suggestion of an Alsatian representative of Chema that the group, like the UUJJ, should adopt a resolution to help with the construction of Jewish settlements in Palestine. Writing in *Chalom* in 1928, Charles Nehama noted that members of the two organizations regularly attended each other's conferences and discussion groups.[49] Nor did the divide between their respective leaderships entirely prevent co-operation between the two groups. They sponsored a joint Hebrew course in Marseilles beginning in February 1929,[50] and both participated in the creation of the Comité d'Entente des Groupements Jeunes in 1931.[51]

---

[47] Opposition to the UUJJ began mounting within the Consistory and rabbinate after the 1928 Strasbourg conference. Ironically, Poujol suggests ('Aimé Pallière', ii. 487–9), much of their criticism stemmed from a lack of understanding of what had actually transpired at the conference. While they objected to the anti-religious immigrant faction, it was in fact the Strasbourg conference that set in motion the departure of this group, and reduced the UUJJ to its religiously oriented leadership.

[48] According to Pallière, it was also opposition from consistorial circles that prevented the UUJJ from branching out in France. By 1928 only two sections, in Marseilles and Tours, existed outside Paris. For a detailed discussion of the tensions between Chema Israël and the UUJJ see Hyman, *From Dreyfus to Vichy*, 187–91.

[49] Charles Nechama, 'Pour un rapprochement', *Chalom* (15 Nov. 1928), 15.

[50] *Chalom* (1 Mar. 1929), 31.

[51] This group, organized by the Cercle d'Etudes Juives in 1931, invited members of five different Parisian youth groups—Chema Israël, the UUJJ, the Eclaireurs, the Jeunesse Libérale,

While the revival of Hebrew as a living language was a product of the Zionist movement, this development was also warmly welcomed by most religious Jews. As a result, encouraging French Jews to study Hebrew and setting up courses and educational societies with that objective in mind was one of the main areas in which groups and individuals with differing political and ideological orientations could collaborate. The French branch of the international Hebrew educational society Tarbout (Culture), presided over by Zionist leader Hillel Zlatopolsky, also counted Maurice Liber as a member.[52] The first modern Hebrew courses in Paris were organized by a small network of Zionist associations at the turn of the century. In the postwar years, Tarbout, Chema Israël, the UUJJ, the Institut des Sciences Juives in Strasbourg, and Hatikva—an educational organization publicizing the Zionist cause in France—all offered Hebrew classes.[53] Though the Union Libérale favoured the use of more French in religious services, studying Hebrew as a living language was also encouraged within this milieu: 'As the general tendency is to abandon the study of ancient Greek and Latin', a contributor to *Le Rayon* suggested in 1924, 'why should our children not replace these truly dead languages with the study of Hebrew . . . which is presently becoming the universal language of the Jews, just as Latin was for humanists and scholars of medieval times?'[54] A 1927 article in *Le Petit Rayon* also encouraged young French Jews to study Hebrew and described its revival as a modern miracle.[55]

The desire of native Jews to speed the acculturation of new immigrants from eastern Europe often shaped youth group politics and programming. The principal motive behind the creation of the Union des Jeunesses Israélites, for example, was native Jews' desire to exercise more influence over immigrant youth and, in particular, to inculcate in them patriotic French values. 'While you must not forget your origins', deputy Jean Fabry reminded his audience at the Union's 1930 banquet, 'you are French and your traditions are those of France.'[56] Shortly thereafter, the group amalgamated with the Union Scolaire, which had shifted its orientation during the

and Rouah Israël, a culturally oriented Zionist group created in 1931—to present their programmes and discuss their shared objectives. See *L'Univers israélite* (12 Feb. 1931), 725.

[52] This group mostly had branches in eastern Europe. See Abitbol, *Les Deux Terres promises*, 270.

[53] Hatikva, described in *Le Peuple juif* as a youth group for the study of Hebrew and Jewish history, was created in 1918 and had branches in Paris, Strasbourg, and Bordeaux by 1924. 'Réunion de Tarbout', *Menorah* (22 Jan. 1924), 31, reported that Tarbout had close to 150 children enrolled in Hebrew classes in Paris.

[54] P.S.T., 'Etude de l'hébreu moderne', *Le Rayon* (15 Aug.–15 Sept. 1924), 26–7.

[55] See 'Hanouka à Tel-Aviv', *Le Petit Rayon* (Jan. 1927), 6.

[56] *L'Univers israélite* (17 Jan. 1930), 502.

1920s to reach out to the immigrant community. The leadership's condescending attitude towards the immigrant population, however, ultimately alienated many within that community.[57]

Whereas east Europeans were often under pressure from natives to 'be more French', this problem was largely non-existent for immigrants from the former Ottoman empire. Because these Sephardi Jews were already French-speaking and familiar with French cultural norms, they tended to have an easier relationship with the native Jewish community.[58] At the same time, however, their experience as a national group within the Ottoman empire gave them an ethnic understanding of Jewish identity very different from the 'religious' model developed by French Jews over the course of the nineteenth century. It is for this reason that the Association Amicale des Israélites Saloniciens (AAIS), an organization created by Salonican immigrants, served as a model of the possibilities for Jewish community-building in France.

The AAIS was originally affiliated with the Association Cultuelle Orientale, an umbrella organization established by Ottoman immigrants in 1909 to provide members with services that followed the Sephardi rite and supervise the Jewish education of their children. The Salonicans split off from the Association Cultuelle in 1923. While this split came in part from power struggles within the organization, it also reflected their particular position within the Ottoman Jewish community. As the economic and social elite of Sephardi immigrants, Salonicans tended to identify even more strongly with French Jews than did other Ottomans.[59] They therefore wanted to create a stronger link between their own community and the Consistory. While the Salonicans organized their own high holy day services in accordance with Sephardi ritual, for example, they did so in consultation with the Consistory and invited rabbis from the native community to attend.[60] The fact that the

[57] Hyman, *From Dreyfus to Vichy*, 139. Hyman describes the group as 'anti-Zionist and smugly assimilationist'. Attitudes towards Zionism within the Union Scolaire may have been more diverse than she suggests, however. One of the driving forces behind the group was Charles-Edouard Lévy, who led most of the weekly discussion groups. Though Lévy does not appear to have collaborated with the Zionist movement in the post-war years, he encouraged French Jews to support Zionism in an article for *L'Echo sioniste* (10 Mar. 1912), 45; in the same year he published a short story entitled 'Du temps qu'on n'était pas encore français', *L'Echo sioniste* (10 Dec. 1912), 245–9 (discussed further in Chapter 8 below).

[58] Jews from North Africa formed another element of the Sephardi population in France during this period. On this community, see Laloum, 'Les Juifs d'Afrique du Nord au Pletzl?'.

[59] The port city of Salonica became a major Jewish cultural centre in the late 19th century and Jews actually formed the majority of the population before the Balkan Wars in 1912–13. At this point, the city was conquered by Greece, and a hostile government policy, which intensified during the First World War, forced the majority of the Jewish population into exile.

[60] On the Salonican Jews and other Ottoman immigrants in Paris during the inter-war

AAIS was close to both the Consistory and the Alliance, however, did not preclude the organization from having a strong relationship with the French Zionist movement. Though the group was officially politically neutral, it was close to French Zionist circles, and both *Menorah* and *La Nouvelle Aurore* reported regularly on its activities.[61]

The AAIS set up new headquarters in 1924, complete with a cafeteria, library, and reading and recreation rooms, and also began to sponsor lecture series and parties. These developments led Aimé Pallière to describe the AAIS as the only existing French equivalent to the American Jewish community centre.[62] The president of the Union des Adhérents Orientaux de l'Alliance Israélite Universelle made a similar observation, praising the AAIS's decision to serve as a 'home for all Sephardi Jews' with the opening of its new community centre. While the Union des Adhérents Orientaux, he noted, had originally been conceived of as an educational society as well as a fundraising committee for the Alliance, the AAIS's willingness to host the group's meetings and welcome members to its own activities made it unnecessary for the former to set up an independent headquarters.[63] The AAIS's hospitality, however, was not limited to the Sephardi community. A number of different associations, including Tarbout and the Union des Femmes Juives Françaises pour la Palestine, held their meetings at the AAIS, as did the UUJJ on several occasions before it opened its own community centre in 1927. The AAIS sponsored regular conferences and lectures, with a range of speakers and topics very similar to that of the UUJJ.

Creating New Forums for Jewish Education and Culture

The first successful Jewish scholarly society to be created in France was the Société des Etudes Juives.[64] Organized in 1880 under the patronage of Baron

years, see Benveniste, *Le Bosphore à la Roquette*. She emphasizes the importance that the Salonicans placed on consistorial approval while at the same time insisting on maintaining many of their own traditions (p. 83).

[61] Jarrassé, 'L'Eveil d'une critique d'art juive', also points to the Salonicans' particular combination of French and Jewish ethnic/national identity, which, he argues, facilitated their participation in the Jewish art world in the 1920s.

[62] *L'Univers israélite* (23 Jan. 1925), 413–15. Though the group was created in 1919, it does not appear to have sponsored anything in the way of social and cultural activities before it moved into its headquarters in 1924. It is interesting to note that an article in the following issue of the *L'Univers israélite* reminded readers that the Union Scolaire was, in fact, the first organization of this kind.

[63] See 'Assemblée Générale de l'Union des Adhérents Orientaux de l'Alliance Israélite', *Menorah* (15 July 1924), 189–90.

[64] In its founding statement the group noted the brief existence of two other similar organizations, La Société des Bons Livres and La Société Scientifique et Littéraire Israélite. See

James H. de Rothschild by a group of prominent Jewish intellectuals,[65] this group aimed to bring scholarship on different areas of Jewish studies together and serve as a forum for diverse aspects of the study of Jewish society and culture. The society, its founders hoped, would become 'an intellectual centre for French Judaism and a new link between different members of Jewish society'.[66] While the group created a library, sponsored lectures, and published a journal, the *Revue des études juives*, these activities were limited to an elite group of scholars doing advanced research in Jewish religion, history, and philology. During the 1920s, these kinds of discussions moved from the realm of high culture to a language and a forum accessible to the broader public.

A new interest in creating a popular Jewish culture was an important development among Jewish communities in both Germany and the United States in the early twentieth century. The *Menorah Journal*, an American magazine dedicated to 'Jewish culture and ideas' that enjoyed great success among American Jews in the 1910s and 1920s, reflected a new interest in the idea of a Jewish culture. This journal was created in 1915 by the Menorah Society, a Jewish student group founded at Harvard in 1906 that had chapters at a number of American universities in the post-war years. The distinguishing feature of both the journal and the society was a commitment to providing Jewish education and cultural programming unconnected to any specific political agenda. By creating a popular forum for Jews to both educate themselves about Judaism and explore the question of Jewish identity in the modern world, the Menorah Society and *Menorah Journal* played a critical role in the redefinition of Jewishness in ethnic terms.[67]

Michael Brenner has tracked a similar phenomenon in Weimar Germany, describing the popularization of the Wissenschaft des Judentums and the creation of new forums for Jewish adult education.[68] In both the United States and Germany, one aspect of this renewed interest in Jewish culture was the creation of a more comprehensive Jewish educational structure.

'Procès-verbaux', *Revue des études juives*, 5 (1880), 154. Albert, *The Modernization of French Jewry*, 251, notes Hippolyte Rodrigues's unsuccessful attempt to create the later organization in 1865.

[65] These included Théodore Reinach, James Darmesteter, Salomon Munk, and the Turkish-born Hebraist scholar Joseph Halévy. On the *Revue des études juives*, see Simon-Nahum, *La Cité investie*, and Schwarzfuchs, 'Les Débuts de la science du judaïsme en France', 214.

[66] See 'Procès-verbaux', 154.

[67] On the Menorah Society and the *Menorah Journal*, see Korelitz, 'The Menorah Idea'; Strauss, 'Staying Afloat in the Melting Pot'; and Joselit, 'Against Ghettoism'. The journal was a completely separate venture from *Menorah*, the French Zionist periodical launched in 1922 (see Chapter 6).

[68] Brenner, *The Renaissance of Jewish Culture in Weimar Germany*, chs 3 and 4.

In the United States, a concern with providing Jewish education for both children and adults started as early as the late nineteenth century, with the Hebrew school and community centre movement.[69] In Germany, the Weimar period saw both the revival of separate Jewish education for children and the Lehrhaus movement, which succeeded in setting up a network of adult education societies in different cities in the early 1920s.[70]

French Jews did not create equivalent structures for Jewish education. Jewish elementary schools, which catered almost exclusively to new immigrants, experienced a steady decline in the inter-war years and the curriculum in the few that did exist had little Jewish educational content.[71] While some attempts were made to reform the synagogue system of religious instruction, the evidence does not suggest that any major changes were made during this period: religious instruction remained mostly limited to providing young boys with a basic reading knowledge of Hebrew for their bar mitzvah. Nonetheless, the new network of Jewish associations and clubs created over the course of the 1920s did provide French Jews with a much greater opportunity to immerse themselves in Jewish culture, broadly speaking, than had existed before the war.

Youth groups provided the most important forum for Jewish education. In his overview of French youth movements in the inter-war years, Gérard Cholvy notes that the category of youth corresponded more to marital status than to age. Longer periods of schooling and later marriages meant that participation in 'youth activities' often extended well into the twenties. The age limit for membership in the Eclaireurs Israélites, he points out, was 29, and Scout leaders were often older.[72] For Jewish groups the particular importance of cultural programming meant that the age barrier was even less crucial than for French youth groups in general. There was also a distinction among the Jewish groups themselves: dances, sporting clubs, and other purely social activities were obviously geared towards adolescents and

[69] On this phenomenon, see Kaufman, *Shul with a Pool*.

[70] The most important of these organizations was the Frankfurt Lehrhaus, which was created by Franz Rosenzweig in 1920. This organization combined the principles of a traditional Jewish *ḥeder* or *beit midrash* with those of the German *Volkshochschulen*, adult education societies (similar to the Universités Populaires movement) which gained popularity during the Weimar years. At the peak of its activity in 1923–4, the Frankfurt Lehrhaus enrolled approximately 1,100 students. Similar institutions for Jewish adult education, Brenner notes in *The Renaissance of Jewish Culture in Weimar Germany*, ch. 3, were created in seven of the largest German cities as well as in several smaller communities over the course of the 1920s.

[71] See Szajkowski, *Jewish Education in France, 1789–1939*. The handful of Jewish schools run by the Consistory, Szajkowski notes, all put much more emphasis on acculturating immigrants than on Jewish education. In Paris, the number of pupils at the three existing Jewish elementary schools declined from 947 in 1915 to 342 in 1925.

[72] Cholvy, *Mouvements de jeunesse chrétiens et juifs*, 16.

singles in their early twenties; lectures, conferences, and discussion groups intended to educate Jews about their particular heritage, however, were much less age-specific.

In heralding the creation of the Union Scolaire in 1897, Louis-Germain Lévy envisaged the group as a forum for Jewish education. In fact, however, the Union's weekly lectures and discussion groups—by far the most successful of its activities[73]—did not, for the most part, deal with specifically Jewish topics.[74] While the group prided itself on providing a forum for Jewish sociability, this was not linked to a concern about educating Jews about Judaism per se. For all the Jewish youth groups created in the 1920s, by contrast, lectures, conferences, and discussion groups on Jewish themes were a central part of the programming. Speakers and topics of course varied from group to group: whereas Chema Israël and the Union Libérale primarily featured conferences on religious subjects, the UUJJ and the AAIS favoured lectures on Jewish history, current events, and contemporary Jewish literature. Nonetheless, there was a fair amount of overlap in these groups' range of interests.

While the Eclaireurs Israélites was primarily a sporting organization, it reserved an important place for Jewish education as well. Scouts earned certificates for participating in various activities, each of which was assigned a certain point value, and the category with the highest number of points was the 'religious certificate'.[75] Although the majority of the UUJJ's lectures focused on Zionism and current affairs, Aimé Pallière spoke frequently on religious themes.[76] The first meeting of the Jeunesse Libérale Israélite featured a debate on Zionism: Théodore Reinach represented the anti-Zionist position while Aimé Pallière, Léon Filderman, and Ferdinand Lop, a regular columnist for both *L'Univers israélite* and *La Tribune juive*, the Strasbourg Jewish weekly, spoke on Jewish nationalism.[77] Zionist sympathizers Pierre

[73] Writing about the group in 1923, Jules Meyer noted that 'neither its adult education courses, its placement services, its artistic evenings or balls gave the Union Scolaire its excellent reputation . . . rather, it owes its success to its conferences and above all its weekly discussion groups'. See 'L'Union Scolaire', *Menorah* (29 Apr. 1923), 275–7: 276.

[74] Conferences for spring 1910, for example, included only one with a Jewish topic: a lecture by Victor Basch entitled 'Judaism and German Thought in the Nineteenth Century'. Other lectures touched on everything from theatre and art to the 'depopulation crisis' in contemporary France and the exploration of the North Pole. The president of the organization, Charles-Edouard Lévy, spoke regularly on scientific and medical subjects. See *L'Union scolaire* (May/June 1910), 4.   [75] Michel, *Juifs, Français et Scouts*, 52.

[76] The UUJJ also organized a conference in 1926 entitled 'Different Aspects of the Jewish Religion'. See 'Nos conférences à Paris', *Chalom* (Mar. 1926), 16.

[77] See 'Séance d'ouverture de la "Jeunesse Libérale Israélite"', *Le Rayon* (15 Feb. 1925), 4–7. Reinach and Pallière participated in a debate on the same topic at the UUJJ in March 1927. See *Chalom* (15 Mar. 1927), 5.

Paraf, Charles Gide, Baruch Hagani, Maurice Level, Victor Basch, and Jean Schrameck (an Alsatian who would become president of the UUJJ's central committee in 1930) were all invited to speak for Chema Israël, whose members were perhaps more sympathetic to Zionism than its leadership: reporting on the popularity of Aimé Pallière's speeches for the group, *L'Univers israélite* reported that some of the audience applauded when he praised the Zionist movement, and others when he spoke about the importance of religion.[78]

The issue of Jewish identity itself—who is a Jew? what is Judaism?—was a common focus for lectures, conferences, and debates. Speaking at the Union Scolaire in 1921, for example, Fernand Lévy-Wogue, a high-school teacher and author of a collection of short stories on Jewish themes published under the pseudonym Kislev, analysed the various ways in which Jews had understood themselves to be linked with one another, from a sense of being part of a common race or religion to a shared sense of moral values and even a sense of humour.[79] To be Jewish, he asserted, was in fact to feel all of these things at once: to be moved by injustice and violence, to attach oneself to the values of 'justice, equality, and charity' that form the 'moral heritage' of Judaism.

The AAIS sponsored a conference in 1924 on 'The Jew in Contemporary Society', in which four speakers elaborated on the tension between assimilation and self-preservation.[80] A 1928 article in *L'Univers israélite* entitled 'What Is a Jew?' commented on the central place this issue had come to occupy in contemporary discussions: after Julien Weill gave a lecture on the subject for Chema Israël, the author noted, Chief Rabbi Israël Lévi also felt compelled to address the question.[81] Another 1928 Chema lecture series entitled 'The Tendencies of Modern Judaism' featured talks by Victor Basch on Zionism, Aimé Pallière on 'the Jewish soul', and Edmond Fleg on Martin Buber and Jewish mysticism. UUJJ conferences the same year featured, among other talks, Zionist leader Léon Filderman and André Spire on the subjects, respectively, of 'Different Ways of Being Jewish' and 'Why I Am a Jew'.[82]

Debating clubs and literary societies provided another forum for discussion of Jewish identity and culture in the public sphere. The most successful

[78] *L'Univers israélite* (17 Feb. 1922), 500–1.

[79] Lévy-Wogue's short-story collection (Kislev, *Contes de Hanouka*), includes an essay entitled 'Etre Juif', which is the text of his 1921 lecture at the Union Scolaire. It was also published in *L'Univers israélite* (28 Jan. 1921), 493–5, and reprinted in *L'Union scolaire* (Mar. 1921), 1–6.

[80] *Menorah* printed a report on the conference. See 'Le Juif dans la société contemporaine', *Menorah* (1 Mar. 1924), 55–8.

[81] Louis Weill, 'Qu'est-ce qu'un Juif?', *L'Univers israélite* (21 Dec. 1928), 454.

[82] Spire's lecture was a commentary on Edmond Fleg's 1928 memoir *Pourquoi je suis Juif*.

was the Club du Faubourg, created by the Jewish journalist, left-wing political activist, and playwright Léo Poldès in 1918.[83] Defined as an 'open forum
for cordial debate' the club, located on the boulevard Perrière in the fashionable sixteenth arrondissement, sponsored debates on politics, literature, and
current affairs. By the mid-1920s the club was meeting three times a week
and attracting thousands of participants.[84] People with radically opposing
viewpoints were often invited to ensure a lively debate: a discussion of 'the
Jewish question' in 1924, for example, featured René Groos, the notorious
Jewish member of Action Française, Reform rabbi Louis-Germain Lévy, and
novelist Josué Jéhouda. The most frequent format for Faubourg meetings
was the 'book trial': several speakers would be invited to debate the issues
raised in a recently published novel or essay. Audience participation was
encouraged.[85] All of the most popular books on Jewish themes published in
the 1920s—from Palestinophile literature, to Geiger's collection of Jewish
jokes, to Jacob Lévy's *Les Juifs d'aujourd'hui* and Sarah Lévy's *O mon goye!*—
were submitted to the tribunal of the Faubourg.[86] The fact that debates on
topics such as antisemitism, Zionism, and mixed marriage were featured
regularly by a debating society best known for sponsoring debates on
provocative political, social, and cultural issues of the day such as communism, race war, gender identity, feminism, and homosexuality helped to make
the 'réveil juif' a focal point of the Parisian cultural revolution of the 1920s.[87]

---

[83] Léo Poldès, whose real name was Léopold Szeszler, was born into a middle-class Parisian
family and studied political science and journalism as a young man. He began his career as a
journalist for a variety of left-wing publications and ran for office on the socialist ticket in 1919.
Poldès was won over by Bolshevism in 1920 and subsequently became active in communist
politics. Running the Faubourg, however, which enjoyed great success through the inter-war
years, was his primary occupation. After spending the Second World War as a refugee in South
America, he returned to Paris and re-established the club, which continued to function until
his death in 1970.

[84] Sowerine, *France Since 1870*, 129. On the Faubourg and its prominence in Parisian cultural life in the inter-war years, see also Goublet, *Léo Poldès, le Faubourg*, and Sowerine and
Maignien, *Madeleine Pelletier*. Pelletier was a regular speaker at the Faubourg, and the club was
sued for 'outrages aux bonnes mœurs' after sponsoring a debate of her 1935 book *La Rationali-
sation sexuelle* (*Madeleine Pelletier*, 221–3).

[85] This was a form of debate popular in the Soviet Union at this time, where trials were often
staged theatre pieces. Actors would represent the various points of view and the audience
would declare a verdict at the end. In France, passing judgement appears to have been less
important: I have found no reference to verdicts at the Faubourg's 'trials'. I am grateful for this
background to Edna Nahshon, who has researched the phenomenon of mock trials internationally for her forthcoming book, *Spectacular Justice: Mock Trials and Public Jewish Discourse*.
Information on Jewish mock trials in the Soviet Union comes from Anna Shternshis's unpublished paper, 'Jewish Theatrical Trials in the Soviet Union (1917–1941)'.

[86] See Appendix I for a list of books on Jewish themes (to which I have found reference) that
were debated at the Club du Faubourg in the 1920s.

[87] A sampling of topics for 1924, for example, includes 'Polygamie', 'Un révolutionnaire:

The Faubourg was a source of inspiration for many in the Jewish community. The UUJJ's 'causeries contradictoires' were modelled on the Faubourg's format, and a club of Jewish journalists created in 1930 invoked the Club du Faubourg as its model.[88] A report on the club in the *Revue littéraire juive* referred to it as 'a forum for open discussion and education that has attracted the attention of the press the world over'.[89] By 1928 the Faubourg had begun to hold its meetings at the Salle de Wagram, one of the largest halls in Paris. A 1928 debate on the Schwartzbard case which coupled Joseph Kessel with an antisemitic journalist drew such a large crowd that people had to be turned away.[90] A barely disguised reference to the club in Jacob Lévy's 1925 novel *Les Pollaks*[91] suggests the club's notoriety and widespread appeal. The story's protagonists attend a meeting of the 'Club de la Rue', a popular debating society run by 'that curious and alert spirit, Géo Moldès'. Lévy refers to the friendly atmosphere of the club, 'a place where people from a wide variety of backgrounds and opinions have the opportunity to mix and share their views'.[92]

Another Parisian debating club with a strong Jewish emphasis was Henry Marx's Université de Connaître. Like the Club du Faubourg, the Université de Connaître, which published a journal by the same name, sponsored lecture series and conferences that often focused on Jewish themes. Marx founded this group after a trip to Salonica in the early 1920s, and it was apparently his encounter with young Jews there that inspired its creation. In particular, Marx, who had both communist and Zionist sympathies, was impressed by the combination of socialism and Jewish cultural nationalism espoused by many of the Salonicans he met.[93] Reconciling these two ideals became an important theme of discussion for the group, which held a particular attraction for Salonican immigrants. By 1928, when the group was planning thirteen lectures on Jewish themes for the year, ranging from 'Zionism: Jewish Honour and Jewish Land' and 'Moses' to 'The Jewish Masterpiece:

Peut-il croire en Dieu?', 'Un conflit: Peut-il éclater entre Noirs et Blancs?', ' Peu ou beaucoup d'enfants', and 'Le Spiritisme'. See Goublet, *Léo Poldès*, 24.

[88] *L'Univers israélite* (3 Jan. 1930), 441.

[89] *Revue littéraire juive* (Sept. 1930), 320.

[90] See *L'Univers israélite* (30 Mar. 1928), 15–16.

[91] Lévy published this novel as part of a four-volume series, *Les Juifs d'aujourd'hui*, which is discussed in more detail in Chapter 7.   [92] *Les Pollaks*, 193.

[93] On this group, see *Connaître*, subtitled *Revue mensuelle juive, sioniste, littéraire et philosophe*, which was launched in August 1924. The journal reported on Marx's trip as well as on the creation of a sister society, the 'Groupe Henry-Marx' in Salonica. See 'La Vie du groupe', *Connaître*, 1 (Aug. 1924), 23. A number of the articles in the two existing issues of the journal (which, *Menorah* indicates, was published for six years) focus on the Jews of Salonica.

The Writing of Georges de Porto-Riche', it had a considerable following both in France and abroad.[94]

French Jews created several Jewish study circles in 1930 and 1931. The most important of these was the Cercle d'Etudes Juives, which brought different elements of the Parisian Jewish intellectual elite together. The group, which met at the home of its president Baron James H. de Rothschild, included Maurice Liber and other members of the Consistory and rabbinate, as well as prominent Zionist sympathizers including André Spire, Fernand Corcos, and writer Lily Jean-Javal. The Cercle organized some lectures in conjunction with the Société des Etudes Juives and, like that group, had a programme consisting mainly of presentations by prominent scholars rather than the kind of sensationalist debate sponsored by the Club du Faubourg. André Siegfried, a professor at the Ecole des Hautes Etudes des Sciences Politiques, gave the opening lecture, entitled 'The People Israel in Modern Democracies'.[95] Other speakers included Salomon Reinach on James Darmesteter, Edmond Fleg on his book *Ma Palestine*, and literary critic René Lalou on the poetry and literary criticism of André Spire. As with youth groups, issues of definition and identity were important for the circle. The first item on the group's agenda, as described in an article in *Le Rayon*, was 'to discuss the issue of our audience so as to be certain that our self-definition is open enough to include the diverse tendencies that make up our community'.[96] The article then outlined these various tendencies, from degrees of religious belief and observance, to an attachment to Jewish tradition or memory, to cultural nationalism and Zionism.

Jewish Associational and Cultural Life in Alsace

The main centre of Jewish life outside Paris was Alsace-Lorraine. After the region was returned to French control following the First World War, the Jews of Alsace maintained a largely independent institutional structure.[97] Alsatian Jews developed their own Zionist institutions and published a weekly paper, *La Tribune juive*.[98] They tended to be more religious than their

---

[94]   See 'Les Conférences de Henry Marx', *Menorah* (1 Feb. 1928), 44.

[95]   'Israël dans les démocraties modernes: Une conférence de M. André Siegfried au "Cercle d'Etudes Juives"', *L'Univers israélite* (23 May 1930), 203–4.

[96]   See the article on the group's formation by Etienne Treves, 'Qu'est ce qu'un Juif?', *Le Rayon* (Oct./Nov. 1931), 15–19.

[97]   Despite its re-annexation to France, Alsace maintained a certain amount of regional autonomy. In particular, the separation of church and state did not apply there, which gave local consistories much more control than in other regions of France.

[98]   This paper was originally published as *Le Juif* by the religious Zionist group Mizrahi, beginning in 1919. It became an independent publication and changed its name to *La Tribune juive* in March 1923. One of the main reasons for Alsatian Jewish autonomy, of course, was

Parisian counterparts, and many of the associations they created reflected this orientation. The Union des Amis de la Tradition Juive was created in Colmar in 1922, and in 1920 Alsatian students started a club for observant Jewish students living in Paris. There was a much stronger alliance between religious leaders and Zionists in Alsace than elsewhere in France. It was there that the Mizrahi movement (of religious Zionists) was strongest, and Zionist organizations often counted local rabbis among their members. Many of the new associations created in Alsace during this period reflected this combination of religious traditionalism and Zionism.

One of the first new adult educational institutions to emerge in Alsace in the post-war years was Emounah (Faith).[99] An association of former religious school students in Strasbourg—inspired, perhaps, by the Lehrhaus movement in Germany—created the group in 1923 in order to continue Jewish education into young adulthood.[100] The group offered a series of lectures and courses on Jewish history and religion, and frequently collaborated with local Zionist groups. It sponsored the Strasbourg opening of Keren Kayemet's film *La Terre promise* in 1925, as well as a conference on Martin Buber in conjunction with the Association Sioniste des Dames Juives. Emounah was joined in 1929 by the Institut des Sciences Juives à Strasbourg, geared specifically towards providing a traditional Jewish education for adults. This group offered courses on Talmud, biblical exegesis, classical and modern Hebrew, Jewish literature, history, and philosophy, as well as 'the physical, economic and human geography of Palestine'.[101] It received a significant amount of attention in the Parisian Jewish press and inspired the Paris Consistory to sponsor a similar series of courses on Judaism the following year.[102] The institute was also used as a meeting-place for other Jewish

linguistic. While French articles appeared with increasing frequency over the course of the decade, the majority were in German.

[99] Several literary and historical societies were already functioning in Alsace in the 1920s, including the Société pour l'Histoire des Israélites en Alsace et Lorraine and the Société d'Histoire et de Littérature Juive de Mulhouse et Metz.

[100] The organizing committee included Jean Schrameck, a member of the Union Régionale des Sionistes de l'Est de la France and the UUJJ. Emounah became a UUJJ affiliate in 1930.

[101] See Meyerkey, 'Un seul judaïsme', *La Tribune juive* (11 Jan. 1930), 1–2.

[102] In an article on the opening of the Institut, Aimé Pallière praised the group's programme and suggested that, even without creating such an organization, Parisian Jews could organize a similar set of courses; see *Chalom* (June 1929), 1–2. The following February several members of the Consistory, including Edouard and Robert de Rothschild and Mme R. A. Olchanski, a member of the Cercle d'Etudes Juives, organized a series of 'Conférences pour la jeunesse'. The founders' statement explaining the objective of the courses—which invoked both young people's renewed interest in Judaism and their lack of knowledge about it—was the same as that of the founders of the institute in Strasbourg. See *L'Univers israélite* (14 Feb. 1930), 632–3.

groups, and moved into larger headquarters in summer 1931. A group of young people in Strasbourg set up a study group that sponsored lectures and meetings at the institute, as did the local Zionist association, the Union des Dames Juives, and Emounah.[103]

One of the most important links between the various Jewish groups created during this period was the ubiquitous Aimé Pallière. In a posthumous tribute to Pallière published in the *Revue de la pensée juive*, contemporaries recalled his impact on French Jewish life in the inter-war years.[104] In addition to playing a leadership role in the UUJJ, he lectured frequently at the AAIS, Chema Israël, and the Jeunesse Libérale Israélite, and wrote numerous articles in support of all of these groups in the Jewish press. It was after a discussion with Pallière that Lily Simon decided to found the Eclaireuses.[105] As someone who was both deeply religious and a committed Zionist, Pallière encouraged the various groups to develop whichever of these aspects of Jewishness he felt they lacked. The importance of religion in the UUJJ's agenda was largely due to the influence of Pallière, for whom Zionism was meaningless if it wasn't accompanied by a commitment to religious spirituality. In his lectures for Chema Israël and the Jeunesse Libérale Israélite, by contrast, Pallière sought to persuade his audiences that the Jewish religious revival of the day was intimately linked to the Zionist movement. His position as the president of the UUJJ does not seem to have made him any less welcome as a speaker at Chema, where he gave a very well-attended three-part lecture series on his trip to Palestine in 1930.[106] As this blossoming of diverse forms of Jewish associational life clearly indicates, whether they defined Judaism as a religion, a culture, a race, or a historical community, French Jews in the 1920s increasingly shared the conviction that it was only by creating new spaces for Jewish sociability that their community would survive into the next generation.

[103] *La Tribune juive* (14 Feb. 1930), 106. The article noted that the institute's own courses were suffering due to all the other activities going on at its own centre. An article several months later reported that, while some courses were attended by as few as ten people, others were overcrowded. See *La Tribune juive* (25 July 1930), 474.

[104] See 'Hommage à Aimé Pallière', special issue of *Revue de la pensée juive*, 8 (July 1951). Contributions included André Zaoui, 'Un grand serviteur de Dieu'; Marcel Greilsammer, 'Aimé Pallière à l'Union Libérale Israélite'; Roger Rebstock, 'Aimé Pallière tel que je l'ai connu'; Rabi, 'Aimé Pallière et notre futile jeunesse'; Joseph Fischer, 'Aimé Pallière, et le Keren Kayemet Leyisrael'; and Robert Aron, 'Visite chez Benamozegh'. The volume also contained excerpts from several of Pallière's essays and books. Poujol, who detailed the critical and unique role that Pallière played in youth, Reform, and Zionist movements in France in the 1920s, underlines the ways in which Pallière's very particular insider/outsider status enabled him to move between milieus in a way that no person born and raised as a Jew could do. See Poujol, *Aimé Pallière*, and also her doctoral thesis of the same title.

[105] Michel, *Juifs, Français et Scouts*, ch. 1.   [106] *L'Univers israélite* (14 Mar. 1930), 750.

CHAPTER 6

The Media and the Arts

'I am profoundly moved by the striking renewal of Judaism to which we are witness', declared writer Fernand Corcos in 1927. 'It is as if a coarse, ancient tree, contorted by a thousand blows, dried up and seemingly lifeless, was suddenly covered with new leaves of an unexpectedly brilliant green.'[1] The *Revue littéraire juive*, which inspired Corcos's comments, was but one of a wide variety of Jewish press organs created over the course of the 1920s. As we saw in Chapter 3, the expansion of the Jewish press began in the pre-war years with the creation of *L'Echo sioniste*, *Foi et réveil*, and *Le Rayon*. These titles were now joined by close to twenty others. Some appeared regularly, while others were very short-lived or were published sporadically. Taken as a whole, these journals created a dynamic of activism and debate that, like the youth groups, social clubs, and literary and debating societies described in Chapter 5, changed the face of French Judaism in the post-war years. The presence of a lively Jewish art and music scene as well as the strengthening of the inter-faith movement also infused new energy into French Jewish life of the day. However, the expansion of Jewish cultural life that took place in these years inspired criticism as well as praise. While some expressed un-bridled enthusiasm for this self-proclaimed Jewish cultural awakening, others were sceptical about its content and long-term viability. In particular, many observers wondered if newly created secular Jewish associations and press organs, with their emphasis on self-questioning and the open-ended definition of Judaism, would prove to be more than a one-generation phenomenon.

The Expansion of the Jewish Press

Menorah, funded by the World Zionist Organization and published bi-monthly from 1922 to 1933, had the longest run of any of the Jewish publications created in the 1920s.[2] The initial inspiration for this journal, whose aim was to increase support for Zionism among French Jews, came from Zionist leader Chaim Weizmann, who then lived in Manchester. The

---

[1] *Revue littéraire juive* (Mar. 1927), 4.
[2] On *Menorah*, see Malinovich, 'Une expression du "Réveil juif" des années vingt'.

journal's co-founders were two Sephardi Jews living in Paris: Jacques Calmy, a Palestine-born Zionist publicist and emissary of Weizmann, and Ovadia Cahmy, the French correspondent for a Zionist newspaper in Jerusalem.[3] Its editorial board was made up primarily of French Jews, including Henri Hertz, Roger Lévy, André Spire, Aimé Pallière, Edmond Fleg, Baruch Hagani, and Gustave Kahn, who became editor-in-chief in 1924. Members of foreign origin included Yehouda Tchernoff, the Russian-born writer and translator Ludmilla Bloch-Savitzky,[4] and the Egyptian-born poet Georges Cattaui. Despite its Zionist affiliation, *Menorah* was conceived in the broadest sense, the hope being to unify different factions within French Jewry: 'We need to build a bridge on which different ideas can cross and meet each other, to create a neutral atmosphere where diverse opinions can fertilize one another', read the journal's opening statement.[5]

Initially *Menorah* solicited the contributions of religious leaders who were not necessarily sympathetic to Zionism. While early collaborators included the rabbis Louis-Germain Lévy, Maurice Liber, Mathieu Wolff, and David Berman, by mid-decade their contributions had tapered off.[6] More successful was the attempt to act as a bridge between native and immigrant Jews. Initial articles were written primarily by members of the east European intellectual community, but by mid-decade native Jews made up at least half of the contributors. In addition to reports on the Zionist movement and Jewish settlement in Palestine, early issues of *Menorah* featured *National Geographic*-style portraits of Jewish communities around the world, as well as articles on Jewish history and famous Jewish personalities. By the mid-1920s this kind of article was supplemented by discussions of the emerging French Jewish literary scene and the issue of Jewish identity in modern France. Heavily illustrated and published in book format on high-quality paper, *Menorah* also had a strong artistic emphasis. It followed the development of both the international Jewish artistic movement and the activities and exhibitions of Jewish artists in Paris. As was to be expected, the journal

---

[3] See the announcement of the journal's creation in *L'Univers israélite* (11 Aug. 1922), 467–8. It was originally called *L'Illustration juive*, but changed its name to *Menorah* after the second issue following a dispute with another paper, *L'Illustration*, which objected that the new journal's name was too similar to its own. It was also at this point that *Menorah* became a bi-monthly rather than weekly publication. See *L'Illustration juive* (15 Sept. 1922), 2, 16.

[4] Bloch-Savitzky, described by André Spire as someone who was 'born in Russia but became French through education and marriage', translated numerous works of both Russian and English literature into French. See Spire, 'La Poésie russe à Montparnasse', *Menorah* (13 May 1923), 290–3.   [5] 'Notre programme', *Illustration juive* (Aug. 1922), 1.

[6] Contributions by these personalities were limited to one or two articles in the paper's early years. While it still featured occasional articles on religion in later years, these were most often written by Aimé Pallière, who was a committed Zionist.

also devoted a significant amount of space to reporting on Zionist-oriented groups and activities in Paris, and frequently reported on lectures given at both the AAIS and the UUJJ.

The next wave of French Zionist journalism began with Albert Cohen's launch of *La Revue juive* in 1925. Cohen was born in Greece but immigrated to France as a child. A Zionist sympathizer, he emerged as a prominent figure on the French Jewish literary scene with the publication of his first book of poems, *Paroles juives*, in 1921. Cohen won Chaim Weizmann's support for the creation of an international Zionist literary journal and obtained the financial backing of the French publisher Gaston Gallimard in 1923. The first edition was published in January 1925. *La Revue juive*, which Cohen hoped would function as 'an intellectual centre of the Jewish renaissance',[7] boasted an international editorial board that included Weizmann himself, the Danish Jewish critic Georges Brandès, Albert Einstein, and Sigmund Freud, as well as Léon Zadoc-Kahn and Charles Gide. The initial 5,200 copies of the review were not sufficient to satisfy international demand, and by November it claimed to have subscribers in fifty-eight countries.[8] In his introductory article, Cohen outlined two principal objectives: to reveal the 'soul' of the Jewish people to both the French and the international community and to follow the activities of the Zionist movement.[9]

The journal featured regular columns on Zionism and current events within the international Jewish community as well as a 'Revue de presse' column. The primary focus, however, was literary and intellectual. The *Revue juive* published essays, fiction, and reviews of contemporary literature that touched primarily, but not exclusively, on Jewish themes. The July 1925 edition, for example, included an essay entitled 'Le Moment historique de Montaigne' by Léon Brunchwicg, a discussion of the Zionist movement by Victor Jacobson, and a story by the German Jewish writer Franz Werfel. Jean-Richard Bloch's novel *La Nuit kurde* was reviewed, as was *Esquisse d'une doctrine juive*, a book by the rabbi David Berman that outlined the fundamental tenets of the Jewish faith. Despite its initial success, *La Revue juive* ceased publication after only eleven months. Reasons for the journal's failure remain obscure, but it appears to have been due at least in part to internal bickering.[10] In his biography of Albert Cohen, Jean Blot also suggests that

---

[7] Blot, *Albert Cohen*, 100.

[8] Ibid. 110. The list of countries appears in the November 1925 issue, the last to appear.

[9] Cohen, 'Déclaration', *La Revue juive* (Jan. 1925), 1.

[10] In a 1979 interview Cohen gave the rather vague explanation that the journal had ceased publication 'à la suite d'intrigues'. See *Magazine littéraire*, 147 (Apr. 1979), special issue entitled 'Dossier Albert Cohen'. According to Abecassis, the failure of the journal was due to Cohen's difficulty in collaborating with Zionist representatives in Paris and Geneva. See *Albert Cohen: Dissonant Voices*, 6.

Septième Année — Nº 10
15 MAI 1928

Prix de ce Numéro:
France: 3 frs   Etranger: 3 fr. 50

MENORAH

FIGURES BIBLIQUES

RUTH   (photo Braun & Co, cliché Menorah)   par Alexandre Cabanel

FIGURE 4 Cover of *Menorah*, 15 May 1928. *Menorah* was the only Jewish magazine in the 1920s with illustrated covers, which varied greatly in theme. In 1928, for example, a series of covers entitled 'Les grandes Figures d'Israël' featuring portraits of men such as Albert Einstein and Adolphe Crémieux, was followed by the more romantic 'Figures bibliques', featured here

Reproduced by permission of the library of the Alliance Israélite Universelle

because the editorial board as well as many of the collaborators were chosen for their status as Jews who had contributed to world culture, they had little to contribute to a specifically Jewish paper after a few issues.[11]

More successful were the *Revue littéraire juive* and *Palestine*, both launched in 1927. The *Revue littéraire juive*, while similar in format to *La Revue juive*, was more thematically Jewish in focus. Edited by Pierre Paraf, its editorial board comprised both prominent Zionist activists and literary figures. These included Léonce Bernheim, Yvonne Netter, Fernand Corcos, Myriam Schach, Hillel Zlatopolsky, Léon Filderman, Edmond Fleg, Henry Marx, Raymond-Raoul Lambert, Joseph Kessel, journalist and literary critic J. Ernest Charles (who was an occasional lecturer at the UUJJ), and artist Maxa Nordau, the Parisian-born daughter of Zionist ideologue Max Nordau. Non-Jewish members included the vice-president of the League of the Rights of Man, André-Ferdinand Hérold, and the Protestant writer Gaston Riou. The journal's opening statement, written by Justin Godart, declared it to be 'a new and important manifestation of the awakening of French Judaism' which, 'with the works that it will publish, will link this movement with that of the intellectual and artistic movement of the international Jewish community'.[12] The *Revue littéraire juive* published both contemporary French fiction on Jewish themes and international literature in translation. Essays and short stories by German authors such as Martin Buber, Stefan Zweig, and Else Lasker-Schüler were all featured, as were the writings of Israel Zangwill and the American author Ludwig Lewisohn, who was living in Paris at the time.[13] The writings of the Yiddish writers I. L. Peretz, Sholem Aleichem, and Sholem Asch also appeared regularly, as did contemporary Hebrew fiction and poetry.

Palestine, launched by the committee France-Palestine and subsidized by the Rieder publishing house, was edited by the group's non-Jewish president, Justin Godart. Though the Jewish writer Henri Hertz served as managing editor, *Palestine*, in keeping with the goals of France-Palestine, was initially intended to promote the Zionist movement in France without functioning as a Jewish journal. In its opening statement, Godart explained that *Palestine* would be neither an organ of Jews of French origin, nor a French-

---

[11] Blot, *Albert Cohen*, 114–17.   [12] *Revue littéraire juive* (Mar. 1927), 1.

[13] Ludwig Lewisohn was an American writer from a highly integrated German Jewish family who experienced a Jewish 'awakening' similar to that of André Spire and Edmond Fleg. After a trip to Palestine in 1924, Lewisohn settled in Paris in 1925, where he remained until the early 1930s. His writings touched on many of the same themes—namely, the nature of Jewish integration in contemporary society—that interested French Jewish authors of the day. For a comparison of themes in French and American Jewish-themed literature in the 1920s, see Malinovich, 'Race and the Construction of Jewish Identity'.

language publication aimed at serving the international Jewish community. Rather, he asserted, it was a journal published by a 'simply French' committee (i.e. France-Palestine) of which both Jews and non-Jews were members.[14] In keeping with this approach, *Palestine* published a number of articles by non-Jews on Zionism and various aspects of 'the Jewish question' more broadly. Contributions for 1927/8, for example, included Albert Thomas ('La Palestine et la politique sociale internationale'), Anatole de Monzie ('Réflexions sur le sionisme), and Elie Faure ('L'Ame juive').[15] Like *Revue littéraire juive* and *Menorah*, *Palestine* also functioned as a literary review, publishing short stories, poetry, and essays by Jewish writers such as André Spire, Armand Lunel, I. L. Peretz, and Georges Cattaui.

The journal ceased publication briefly between December 1929 and March 1930, at which point it became more explicitly literary in orientation. Now subtitled *La Nouvelle Revue juive*, it informed its readers that, while it would continue to present the Zionist movement to the French public, the importance of its political programme would not hinder it from publishing 'spiritual studies' relevant to Judaism. Rather, in the tradition of Cohen's now defunct *Revue juive*, it would publish a wide variety of literary, artistic, and philosophical articles related to Judaism.[16] The format of the journal also changed with the new approach: each issue now grouped together articles on specific themes. Topics for 1930 and 1931 included American and British Zionists, Jews in the Soviet Union, Jewish theatre, and a historical retrospective on the Dreyfus affair.

All of the major Jewish youth movements created in the 1920s—Chema Israël, the UUJJ, and the Eclaireurs Israélites—published newspapers and magazines, as did the Club de la Jeunesse Juive, Bené-Mizrah, La Fraternité, and the Union des Jeunesses Israélites. The most successful and widely read of these was the UUJJ's publication *Chalom*, which had 2,000 subscribers in 1928.[17] As well as reporting on activities and debates within the UUJJ, the journal featured columns on literature, religion, theatre, and the arts, as well as excerpts from contemporary Jewish fiction and poetry.

The Alliance Israélite Universelle created its own monthly publication, *Paix et droit*, in 1921. The major impetus for the journal was the new impor-

---

[14] Justin Godart, 'Le Sens d'une revue française: "Palestine"', *Palestine* (Oct. 1927), 1.

[15] See *Palestine* (Nov. 1927), 49–53; (Feb. 1928), 193–5; (Jan. 1928), 151–69.

[16] The group's revised statement of purpose was printed on the inside flap of each issue after March 1930.

[17] See 'Un rapport sur *Chalom*', *Chalom* (15 Aug.–15 Sept. 1928), 19–21. This figure represents the journal's readership at the peak of the UUJJ's success, just before the 1928 crisis that marked the beginning of the decline of the organization. On *Chalom*, see Poujol, 'Une exception dans la presse des mouvements de jeunesse'.

tance of Zionism on the world stage and the endorsement of national minority rights at the Paris Peace Conference, both of which the Alliance firmly
opposed. The first issue affirmed the Alliance's opposition to a 'national'
solution of any kind to Jewish oppression and declared its own commitment
to advocating individual political rights for Jews 'in the Orient and anywhere
else that they are denied civil emancipation'.[18] While the majority of the
journal's space was devoted to reporting on the Alliance's international
charitable and educational projects, it also included articles on a variety of
contemporary political and social issues. *Paix et droit* reported more system-
atically and thoroughly on the antisemitic movement, both in France and
abroad, than most Jewish press organs of the day, and often tried to link the
Zionists' 'racialized' understanding of Jewishness with antisemitism. The
strongly anti-Zionist Alfred Berl was the journal's most prolific contributor.
One of his first contributions was an article objecting to the confusion of
'race' and 'nationality' in contemporary discourse, and arguing for the
nation as a 'community of consent'.[19] Though the focus of the paper was
political rather than literary or religious, it occasionally published articles by
Maurice Liber on religious subjects,[20] and several short stories by the
Tunisian Jewish folklorist Ryvel appeared in 1929.[21]

Both *Foi et réveil* and *Le Rayon* ceased publication during the First World
War, but they resumed again afterwards. *Foi et réveil*'s first post-war issue
came out in 1918, and the journal moved from Nice to Paris a year later
when its editor, Jules Bauer, accepted a position as the head of the Ecole
Rabbinique. As we saw in Chapter 3, this journal was originally founded as a
response to the Union Libérale, and many of its pre-war articles criticized the
Reform movement. This polemical orientation was largely abandoned in the
post-war years as the liberals were integrated into the mainstream Jewish
religious community. As well as articles on religious themes, *Foi et réveil*
published short stories, poetry, and essays on various social and cultural
issues, as well as discussions of contemporary Jewish literature. Rabbis
Liber, Bauer, and Weill continued to contribute regularly, as did Aimé Pallière, Armand Lipman, and David Berman. While some contributors—in
particular Liber and Lipman—occasionally wrote articles attacking Zionism,
overall the journal reflected an even-handed and often sympathetic attitude

---

[18] *Paix et droit* (Sept. 1921), 1.
[19] See Berl, 'Race et nationalité', *Paix et droit* (Nov. 1921), 1–3.
[20] See e.g. 'La Protection de la femme juive', *Paix et droit* (Mar. 1925), 4–6.
[21] This was a pseudonym for Raphaël Lévy, a rabbi and teacher at one of the Alliance schools
in Tunis. *Paix et droit* published several stories from his 1929 book, *La Hara conte: Folklore
judéo-tunisien*. See 'La Légende de la chouette', *Paix et droit* (Mar. 1929), 11–12, and 'Keppara:
Fragments du journal d'une institutrice', *Paix et droit* (May 1929), 10–11.

towards Jewish nationalism. In several instances, we find debates between Zionists and non-Zionists. A 1920 article by Lipman attacking Zionism, for example, was followed by a response by H. Stourdzé, the head of the French Mizrahi movement.[22]

Le Rayon's first post-war issue came out in 1921. While a 'Choses et autres' column continued to feature 'words of wisdom' from other religions, these short quotes and extracts now gave way to a much wider range of articles on Jewish themes. Though defending Reform against its detractors remained a concern of the journal in the early 1920s, this was much less the case after the group's 1924 rapprochement with the Consistory. Both David Berman and Aimé Pallière were regular contributors. *Le Petit Rayon*, created in 1926 for young adults, published short stories and essays explaining the underlying significance of Jewish holidays and rituals as well as reporting on the activities of the Jeunesse Libérale Israélite. Like *Foi et réveil*, *Le Rayon* maintained an open attitude towards Zionism, publishing both sympathetic and critical articles as well as exchanges between contributors with opposing views.

A number of other journals of differing political and ideological orientations also peppered the Jewish landscape in the 1920s. *Le Réveil israélite* appeared in 1919 and *La Revue israélite*, a collaborative effort between Sephardi immigrants and native French Jews, was launched in 1923. Henry Marx created *Connaître: Revue mensuelle juive sioniste, littéraire et philosophe*, which grew out of his debating society, the next year. Meyerkey helped to create a weekly paper, *Les Flambeaux*, in 1926.[23] While many of these smaller journals were only published for a brief period, they can nonetheless be seen as indicative of the new energy that characterized French Jewish life at the time.

Jewish Music and Art

At the forefront of avant-garde literary, musical, and artistic production in the 1920s, Paris became a magnet for artists, writers, and musicians the world over. While earlier generations of artists had come for training and

---

[22] See Commandant A. Lipman, 'Etre ou n'être pas', *Foi et réveil*, 13 (1920), 206–17, and H. Stourdzé, 'Etre ou n'être pas: Une réponse', *Foi et réveil*, 15 (1921), 83–94.

[23] Very few editions of these journals exist. We often find notices announcing their creation in *L'Univers israélite* or other regular publications, but few or no subsequent references. The creation of *Les Flambeaux*, for example, was announced in *L'Univers israélite* (7 May 1926), 178, but I have not found any reference to the paper after this date. Only one copy (23 Apr. 1926) remains in the library of the Alliance Israélite Universelle. Catherine Poujol found some additional copies at the Central Zionist Archives in Jerusalem: see 'Aimé Pallière', vol. ii.

eventually returned home, from the early years of the twentieth century a growing number made Paris their permanent home. It was this international group, centred in the Parisian neighbourhood of Montparnasse, that came to be known as the Ecole de Paris. Immigrant Jewish artists, most of them from eastern Europe, comprised one important component of this community. It was in the years just before the First World War that figures such as Marc Chagall, Chaim Soutine, Mané-Katz, and Chana Orloff, attracted by the cubist revolution and an opportunity to study art that was generally denied them in the tsarist empire, began to settle there.[24] While some of these Jewish artists were expelled from France or returned to their home countries during the war, it was in these years that others first began to make their presence felt on the Parisian art scene.[25] Several of the returnees —including Marc Chagall and Mané-Katz—initially chose to remain in the newly created Soviet Union. By the early 1920s, however, disappointed by the Soviet turn towards a dogmatic social realism, most had returned to the French capital, where they were joined by a flood of new arrivals.[26] By the mid-1920s, many of these Jewish artists had achieved considerable success within the French art world.

Benefiting from the ebb of antisemitism and the general sense of optimism of the Jewish community during this period, these artists integrated easily into the Parisian artistic world. At the same time, however, many were involved in the larger Jewish cultural scene of the day. The Jewish press, in particular *Menorah*, reported regularly on their activities and exhibitions, and both the AAIS and *Menorah* organized special exhibitions featuring their work. *Menorah* informed its readers in 1924, for example, that the AAIS had sponsored a very successful show for Jewish artists organized by the journal's editor Gustave Kahn. Both Maurice Liber and Julien Weill attended the opening.[27] Although dominated by Jews of foreign origin, this lively Jewish art scene inspired a number of French-born artists—including, for example, Laurance Lévy-Bloch, who always accompanied her signature with a menorah (a branched candelabrum)—to proudly affirm their Jewish heritage.[28]

The Société des Amis de la Culture Juive, created by a group of Russian Jewish artists in 1923, organized concerts and conferences on subjects

[24] On this group of Russian émigré artists, see Silver and Golan (eds), *The Circle of Montparnasse*; Roditi, 'Les Peintres russes de Montparnasse'; and Brigitte Haus, 'Les Artistes juifs de l'Ecole de Paris'.　　　　[25] Silver and Golan (eds), *The Circle of Montparnasse*, 36–7.

[26] The last wave of Jewish immigrant artists arrived between 1922 and 1926. See Haus, 'Les Artistes juifs de l'Ecole de Paris', 46.

[27] See S. David, 'L'Exposition des artistes israélites', *Menorah* (1 May 1924), 121.

[28] See Jarrassé, 'L'Eveil d'une critique d'art juive', 69.

FIGURE 5 Bust of Edmond
Fleg by Chana Orloff. The
photograph was featured in
the first issue of *Illustration
juive*, August 1922 (p. 8),
accompanied by the
publication of Fleg's poem 'La
Ruine du temple'
Reproduced by permission of
the library of the Alliance
Israélite Universelle

ranging from the situation of Jews in Poland to Jews in modern music,[29] and
the Cercle Artistique de Montparnasse was created in 1931. Interestingly, the
impetus for this group came from the Union Libérale, which had begun collaborating with certain members of this community to organize high holy
day services in private homes. The circle's founders included Louis-Germain
Lévy, Clarisse Eugène-Simon, a regular contributor to *Le Rayon*,[30] Mané-
Katz, Jacques Bielinky, and Aimé Pallière.[31] Intended to function as 'an
organism able to bring this community the benefits of Jewish solidarity and
spirituality', the group, which was soon renamed Cercle Spirituel et Artistique Israélite, began to sponsor lectures focusing on Jews and art. Initial
speakers included Louis-Germain Lévy on 'Moses: Legislator and Artist' and
Aimé Pallière on 'The Perpetuity of the Jewish People and its Role in Art'.[32]

---

[29] See *Menorah* (1 Apr. 1924), 86, which reported that the group was just over a year old.
[30] Simon, who began writing for *Le Rayon* in the 1920s, was active in the Union Libérale as
early as 1905. It was in that year that she sent a letter to *L'Univers israélite* with the text of Louis-
Germain Lévy's 1905 lecture at the Congrès du Christianisme Libéral et de Toutes les Religions
in Geneva, as well as the response of Pastor Charles Wagner.
[31] *L'Univers israélite* (30 Jan. 1931), 624.   [32] See *L'Univers israélite* (3 Apr. 1931), 18.

FIGURE 6 Sketch of André Spire by Maxa Nordau, *Menorah*, 16 September 1923 (p. 387). *Menorah* regularly featured sketches of contributors alongside their articles. Nordau was one of the paper's regular artistic contributors, and this portrait was accompanied by an essay by Spire on women and education

Reproduced by permission of the library of the Alliance Israélite Universelle

Creating new spaces in which to perform Jewish music—from traditional religious compositions to Yiddish folk songs—was another important development in Jewish cultural life during the 1920s. In a review of a Jewish musical performance in 1914, a commentator for *L'Univers israélite* praised the singer's rendition of Jewish folk songs as a welcome window on to 'the sentiment of the Jewish soul'. He was critical, however, of her decision to include traditional religious melodies, which he deemed inappropriate for a secular setting.[33] As this comment indicates, performing Jewish liturgical music outside a synagogue setting was rare before the early twentieth century. By the mid-1920s, however, such performances had become much more common both in France and elsewhere in western Europe and the United States. Remarking on this phenomenon in Germany, Michael Brenner notes that 'an increasing number of Jews experienced Jewish music by attending a Sunday matinée or turning on their radios. They listened to Klezmer music, Yemenite Jewish dances and . . . contemporary renditions of

---

[33] 'Autour d'un concert', *L'Univers israélite* (29 May 1914), 206–7.

Jewish liturgy in the same way that they listened to Beethoven's symphonies and Wagner's operas: as concert audiences.'[34]

In France, the Société des Amis de la Musique Juive, comprised principally of Russian Jewish musicians living in Paris, was created in 1928 on the initiative of the sculptor Nahum Aronson.[35] One of its first performances was a Hebrew concert at the Union Libérale, with a programme that included both a rendition of Kol Nidre and hasidic dances.[36] As well as organizing concerts, the group was involved in creating orchestras and choruses in Parisian Jewish youth groups. The proceeds from one of their 1929 concerts, *L'Univers israélite* reported, were being used to create an orchestra for the Maccabi club.[37] It was also under the auspices of this group that Léon Algazi, director of the UUJJ's chorus created in 1924, organized the Mizmor choir for Jewish youth in 1929. The group, which as Algazi explained in an article in *L'Univers israélite* was 'an artistic rather than confessional organization', counted thirty members in 1931 and performed on several occasions for Radio Paris.[38] *L'Univers israélite* reported regularly on the concerts of the Chorale Israélite du Chant Sacré founded in Strasbourg in 1923, and *La Tribune juive* noted that a Jewish chorus created in Metz in the late 1920s limited its membership to single men and women and organized group excursions as well as concerts.[39]

The Beginnings of an Inter-Faith Movement

An important characteristic of many of the Jewish associations and publications created during the 1920s was the extent to which they sought the participation and contributions of non-Jews. This participation was undoubtedly solicited in part because of the legitimacy that it would offer: as we have seen, this kind of thinking was at the core of the creation of France-Palestine, which specifically sought the help of non-Jews in order to prove that the Zionist movement, rather than representing narrowly Jewish interests, had a broader 'universalist' programme. The editors of the *Revue littéraire juive* probably had a similar agenda in mind when they recruited an impressive list of non-Jewish spokesmen to endorse the opening issue of the

---

[34] Brenner, *The Renaissance of Jewish Culture in Weimar Germany*, 61.

[35] This group was in fact a revival of a Jewish musical society by the same name formed in St Petersburg in 1908. Its founders in France included a number of prominent Zionist personalities, including Hillel Zlatopolsky, Isaac Naïditch, Vladimir Haffkine, Victor Jacobson, Léon Filderman, Myriam Schach, Yvonne Netter, and Léon Zadoc-Kahn. See *L'Univers israélite* (13 Jan. 1928), 526–7.   [36] Ibid.   [37] *L'Univers israélite* (7 June 1929), 243–4.

[38] Algazi, 'La Chorale Mizmor', *L'Univers israélite* (2 Oct. 1931), 113.

[39] See *La Tribune juive* (6 June 1930).

journal in 1928,[40] as did the members of the AAIS when they included only one Jewish speaker at their 1924 conference, 'The Jew in Contemporary Society'.[41]

This non-Jewish participation was also a reflection of a new openness towards Judaism within liberal Christian circles.[42] In some instances 'sympathetic' Christian interest was ultimately aimed at encouraging conversion. The society of Notre Dame de Sion, for example, sought to convert Jews to Catholicism by emphasizing the similarities between Judaism and Christianity. In a 1926 article for *Foi et réveil*, Aimé Pallière noted a similar kind of 'sympathetic' conversionary rhetoric in the sermons of Pierre Sanson, the orator at Notre Dame between 1925 and 1928. Though Sanson was castigated in the right-wing Catholic press for his vehement stand against antisemitism, Pallière noted that his sermons were still caught up in an apologist Christian discourse that posited Christianity as the fulfilment of Judaism.[43] Pallière unequivocally praised the more radical 1928 decision of Notre Dame de Sion to change its focus from converting Jews to encouraging inter-faith dialogue. It was at this point that the group changed the name of its bulletin, *Le Retour d'Israël*, to *Bulletin catholique de la question d'Israël*.[44]

The waning of antisemitism within mainstream Catholicism, and in particular within youth groups, was an important factor in encouraging the beginnings of an inter-faith movement. As we saw in Chapter 3, leaders of the Union Libérale were close to both liberal Protestant circles and the Ecole de Lyon, a branch of the modernist Catholic movement. An important feature of both of these movements was an interest in dialogue. Rather than taking conversion as the ultimate objective of Christian–Jewish exchange, they sought to establish a basis for mutual understanding. In the 1920s this kind of dialogue became much more common. At a conference on the religious revival in contemporary France sponsored by the Ecole de Philosophie

[40] These included Justin Godart, Henri Barbusse, Georges Bonnet, Arthur Levasseur, Louis-Jean Finot, André Lamande, and Gaston Riou.

[41] Speakers included the Abbé Brugerette, a professor of philosophy and history, Anatole de Monzie, and Justin Godart. The fourth speaker was Eva Leon, a visiting Zionist spokeswoman from the United States. See 'Le Juif dans la société contemporaine', *Menorah* (24 Feb. 1924), 55–8.

[42] Both Pierrard, *Juifs et catholiques français, 1886–1945* (p. 248), and Gugelot, *La Conversion des intellectuels au catholicisme en France, 1885–1935* (pp. 203–6), note this change in Catholic attitudes in the late 1920s and early 1930s. [43] *Foi et réveil*, 24/5 (1926), 129–45.

[44] Pallière, 'Le Peuple témoin', *Palestine* (July/Aug. 1929), 5. There is some doubt among historians as to whether the group's official anti-conversionary stance should be taken at face value. I would tend to agree with Poujol's analysis (*Aimé Pallière*, 288) that, while the group did not abandon the traditional Christian belief that 'the Jews' would be converted with the Second Coming, it genuinely abandoned its original mission of converting individual Jews in the here and now. For an overview of the order's attitudes towards and relationship with Jews, see Comte, 'De la conversion à la rencontre', 102–19.

in 1926, both Julien Weill and André Spire were invited as representatives of Judaism.[45] Rapprochement between Judaism and Christianity was also an important theme at the Semaine des Ecrivains Catholiques which took place in Paris in 1927. Several Catholic speakers focused on points of commonality between the two religions, and Edmond Fleg was invited to speak on Judaism.[46] Another figure who helped to create a Jewish–Christian dialogue was Joseph Bonsirven, who disputed Renan's contention that Judaism was a 'dead trunk' of Christianity in *Sur les ruines du Temple*. Bonsirven began publishing a column, 'Bulletin du judaïsme français', for the Catholic journal *Etudes* in 1927, which reported on developments and trends within the Jewish community in an objective fashion.[47]

The UUJJ featured several lectures by liberal Christian theologians, including Paul Vulliaud and Marie-André Dieux, a priest and former missionary who became a popular speaker against antisemitism in the 1920s.[48] While non-Jews rarely spoke at Chema Israël, the group sponsored a number of lectures and discussions on the relationship between Judaism and Christianity that went beyond apologetics. In 1923, for example, a speaker addressed the question, 'Should We Show an Interest in Christianity and its Founder?' While Christianity was not an appropriate subject for sermons, the speaker concluded, it was imperative for Jews to educate themselves about Christianity in other settings (such as Chema), not only to be equipped to respond effectively to conversionary efforts, but also because 'the history of the origins of Christianity is a chapter in our own history, and thus the Jewish historian must study it, and the cultivated Jew must be knowledgeable of it'.[49] This inter-faith dialogue made an impression on contempor-

[45] The proceedings were subsequently published in a book entitled *La Renaissance religieuse*. In his introduction, the editor Georges Guy-Grand calls Judaism, along with Catholicism and Protestantism, 'one of the three great religions of France' (p. 2).

[46] Pro-Jewish speakers included Alfred Poizat, who published a book called *Le Miracle juif* in 1932, in which he argued that 'Christianity is Judaism in its essence', and P. Joussé, who focused on the possibilities for the collaborative study of sacred texts between Catholics and Jews. See Pierrard, *Juifs et catholiques français*, 251–2.

[47] *L'Univers israélite* (30 Jan. 1931), 613–16, reported on an issue that he devoted to Zionism in 1930. *L'Univers israélite* reprinted an excerpt from the column devoted to Zionism in 1930; see *L'Univers israélite* (30 Jan. 1931), 617–18.

[48] See Chapter 5 above. Vulliaud, a scholar of Jewish mysticism, dated the Zohar to talmudic times, thus disputing the view of scholars who claimed it was a medieval 'forgery' with no authentic Jewish content. In addition to his discussion of Jewish symbolic poetry, he gave a lecture on Jewish mysticism for the UUJJ in 1926. On Dieux, who developed a reputation as the 'bête noire of antisemites', see Pierrard, *Juifs et catholiques français*, 248–50, and Poujol, *Aimé Pallière*, 289–396.

[49] *L'Univers israélite* (23 Mar. 1923), 18. The Paris section of Chema also sponsored a conference series entitled 'Judaism and Christianity in History' in 1927. See *L'Univers israélite* (4 Nov. 1927), 216.

aries. Writing in his column 'Chronique parisienne' for *Chalom* in 1927, Meyerkey commented approvingly on the new 'état d'esprit' in Christian circles. For the first time, he remarked, certain Christians are actually showing an interest in trying to understand Jews and Judaism on their own terms.[50] Reporting on the Semaine des Ecrivains Catholiques, the *Revue catholique des idées et des faits* noted with similar surprise that a newly sympathetic atmosphere in Catholic circles towards the Eastern Orthodox Church and Anglican Church had now been extended to Jews.[51]

Confidence and Doubts

Writing in *Le Rayon* in 1927, Meyerkey offered a dramatic comparison between the situation of French Jewry in his own day and at the turn of the century:

At the beginning of the century, we feared for the future of Judaism. Young people no longer practised their religion and had no interest in learning more about it. In the aftermath of the war, things changed. Our brothers experienced an awakening that was both religious and ethnic. We can only feel sorry for those who let this golden opportunity pass them by.[52]

The first issue of the *Revue littéraire juive* conveyed a similar sense of optimism. More than a dozen literary and political figures, both Jews and non-Jews, were invited to write short statements of endorsement, all of which hailed the journal as a sign of the new spirit of French Judaism. French Jews had once believed that in order to be accepted as equals they had to suppress all that made them distinctive, a number of commentators observed. Now, by contrast, they were finally secure in their place in French society and thus felt free to explore their own particularism. 'We have been endowed with a remarkable history', marvelled writer Henry Marx, 'let us not cease to be faithful to it, even though we are fully modern.'[53] However, this enthusiasm was often tempered by concerns both about the content of the Judaism being 'revived' and the lasting impact that this phenomenon would have on the French Jewish community. It is to some of these criticisms and concerns that I will now turn.

Religiously minded Jews often criticized the secular quality of many of these new organizations and activities. This issue had already come up before the war for the Union Scolaire. Writing in the group's journal in 1912,

---

[50] *Chalom* (Apr. 1927), 19–20.
[51] Pierrard, *Juifs et catholiques français*, 252. This inter-faith dialogue is a central theme in Poujol's biography: see especially *Aimé Pallière*, 287–332.
[52] 'Le Réveil de la jeunesse juive', *Le Rayon* (15 Apr. 1927), 13–15.   [53] Ibid.

Hippolyte Prague, the editor of the *Archives juives*, objected to a conference on Freud's *Totem and Taboo*. From Prague's perspective, it was problematic for a Jewish organization to sponsor a conference on a book that treated religion as an atavistic superstition, in particular given the secular orientation of Jewish youth and their general ignorance of the basic precepts of Judaism.[54]

Prague's concerns remained alive in the 1920s, as secular associations and activities became a regular feature of Jewish life. A common target of criticism was the Club du Faubourg. While the group was a source of inspiration for many French Jews, its flamboyant style, range of discussion topics, and, above all, growing popularity drew criticism from others. *L'Univers israélite* grudgingly began announcing the club's debates in the mid-1920s, but its reports were often accompanied by acerbic criticism. What was most shocking to the *Univers israélite*, it seems, was that the club brought Jews together to discuss Jewish issues in a flagrantly secular setting. Referring to it as a 'Jewish Salon', one commentator suggested that the Faubourg, rather than providing an environment in which to reconnect with one's Jewish heritage, was a place where Jews were in the process of 'de-Judaizing'.[55] While the Faubourg put the important issues of assimilation and Zionism on the table, Aimé Pallière commented in a similar vein, it devoted no attention to the Jewish religion.[56] Reporting on an event sponsored by the group in Strasbourg, a reporter for *La Tribune juive* was even more critical. While the group's 'spirit and activity' might be approved of in the capital, he asserted, in Strasbourg 'it makes an unfavourable, if not downright disagreeable, impression'.[57]

Writing in 1929 from the perspective of someone 'who was young half a century ago', a contributor to *L'Univers israélite* reflected on the Jewish renaissance of the day. Taking the UUJJ as the example par excellence of the spirit of the new generation, he praised the organization for its 'conferences, discussions, and international exchanges on all subjects touching on Judaism' as a phenomenon of 'real importance' for the Jewish community. He went on, however, to express concern that the success of this organization did not appear to have translated into a rise in religious observance: there was no indication, he noted, that religious laws were being observed more scrupulously or that attendance at services was up: 'It seems that this youth is only interested in Judaism from an intellectual perspective', he remarked, 'and that religious observance . . . will remain in the background of its concerns.'[58] As we saw in Chapter 5, the issue of religious observance was in fact

[54] *L'Union scolaire* (Feb./Apr. 1912), 4.   [55] *L'Univers israélite* (8 Feb. 1924), 529.
[56] *L'Univers israélite* (13 June 1924), 197–9.   [57] *La Tribune juive* (12 Dec. 1930), 773.
[58] Adam Dreyfus, 'Tribune des lecteurs: Renouveau juif?', *L'Univers israélite* (12 Apr. 1929), 983.

a major source of conflict within the Parisian section of the organization, and Meyerkey, writing two years earlier in his regular column for *Chalom*, in fact expressed concerns not that different from those of the commenter in the *Univers*. One of the most noteworthy phenomena in the contemporary Jewish community, he observed, was that 'even the non-believers want to be Jews', which he took as 'proof that we are as much a people as a religion . . . one is a child of Israel as long as one has not "broken ethnically" with it'. He went on, however, to express uncertainty about how and whether the kind of individually determined, self-reflective Judaism that the group encouraged would be successfully transmitted to the next generation.[59]

For the majority of young French people—both Jews and non-Jews—the 1920s were a time in which religious practice and belief were on the decline. The comments of young people in *Chalom* often reflected the reigning mood of secularism. Writing in *Chalom*'s 'Journal de l'UUJJiste' column in 1927, for example, one member declared unequivocally, 'I am not religious. It is not faith that inspires me to Jewish practice. I think that many of my friends are in the same situation. What kind of return to Jewish life is thus possible for us?' In response, he drew on an idea that several other UUJJ members had already developed, that of 'a Jewish spiritual state': rather than thinking of religious obligations as 'an affair between oneself and God, one feels that one belongs to the Jewish people and that the laws of the collectivity are thus incumbent upon the individual'.[60] Reflecting on what she took away from her attendance at a Zionist congress, another UUJJ member linked her discovery of Zionism to her renewed commitment to her Jewish heritage and a process of introspection about the content of Jewish identity in the diaspora: 'the essential thing', she noted, 'is not so much to resolve the "Jewish question" as to conserve the unique, forty-centuries-old phenomenon that we call Judaism'. Zionism, she went on to explain, was for her the only vibrant element of Judaism with something to offer the modern Jew: 'I finally understand', she concluded, 'that to work with the Zionists could be something grand, but that above all I must work to remake myself.'[61]

While this kind of soul-searching and emphasis on an open-ended definition of Judaism was a source of inspiration to many young French Jews of the day, it also provoked criticism and concern. The lack of any kind of substantive Jewish culture in France, a contributor to *Chalom* suggested, inevitably limited the possibilities for a true Jewish renaissance: in comparison

[59] Meyerkey, 'Chronique parisienne', *Chalom* (Apr. 1927), 19.

[60] Max, 'Le Carnet de l'UUJJiste: Le Respect du Shabbat', *Chalom* (Apr. 1927), 20. Max's comments were followed by two other reflections on Jewish identity: P. Escat, 'A la recherche d'une doctrine', and Rabbi Waldemar, 'Confession d'un jeune Juif'.

[61] Raphaella, 'Badinage autour d'un meeting', *Chalom* (Dec. 1927/Jan. 1928), 22.

with countries with large Jewish populations, the so-called Jewish renaissance in France would necessarily remain superficial because it did not include any substantial educational reforms: 'The education of French Jews', he concluded pessimistically, 'is purely and exclusively French.' Lectures and conferences offered by various youth groups and 'circles' were not substantive enough to transmit Jewish culture from one generation to the next: an intellectual interest in 'identity' could not be equated with creating a generation of French Jews with a real depth of knowledge about Judaism itself. Objecting to the use of the word 'renaissance' to describe what was going on within the French Jewish community, this sceptic asked his readers rhetorically: 'Will we be able to hand on this torch of Judaism to our descendants?', and concluded pessimistically that 'it is possible that it is in fact a torch with a very feeble light, likely to be extinguished in the generation that follows us'.[62] As this article suggests, for many people involved in Jewish cultural life of the day, writing on Jewish themes or participating in Jewish activities was linked more to personal identity quests than to concern about 'handing on the torch' to future generations. The personal lives of some of the more prominent Jewish intellectuals of this period are revealing on this point: it is interesting to note that André Spire, Gustave Kahn, and Albert Cohen all married Christian women.[63] For Victor Basch, lending support to the Zionist movement was in fact a way to express a sense of Jewish identity that he felt incapable of transmitting to the next generation.[64] Clearly, for these men—and undoubtedly for many other French Jews of the day—a 'revived' sense of Jewish identity did not necessarily lead to an embrace of traditional Jewish communal concerns, of which opposition to intermarriage was primary.

Writing in the *Revue littéraire juive* in 1928, Raymond-Raoul Lambert remarked on the changes that were taking place in how Jews thought about

[62] See Jaime Azancot, 'Le Judaïsme de demain', *Chalom* (1 Mar. 1929), 18–19. This article was a response to a lecturer at the UUJJ who had spoken enthusiastically of 'handing on the torch of Judaism'.

[63] For both Spire and Cohen, these marriages were followed by subsequent long-term unions with Jewish women. Spire's first wife Gabrielle died in the late 1930s. He then married a second cousin with whom he had one daughter, Marie-Brunette, who was born during the Second World War in New York. Albert Cohen married Elisabeth Brocher, the daughter of a Protestant pastor in Geneva, in 1919, with whom he had a daughter, Myriam. Elisabeth died in 1924, and in 1931 he remarried another Protestant woman, Marianne Goss. This second marriage broke up in 1944, at which point Cohen became acquainted with Bella Berkowith, a (Jewish) friend of his daughter, who became his third wife. Gustave Kahn married Elizabeth Conrati in 1898. She converted to Judaism at the height of the Dreyfus affair, apparently on her own initiative rather than as a result of any express desire of Kahn. The couple did not have children. I am grateful to Catherine Fhima for sharing biographical information on Spire and Kahn with me. On Albert Cohen, see Jean Blot's biography, *Albert Cohen*.

[64] See Fhima and Nicault, 'Victor Basch et la judéité', 236.

themselves and their place in French society. The present generation, he asserted, was united by its readiness to publicly affirm a Judaism 'devoid of proselytizing or even religious pride'. Whereas Jewishness was once relegated to the private sphere, it could now be openly discussed, debated, and explored with confidence.[65] For Lambert, this phenomenon was a product of the decrease in antisemitism in contemporary French society which began in the aftermath of the Dreyfus affair and was hastened by the war: 'In the lycée, in the army', he affirmed, the young Jew 'no longer suffers from persecution'. Lack of prejudice, he reasoned, encouraged solidarity. Once the stigma of Jewishness had been removed, 'the young French Jew is happy to meet co-religionists with whom he feels freer, more at ease'. Importantly, however, this new brand of Jewish solidarity and pride had not lessened young people's tendency to look at the world from a 'strictly human' perspective, to understand that happiness comes from interaction with different kinds of people. Most often, Lambert commented with approval, the best friend of this proud young Jew was a Christian.[66]

Lambert's article is very positive in tone. He saw no contradiction between his generation's dual desire for Jewish affirmation and integration, and he expressed confidence that this sense of pride and self-assurance would translate into a lasting commitment to Judaism: the young Jew of today, he asserted, 'at last has the consciousness that he must transmit a heritage, intact, to his children'.[67] As his own discussion clearly indicates, however, for all of the young people he described, being Jewish was much more about an internal 'feeling' than about any kind of commitment to the maintenance and perpetuation of Jewish communal distinctiveness. The examples that he gives are telling. Marcel, though he has 'little time to devote to Jewish problems', attends his family synagogue for major holidays and feels a sense of affinity with things Jewish, from liturgy to literature to food. David, the son of German Jewish immigrants, hails from a strictly Orthodox family and remains very pious by 'habit, superstition, and love for his grandmother'. Serge, who has a typically Jewish physiognomy and is the grandson of a chief rabbi, has lost all sense of connection with the Jewish religion, but will undoubtedly marry at the Synagogue de la Victoire to 'make his future wife happy'. Samuel began to 'feel Jewish' at the Sorbonne where he came into contact with east European Jewish students, 'understands' Zionism, and respects the 'force of heredity', but has no religious education or interest therein.[68]

It is exactly this kind of Judaism that Maurice Liber criticized in a 1926 exchange with André Spire in *L'Univers israélite*. In an article entitled 'Les

[65] Lambert, 'Recherche d'une jeunesse juive', *Revue littéraire juive* (July 1928), 598.
[66] Ibid. 599.　　　　　　[67] Ibid. 598.　　　　　　[68] Ibid. 596–7.

Paradoxes de M. Spire', Liber suggested that the Judaism of Spire and others like him was untenable because it was rooted in ethnic posturing rather than an attachment to a viable ideology or way of life. The hero of Zangwill's 'Chad-gad-ya', to whom Spire attributed his 'return' to Judaism, Liber reminded the reader, was a tragic figure: an intellectual who commits suicide because he is unable to find a sense of equilibrium between Western culture and his Jewish heritage. This story and Spire's reaction to it, Liber argued, did not provide a viable model of Jewish identity: 'To affirm one's Judaism, to be proud of it, is an attitude or a pose; it is not a doctrine. To want to be Jewish is an intention or a pretension; it is not a system or a discipline.'[69] In response, Spire defended his position as a 'Juif de race' and responded to Liber's comments by comparing the situation in contemporary France with that in the late 1880s, when he came of age: the transformation of the community, Spire asserted, was nothing short of miraculous: 'French Judaism today is livelier, stronger than during my youth. There are hundreds of young French Jews who want to know what Judaism is, who are asking their parents who are non-believers or sceptics to teach them what Judaism is, who want to know why their ancestors struggled and suffered.'[70] For Spire, the fact that young Jews were interested in Judaism was evidence of a Jewish renaissance. For Liber, by contrast, being 'interested' in Judaism was only valuable if it led to a return to religious practice and a commitment to Jewish continuity. While both Spire and Liber strongly opposed 'assimilation', they understood this term very differently. For Spire, assimilation was first and foremost a state of mind: an assimilated Jew was someone who was ashamed of his origins and felt that he must dissimulate them in order to be fully French. For Liber, by contrast, assimilation was linked to action: an assimilated Jew was someone who had abandoned religious practice and/or ceased to participate in Jewish community life. While Liber's article was largely a polemic against secularism, both his article and Lambert's raised an important point: understanding one's Jewishness in ethnic or cultural terms was not necessarily synonymous with maintaining a long-term commitment to Judaism or Jewish community life per se.

In this context it is perhaps interesting to consider the fact that two people who were active in Jewish literary and communal life in the 1920s—Yvonne Netter and Georges Cattaui—later converted to Catholicism. Cattaui, who converted in 1928, was a personal friend of André Spire and active

---

[69] 'Les Paradoxes de M. Spire', *L'Univers israélite* (31 Dec. 1926), 517–19. Liber's article was written in the context of criticizing the decision of the Ecole de Philosophie to invite Spire as well as Julien Weill to participate in its series of conferences on the religious revival in contemporary France. See p. 152 above.
[70] 'Une lettre de M. Spire', *L'Univers israélite* (7 Jan. 1927), 552–3.

in French Zionist circles in the mid-1920s. As noted above, he joined the editorial board of *Menorah* in 1923 and published a number of essays and poems in various Jewish press organs. He wrote an enthusiastic article in favour of the creation of the Hebrew University of Jerusalem for *La Revue juive* in 1925, and his poems expressing enthusiasm for the Zionist movement appeared in *Le Peuple juif, Chalom, Menorah*, and *Foi et réveil* in the early 1920s. In a 1924 lecture for the AAIS that was subsequently published in *Menorah*, Jacques Calmy included Cattaui, along with Henri Franck, Edmond Fleg, André Spire, and Albert Cohen, as one of the new voices of French Jewry.[71]

Yvonne Netter, who converted in 1940, was a Parisian-born lawyer, feminist, and Zionist activist in the mid-1920s. She created the Union des Femmes Juives Françaises pour la Palestine, the French affiliate of the World Zionist Organization, in 1924. She presided over the short-lived Union Sioniste Française in 1926, was a member of the central committee of the UUJJ, and contributed regularly to the Jewish press. In a brief biography of Netter for *Archives juives,* Catherine Nicault suggests that the motives behind her 1940 baptism are open to interpretation: ultimately, it is impossible to know if it represented a sincere reaction to a difficult period in her life (the mobilization of her only son) or an attempt to escape persecution. In discussing Netter's Zionist activism, however, Nicault suggests that her 'Diasporic Zionism', rather than a 'simple battle for equality', was part of her own search for identity.[72] While the reasons for both Netter's and Cattaui's conversions were undoubtedly overdetermined, it seems fair to surmise that they grew out of the same identity quest that initially sparked their interest in Jewish nationalism.

For many German Jews, Michael Brenner notes, involvement with the Lehrhaus, the most successful Jewish educational society of the Weimar period, grew out of the realization that their parents' and grandparents' integration was chimerical. While they had become culturally German, their social circle and professional opportunities remained circumscribed by their Jewishness. The new generation, by contrast, sought to immerse themselves in Jewish learning as part of a desire to affirm their cultural distinctiveness.[73] In France, by contrast, no such motivation existed. Social and political integration, which had been a reality since the mid-nineteenth century, continued in the 1920s. Overall, French Jews who emphasized their distinctiveness did not do so as a result of their failed integration into French society,

[71] Calmy, 'Poètes juifs de la langue française', *Menorah* (1 Apr. 1924), 89.
[72] Nicault, 'Yvonne Netter, avocate, militante féministe et sioniste'.
[73] Brenner, *The Renaissance of Jewish Culture in Weimar Germany*, 81.

but rather because they felt a new sense of freedom to affirm their identity. If this translated into a lasting commitment to Judaism for some, for Cattaui, Netter, and others it may have represented a phase as much as anything else. While the transitory nature of some Jews' interest in their religious heritage was undoubtedly an aspect of Jewish life in other countries as well, the extent of Jewish cultural and social integration in France perhaps made trajectories like Cattui's and Netter's more common in France than elsewhere.

The example of Jewish converts to Catholicism raises another interesting point. While the conversion of Netter and Cattaui might initially appear surprising given their Zionist sympathies and obviously strong sense of themselves as Jews, it may not have represented as much of an opposition to their 'Jewishness' as one might think. While Netter and Cattaui were unique in that they were Zionists and active in Jewish communal circles prior to conversion, they were not alone in their decision to embrace Catholicism. As Frédéric Gugelot notes in his study of conversion to Catholicism among French intellectuals between 1885 and 1935,[74] Jews were over-represented among converts to Catholicism in the inter-war years. Jewish conversions, Gugelot shows, peaked during and in the immediate aftermath of the First World War and again in the late 1920s.[75] Interestingly, he points out, for many Jewish converts during this period conversion itself became a form of re-Judaization. Many were baptized under the patronage of Jacques and Raïssa Maritain, who convinced them that they need not abandon their Judaism in order to embrace Christianity. By latching on to the philosemitic Catholicism of someone like Charles Péguy, for whom the Jews remained the chosen people, these converts were able to understand their baptisms as an act of fulfilment rather than as treason.[76]

We see a similar, if less extreme, mechanism at work in the attraction of many French Jewish intellectuals and writers of the day towards the personality of Jesus. This was part of a larger European and American trend, as the attempt on the part of certain Christian theologians to discover a 'human Jesus' opened the door to a new interest in Jesus in liberal Jewish circles.[77] The most striking example of this phenomenon is undoubtedly the paintings of Marc Chagall, who reclaimed the crucifix as a Jewish symbol of suffering. In articles for both *Menorah* and *Palestine*, Maurice Level (who contributed regularly to both journals) encouraged readers to accept Jesus as a Jewish prophet. Traditional Jewish apologetics focused on the idea that

[74] Gugelot, *La Conversion des intellectuels au catholicisme en France, 1885–1935*, 169–210.

[75] They began to taper off in the mid-1930s (ibid. 199–200), a decrease that Gugelot correlates with the shift away from conversionary efforts on the part of the Société de Notre Dame and other like-minded groups and individuals.

[76] For a succinct summary of this argument, see also Gugelot's article, 'De Ratisbonne à Lustiger'.   [77] See Novak, 'The Quest for the Jewish Jesus'.

Jesus's message was not original, but rather could be found in the teachings of Rabbi Hillel. Level, by contrast, argued that Jesus's teachings built on and surpassed Hillel's and thus represented the 'supreme flower' of Judaism.[78] The most prominent Jewish writer to express this kind of sympathetic attitude towards Jesus was Edmond Fleg. In a series of books published between 1926 and 1933—*L'Enfant prophète, Pourquoi je suis juif, Ma Palestine,* and *Jésus raconté par le Juif errant*—Fleg revealed a fascination with the message and significance of Jesus from a Jewish perspective. Somewhat paradoxically, Catherine Fhima suggests, Fleg's progressive interest in Jesus actually represented the solidification of his identity as a Jew. *L'Enfant prophète* and *Pourquoi je suis juif* represent the perspective of the 'assimilated Jew', unequipped to answer to the Christian charge of deicide. In *Ma Palestine* and even more so in *Jésus raconté par le Juif errant,* Fleg, by contrast, developed the idea that Jesus was neither God nor messiah but a Jew who deserved his place in the line of Hebrew prophets. The more Fleg became interested in Jesus, Fhima concludes, the more he became Jewish.[79]

As this analysis of Fleg suggests, the move towards an ethnic understanding of Jewishness played an important role in legitimating this kind of sympathetic interest in Jesus in Jewish circles. Fleg, Level, and others writing in secular Jewish journals such as *Palestine* or the *Revue littéraire juive* understood Judaism as an ethno-cultural heritage rather than a religious tradition that was necessarily separated from Christianity by certain beliefs. As a result, they did not see their fascination with or attraction to the figure of Jesus as antithetical to their strong sense of identification as Jews. The circle of converts that Gugelot describes, to be sure, took this engagement with Christianity much further. Nonetheless, they socialized together, gathered together for specific prayer ceremonies, and were generally encouraged by Maritain and others—including the Société de Notre Dame de Sion—to maintain an 'ethnic' sense of Jewish identity. As this evidence suggests, while opening up the category of ethnic identity provided a basis for some to renew their links with the Jewish community, for others it may have provided the necessary psychological tools to leave the boundaries of Judaism as they are traditionally defined.

---

[78] For Level, the subsequent development of Christianity, in which Jesus became a vindictive God of judgement, represented a return to a more primitive kind of Judaism. Maurice Level, 'Après l'Omega', *Palestine* (Apr. 1929), 168–73. Level developed a similar line of argument in a 1930 article for *Menorah* entitled 'L'Armée sans uniforme' (1 May 1930), 134. This article was an instalment of his regular column for the journal, 'Le Minora de *Menorah*'.

[79] Fhima, 'Aux sources d'un renouveau identitaire juif en France', 188. On Fleg and Christianity see also 'Hommage à Edmond Fleg', special issue of *Revue de la pensée juive*, 2 (Jan. 1950), especially Daniélou, 'Edmond Fleg et le christianisme', and Fumet, 'Réflexions sur "Pourquoi je suis Juif"'.

CHAPTER 7

Jewish Literature in France
1920–1932

'WITH the exceptions of Fleg, Spire, Bloch, and the Tharaud brothers', remarked Jewish writer and literary critic Benjamin Crémieux in 1925, 'Judaism was of no interest to anyone in France until 1914.'[1] Crémieux went on to contrast this state of affairs with that of the France of his own day:

Today, two major Jewish journals, *La Revue juive* and *Menorah*, come out regularly. The Rieder publishing house puts out a Judaism collection, directed by Edmond Fleg. Everyone has read Geiger's *Histoires juives*. The Tharaud brothers have published three subsequent books on Jewish subjects. Even Pierre Benoît has sacrificed himself to this vogue, publishing *Le Puits de Jacob*, a novel about Zionism.[2]

As we saw in Chapter 2, the first wave of writers to explore Jewish themes in their essays, fiction, and poetry wrote in the years before the First World War. Over the course of the 1920s, what had been the novelty of a few maverick intellectuals became a recognized genre of writing, as the titles cited by Crémieux were joined by dozens of novels, poems, plays, collections of folklore, and short stories that explored different aspects of Jewish life and the issues of assimilation and acculturation in modern society.[3] A vogue for Jewish themes inspired French publishing houses to translate both contemporary and classical Jewish authors and sparked the creation of several specialized series. The most important of these, as Crémieux's article indicates, was the Rieder publishing house's 'Judaïsme'. Created in 1925, this series was divided into two sections: 'Œuvres', overseen by Edmond Fleg, which published contemporary scholarly studies of Judaism, and 'Etudes', overseen by Paul-Louis Couchoud, a controversial Christian Bible scholar

---

[1] The article in which these remarks appeared, entitled 'Judaïsme et littérature', was first published in *Les Nouvelles littéraires* and was reprinted in the literary supplement of *L'Univers israélite* (23 Oct. 1925), 18–20. [2] Ibid. 19.

[3] Appendix III, which includes many more titles than I have been able to discuss in the present book, is intended to give the reader a sense of the range and volume of fiction on Jewish themes published in France from the beginning of the 20th century to the early 1930s. While I have generally limited the list to the period before 1932, if a particular author's work is discussed in the text I have included his or her subsequent publications, if any, up to 1940.

who questioned the historical existence of Jesus, which published translations of both classical and modern Jewish literature.[4] In addition Le Triangle,
a small publishing house that focused on artistic themes, began an 'Artistes
juifs' series in 1927, featuring monographs in both Yiddish and French,[5]
and in 1928 the *Revue littéraire juive* created a small publishing house, Les
Editions ERELJI, devoted to the publication of books on Jewish themes.[6]
This wave of Jewish literature made an impression in the broader French literary world. 'When we take stock of the fiction of this century', the *Mercure de
France* suggested in 1925, 'we must consider the discovery of the Jewish soul
as one important element of it.'[7]

Below I examine the different facets of Jewish literature of the 1920s. Discussion of this new genre in the French Jewish press of the day reveals the
extent to which, like the new forms of associational life and cultural activity,
it was a source of both optimism and anxiety within the Jewish community.
In order to gauge the response to this genre of writing in French society at
large and compare it with that of French Jews, I have also looked systemati-
cally at discussions of literature on Jewish themes in the *Mercure de France*,
one of the most important French literary journals of the day.

Jewish Literature from Foreign Lands

The expansion of the Jewish press in post-war France played an important
role in making international Jewish literature accessible to French readers.

---

[4] See Appendix II for a complete list of works published in the series, which was the fruit of
Edmond Fleg's labours. Fleg first tried to interest the editor Georges Crès, who published his
Anthologie juive, in underwriting a series entitled 'Cahiers d'Israël' that Fleg would edit. When
this did not work out, Fleg successfully enlisted the support of Jean-Richard Bloch, who had
just been named general editor of the series 'Les Prosateurs français contemporains' at Rieder
in 1925, in the creation of a 'Judaïsme' series at that publishing house. Rieder went on to
become one of two major French publishing houses—the other being Gallimard—to publish
literature on Jewish themes in the inter-war years. See Fhima, 'Au cœur de la "renaissance
juive"', 37.

[5] This series, which was created on the initiative of Michel Kiveliovitch, a mathematician of
Polish origin, was published through the early 1930s. See Jarrassé, 'L'Eveil d'une critique d'art
juive', 70–3.

[6] 'Les Editions ERELJI . . . created in response to the express desire of a number of readers'
was announced in the *Revue littéraire juive* (Nov. 1928), 1. Its first publication was a collection of
biblical stories by M. Eisenstadt entitled *Le Bouclier de David: Contes bibliques*. Other publications, also from 1929, included Simon Dubnow, *Histoire d'un soldat juif*; Dr Schapiro, *L'Hygiène
alimentaire des Juifs devant la science moderne*; a novella by S. C. Cohen, *La Renégate*, which was
also published in instalments in the *Revue littéraire juive* in 1929; and *Le Herem*, a novel by a
Salonican writer, Uriel de Medonça, with a preface by Pierre Paraf. Paraf's preface and a short
segment of the novel also appeared in the *Revue littéraire juive* (Nov./Dec. 1929). This publishing venture does not appear to have been very long-lived: I have found no reference to any publications after 1929.   [7] *Mercure de France* (15 Dec. 1925), 713.

By the mid-1920s, Yiddish and Hebrew fiction in translation was appearing regularly in the Jewish press of the day—in particular *Menorah* and the *Revue littéraire juive*—as were short stories and novels on Jewish life in eastern Europe by figures such as the German Jewish poet Else Lasker-Schüler and the philosopher and interpreter of hasidism Martin Buber.[8] Yiddish and Hebrew theatre also became popular in Paris in the 1920s. Alongside the Yiddish theatre created by and for the immigrants themselves, several Yiddish and Hebrew plays were translated and performed for the wider Parisian public.

The first Yiddish play performed in French was Sholem Asch's *Dieu de vengeance* (*Got fun nekome*), which opened in 1925 at the Théâtre de l'Atelier. In 1926 the Habima theatre company of Moscow performed S. Ansky's *Dybbuk* in Paris and Chajim Bloch's *Golem* in both Paris and Strasbourg. It was the success of these performances that inspired Gaston Baty, the Christian director of the Studio des Champs Elysées, to produce a French version of the *Dybbuk* in 1928.[9] Léon Algazi wrote the music for the production and, as Baty explained in an interview in *L'Univers israélite*, also filled him in on details of traditional Jewish religion and culture.[10]

French readers were also introduced to the world of east European Jewry through novels and short stories written in French by writers of east European origin, who had often immigrated as children or young adults. The most successful novel of this genre was a trilogy entitled *L'Epopée de Ménaché Foigel*, the collaborative effort of Moïse Twersky, an immigrant from the Ukraine, and the prominent French novelist and literary critic André Billy.[11]

---

[8] While Buber's writings appeared mostly in the Zionist press, *Foi et réveil* also published an excerpt from his *Legends of the Ba'al Shem Tov* in 1927. See Martin Buber, 'Le Livre de prière (légende du Baal-Schem)', *Foi et réveil*, 27 (1927), 44–8. I. L. Peretz and Sholem Asch were the Yiddish writers most often translated into French in the inter-war years. Between 1927 and 1929, Peretz's stories appeared in almost every issue of the *Revue littéraire juive*. These included selections from his *Folkstimlekhe geshikhtn* (1909) and *Hsidish* (1911), as well as earlier stories such as 'La Rose' ('Di Royz', 1894) and 'Paroles sous la lune' ('Di Levone Derseylt', from *Kleyne Mayses Far Groyse Mentchn* (1894)). Pre-Second World War translations of Sholem Asch into French include *La Chaise électrique*, *Pétersbourg*, and *Le Juif aux psaumes*. For a complete list of Yiddish literature translated into French, see the bibliography compiled by Ksiazenicer and Ertel, *Une maisonnette au bord de la Vistule, et autres nouvelles du monde yiddish*. The folklorist Raymond Geiger, who had introduced Morris Rosenfeld's poetry to *La Phalange* and *Pages libres* in the pre-war years, continued to translate his writings for *L'Echo sioniste*, *Chalom*, and *Menorah* in the 1920s, and both Edmond Fleg and Ovadia Cahmy, the editor of *Menorah*, translated the Hebrew poetry of Hayim Nahman Bialik as well as the essays of the Zionist writer and activist Ahad Ha'am.

[9] The play was translated into French as part of the Rieder series in 1927.

[10] 'Le Dibbouk au studio des Champs Elysées', *L'Univers israélite* (27 Jan. 1928), 591–2.

[11] As Billy explained in his preface to a post-war edition of the trilogy, he based the novels on details of Jewish history and culture that Twersky, whom he had met at an artist's studio in

The novels recount the adventures of Ménaché and his wife Havele, first in tsarist Russia, then in Paris, and finally in England during the First World War. 'Collect . . . innumerable descriptions of the tragic-comic episodes of the most remote Jewish communities in Russia and parade before us pictur-esque characters from all the Jewish communities of Europe', a reviewer for *L'Univers israélite* remarked, 'and you will get an idea of the extreme pleasure that even the reader most removed from Judaism gets from reading this realistic and undoubtedly true story.'[12]

In the early 1920s *Foi et réveil* published a series of sketches by Fanny Frenkel, a young woman who had left Poland as a child, describing her return to her native village after the First World War.[13] Many of the stories depict the suffering and poverty of the local population, while others evoke a nostalgic image of a world that still moved to the rhythm of Jewish ritual and tradition. In a series entitled 'Silhouettes polonaises', Frenkel introduces us to Riwka, a 6-year-old girl too hungry to play, as well as two beggars: a young man who prefers to study Talmud rather than work and an old man too weary to even notice when Frenkel gives him money. Her 'Silhouettes juives', which appeared several months later, are more playful in character, evoking themes such as the complications of keeping kosher and the piety of children brought up within the strictures of Jewish tradition.[14]

While most of the picturesque Jewish literature of this period describes life in the Ashkenazi world, several authors of Sephardi origin achieved prominence. Elissa Rhaïs wrote novels and short stories about Jewish life in her native Algeria, told in the style of an oral storyteller. 'We are terribly fond of exoticism in France', a reviewer for the *Mercure de France* remarked of Rhaïs's 1920 novel, *Saâda la Marocaine*: 'Mme Elissa Rhaïs, who has barely arrived from Algeria, has had such success in literary society that one wants to give her all the prizes.' It was her ability to describe the North African Jew-ish milieu in minute detail and make it come alive for French readers, the reviewer concluded, that accounted for her success.[15]

Montparnasse, provided him with. According to Billy, Twersky had in fact collaborated in a similar manner on a number of other 'Jewish novels' but had always insisted on remaining anonymous. In particular, he suggested that Twersky's father, a 'rabbin miraculeux', was the model for one of the characters in the Tharaud brothers' 1920 novel, *Un Royaume de Dieu*. See the preface to *Le Fléau du savoir* (pp. i–viii). Billy dedicated this edition to the memory of Twer-sky, who committed suicide on the day the Germans marched into Paris. The only other book for which Twersky is named as a co-author is Twersky and Guédy, *Israël à New York*.

[12] Georges Huisman in *L'Univers israélite* (7 Oct. 1927), 79.
[13] As the author explains in a short preface, she left Poland at the age of 10 and was 18 when she returned to visit. See 'Silhouettes polonaises', *Foi et réveil*, 17 (1922), 245–52.
[14] 'Silhouettes juives', *Foi et réveil*, 21 (1923), 247–55.
[15] Rhaïs, *Saâda la Marocaine*. See *Le Mercure de France* (15 Jan. 1920), 472. Elissa Rhaïs was

Albert Cohen, the author associated with the Jewish renaissance of the 1920s who left the most lasting impact on French literature, was also of Sephardi origin.[16] His first novel, *Solal*, was published in 1930. The first half of the book, which tells the story of a Greek Jew who immigrates to Paris, is set in the city of Salonica, and through Cohen's vivid descriptions we learn of the religious customs, dress, and outlook of Greek Jews.[17] A. H. Navon,[18] another Ottoman Jew, similarly punctuated his 1925 novel *Joseph Pérez: Juif du ghetto* with colourful descriptions of Sephardi culture and tradition, including, for example, a description of a ceremony designed to ward off evil spirits that is performed at the time of Joseph's circumcision, as well as a lengthy description of the bar mitzvah ceremony and its significance.[19]

In a review of Edmond Fleg's 1925 translation for the Rieder series of Sholem Aleichem's *Tevye der Milkhiker*, entitled *L'Histoire de Tévié*,[20] Benjamin Crémieux remarked approvingly that Yiddish literature enabled

in fact a pen name for Rosine Boumedine, who was born into a modest Algerian Jewish family in 1876. Her youthful marriage to a rabbi, with whom she had three children, ended in divorce in 1914. Her second marriage, to a wealthy merchant, brought her first to Algiers, where she held a salon and charmed her guests with her stories, then eventually to Paris, where she arrived in 1919 and immediately interested the publisher Plon in *Saâda la Marocaine*. In order to create an exotic aura around Boumedine, Plon changed her name and spread the rumour that she had been brought up in a harem. This in turn led to multiple speculations as to her actual biography and origins. In a short essay written in 1929, for example, André Spire described Rhaïs, whom he admired greatly, as the daughter of a Muslim mother and a Jewish father, who came to Paris because she was 'ruined by the war', a version of events that I have found no reference to elsewhere. See Spire, 'Elissa Rhaïs', in *Souvenirs à bâtons rompus*, 248–55. On Rhaïs and the scandal surrounding her origins and biography, see Bitton, *Présences féminines juives en France*, 200–2.

[16] Cohen's oeuvre, unlike that of most 1920s writers on Jewish themes, has entered the canon of high French literature. He is the subject of two biographies—Blot, *Albert Cohen*, and Valbert, *Albert Cohen, le seigneur*—as well as a body of literary criticism centred around the *Cahiers Albert Cohen*. In his recent study, *Albert Cohen: Dissonant Voices*, however, Abecassis focuses on what he calls 'the Cohen paradox': while Cohen is generally categorized as among the most important French writers of the 20th century, his works are not widely translated and have inspired relatively little scholarly attention. For Abecassis, the fact that Jewishness is at the very centre of all of Cohen's writings is a primary factor in understanding this relative marginality.   [17] Page references to *Solal* are to the reprinted text in Cohen, *Œuvres*.

[18] Navon is identified as the director of the Ecole Normale d'Auteuil in *Menorah*, where he published a short story describing an incident from his childhood in an unnamed city in the Ottoman empire. See A. H. Navon, 'Souvenirs des temps jadis', *Menorah* (1 Mar. 1930), 68–9.

[19] As noted in Chapter 6, the fiction of Ryvel (Raphaël Lévy), a rabbi and teacher at one of the Alliance schools in Tunis, was published in *Paix et droit* in 1929. Ryvel published several collections of stories set within the pious and often superstitious world of the Tunisian ghetto. These included *La Hara conte: Folklore judéo-tunisien* and *L'Enfant de l'oukala et autres contes de la Hara*. This collection includes stories dedicated to both Maurice Liber ('L'Aveugle') and André Spire ('Le Miracle').

[20] Fleg chose to translate this book into Judaeo-French, the dialect of Alsatian Jews, rather than standard French.

French Jews to connect with the regionalist revival on their own terms. This literature, he noted, 'provides us with exactly the same range of characters that we would find in regionalist literature: heroes chosen from the poor artisans and peasants of Poland and the Ukraine, anecdotes that are folkloric in style and most often drawn from the most mundane life experiences, with a tone that is always humorous and often satirical'.[21] Gaston Baty expressed his reasons for producing a French version of the *Dybbuk* in similar terms: the play, 'a work of mystical beauty', he explained, represented for him 'the traditional Israelite soul' in the same way that Paul Claudel's plays were representative of the Catholic soul.[22] As these comments indicate, Jewish folklore helped to 'normalize' the position of the Jews in French society by conveying the social and cultural basis for Jewish difference: like any other 'regional' group, Jews had a distinct set of character traits and cultural traditions that had grown out of their particular history and experience.

The primary appeal of Yiddish literature for French Jewish readers was that it provided a window into the world of the east European shtetl where, in contrast to contemporary French society, Judaism pervaded all aspects of life. For a reviewer of *L'Histoire de Tévié* in *L'Univers israélite*, for example, what was most interesting about the story was its penetrating portrait of the state of mind of Tevye, a pious and simple Jew who functions within a completely Jewish universe.[23] In a 1929 article for *L'Univers israélite* André Spire suggested, in a similar vein, that the appeal of both Israel Zangwill's fiction and the Yiddish writers Sholem Abramovitsh (Mendele Moykher Sforim), I. L. Peretz, and Sholem Aleichem was that they were able to combine tragedy and comedy in a way only possible for someone who had grown up in a wholly Jewish environment. This kind of honesty, he concluded, was impossible for French authors who might write on Jewish themes but who had never 'seen, breathed the light, the shadows, the atmosphere of a real ghetto'.[24]

Both Zangwill's writings, which were immensely popular in France in the 1920s,[25] and modern Yiddish literature could be read on many levels.

[21] Crémieux, literary supplement of *L'Univers israélite* (23 Oct. 1925), 19.

[22] 'Le Dibbouk au studio des Champs Elysées', 591–2. René Wisner, a literary critic for *Menorah*, praised Baty's production as the attempt of a Catholic mystic to gain a better understanding of Jewish mysticism and, by extension, a symbol of the spirit of Christian–Jewish unity of the day. The French audience, he noted, watched the play with great respect. 'Le Dibbouk', *Menorah* (15 Feb. 1928), 55.

[23] U.C., 'L'Histoire de Tévié', *L'Univers israélite*, literary supplement (22 May 1925), 248.

[24] See André Spire, *L'Univers israélite* (4 Jan. 1929), 517–19. Joseph Milbauer similarly emphasized the 'tragi-comic' aspect of Zangwill's *Comédies du ghetto* in *Palestine* (Apr. 1929), 190.

[25] Almost all of Zangwill's books were translated into French. The Israel Zangwill Committee, presided over by André Spire, was created after Zangwill's death in 1928 and counted

These writers had, for the most part, abandoned religious practice and embraced socialism and Jewish nationalism as adults, but their fiction nevertheless aimed to preserve and transmit the cultural heritage of the traditional Jewish world that they had grown up in. At the same time, however, these writers were very critical of the outlook and traditions of 'ghetto' Jews, and often made them the object of parody and biting satire in their fiction. Contemporary French critics hailed Peretz's *Bontché le silencieux* (*Bontche Schweig*), for example, as a welcome counterpoint to the Western stereotype of the Jew as urban and middle-class, and praised Peretz for providing an authentic image of Jewish ghetto society little known to either Jews or Christians in the Western world.[26]

As Ken Frieden notes, however, the story, which describes the quiet, suffering life of an impoverished shtetl Jew, can be read in a variety of different lights: while some readers appreciated it as 'folklore'—a window on to the world-view of a pious east European Jew—others understood it as an attack on the values of traditional Jewish religious culture.[27] In his discussion of Israel Zangwill's fiction, Joseph Udelson similarly notes that though Zangwill provided readers with 'folkloric' details about Jewish culture and tradition, he did not present a nostalgic or romanticized image of Jewish ghetto life. Rather, his literature was very critical of the insular Jewish world that he had left behind, and often betrayed a strong tension between his desire for Jewish self-affirmation and for assimilation.[28] As these analyses suggest, the appeal of this kind of writing for French Jews in the 1920s was perhaps twofold. At the same time as providing an image of an apparently authentic Jewish world, it dealt with many of the same issues—the weight of tradition, the temptations of 'universal' culture versus the pull of one's Jewish heritage—with which they were struggling in contemporary France.[29]

among its membership close to thirty prominent Jewish artists and writers of the day. See 'Un comité Israel Zangwill', *L'Univers israélite* (30 Nov. 1928), 69. This French group was a branch of the English Zangwill Committee, which established a prize to be awarded to an emerging Jewish savant, writer, or artist. Lord Reading, the head of the English committee, *L'Univers israélite* noted, correctly reasoned that France, 'where Zangwill had so many admirers and disciples', would be very supportive of this idea. An announcement of Zangwill's death in the *Mercure de France* (15 July 1926), 248–9, which described his literature as 'satirical, humorous, and sociological all at once', included a list of over thirty of his publications.

[26] This short story appeared in French in 1914 as part of a collection, *Bontché le silencieux et autres contes juifs*, with a preface by Pierre Mille. This was the first book of Yiddish fiction to be translated into French. See M. R. Gustalla's review in *Foi et réveil* (May 1914), 96. Gustalla would later become the head of Chema Israël in Marseilles.

[27] Frieden, *Classic Yiddish Fiction*, 288.   [28] Udelson, *Dreamer of the Ghetto*.

[29] As noted in Chapter 1, it was Zangwill's story 'Chad-gad-ya', which focuses on a modern Jew's inability to bridge the gap between his Jewish heritage and his attachment to secular European culture, that had such an impact on André Spire and other Jewish intellectuals in the years before the First World War.

A common denominator in literature on Jewish themes in Weimar Germany was an image of the assimilated 'non-Jewish' German Jew, most often portrayed as uprooted and torn between antisemitism and self-denial. Plagued by mounting antisemitism and a sense of the impossibility of being both German and Jewish, many authors and readers found refuge in counter-images of 'authentic' Jewish types—whether east European, Oriental, or historical.[30] While French Jews were also attracted to fiction describing Jews in historical settings and foreign locales, some commentators expressed concern that this genre of literature presented a one-sided image of Jewish life. In a 1927 article for the *Revue littéraire juive*, for example, Pierre Paraf remarked that the literature of 'Peretz, Sholem Asch, Sholem Aleichem, and Bialik shows us the living cemetery of Judaism with its mysticism, its ghosts . . . and the shadow of pogroms on its walls'.[31] Though he was an enthusiastic supporter of the Zionist movement and frequently emphasized Jewish uniqueness in his writings, Paraf did not consider the shtetl Jew, whose life was shaped by persecution and isolation from the surrounding society, to represent an 'authentic' Judaism. Rather, he impressed upon his readers, French Jews' experience of integration and acceptance by the wider society was an equally compelling example of the Jewish experience in the modern world.

French Jewish Writers

At a conference of the Société des Etudes Juives on 23 March 1907, writer Robert Dreyfus referred to a conversation he had had with Maurice Barrès several years before.[32] Barrès, he noted, had expressed his surprise that so few French Jews had written the folklore of their own people using 'personal instincts, childhood memories, family papers, in order to depict the Jewish soul in the work of the imagination, just as he was doing for the soul of Lorraine'.[33] The first twentieth-century French Jewish writer to show this kind of concern with historical and cultural transmission was undoubtedly

---

[30] Brenner, *The Renaissance of Jewish Culture in Weimar Germany*, ch. 5.

[31] Paraf, 'Montaigne et l'esprit juif', *Revue littéraire juive* (Dec. 1927), 823.

[32] Société des Etudes Juives, *Actes et conférences*, 53 (1907), pp. xlviii–xlix. The lecture, entitled 'Alexandre Weill ou le prophète du Faubourg St. Honoré', was originally published in the *Revue des études juives* in 1907 and subsequently as part of the collection 'Vue des hommes obscurs' in *Les Cahiers de la Quinzaine*, 9/9 (1908). Citations are taken from the second publication.

[33] Ibid. 13. It was Barrès's comment, however, that inspired Dreyfus to write his essay on Alexandre Weill, who was in fact one of a small group of Alsatian Jews who wrote about Jewish life in their native villages. Weill's writings and their relationship to the body of Jewish folklore that emerged in the 1920s are addressed below.

Jean-Richard Bloch, whose 1918 novel *...et Cie* is peppered with Yiddish expressions and references to Jewish holidays and religious practices meticulously explained to readers in the footnotes. In the 1920s numerous other French-language novels, plays, and short stories similarly sought to convey the distinctiveness and colour of Jewish history and culture.

The most prominent French Jewish folklorist of the day was Armand Lunel, a member of the Jewish community of Avignon, which traced its roots back to the medieval papal protectorate.[34] A graduate of the Ecole Normale and professor of philosophy, Lunel began writing fiction in the mid-1920s.[35] In an essay written in 1938 as part of a tribute to André Spire, Lunel reflected on the influence of reading Spire's *Quelques Juifs* on his own decision to write the folklore of the Jews of Provence. Spire's insistence that Jews have a distinct history and culture of which they should be proud, Lunel recalled, sparked his interest in a great-uncle of his, 'a colourful *shnorrer* from Provence',[36] who was in fact the inspiration for Isaac de Pampelune, a character in his first novel, *L'Imagerie du cordier*. A playful, folkloristic interest in the Jews of the Midi was the defining characteristic of Lunel's fiction, which was acclaimed in both the Jewish community and the wider French literary world. His 1926 novel *Esther de Carpentras*, a modern version of a Provençal *purimspiel*,[37] first appeared in instalments in *Europe*, a progressive journal founded by French Zionist sympathizers in 1923, and served as the libretto for an *opéra bouffe* by the prominent composer Darius Milhaud, who was also from an old Jewish family in Provence.

Lunel's best-known novel was *Nicolo-Peccavi, ou l'affaire Dreyfus à Carpentras*, which won the Renaudot literary prize in 1926, the first time, according to Wladimir Rabinovitch, that a major literary prize had been awarded to such a 'profoundly Jewish work'.[38] The title character Nicolo-Peccavi, a staunch Catholic and leader of the anti-Dreyfusard movement, discovers that he is in fact the descendant of a Jewish convert. He is maligned and misunderstood by both the Christian and Jewish communities, and ends his life as an itinerant salesman, like his great-grandfather, the first in the family to convert to Catholicism. Lunel's narrative alternates between the

---

[34] It traced its origins to the 12th century, when the papacy was located in Avignon. Jews within the papal city were considered subjects of the pope rather than the king of France. While they were subject to special laws and restrictions, they were free of the threat of expulsion and thus enjoyed an unusual degree of communal stability.

[35] For more information on Lunel, see Jessula, 'Armand Lunel'.

[36] Lunel, 'André Spire et notre génération'. Lunel recalled that he had intended to interview his uncle, but that he had died before he had a chance to do so.

[37] The original Provençal version of this play, which re-enacted the biblical story of Esther, was entitled *La Tragédie d'Esther* and written in 1774.

[38] Rabi, *Anatomie du judaïsme français*, 103.

crisis that Peccavi faces in the midst of the Dreyfus affair in *fin-de-siècle* France and a history of the papal Jewish community, describing the hardships that it faced: economic restrictions, forced baptisms, and a dress code, most notably the obligatory wearing of a distinctive yellow hat. At the same time, however, Lunel gives his readers a feeling for these Jews' strong sense of solidarity and their disdain for the surrounding population, which remains largely hostile even when the Jews become their theoretical equals in the aftermath of the revolution.[39] While this community came to share many of the cultural traditions and customs of the non-Jewish population over the course of the following century, it nonetheless maintained a strong sense of independence and pride in its particular history. In the novel this comes across very strongly in the character of Abramet, who sets up a kind of informal museum in his home featuring 'a unique marvel, a yellow Jewish hat hung as proudly from the ceiling as a cardinal's hat might hang in a cathedral'.[40]

For critics of the day, the book's merit lay above all in the detailed information that it provided about the history and culture of the Jews of Carpentras. 'The author takes the pretext of a dramatic plot in order to interest us in the Jewish ghettos of the Holy See', noted a reviewer in the *Nouvelle Revue française*, who went on to speculate that the aspect of the novel that would be of greatest interest to Jewish readers would be the documentation of Jewish family life in the region.[41] Abramet, along with many other figures in the story, is based on a real person from Carpentras at the turn of the century, as Jules Bauer noted in his review of the novel for *Foi et réveil*: 'All the people from Carpentras who knew Abramet will be delighted to read *Nicolo-Peccavi*. And those who have never lived [there] will at least have a taste of [Lunel's] literary talent and the art with which he evokes both the melancholy and picturesque aspect of our past.'[42]

In the 1920s, several collections of Jewish stories and fables were published in French. In some instances, these focused on a particular theme or group of writings, such as Lupus Blumenfeld's *Anthologie des conteurs yiddish* and Léon Berman's *Contes du Talmud*.[43] Both Edmond Fleg and Gustave Kahn assembled collections which took a much broader approach, combining diverse elements of Jewish literature and folklore into single anthologies or collections of writings. The first edition of Fleg's *Anthologie juive*, commissioned by Georges Crès for a series of anthologies on literature and religion, appeared in 1923.[44] Fleg's collection, which assembled a wide variety of

---

[39] *Nicolo-Peccavi*, 109.   [40] Ibid. 127.   [41] Cited in *L'Univers israélite* (10 Dec. 1926), 425.
[42] Bauer, *Foi et réveil*, 27 (1927), 62.   [43] Both titles appeared in the Rieder series.
[44] See Berg, 'Traducteur parce qu'anthologiste', 37. A Catholic anthology was compiled by Abbé Henri Bremon and Père Vallery-Radot, and a Protestant collection by Raoul Allier.

Jewish texts in translation—passages from the Bible and Talmud, modern Hebrew and Yiddish poetry, a segment of Henri Franck's *La Danse devant l'arche*—was published to great critical acclaim. The book's pedagogical value was greatly enhanced by the extensive notes that Fleg provided for each passage he included.[45]

Despite this pedagogical approach, the *Anthologie*, like *Ecoute Israël*, represented a very different kind of Jewish scholarship to that undertaken by the Wissenschaft scholars in the nineteenth century. These volumes do not speak to scholars but rather were intended to make Jewish history and folklore accessible to a broader audience. Jewish religious leaders of the day greatly appreciated this approach. In a discussion of the anthology in the *Review des études juives*, for example, Julien Weill, while pointing to the inaccuracy of certain of Fleg's biblical translations, praised the collection as a kind of 'talmudic gospel' that definitively illustrated the vitality of Jewish thought throughout the ages.[46] One of the original features of both the anthology and *Ecoute Israël* was their juxtaposition of stories, poems, and legends from biblical times to the present, creating a picture of Judaism and Jewish history as a cohesive whole. Reflecting on the guiding theme of the anthology almost thirty years after it was originally published, Fleg said: 'The Jewish people has traversed so many eras, lived among so many peoples, it speaks all languages, and though it has always linked its own story with that of humanity as a whole, it has never completely separated the religious from the profane, the moral from the sacred in its meditations.'[47]

We see a similar interest in evoking a connection between Jews of different eras and regions in Gustave Kahn's *Contes juifs*, which included both biblical stories and tales set in the pre-modern and contemporary Ashkenazi world.[48] In this collection we find stories on the biblical figures of Jephthah, Dinah, Boaz, and Isaac, on the pre-modern shtetls of Alsace and eastern and central Europe, and on Jewish life in modern France, Vienna, Holland, and Russia. Despite the geographical range of Kahn's *Contes*, a reviewer for *L'Univers israélite* noted, the book 'leaves us with the satisfying taste of regional literature'.[49] In an era in which regional literature, folklore, and tales set in foreign, 'exotic' lands were all very much in vogue, this post-war

---

[45] See 'L'Anthologie juive de M. Fleg et la critique', *L'Univers israélite* (31 Aug. 1923), 566–9, and *Paix et droit* (Nov. 1923), 12.   [46] 'L'Anthologie juive de M. Fleg', 566–7.

[47] Algazi, 'Un entretien avec Edmond Fleg', 106.

[48] Only one story in *Contes juifs*, 'La Sagesse du rabbin', takes place in a Sephardi setting—the Jewish community of Sousse in modern Tunisia.

[49] Marius Lorar, '*Les Contes juifs* de M. Gustave Kahn', supplement to *L'Univers israélite* (1 Jan. 1926), 62.

wave of Jewish writing, from Yiddish literature in translation to Lunel, Fleg, and Kahn, resonated among many French Jews.[50]

This wave of Jewish folklore or 'regionalist' literature bears certain similarities to an earlier genre of romantic writing and art that developed in both France and Germany in the mid-nineteenth century. From as early as the 1830s, writers such as Alexandre Weill, Daniel Stauben (Auguste Widal), and Georges Stenne wrote novels and short stories set in rural Alsatian villages.[51] The objective of these early Alsatian Jewish writers who themselves grew up in traditional homes, Richard Cohen argues, was to render a sympathetic portrait of traditional Jewish life and customs as they existed in pre-modern times. Cohen characterizes this genre of fiction as 'a dialogue with a vanishing world'.[52] Envisioning a future where traditional Judaism would disappear completely, certain newly urbanized Jewish writers and artists felt a duty to represent it for future generations. Creating a nostalgic image of Jewish ghetto life, Cohen suggests, enabled nineteenth-century folklorists such as Weill and Stauben to counter a sense of disorientation and emptiness that resulted from their rapid integration into modern European society.

Like the earlier Alsatian folklore, Jewish writing in the 1920s betrayed a strong concern with the act of cultural and historical transmission. Jewish writers who came of age in the late nineteenth and early twentieth centuries, however, had grown up for the most part in secular, urban settings. To the extent that they did seek to represent traditional Jewish life, they did so as a way of reconnecting with a Jewish past outside the realm of their own personal experience. Rather than depicting a 'dying world', they wanted to create a usable past for those contemporary French Jews who, like their non-Jewish counterparts, were eager to reconnect with the history and culture of their ancestors. Just as French folklorists evoked the bond between modern French citizens and their ancestors from Provence or Brittany, Fleg and Kahn sought to create a mythic heritage for urbanized French Jews.

For many Jewish writers, the vogue for Jewish themes in French literary and intellectual circles provided an opportunity to counter traditional stereotypes about Jews and convey the history, values, concerns, and traditions of Judaism and the Jewish people to the French public. In an interview in *L'Univers israélite* in 1927, the novelist Josué Jéhouda explained that he had decided to focus exclusively on Jewish themes in his literature 'because I

[50] On the emergence of the academic discipline of folklore studies, see Lebovics, *True France*, 136. On the prominence of regionalist literature in France in the 1920s, see Thiesse, 'Le Mouvement littéraire régionaliste, 1900–1945'.

[51] See Richard Cohen, 'Nostalgia and "Return to the Ghetto"'. Cohen's article treats this theme in both German and French Jewish art and fiction.   [52] Ibid. 135.

believe I understand this people that everyone is talking about so much today and, in my opinion, remains misunderstood by western Jews as well as Christians. If, after having read my literature, the reader understands Jews a little bit better, I will not have worked in vain.'[53] Jacob Lévy, the author of *Les Juifs d'aujourd'hui*, expressed a similar sense of mission: 'the source of anti-semitism is the non-Jews' total ignorance of the Jewish mentality. To help us better understand each other: this is my agenda.'[54] Convinced that anti-semitism was waning precisely because Jews and Christians were coming to know and understand each other better, Lévy, Jéhouda, and many other Jew-ish authors of the day saw their own fiction as part of this process of rap-prochement and reconciliation.

In each volume of *Les Juifs d'aujourd'hui*, Lévy, an art expert and critic whose real name was Gaston Edinger,[55] explored a different stratum of the contemporary Parisian Jewish community. The first, *Les Pollaks*, focuses on the rivalry between native and immigrant Jews. The second, *Les Demi-Juifs*, is the story of the son of a Catholic mother and a Jewish father who struggles to define his own identity, while the third, *Les Doubles-Juifs*, focuses on an Orthodox Jewish family in contemporary Paris. The trilogy's connecting thread is a family of the Parisian haute bourgeoisie whose patriarch, Samuel Springer, is a prominent art dealer and observant Jew. One of Lévy's con-cerns in writing about the Springer family is to put their religious practices and beliefs, which could be read as superficial or hypocritical, into their social and historical context. The opening scene of *Les Pollaks* serves as a vehicle to distinguish Jewish and Christian religious culture. In the course of his sermon, the rabbi of the Synagogue de la Victoire, frequented primarily by the Parisian Jewish elite, laments the fact that so few members of the con-gregation attend services on a regular basis. Samuel's sons, we soon learn, are examples of this phenomenon. Though they go to synagogue to please their father, they do not believe in God. Rather than presenting this state of affairs in an entirely negative light, however, Lévy gives his readers a sympa-thetic impression of the Springer family. While such behaviour might appear hypocritical from a Christian perspective, in which faith is of critical

[53] 'Un quart d'heure avec Josué Jéhouda', *L'Univers israélite* (21 Oct. 1927), 142.

[54] Lévy, *Les Juifs d'aujourd'hui* (1925–7), vol. iii: *Les Doubles-Juifs*, p. vii. An additional volume, *Les Chrétiens*, was published in 1928.

[55] As Edinger he was the co-author of a guide to ancient ceramics, the *Dictionnaire pratique de céramique ancienne*, published by Albin Michel in 1925. Edinger may also have been the author of sixteen novels published between 1917 and 1935 under the pseudonym Sheridan, and there is some speculation that he also penned *Mon Rabbin chez les riches* as Pierre Samuël. See the cross-references for Jacob Lévy in the catalogue of the Bibliothèque Nationale de France and the Library of Congress.

importance, the Springer sons' decision to continue to go through the motions of religious ritual, Lévy explains, grows out of the strength of the Jewish family and respect for tradition, both essential aspects of Judaism. Samuel, in turn, knows that his sons are not religious at heart but is nonetheless content that they spare him the pain of openly admitting it. Despite their lack of religious faith, Lévy goes on to assure his readers, both sons respect Judaism as a broad philosophical system. Jews have their own way of relating to their religious heritage, Lévy wants to impress upon the reader, which should not be dismissed as hypocritical or devoid of spirituality by using the yardstick of Christian religious thinking.

In Edmond Cahen's novel *Juif, non! . . . Israélite*, Simon Lévy, a Jewish army officer, constantly surprises his Christian wife Suzanne by failing to conform to her prejudices. Whereas she remembers the Jews from her home town of Toulouse as swarthy and obsequious, Suzanne is taken with Simon's blond hair, blue eyes, and discreet personal style. When she confronts him with this discrepancy he explains passionately that most French Jews, like himself, are indistinguishable from the broader population: unfortunately, she and the rest of gentile society only 'see' those Jews who exhibit distinctive physical or moral traits.[56] Suzanne is further intrigued to learn that Lévy has left Paris and the promise of a successful future in politics to follow the very 'French' career of a gentleman farmer in the south of France. She is also delighted to discover that he is much more generous with his money than her former husband: 'another one of my old prejudices against the Jewish people', she remarks, 'that crumbled away'.[57]

Many authors aimed to give their readers a sense of the diversity and complexity of contemporary Jewish society by presenting a wide range of Jewish personalities and types. Lily Jean-Javal, a Parisian-born *femme de lettres* and Zionist activist who came from a French Jewish family of long standing,[58] presents us with a host of Jewish characters in her novels *Noémi* and *L'Inquiète*, the saga of a young Jewish woman from the south of France. Noémi Valdès is a young woman from a wealthy Jewish family in the southern

---

[56] *Juif, non!... Israélite*, 80.   [57] Ibid. 93.

[58] Lily Jean-Javal was born Lily Lévy to a mother who traced her origins to the Comtadine papal protectorate. Both her father, an engineer, and her husband, an industrialist who served as a deputy in the *département* of Yonne, hailed from the Alsatian Jewish bourgeoisie. Lily never remarried after her husband, Jean Javal, was killed in action during the First World War. She used the name Lily Jean-Javal for the many novels, essays, collections of poetry, and stories for children that she wrote in the inter-war years. A regular contributor to *L'Univers israélite*, *Menorah*, and *L'Appui français*, she was a member of the Zionist fundraising organization Keren Hayesod, and lectured widely on her 1930 trip to Palestine, which she also wrote about in the Jewish press. On Jean-Javal see Bitton, *Présences féminines juives en France*, 203–5, and Eladan, *Poètes juifs de langue française*, 101–5.

city of Bayonne, whose Jewish community dates back to the fifteenth century. Her grandfather is a modern prophet who successfully combines traditional Judaism with a strong commitment to humanitarian universalism. Her cousin Joseph, a young rabbi who writes letters to Noémi complaining about assimilation and intermarriage among the younger generation, represents the choice of generational continuity. Radical assimilation is presented in the character of Lazare, a cousin who has moved to the United States and converted to Christianity.

A similar panorama of Jewish personalities colours the fiction of Josué Jéhouda. Born into a hasidic family in the Ukraine, Jéhouda settled in Geneva in 1912 after travelling extensively through central Europe and the Middle East. In the post-war years, he divided his time between Paris and Geneva and became a prominent figure on the Parisian Jewish literary scene.[59] In Jéhouda's two-volume novel *La Tragédie d'Israël* we find both a simple, pious Russian Jew who would never think to question Jewish tradition and a modern rabbi who studies world religions in order to better understand the 'true mission' of Judaism. Esther is a virtuous young wife who takes responsibility for perpetuating Jewish tradition in the home. Her husband Joseph, who no longer has any religious faith, translates his commitment to Jewish tradition into support for Zionism. Rachel, a family friend, casts off the yoke of tradition and sets out for Paris to try her chances as a musician, while her sister Miriam remains at home, reading spiritualist literature and experiencing a personal sense of Jewish rebirth. The cynical modern Jew is conveyed through the character of Goldglaub, who leads David, the novel's protagonist, down the path of materialism. The secular French 'Israelite' is represented through the character of Lucien Dreyfus, for whom Judaism is simply a confession in which he no longer believes.

Generational Conflict: Towards a 'Spiritual' Judaism

In Jewish fiction in the 1920s we see a new character type emerging: the spiritually oriented young French Jew, torn between the need to carve out an individual identity and maintain a link with Jewish tradition. While some authors created male characters that fitted this model, this 'new spiritual Jew' was most often a young woman. Jean-Javal's Noémi is exemplary of this type. Disenchanted with her family's materialistic values and the limited options open to her, she sets out for Paris against her family's wishes to work as a nurse to the poor. While she gets great satisfaction from this, she has

---

[59] For biographical details on Jéhouda, see Raymond-Raoul Lambert's review of *De père en fils* in *Chalom* (Nov. 1927), 25–7.

difficulty integrating into the hierarchical structure of the hospital where she is working, and after a series of adventures, including a failed romance with a Protestant minister and a battle between clerical and anti-clerical elements at 'Le Nid', a school she founds in Paris, Noémi ultimately returns to Bayonne. There she marries Paul Dias, a fellow Jew with a similar family background, and founds a summer camp for disadvantaged Parisian children on her family's estate.

Josué Jéhouda's hero David follows a similar path of revolt and return. Jéhouda, like Jean-Javal, paints David's dissatisfaction in generational terms: 'like all those of his generation', he explains, 'David ardently aspired to an individual existence'.[60] David's revolt takes the opposite form to Noémi's: he is from a poor immigrant family and breaks away by devoting himself to material gain. Ultimately however, he falls ill and realizes the error of his ways; under the influence of two mystically oriented friends, Miriam and Leister, he reconnects with his Jewish heritage and marries Miriam, a pious young woman and the daughter of a rabbi. Both Jean-Javal and Jéhouda created heroes whose central problem is whether or not they can make a successful break with their family in order to carve out lives for themselves unconnected to their Jewish heritage. Ultimately, David, like Noémi, finds that this is impossible. As Miriam and Leister show him while he is in the sanatorium, his illness is in fact a result of his turning his back on Judaism. It is in this section of the novel, entitled 'La Maladie est un bonheur' ('Illness is a Godsend'), that Jéhouda develops a rather eclectic theory that brings biblical and kabbalistic wisdom to bear on tuberculosis: the only way to cure the disease, David's friends explain, is 'to unlock the spiritual force which is in each of us'.[61] Here, Jéhouda shares his anti-rationalist critique of modern society, influenced perhaps by his hasidic background, with the reader: both the quest for material gain and a belief in pure science are flawed ideologies because they do not take into account the needs of the soul, which is in fact the driving force of human existence. For Jéhouda, this spirituality was necessarily linked to one's particular ethnic heritage. Leister tells David the story of an unfortunate Jewish doctor, also the victim of tuberculosis, whose illness grew out of his stubborn search for 'universal' truth. The cause of his illness, Leister explains, is his intellectual generosity, his failure to realize that 'it is only when a Jew becomes a Jew that he can become completely universal. Each individual must have his spiritual home.'[62] In a

---

[60] *La Tragédie d'Israël*, i: *De père en fils*, 66.   [61] *La Tragédie d'Israël*, ii: *Miriam*, 155.

[62] Ibid. 187. The link that Jéhouda makes here between the maintenance of one's ethnic identity and one's physical and mental health was similar to that of the American Jewish writer Ludwig Lewisohn. Lewisohn lived in France from the mid-1920s to the early 1930s, and his novels, memoirs, and essays were widely translated into French. Like Jéhouda, he criticized

similar vein, Noémi can only fulfil her 'universal' dream of helping poor children by renewing her connection with her Jewish heritage: 'Her desire to help her fellow man had not diminished', Jean-Javal explains, 'but she felt she could only regain her strength by returning to the home of her ancestors.'[63]

Simone, a character in Lévy's *Les Juifs d'aujourd'hui*, also combines a strong sense of spirituality with a sense of her Jewish identity: 'I feel Jewish through and through', she explains to her uncle. 'But let us be clear. Not Jewish like the worldly women covered in jewels with whom we are all familiar . . . No, I am Jewish in the largest sense of the word: a moral Jew you might say, in keeping with the scriptures.'[64] Like the Springer sons, Simone does not express her Judaism through traditional religious observance. Rather, she directs this energy towards charitable activity: 'All the faith and mysticism that others bring to religion', Lévy explains, 'Simone offered to the day-care centre she created.'[65] Charitable activity enables Simone to set herself apart from what she perceives as the crass materialism of the previous generation. We see a similar pattern in *Noémi*. Noémi has lost her faith in Jewish religious doctrine and senses an atmosphere of hypocrisy and shallowness among her friends and family, who go through the motions of prayer but are in fact very materialistically oriented. Inspired by the wisdom of her grandfather, who reminds her of 'the tradition of our race transmitted from century to century at the price of many a bloody encounter: the cult of justice',[66] Noémi, like Simone, throws herself into charitable work.

The character of Simon Lévy in *Juif, non!... Israélite* is also very spiritually minded. In one of the opening scenes of the novel Suzanne, who is working as a volunteer nurse, is surprised to find Simon talking with a rabbi, and remarks that she thought that modern Jews had all become atheists. This was true for the previous generation, Simon explains, but 'our generation, the generation that fought in the war, tend to be believers'. As he is preparing for an operation, he goes on to explain, he needs spiritual reassurance: 'at a time when courage is needed, it is not useless to immerse ourselves in the tender beliefs of childhood'.[67] Simon differs from the other young Jewish

melting-pot-style assimilation, favouring instead cultural pluralism. For both authors, however, the maintenance of Jewish distinctiveness was more a matter of destiny than choice: the Jew who attempts assimilation suffers both physically and mentally, because he has betrayed the calling of his inner soul. See in particular Lewisohn's *The Island Within*. His writings were part of a broader trend in American Jewish fiction. Whereas late 19th- and early 20th-century novels on Jewish themes tended to glorify integration, by the early 1920s there was a shift towards narratives focused on the dilemmas posed by absorption. See Fine, 'In the Beginning: American-Jewish fiction, 1880–1930'.

[63] *L'Inquiète*, 240.   [64] *Les Demi-Juifs*, 75.   [65] Ibid. 16.
[66] Ibid. 25–6.   [67] Cahen, *Juif, non!... Israélite*, 55.

characters in that he marries a non-Jew: he does not feel a contradiction between his strong sense of spiritual connection to the Jewish people and his decision to marry Suzanne, a devout Catholic. For Simon, however, inter-marriage does not mean assimilation. His Jewish heritage continues to exer-cise a critical influence on his way of life and mode of thinking throughout the novel, as he frequently explains to his Christian wife. We see this, for example, in his explanation of his decision not to run for public office in a town in the south of France where he manages an agricultural estate. Such a decision, he explains to Suzanne, would force him to give up his career in farming, a profession that is dear to him precisely because he is a Jew: 'The land that I cultivate each day is a testimony to my compatriots', he declares, sure that 'one can be both fully Jewish and fully French'.[68] As Simon explains to Suzanne early on in the novel, his religiosity is not related to the specificity of Jewish religious practice but rather reflects an internal state of being: 'I am intuitively religious; my heart needs to believe. I am strengthened by the idea of the great beyond.'[69] While a generation earlier this sentiment would most likely have led the character to abandon all sense of belonging to the Jewish people, for Simon it is no longer necessary to 'choose' between universalism and particularism. He understands Jewishness as a strong spiritual heritage that will continue to define his actions and sentiments even if he does not marry a Jewish woman or observe Jewish ritual.

This character type embodies many of the ideals espoused by Jewish youth movements of the day. One of the central criticisms that the UUJJ and Chema Israël made of their parents' Judaism was that it was more form than content: they went through the motions of religious observance without any real appreciation of Judaism's spiritual value. An assimilated Jew, Aimé Pal-lière explained in an article for *Chalom*, is someone who hides behind his vacuous assertion of belonging to the Jewish race: though this person might show a preference for Jewish women or socialize primarily with Jews, he has nothing of Jewish value to transmit to his children, who are thus sure of being completely absorbed into the surrounding society.[70] Pallière's critique of 'Franco-Judaism' is similar to that of historian Michael Marrus. Jews often used the language of race to express their sense of solidarity with other Jews, Marrus argues, even as they abandoned religious observance or any kind of cultural activity that would distinguish them as Jews in the public sphere.[71] For Pallière, who defined an 'unassimilated Jew' as someone with either a

[68] Ibid. 261.   [69] Ibid. 56.
[70] Pallière, 'Questions et réponses', *Chalom* (Mar. 1928), 4–7. In the same issue of *Chalom* we find an article by David Berman criticizing the tendency of Jews to 'hide behind the idea of race' rather than actively doing anything to perpetuate Jewish tradition. See 'Le Mysticisme de la race', *Chalom* (Mar. 1928), 7–9.   [71] See Marrus, *The Politics of Assimilation*, ch. 1.

religious or a nationalist commitment to Judaism, what distinguished members of the UUJJ was their commitment to perpetuating Judaism for generations to come.[72]

As we saw in Chapter 6, a number of people expressed concern that the newly created Jewish associations and activities had little in the way of Jewish content and thus did not provide a viable model for perpetuating Jewish identity. Discussions of Jewish literature often revolved around similar themes. Nina Gourfinkel, a regular reviewer for *Palestine*, suggested that the character of Simon Lévy in *Juif, non! ... Israélite* is unrealistic. That someone so thoroughly integrated to the point of having no qualms about intermarriage would continue to have such a strong sense of Jewish identity, she suggested, is scarcely believable: 'that Simon Lévy does not differ from other Frenchmen, so be it. That he does not want to be a Jew, that is his business. But that given this state of affairs he is able to retain the psychological mindset of a Jew is very unrealistic.' Cahen's hero, she concluded, 'is neither a Jew nor an Israelite'.[73] Cahen's position was problematic for Gourfinkel because it assumed that it is possible to preserve one's Jewishness without actively doing anything that distinguishes one as a Jew. In fact, as both she and another reviewer for *L'Univers israélite* suggested,[74] it is exactly this kind of attitude that makes Jews vulnerable to complete assimilation.

Another reviewer for *Palestine* objected to *Pourquoi je suis Juif* in a tone similar to Maurice Liber's critique of André Spire's 'Judaism without religion'. Fleg's tale of the loss and rediscovery of Jewishness, he suggested, was representative of a whole genre of literature characterized by a kind of self-inflated angst. In these writers' tendency to 'flagellate themselves to an exaggerated degree with their "newly discovered" Judaism', the reviewer argued, we see the same kind of psychological mechanism that has led other Jewish intellectuals to a passionate conversion to Catholicism. This kind of Jewish 'rebirth' is fickle, he concluded, and ultimately has little to contribute to Judaism itself.[75]

Beyond Apologetics: Critical Images and Ambivalence

Many Jewish writers in the 1920s were committed to the idea of creating a 'realistic' rather than idealized image of Jewish society, and often conveyed negative as well as positive images of Jewish culture and society in their

[72] See 'Questions et réponses', 6.
[73] Gourfinkel, 'Les Lettres', *Palestine* (June 1930), 67–8.
[74] Ben Eliaquim, 'Commentaires', *L'Univers israélite* (13 June 1930), 295.
[75] 'Revue du mois', *Palestine* (Apr. 1928), 90–1.

fiction. Jacob Lévy's *Les Pollaks*, for example, exposed the prejudice of native Jews against east European immigrants. The novel begins as two young Jewish lawyers, Pierre Springer and Olga Bérinsky, decide to marry, a decision that Pierre's father protests vehemently against. Despite the fact that she grew up in France and attended the Sorbonne, for the elder Springer Olga's immigrant origins make her a 'Pollack' and thus an unfitting mate for his son. Ultimately, Pierre gives in to his father and breaks off the engagement. Meanwhile, Olga falls in love with Dussinger, an artist who is a friend of Pierre and protégé of his father. In the novel's dramatic climax, we learn that Dussinger himself is of east European Jewish origin, but the elder Springer's prejudice has led him to masquerade as a Christian. Lévy presents the novel's central thesis through the device of a conversation between the rabbi at the Synagogue de la Victoire and Dussinger. Posing as a non-Jewish outside observer, Dussinger points to the glaring contradiction between the synagogue's inscription: 'Love your neighbour as yourself' and the actual disdain that French Jews have for their east European brethren.[76]

Les Pollaks created a lively debate in Jewish circles of the day, including a discussion at the Club du Faubourg on the question: 'Is there antagonism between Polish and French Jews?'[77] While some criticized the book for exaggerating antagonism between immigrants and natives,[78] others took its accusations seriously and sought to dispel the prejudices and misconceptions that it exposed. In May 1925 a number of prominent figures in the Jewish community organized a meeting to assert their solidarity with immigrants. Raymond-Raoul Lambert, a reporter for *L'Univers israélite*, implored his fellow Jews to welcome the newcomers as brothers, while Yvonne Netter spoke of the need to study the lives of the immigrants so as to better understand them. Jacques Bielinky, who was himself of east European origin, reminded his readers that the immigrant community comprised not only impoverished itinerant merchants but also educated professionals and artists.[79]

Women often highlighted the sexism of traditional Judaism in their writing. The lack of respect that Noémi receives within the patriarchal milieu of her family, for example, is the major catalyst for her decision to leave it

---

[76] *Les Pollaks*, 52–3.

[77] See 'On parle trop de nous', *L'Univers israélite* (13 Mar. 1925), 577.

[78] A reviewer for *Foi et réveil*, for example, suggested that the book posed this conflict in too extreme terms: 'We can criticize the author for having taken offhand comments seriously, and having made a thesis out of them'. Auber, '*Les Pollaks*', *Foi et réveil*, 22/3 (1925), 64.

[79] See the article by Jacques Bielinky on this meeting, which took place at the Salle du Journal, in *L'Univers israélite* (29 May 1925), 204–6. The poet Pierre Créange referred to the controversy that the novel sparked in 'Les Juifs polonais... et les autres' in *Epîtres aux Juifs*.

behind and strike out on her own. The most common stereotype associated with Jews, however, was that of materialism and *arrivisme*. We see this image in the portrayal of Noémi's situation and in Sarah Lévy's 1930 novel *O mon goye!*, both of which portray female protagonists struggling to free themselves from what they perceive as the superficial, materialist nature of the Jewish world into which they have been born. Both of these novels convey a negative picture of bourgeois Jewish women. Noémi's mother and aunts are concerned with little else than preserving their privileged lifestyle and marrying their daughters to wealthy men. In *O mon goye!* Sarah Lévy describes the typical Jewish wife as over-controlling and obsessed with her husband's business success: the first thing she utters when he arrives home is 'How much?'[80]

Characters in these novels display a profoundly ambivalent attitude towards being Jewish.[81] Noémi is caught between a desire to create a new identity for herself in Paris and a strong sense of connection to her heritage. She associates Jewishness with materialism and sexism, while at the same time crediting her Jewish heritage with giving her a strong will and passion for justice. In *O mon goye!* Sarah Lévy constantly fluctuates between feelings of revulsion and attraction to Judaism and the Jewish people. At some points in the novel, she expresses a sense of relief that her relationship with a non-Jew has freed her from the Parisian Jewish society of her childhood and first marriage, a world peopled by mundane businessmen and their showy, shallow wives. On the other hand, she feels a sense of warmth and honesty among Jews that stands in sharp contrast to the cold, polite, and often hypocritical Christian milieu of her lover. Lévy's characterization of the Jewish wife as obsessively controlling and materialistic, for example, is tempered several paragraphs later by her observation that as a child she learned to hear, in the wife's blunt 'How much?', 'all the love that the wife owes to her husband, all the help he gives her, the support'.[82]

Confident that antisemitism was on the wane in France, many Jewish authors felt no need to censor themselves. Defending his choice of themes, Jacob Lévy argued that Jewish writers would accomplish much more in the cause of Christian–Jewish relations by presenting Jewish society honestly, faults as well as virtues, than if they were to engage simplistically in apologetics. 'Like all other men, the Jew has his faults: is it by ignoring them that they

[80] *O mon goye!*, 162.

[81] Writing about early 20th-century American Jewish fiction, Eric Homberger suggests that, rather than categorizing writers' sometimes negative feelings about being Jewish as 'self-hatred', it is more useful to 'open up a terrain for analysis; not of Jewish "self-hatred" but Jewish ambivalence, the burden of being of two minds about Jewishness itself'. 'Some Uses for Jewish Ambivalence', 168.   [82] *O mon goye!*, 162.

will go away?'[83] Folklorist Raymond Geiger, whose collections of Jewish jokes were perhaps the most widely read Jewish books of the day,[84] expressed a similar sense of confidence. Geiger's anthology, as many critics noted, contained many jokes and vignettes that could easily be considered antisemitic. By far the greatest number of jokes revolve around Jews' 'love of money' and many others touch on subjects such as lack of hygiene or dishonesty in business. For Geiger, however, those who objected to his collection missed its point entirely. His objective in compiling these stories (which, he assured the reader, were drawn from Jewish sources) was, first and foremost, 'to amuse' and, secondly, to make a contribution to the folklore of the Jewish people. 'Whether we like it or not and for very obvious reasons', he asserted, 'Jews are a group of people endowed with a particular set of reactions and character traits. Jewish humour is a fact. Cannot [this collection] serve as contribution to the study of group psychology? Does not such a collection of oral traditions serve the cause of folklore?'[85]

To a certain extent, this author's confidence betrays a strong sense of security about the place of the Jews in French society. At the same time, however, discussion in the Jewish press of the day (as well as the fact, of course, that both Geiger and Lévy felt the need to defend themselves) indicates that their choice of themes raised a number of fears and concerns within the Jewish community. In an article in *L'Univers israélite* in 1925, Jules Meyer, one of the paper's regular columnists, expressed some of his misgivings about the proliferation of Jewish writing and activities:

we French Jews are a bit perturbed by this profusion of public demonstrations of all kinds (novels, plays, films, posters, meetings) . . . And if we are shocked, what must non-Jews think? Certainly, here in France . . . the interest that people are showing in us is friendly. But antisemitism has existed and prospered in France. It has perhaps not said its final word. We must not forget that we are not at an oriental bazaar: we are here in Paris, in France.[86]

Meyer expressed a similar sentiment in his review of Bernard Lecache's 1925 novel *Jacob*, in which Lecache, who was himself born in Paris of immigrant parents, tells the story of the French-born son of Polish immigrants who sacrifices himself at the altar of material success. Lecache, Meyer noted, felt no need to censor his portrait of Jewish society for the outside world.

---

[83] *Les Doubles-Juifs*, p. vii.

[84] *Histoires juives* and *Nouvelles histoires juives*. Crémieux's comment that 'everyone has read Geiger's *Histoires juives*' indicates the popularity of the collection, which went through 104 reprints within a year of its publication.

[85] Geiger, '*Histoires juives*', *La Revue juive* (15 Jan. 1925), 78–9.

[86] Meyer, 'Les Juifs et la littérature', *L'Univers israélite* (30 Oct. 1925), 140–1.

While this may have made for compelling literature it went against common sense: it was not necessary to reveal everything that one felt about Jews in a book aimed at the general public: 'What scientist would dare announce to an ignorant, rowdy crowd that the end of the world is at hand?', he asked by way of analogy.[87] Nina Gourfinkel raised a similar set of objections to the image of Jewish society that the Russian-born author Irène Némirovsky created in her 1929 novel *David Golder*.[88] The novel tells the story of a Russian Jewish immigrant who, like Lecache's character in *Jacob*, is ruined by his obsession with material gain. Though he has achieved great material success, Golder is left at the end of his life with a greedy, spiteful wife and a daughter whose only interest in him is financial. 'Could you not have given your characters some sympathetic qualities to temper the kind of decadent materialism that you are describing?', Gourfinkel asked in an interview with the author, to which Némirovsky simply responded, 'That is how I saw them.'[89] In this exchange we see a young Jewish author's sense of confidence in her choice of theme. Némirovsky, like Lévy, Geiger, and Lecache, felt free to create an image of a certain Jewish milieu 'as she saw it' with no compunction to tailor her writing to any kind of apologist agenda. For Gourfinkel, by contrast, Némirovsky showed bad judgement in including such crass, decadent Jewish characters in a novel aimed at the general public.

Novels such as *Noémi*, *L'Inquiète*, and *La Tragédie d'Israël*, which portrayed protagonists successfully coming to terms with their Jewish heritage, received little critical attention outside Jewish circles. More sensationalist books such as *Jacob*, *David Golder*, *O mon goye!*, and Geiger's *Histoires juives*, by contrast, were widely reviewed, debated at the Club du Faubourg, and in some instances went into multiple editions.[90] This undoubtedly heightened

[87]   Meyer, '*Jacob*', *L'Univers israélite* (27 Nov. 1925), 252.

[88]   Némirovsky was born in Kiev into a cosmopolitan merchant family forced out of Russia by the October Revolution. The family moved to France in 1919, where she studied literature at the Sorbonne. The publication of *David Golder* marked the beginning of a very successful literary career, and she went on to publish five well-received novels in the 1930s. While her two daughters survived the war, both Némirovsky and her husband, neither of whom had French nationality, were murdered at Auschwitz. Fifty years after their death their daughter, Elisabeth Gille, wrote a fictional biography of her mother entitled *Le Mirador*, which was re-edited in 2000 along with a collection of short stories that Némirovsky had published in the French press in the 1930s. Némirovsky's unfinished last novel, *Suite française*, which she wrote in hiding before being arrested in 1942, was recently published with a bibliographical preface by Myriam Anissimov. For a brief biography of Némirovsky, see Bitton, *Présences féminines juives en France*, 230–1.

[89]   Gourfinkel, 'L'Expérience juive d'Irène Némirovsky: Un interview de l'auteur de *David Golder*', *L'Univers israélite* (28 Feb. 1930), 677–8.

[90]   For books debated at the Faubourg, see Appendix I. *Jacob* was reprinted eleven times in the first year of its publication. *David Golder* was republished twice before the Second World

the concern of many Jewish commentators that images of specific families and individuals could easily be misread as paradigms of 'the Jewish personality' or Jewish society. In the broader French press, these novels tended to be understood as representative of Judaism or the Jewish people in general. Reviewers in Jewish journals, by contrast, often suggested that their principal themes could have been explored in a non-Jewish context. A review of *Jacob* in the *Mercure de France*, for example, praised it as part of a new genre of Jewish literature that 'enables us to educate ourselves outside the works of historians or sociologists as to the genius of the "chosen people" . . . to live with them, in intimacy'.[91] Writing in *La Revue juive*, Henri Hertz by contrast suggested that the underlying factors in *Jacob* that influence the protagonist's personality and the choices that he makes 'do not originate in the Jewish world, nor in any foreign country, but simply in various French provinces and social classes'.[92] Nina Gourfinkel argued in a similar vein that Némirovsky's novel could just as easily have revolved around Christian characters.[93] The very different tone of reviews of *O mon goye!* in the *Mercure de France* and the Jewish press also speaks to this issue. 'Mme Sarah Lévy, as her name indicates', declared a reviewer for the *Mercure*, 'is Jewish and familiar with the people of her race, and is thus able to detect their faults and failings —let us say their particularities—with remarkable objectivity.'[94] Writing in *Chalom*, Raymond-Raoul Lambert, by contrast, suggested that Lévy took great liberties in generalizing about Jews when in fact she was 'familiar with Judaism in only the most superficial manner'.[95] 'The puppet-like characters of Sarah Lévy no more personify the Jewish people than do those of her *goy*, disguised as a knight in shining armour, incarnate Christianity', Jules Meyer concurred in his review of the novel for *L'Univers israélite*.[96] These kinds of concerns were heightened by the fact that an essentialized image of Jewish difference was becoming increasingly commonplace in French society in the 1920s.

War. The original edition was published by Gallimard in 1929. An illustrated version was issued in 1931 by Ferenczi as part of a series entitled 'Le Livre moderne illustré'. The book was reissued by Flammarion in 1939, and numerous editions were published in the post-war years as well. In his review of *O mon goye!* for *Chalom*, Raymond-Raoul Lambert noted that he was eager to give his impressions of the book because it had recently been the object of widespread publicity. See 'Chronique des livres', *Chalom* (15 Apr. 1929), 13–14. As already noted, Geiger's *Histoires juives* was reprinted 104 times.

91 *Le Mercure de France* (15 Dec. 1925), 713.
92 Hertz, '*Jacob*', *La Revue juive* (Nov. 1925), 749.
93 Gourfinkel, 'De Palestine à *David Golder*', *Palestine* (Mar. 1930), 32–8.
94 *Le Mercure de France* (1 Apr. 1929), 168.
95 Lambert, 'Chronique des livres', *Chalom* (15 Apr. 1929), 13.
96 Meyer, '*O mon goy!*', *L'Univers israélite* (8 Mar. 1929), 815.

Reinventing Jewish Difference

As we saw in Chapter 2, those intellectuals who experienced a Jewish 'awakening' in the years before the First World War struggled very consciously with, on the one hand, a 'racial' sense of themselves as Jews and, on the other, a commitment to a liberal, individualist model of national identity. By the mid-1920s, by contrast, the idea that there are certain distinct, unalterable traits that set Jews apart from the rest of the population had become much more widely acceptable, both among Jews and in French society as a whole. A comparison of reactions to Maurice Donnay's play *Le Retour de Jérusalem* at its première in 1903 and during a 1928 revival gives us a sense of this change of mood. The play focuses on the unsuccessful relationship between a Jewish woman and a Christian man, the failure of which is blamed on the essential racial differences between them. Donnay, who was not Jewish, contended that his thesis—that the French and the Jews possess different 'spirits'—was not intended as antisemitic. Rather, he asserted, the play was about a conflict between 'two truths': France and Israel.[97] Most theatre-goers and reviewers in 1903, however, viewed *Le Retour de Jérusalem* as antisemitic. The play inspired strong emotions, including anti-Jewish outbursts at the theatre and numerous articles in both the Jewish and liberal French press denouncing its thesis.[98]

Donnay's play was shocking to audiences at the turn of the century because he created an image of the Jew as 'other' very different from negative Jewish stereotypes that had traditionally existed in French theatre and literature. A stock Jewish character associated with moneylending and dishonest business practices dated back to the Middle Ages and persisted as a familiar trope in modern French fiction. However, these Shylock-like Jewish characters functioned primarily as literary devices that were largely divorced from a particular writer's feelings about Jews in contemporary society.[99] Donnay, by contrast, presented his audience with modern Jews who appear to be fully

[97] Donnay defended his position in a long preface that preceded the first printed version of the play. See *Le Retour de Jérusalem* (1904). The play was reprinted in *La Petite Illustration* (9 Jan. 1929) with an introduction and press review by Robert de Beauplan.

[98] For a reviewer in *L'Univers israélite*, Donnay's opposition between the 'Semitic' and 'Aryan' races made the play little more than an exposé of the antisemitic ideology of the day. See B.M., '*Le Retour de Jérusalem*', *L'Univers israélite* (11 Dec. 1903), 361–4, and 'L'Antisémitisme au théâtre', *L'Univers israélite* (18 Dec. 1903), 389–95. The second piece includes a long excerpt from an article criticizing the play on a similar basis in *L'Aurore*, the voice of the Radical Party.

[99] French writers of the Romantic era, Lehrmann argues in *The Jewish Element in French Literature*, 152–6, often drew upon the medieval fable of the Jew as usurer, which had strong resonance in French culture, even as they supported the liberal, universalist ideals of the French Revolution.

French, but in fact exhibit biologically inscribed character traits that make them fundamentally incompatible with their 'Aryan' compatriots. While in 1903 this thesis appeared to most to be synonymous with the blatant anti-semitism of Drumont or Maurras,[100] a quarter of a century later this was no longer the case. The 1928 production of *Le Retour de Jérusalem* sparked almost no reaction in the Jewish press,[101] and was generally reviewed in the wider French press as a well-structured, entertaining study of the 'Jewish–Aryan drama' that French audiences, no longer in the heat of the Dreyfus affair, were now prepared to hear without rancour or uproar.[102] In an intro-duction to the printed version of the play that appeared in *La Petite Illustra-tion* in 1929, the author suggested the primary reason for this change: while Donnay's thesis that Jew and Christian have divergent character and person-ality traits was once scandalous, 'today it has become fashionable to study semitic psychology. Far from taking offence at certain personality traits that Donnay highlighted, today's Jews are proud of those characteristic traits which ensure the endurance of their race.'[103] As this commentator indi-cates, by the mid-1920s a 'semitic discourse' that placed a positive value on Jewish distinctiveness had become standard among Jewish writers and publicists. The emergence of a positive image of the Jew as Oriental provides a striking example of its prevalence.

One of the major objectives of nineteenth-century Jewish intellectuals and communal leaders was to create a modern Jewish identity rooted in Western, rather than Eastern, civilization and culture. An important theme running through the Jewish press and Jewish literature in the 1920s, by con-

[100] As Paula Hyman has noted, for antisemitic nationalists it was precisely the fact that the Jews *appeared* to be fully French that made them so dangerous. For Drumont, Barrès, Maurras, and their followers, 'The French veneer of assimilated Jews was considered to be woefully superficial. Within the depths of their being, [according to the antisemites] French Jews have their own distinctive and alien culture.' Hyman, *From Dreyfus to Vichy*, 19.

[101] The only article the play inspired was a brief discussion by Raymond-Raoul Lambert in *L'Univers israélite* focusing precisely on the very different reactions to the play in 1903 and 1928. *Le Retour de Jérusalem*, he noted, 'which first played in 1903 when the passions of the Dreyfus affair were running strong, did not inspire any demonstration or polemic this year'. While Lambert went on to criticize the play's superficial characters and remarked that it belonged more to the genre of junk novels than high literature, he argued that one would be wrong to categorize *Le Retour de Jérusalem* as an antisemitic play. Rather, he suggested, it was a kind of innocuous, misguided attempt to explore 'the Jewish question' on the French stage. 'Maurice Donnay et le problème juif', *L'Univers israélite* (1 Feb. 1929), 645–6.

[102] See the press comments preceding the 1929 printing in *La Petite Illustration*. For reactions to the play in 1903 and 1928 see also Meyer-Plantureux, *Les Enfants de Shylock ou l'antisémitisme sur scène*, 32–8, 61–3.

[103] De Beauplan, '*Le Retour de Jérusalem* au théâtre de la Porte Saint-Martin', *La Petite Illus-tration* (9 Jan. 1929), unpaginated. At the end of his essay de Beauplan cites excerpts from numerous reviews of the play.

trast, was the idea that Jews, while acculturating outwardly to the Western world, had retained an Oriental soul. 'The Jew has brought the Orient with him', Pierre Paraf remarked in a lecture for the Union des Femmes Juives Françaises pour la Palestine:

No matter how far away he may be, from the Americas to cold Lithuania, he carries it with him in his Torah, in his talit, in the warmth of his regard . . . may the ungracious customs of the West never let him forget this invincible attraction. Poets, novelists, when your interest turns towards us, may you recognize our true face, the face of a great, ancient people . . . in which the warmth of the Orient will forever nurture lofty dreams and invincible faith.[104]

For UUJJ leader Wladimir Rabinovitch, it was the Jews' Oriental essence that might hold the key to the redemption of Western civilization. The Jews had retained the 'Oriental' values of ancient Israel, namely a strong sense of social justice and equality, and it was by working to bring these values to contemporary French society, he concluded, that they would best expend their energy.[105]

Whereas the European Jewish link with the 'Orient' had been purely historical for centuries, the Zionist movement created a modern, concrete connection. A whole series of novels and travelogues describing Jewish pioneering efforts in Palestine published over the course of the 1920s reinforced a romantic idea of the Jew as spiritually linked to the Orient.[106] By far the most popular of these was Myriam Harry's *Les Amants de Sion*, which was translated into German and English and widely read in England, Germany, and the United States as well as in France.[107] Harry was born in Jerusalem to a Protestant mother and Russian Jewish father who had converted to Protestantism. She immigrated to France as a young woman, and under the guidance of the novelist Jules Lemaître became a prominent figure in the French literary scene by the turn of the century. The glowing images of Jewish Palestine that Harry presented in *Les Amants de Sion* were drawn from her return home in the 1920s and stand in sharp contrast to her childhood image of the Jews of Jerusalem as haggard relics of the past. For André Spire, Harry's narrative was testimony to her reattachment to her

---

[104] The lecture was published as 'Le Réveil du judaïsme français', in the *Revue littéraire juive* (July 1928), 577–94.

[105] Rabinovitch, 'Tempête sur l'Occident', *Chalom* (Oct. 1931), 21–3.

[106] These include Pierre Paraf, *Quand Israël aima*; Fleg, *Ma Palestine*; Kessel, *Terre d'amour*; Corcos, *Le Sionisme au travail*; Jéhouda, *La Terre promise*; and Roukhomovsky, *Palestine dernière heure*.

[107] Michael Berkowitz cites the English translation of this book, *Springtide in Jerusalem*, along with the Hadassah president's *The Immortal Adventure* as among the most popular Zionist books published between the two world wars. See *The Reception of Zionism*, 138.

FIGURE 7 Portrait of Myriam Harry, *Menorah* , 15 October 1922 (p. 51).
It was accompanied by a laudatory article entitled 'Myriam Harry et La Palestine'.
Harry was an eccentric character who cultivated an image of herself as oriental
by appearing in public in Arab-style dress

Reproduced by permission of the library of the Alliance Israélite Universelle

Jewish roots, to 'the blood that was sleeping within her, the race that she had doubted for so long'.[108]

A number of non-Jewish writers also published accounts of their trips to Palestine in the 1920s and early 1930s, many of which conveyed great sympathy for the Zionist movement. Whereas expressing support for a liberal model of Jewish integration and acculturation had once appeared as the only possible option for sympathetic non-Jews, for many of them the success of the Zionist movement illustrated that Jews had maintained a unique spirit despite a century of acculturation. In his richly illustrated travelogue *Le Retour à Jerusalem,* for example, Pierre Bonardi described Zionism as 'one of the greatest human enterprises: the return of a race to its land of origin'.[109] According to the novelist Pierre Benoît, a French nationalist who was sympathetic to the ideas of Maurice Barrès and Edouard Drumont, it was a trip to Palestine in the early 1920s that converted him from antisemite to philosemite. During his trip, Benoît explained, he was overcome by the Jews' enthusiasm for their ancestral home. While he had previously thought of Zionism as simply a European colonialist venture, as a French nationalist he came to admire the ardent sense of Jewish nationalism that he encountered in Palestine. Benoît went on to write *Le Puits de Jacob,* a novel that sought to convey the pull of the Orient on the modern Jew.[110]

Both of these books were very well received in Jewish circles. 'M. Pierre Benoît is audacious', declared Yvonne Netter in *Le Rayon*: 'He dares to present to Jews a variety of different characters, all of which they recognize as their own.' As well as rallying the support of 'all the Jews', she concluded, 'his novel has proven to be of interest to numerous gentile readers as well'.[111] Writing in *Menorah* in 1928, Léon Algazi discussed the appeal of Jewish music for contemporary audiences in similar terms. Invoking the marked interest in 'national particularisms' in the post-war years, he suggested that 'we are finally beginning to understand that true harmony among peoples is achieved, not through the levelling of individualisms, but through an intelli-

[108] Spire, '*Les Amants de Sion*', *La Revue juive* (15 May 1925), 392.

[109] Bonardi, *Le Retour à Jerusalem*, 181. This book was part of a series called 'L'Invitation au voyage'.

[110] The story revolves around a young Jewish woman from Constantinople who emigrates to a kibbutz in Palestine. At a certain point she travels to Paris to request money from the Baron de Rothschild and, charmed by the ease of Parisian life, remains in France. Despite the luxuries that she enjoys, however, she feels empty and unsatisfied, and ultimately returns to Palestine.

[111] See Netter, 'A propos du *Puits de Jacob*', *Le Rayon* (15 Apr. 1925), 9–11. We also find a glowing review of Bonardi's book by Bielinky in *L'Univers israélite*. Of all the Zionist travel literature to come out in recent years, he declared, Bonardi's was by far the best. See Jacques Bielinky, '*Le Retour à Jérusalem*', *L'Univers israélite* (23 Dec. 1927), 436.

gent and skilful utilization of diverse elements: we are beginning to see that we must try to understand one another'.[112]

In a cultural climate in which the persistence of ethnic and national particularism was increasingly understood as compatible with universal, republican culture, French Jews experienced a new freedom to express their own sense of 'feeling different'. At the same time, however, this sense of difference could also be associated with strong feelings of alienation and loss.

The Jew as Outsider

While French Jews in the 1920s often projected a positive image of themselves as Semitic or Oriental, these kinds of ideas also reinforced the image of the Jew as an eternal outsider. This comes across very strongly in fiction dealing with the themes of intermarriage and conversion. Characters in Jewish fiction in the 1920s often feel torn between embracing and rejecting their Jewish heritage precisely because they experience their Jewishness as an all-encompassing primal force over which they have little control. In almost all of these stories, we are presented with a Jew who attempts and fails to transcend his or her Jewish roots and blend unobtrusively into the surrounding society. We see this theme in its most extreme form in Albert Cohen's *Solal*, in which the Greek Jewish protagonist obtains a position as a minister in the French government and marries a French aristocrat. But as soon as he has achieved this incredible success, Solal's world begins to fall apart. He is constantly caught between his French wife Aude and his Greek family, neither of whom respects or understands the other. In the end he is left with nothing; he rejects his family and loses his fortune, his wife leaves him for her former Christian fiancé, and Solal commits suicide.

In his 1928 play *L'Eternel ghetto*, Léo Poldès, the director of the Club du Faubourg, also portrayed an image of a failed Jewish–Christian union.[113] The action centres on Max, a young man whose father is a pious Jew and the 'chef des sionistes', in the process of planning his family's departure for Palestine. The play begins with the dramatic revelation that Max has converted to Catholicism and plans to marry Jeanne, a Christian. Max does not simply undergo a religious conversion but rather becomes a kind of anti-Jewish zealot. He formally denounces Zionism, becomes friendly with a leader of the antisemitic movement, and denies all sense of solidarity with the Jewish people. In *Solal* and *L'Eternel ghetto*, to be a Jew is to be burdened with filial responsibility and the curse of being an outsider, a fate that both protagonists attempt to escape by marrying Christian women. For both Solal

---

[112] Algazi, 'L'Année musicale', *Menorah* (15 Jan. 1928), 24.   [113] Poldès, *L'Eternel ghetto*.

and Max, however, this proves to be impossible. Jewishness is not a cultural heritage that one can opt out of but rather a biologically inscribed trait, transmitted inevitably from generation to generation.

While Solal and Aude come from very different backgrounds—Solal is not a French Jew, but a Greek immigrant—Cohen does not portray their failed marriage as the result of 'cultural differences'. Rather, he reinforces the idea that there are certain inescapable personality traits associated with the Jew, such as passion and sensuality, that make the union impossible. For Solal, the fact of his Jewishness functions throughout the novel as an irrational force that constantly thwarts his intellectual desire for integration. In one scene, for example, he is praying in the company of visiting relatives from Greece. When Aude and her father enter the room, Solal deliberately ignores them, intensifying the swaying body motion that accompanies traditional Jewish prayer. Later, reflecting on this moment, he wonders, 'What demon, stronger than he, had possessed him at that moment? Now she will for ever have the despicable memory of these two swaying Orientals, cringing in fear before a daughter of Europe.'[114] In a showdown between father and son, Poldès similarly put the question of the 'escapability' of Jewishness on the table. 'I am a Christian', Max asserts with confidence, 'just because by random chance I was born a Jew, [why] must I remain one all my life even if I am disgusted with this race that I renounce?' 'No matter what you do', his father David challenges him, 'you will still have Jewish blood in your veins . . . look at your face. Recognize the mask on which the age-old mark of our race is inscribed.'[115] In the end, it is the father who is proven right. Max ultimately decides to break off his engagement and emigrate to Palestine with his family. While this decision comes in part as a result of his fiancée hurling antisemitic epithets at him during an argument, ultimately, like Solal, it is his own sense of the impossibility of bridging the gap between the French and Jewish worlds that leads him to abandon the engagement. 'I love you Jeanne', he declares, 'but I am not alone. You are not alone. There is around us and between us the invisible presence of our fathers, our grandfathers and our ancestors. It weighs upon us. It is inscribed in our flesh and in our blood.' She sadly agrees, and the couple part definitively.[116]

The idea that there are certain inescapable Jewish personality traits that are independent of any kind of individual will comes across very strongly in the confrontation between father and son in *L'Eternel ghetto*. Even the style of his passionate embrace of Christianity and negation of his Jewishness, David impresses upon his son, betray his Jewish heritage: 'this pride that smothers you, this exaltation towards a new faith is in fact testimony to the

---

[114] Cohen, *Solal*, 251.   [115] Poldès, *L'Eternel ghetto*, 44–5.   [116] Ibid. 122.

fiery Jewish blood that runs through your veins!'[117] Poldès's idea of the Jew's 'Jewishness' being manifest even in the passion and energy that he brings to his hatred of Judaism was perhaps influenced by Henri Bernstein's very popular and controversial play, *Israël*. This play, first performed in Paris in 1908, is the story of Thibauld, a virulently antisemitic young man who discovers that his biological father, Gutlieb, is in fact Jewish. Thibauld is devastated by this revelation and commits suicide rather than be condemned to live out his life knowing that he is 'tainted' by Jewish blood. At one point in the play Gutlieb, like David, concludes that it is his son's passionate hatred of Jews that is, in fact, evidence of his Jewish origins: 'to persuade twenty-eight million Christians that sixty thousand Jews pose a national danger', he reflects, 'one must have the strength and passion of a Jew'.[118]

Even those novels in which the Christian–Jewish union is ultimately successful often present Jew and Christian as diametrically opposed. Unlike *L'Eternel ghetto* and *Solal*, Sarah Lévy's story, in *O mon goye!*, of a young Jewish widow who falls in love with Henri, a Christian, ends with the successful marriage of the Jewish and Christian protagonists. While the widow Sarah ultimately decides that her love for Henri is strong enough to overcome her doubts about the relationship, the focus of the novel is nonetheless on her angst as she feels constantly pulled between her love for Henri and the burden of her Jewish roots. Throughout, Lévy presents us with dichotomous Christian/Jewish traits: the Christian feels at ease in his interactions with the world, confident that everything will work out for the best, whereas the Jew is affected and insecure, always worrying about imminent disaster and on the lookout for financial opportunities. At one point, Henri is horrified when one of Sarah's friends suggests that he open a restaurant on his family's estate: for him, this land is sacred and must be conserved as it has been for generations, whereas for the Jew it is simply a business opportunity to be exploited. At this point Sarah, like Max and Solal, understands that the gulf that separates her from her Christian lover is visceral and impossible to transcend.[119]

This kind of essentialized understanding of the role that ethnic or racial heritage plays in shaping a person's feelings, personality, and, ultimately, destiny was not limited to discussions of Jews, but rather was characteristic of an age in which 'exotic others' were simultaneously romanticized for their difference and rejected as ultimately incapable of assimilation. The film *Zouzou*, a popular hit starring Josephine Baker, for example, makes racial difference the supreme obstacle to a romance between Zouzou, a native of Martinique raised in France by an adoptive (white) French father, and her

[117] Ibid. 45.   [118] Bernstein, *Israël*, 201–4.   [119] *O mon goye!*, 139.

French lover, Jean. Another of Baker's films, *Princess Tam-Tam*, tells the story of Alwina, a Tunisian princess whose integration into contemporary France is undone by the inevitable inability of the native to become anything but superficially civilized.[120] In a similar vein, Paul Morand, one of the most popular writers of the inter-war years, penned a 1928 collection of stories entitled *Black Magic*, all centred on black characters whose essential African nature ultimately undoes their civilized pretensions.[121] The fact that Morand, known for his world travels and cosmopolitan lifestyle, was in fact a proponent of ethnic separatism, Elizabeth Ezra notes, reflects a larger truth about France of the inter-war years: 'often identified with a love of the exotic (the Jazz Age) and assimilationist rhetoric, time and time again its cultural representations emphasized (or invented) difference, denying the very possibility of assimilation'.[122] Given the Jews' status as long-standing residents of France whose very existence was bound up with their political status as integral French citizens, it is not surprising that this discourse reinventing the Jew as racially distinct and, ultimately, as incapable of assimilation as non-white colonial subjects, provoked criticism and concern within the Jewish community.

In their response to this kind of literature, reviewers often expressed a strong sense of anxiety about the dangers of pushing an emphasis on Jewish difference too far. *Solal* was received with great critical acclaim, and reviewers for the general French press tended to characterize the novel as representative of 'the Jewish soul'.[123] Reviewers for the Jewish press, by contrast, objected that Cohen portrayed the Jew in an exoticized manner that bordered on the antisemitic: 'It is noteworthy that next to this extraordinary Solal', Gustave Kahn wrote in *Menorah*, 'the book presents no moderate Jew, no real Jew . . . this is at the very least a shortcoming in a book that presents only stilted and improbable Jews'. *Solal*, declared Raymond-Raoul Lambert in a similar vein in *La Terre retrouvée*, 'appears to me as very misguided . . . Judaism does not equal rags, squalor, disorder, and barbarism'.[124] For these commentators, it was not only Cohen's presentation of stereotyped Jewish characters that was problematic but also the fact that he presented them as the embodiment of a kind of eternal Jewish essence.[125]

[120]   See Ezra, *The Colonial Unconscious*, ch. 4   [121]   Ibid., ch. 5.   [122]   Ibid. 20.
[123]   For numerous reviews of the novel, see 'Dossier de presse de *Solal*', in Cohen, *Œuvres*, 1238–48. We read in *Le Soir*, for example, that 'Cohen's story is profoundly Jewish: under the surface of a mocking and corrupted spirit, the mystique of the chosen people shines through'; or, in *La République*, '*Solal* brings an unexpected revelation of the Jewish soul in all its complexity, it reveals its most moving, its most contradictory and most passionate aspects.'
[124]   Quoted in Albert Cohen, *Œuvres*, 1241–2.
[125]   Cohen's literature would become even more controversial in the 1930s, when his ambiguous images of Jews were increasingly criticized as feeding the flames of antisemitism.

In a 1925 article for *La Revue juive,* Henri Hertz similarly criticized a kind of essentialized Semitic discourse that had become common in discussions of Jewish music and art in the post-war years. It had become high fashion among Jewish intellectuals, he noted, to discuss the concept of a Jewish art in a deterministic fashion, in some instances to the point of invoking the allegedly Jewish origins of Catholic artists and writers and suggesting that their 'Semitic blood' has been a determining factor in their art.[126] 'As for myself', Hertz declared, 'I am very sceptical about this trend. It leads to over-ingenious and perfidious conclusions.'[127] Writing in *Menorah,* Léon Algazi objected to a similar trend in discussions of 'Jewish music'. No particular relationship existed between Judaism and Milhaud's *Malheurs d'Orphée* or Schoenberg's *Le Pierrot lunaire,* he suggested, and he went on to ask rhetorically: 'Do we not all know more than one French musician whose work seems to be more reflective of German than French musical styles?'[128] For Hertz, as for Algazi, the fact that certain Jews were themselves propagating an image of the Jew as other could only serve to strengthen the arguments of those who considered them to be a dangerous influence on the 'true' French nation.

This kind of over-deterministic discourse and the concerns that it raised comes across very strongly in Isaac Kadmi-Cohen's 1929 book *Nomades: Essai sur l'âme juive* and reactions to it within the Jewish community. The Polish-born Kadmi-Cohen spent time in Palestine before immigrating to France as a young man. He served in the French army and was president of the Association des Anciens Combattants Juifs, a veterans' society created in 1928, and became active in the Zionist movement. The central argument of his book is that the Jews, a Semitic, Oriental people who share the blood of Arab nomads, are essentially wanderers, spiritually incapable of becoming attached to any particular country or place. While Kadmi-Cohen claimed that

On the virulently negative reactions to his ill-timed play *Ezéchiel,* which played at the Comédie-Française in the same year that Hitler was elected Chancellor of Germany, see Meyer-Plantureux, 'Du Baron de Horn à Ezéchiel', 82–6.

[126] As Hertz suggested, some commentators took this kind of biological essentialism even further, pointing, for example, to Pablo Picasso's alleged 'semitic origins' as a determining factor in shaping his artistic vision. See e.g. Elie Faure, 'L'Ame juive', *Palestine* (Jan. 1928), 151–69. In fact, as Jarrassé indicates ('L'Eveil d'une critique d'art juive', 69), Picasso was regularly referred to as a Jew by Parisian art critics in the 1920s. On the prevalence of this kind of biological/essentialist discourse within the Jewish art world of the 1920s, see also Haus, 'Les Artistes juifs de l'Ecole de Paris'.   [127] Hertz, 'André Spire', *La Revue juive* (15 May 1925), 303–4.

[128] Algazi, 'L'Année musicale', 24. He made the same point several years later in an interview for *La Joie musicale* on the question, 'Y-at-il une musique juive?' Algazi answered in the affirmative, and went on to discuss traditional religious and folk music—rather than music by contemporary Jewish composers—as examples of Jewish music. The interview was reprinted in *L'Univers israélite* (6 Mar. 1931), 780–1.

'*Nomades* is nothing other than the most fervent extolling of the strength and originality of our race', Maurice Level, one of the regular columnists for *Menorah*, objected to the biological essentialism of Cohen's thesis and pointed to its strong parallels with antisemitic discourse of the day. In particular, Level criticized Cohen's reliance on Barrès's ideology of 'les morts qui parlent', which led him to a simplistic association of the supposed character traits of present-day Jews with those of their ancestors. 'M. Kadmi-Cohen has managed to derive, in a much stronger and more effective manner than the Drumonts of this earth', Level noted sarcastically, 'that which is specific and dangerous about the Jewish character for the western temperament.'[129] Interestingly, in his response to Level, Kadmi-Cohen referred to a recent exchange that he had had in a right-wing newspaper, *La Lanterne*, with an antisemitic royalist, René de Planhol. In response to Planhol's insistence that the Jews must 'choose between France and Israel', Kadmi-Cohen attempted to convince him of the value of Jewish particularism, insisting that 'the glowing richness of [the Jews'] moral and intellectual heritage is of great benefit to France'.[130] While he was not able to change entirely the views of his opponent, Kadmi-Cohen affirmed, Planhol nonetheless went away with 'a greater appreciation of the values of spiritual unity and moral cohesion' that had kept the Jewish people together through the centuries.

Jewish concerns about blurring the boundaries between antisemitism and philosemitism in these exchanges was heightened by the fact that writing on Jewish themes, and the kind of Semitic discourse which so often went along with it, was not limited to Jewish authors. As we saw in Chapter 2, writers such as Romain Rolland and Charles Péguy began introducing Jewish themes into their essays and fiction in the aftermath of the Dreyfus affair. This trend intensified during the 1910s and 1920s as French essayists, playwrights, and novelists felt an increasing freedom to include Jewish characters in their fiction and speculate on the nature of Jewish particularism. While Jewish critics often welcomed what they saw as 'friendly' non-Jewish interest, this genre of writing could be controversial.

Jean and Jérôme Tharaud were the most prominent non-Jewish authors to write on Jewish themes in the inter-war years. They first published romantic stories with east European and biblical settings in Charles Péguy's *Cahiers de la Quinzaine* at the turn of the century,[131] and over the course of

---

[129] See Maurice Level, 'Les Pavés de l'ours', *Menorah* (15 Jan. 1930), 18–21, and Kadmi-Cohen's response in the form of a letter to the editor followed by Level's rebuttal (15 Feb. 1930), 62–4.   [130] Kadmi-Cohen in *Menorah* (15 Feb. 1930), 63.
[131] 'Bar Kochbas, notre honneur', constituted the whole issue of *Les Cahiers de la Quinzaine*, 8/11 (1907).

the 1920s published seven books with Jewish themes, both fictional and historical. The Tharauds covered a wide territory. Their writings included two novels set in east European shtetls, two books on Palestine and the Zionist movement, an essay on the role of the Jews in the Hungarian revolution, a synthetic Jewish history, and a novel set in biblical times.[132] The Tharauds initially enjoyed great popularity in Jewish circles. They were considered sympathetic outsiders with a keen interest in Jewish folklore. Throughout the 1920s, people referring to the 'réveil juif' included the Tharauds' writings as a positive example of new interest of non-Jews in Jewish themes. Excerpts from their books appeared in the Jewish press and they were invited to lecture on several occasions to Jewish youth groups and cultural associations. As the decade wore on, however, there was increasing controversy in Jewish circles about the Tharauds' writing, as many began to feel that the images and ideas about Jews that they were creating were both inaccurate and potentially harmful.

The Tharauds' earliest books on Jewish themes were *L'Ombre de la croix* and *Un Royaume de Dieu*, novels set in east European shtetls and based on actual visits to Hungary and the Ukraine. These books provide readers with detailed information about traditional Jewish religious practice and beliefs and portray the Jews as an impoverished, persecuted people whose religious faith has helped them to maintain a lively, vibrant spirit through the centuries. At the same time, however, the Jews are depicted as a strange, exotic sect marked by physical and psychological deformities. This comes across very strongly in a scene describing hasidic children at play:

the long, traditional sidelocks that must never be cut, black, blond, or brown, float around these young faces, a religious symbol and a charm of human grace. Is it thus from these small, admirable people that one day this talkative, gesticulating, sordid mass of humanity will arise? All these lovely faces will become anxious and preoccupied! These lithe young bird-like bodies will take on this long, hunched-over form with strangely ballooning stomachs! But as our gaze rests on them, our surprise dissipates. We can make out on most of these faces . . . too much excitement, tics, the symptoms of usury and fatigue . . . an immense fatigue: ancient, laid upon them by the centuries, so that in the end on the faces of these children we see only the traits of a very ancient civilization.[133]

Interestingly, passages like this were not, by and large, read as antisemitic by French Jewish contemporaries. *L'Ombre de la croix* was welcomed by most Jewish critics as a well-intentioned, folkloric study of Jewish customs in

---

[132] *L'Ombre de la croix* and *Un royaume de Dieu*; *L'Année prochaine à Jérusalem* and *La Palestine*; *Quand Israël est roi*; *Petite histoire des Juifs* and *La Rose de Saron*.

[133] *L'Ombre de la croix*, 37.

eastern Europe. In a review of the novel in *Le Peuple juif,* for example, Baruch Hagani praised the authors for their ability to evoke 'in successive and strongly coloured brush strokes the atmosphere of Jewish life in far-away communities in eastern Europe'.[134]

The publication of *Quand Israël est roi* in 1924, by contrast, was much more controversial. This book, a pseudo-history of the fall of the old regime and the rise of communism in Hungary, aimed to illustrate the decisive role that the Jews played in the Hungarian revolution. The book was apparently intended as a sequel to *Un royaume de Dieu,* thus presenting the reader with the image of the Jew being transformed overnight from an impoverished, isolated shtetl resident to a revolutionary leader.[135] In this instance, most Jews were outraged by the book's historical inaccuracies and protested at the Tharauds' exaggeration of the role of the Jews in the Hungarian (or any other) revolution.[136] With the publication of their *Petite histoire des Juifs* in 1927, however, the Tharauds once again drew support from certain Jewish critics. In a review in *L'Univers israélite,* Maurice Liber sharply criticized the book for equating Jewish history with the history of life in the shtetl and even more importantly for suggesting that the Jews' ghettoized existence in eastern Europe was itself a product of Judaism.[137] In a review in *Paix et droit,* by contrast, Alfred Berl, one of the leaders of the Alliance Israélite Universelle, admired 'the will with which [the Tharauds] attempt to penetrate and understand the Jewish mentality'.[138] Writing in 1928, a columnist for *Le Rayon* expressed his mixed feelings about the Tharaud brothers in a way that captured many of his fellow Jews' ambivalence:

We assume that they have good faith. I would very much like that to be so. Nonetheless, I find something objectionable in their literature, which lets the readers think that all the strange habits and customs that they describe are integral parts of Judaism rather than simply local customs, 'minhagim' more or less tolerated by Judaism per se. At the very least, we need to point out their ignorance.[139]

---

[134] Hagani, 'L'Ombre de la croix', *Le Peuple juif* (15 Apr. 1917), 6–7.

[135] See Judaeus, 'Antisémitisme et fausse monnaie', *L'Univers israélite* (5 Feb. 1926), 528–9.

[136] Ibid., and Benjamin Crémieux, 'Les Frères Tharaud et le judaïsme', *Menorah* (1 Jan. 1924), 195–6. While Liber's tone is much stronger, both agreed that *Quand Israël est roi* must be classified as maliciously anti-Jewish.

[137] Liber, 'Les Frères Tharaud, historiens du judaïsme', *L'Univers israélite* (13 Jan. 1928), 517–19.

[138] Berl, 'Israël et les Tharaud', *Paix et droit* (Nov. 1927), 1–3. The Tharauds' account of their trip to Palestine, *L'Année prochaine à Jérusalem,* also met with mixed responses. The brothers were very critical of the Zionist movement, which they saw as a misguided attempt by Jews to transform their traditional religious messianism into modern politics. While the book unsurprisingly received very negative reviews in journals such as *Menorah* and *Chalom,* Berl expressed sympathy for the Tharauds' thesis in the anti-Zionist *Paix et droit.*

[139] Baumgarten pointed out, for example, that in *L'Ombre de la croix* the Tharauds place the summer holiday of Shavuot in the middle of winter. See *Le Rayon* (July 1928), 14.

André Spire conveyed a similar sentiment in a 1928 essay on Jacques de Lacretelle's *Silbermann*, one of the most successful novels on Jewish themes of the decade. The story, set during the Dreyfus affair, tells of a Protestant schoolboy who befriends the Jewish David Silbermann when the latter is viciously attacked by his Catholic classmates. Though the novel was intended as a critique of antisemitism, Lacretelle's portrait of Silbermann as intellectually precocious, insecure, and physically weak reinforced many commonly held stereotypes about Jews. Jewish reactions to this novel when it was first published in 1922, however, were relatively positive. Reviewers took care to note that it was not antisemitic in intention, and pointed out that Lacretelle criticized Catholics and Protestants as well as Jews, to whom he ascribed positive as well as negative traits.[140] Writing in 1928, at the height of the 'mode juif', André Spire was more sceptical about the good intentions of either Lacretelle or the Tharaud brothers. While he had initially believed that they were making a sincere effort to be fair towards the Jews, Spire explained, he had come to realize that there was an important difference between non-Jewish writers like the Tharauds and Jacques de Lacretelle and someone like Israel Zangwill. 'When Zangwill describes a Jewish flaw, we feel his heart bleeding'; the Tharauds, by contrast, 'seem to take pleasure in it . . . they are on the side of those who mock'.[141]

Michel Leymarie's recent study of the Tharauds' personal correspondence and preparatory notes for their novels and essays confirms Spire's suspicions. The brother's 1933 publication of *Quand Israël n'est plus roi*, a book which actually expresses support for Nazism, has generally been seen as a turning-point at which the Tharauds' ambivalent stance with regard to the Jews became clear. Leymarie shows, to the contrary, that the Tharauds' interest in Jews and Judaism was voyeuristic and exploitative from the beginning. Unlike Charles Péguy, who in publishing their work in the *Cahiers de la Quinzaine* revealed a blind spot for the Tharauds' antisemitism similar to that of many French Jews of the 1920s, Leymarie argues, the Tharaud brothers were never touched by the plight of the Jewish people. Their journey to the ghettos of eastern Europe at the turn of the century coincided with a vogue for exoticism in French popular culture, and the 'Jewish awakening' of the 1920s, in turn, provided them with an irresistible opportunity for fame and financial gain. There is perhaps a sad irony in the fact that the Tharauds' popularity and financial success were unparalleled by that of any Jewish author of the day.[142]

---

[140] See 'A propos de *Silbermann*', *L'Univers israélite* (19 Jan. 1923), 413–14, and J. Auber, 'Silbermann', *Foi et réveil*, 18 (1923), 51.

[141] Spire, *Quelques Juifs et Demi-Juifs*, 89.   [142] Leymarie, 'Les Frères Tharaud'.

During the 1920s, however, both the mixed images of Jews that the Tharauds created, as well as the Jewish community's own diverse reactions to their writing, can be seen as reflective of an era in which the line between celebrating ethnic difference and reinforcing racist stereotypes was easily blurred. Furthermore, in a world that did not yet know the crimes that would be committed in the name of Jewish difference, the distinction between interest in and disdain for Jews and Judaism was often difficult to discern.

CHAPTER 8

Reshaping Franco-Judaism
1920-1932

IN HIS OPENING STATEMENT for *La Revue juive*, Albert Cohen expressed a strong sense of what distinguished his generation of French Jews from those who came before them:

We are less profoundly Jewish than our fathers, more in love than them with the delights of the Western world, but we want to be more Jewish than they were . . . They believed in the principle of humanitarianism that broke open the ghetto wall. Please excuse us: we have faith.[1]

Cohen's statement is revealing in a number of ways. On the one hand, it suggests a profound change in French Jewish identity after the First World War. The lonely voice of André Spire in *Poèmes juives* and *Quelques Juifs* has become the ethos of a generation intent on reclaiming the Jewish heritage that their parents and grandparents sacrificed in favour of a broad humanism. Interestingly, however, Cohen described himself and his contemporaries as 'more in love with . . . the Western world' than their parents or grandparents. The very desire to be 'more Jewish', Cohen suggested, was a product of the success of their integration.

The primary objective of Jewish religious and intellectual discourse in the nineteenth century was to demonstrate the Jewish contribution to Western culture and to prove that the maintenance of Jewish particularism did not prevent either the Jewish people, or Judaism itself, from contributing to a 'universalist' French culture. While French Jews writing and lecturing about Judaism in the 1920s shared many of the concerns of their predecessors, as Cohen's statement suggests, the centre of gravity had shifted. Rather than demonstrating Judaism's compatibility with universalism, Jewish writers, spokesmen, and religious leaders now focused on the idea that a commitment to universalism and sense of belonging to France need not entail a lessening of one's attachment to Judaism.

The influence of Zionism on Franco-Judaism in the 1920s was critical. Whether rejected, embraced, or critically examined, the Zionists' reframing

---

[1] 'Déclaration', *La Revue juive* (15 Jan. 1925), 6–7.

of Jewishness as an ethnic or national heritage provided a changed concep-
tual framework through which to understand the place of the Jew and
Judaism in the modern world. As we shall see, France's position as a colonial
power in the 1920s also played a critical role in reshaping Franco-Judaism
during this period.

Discourses of Dualism: Zionism and French Judaism in the 1920s

Zionism in America, Melvin Urofsky argues, 'has enjoyed its greatest suc-
cesses when its goals and methods have coincided with the dominant trends
in the broader society'.[2] American Zionists in the inter-war years, he shows,
widened the appeal of their movement beyond a small group of east European immigrants by drawing parallels between the aims and ideals of the
Zionist movement and those of American society. The social protest aspect
of the movement won Zionism a sympathetic response in progressive ranks,
as did the idea of a 'homeland' for American Jews in a cultural context in
which all immigrant groups—Irish, Italian, Polish, and so forth—continued
to have a sentimental attachment to their country of origin. In a similar vein,
the themes that French Zionists focused on reflected the larger ethos of the
era. Zionism was translated through both internationalism and pacifism,
the dominant ideological currents on the French left during this period. Support for a Jewish homeland was integrated into a broader left-wing schema,
as the protection and defence of ethnic minorities came to be accepted as
part of a progressive mindset.

The idea that particular religious, national, or ethnic groups have
'essences' that must be respected and understood played a critical role in
reshaping the parameters of Franco-Judaism. As we saw in Chapter 7, by the
early 1930s the idea that the Jew had certain essential differences that distinguished him from the broader French population was more widely articulated in French society as a whole. While this kind of discourse could be used
to reinforce antisemitism, it could also be integrated into progressive, left-
wing thinking. Whereas the nineteenth-century French left was associated
with the promotion of individual human rights, progressive French intellectual culture in the 1920s was more oriented towards defending and valuing
group difference.[3] This reorientation had a profound impact on French Jew-

[2] Urofsky, *American Zionism*, 2.
[3] Herman Lebovics notes this progressive intellectual reorientation of the French left. By
the mid-1930s, he argues, important cultural spokesmen on the left, even in attacking the
right, 'continued to think within the Maurrasian paradigm' (*True France*, 159). For a detailed

ish intellectual life. Jews could best contribute to the universal ideals of world peace and mutual understanding, many Jews and sympathetic non-Jews argued, by exploring their own particularism and presenting Jewish ideals, culture, and values to the broader non-Jewish world.

For German Zionists, Stephen Poppel argues, the embrace of Jewish nationalism meant the replacement of 'Deutschtum' with 'Judentum': the realization that the dream of integration into German society was illusory, and that Jews could only be fulfilled through the 'liberation of self-affirmation'.[4] French Jews, by contrast, rarely posited 'Frenchness' and 'Jewishness' in oppositional terms. The principal arguments that they used to promote and defend the movement among their compatriots were centred on discourses of dualism. Rather than rejecting either the Jews' loyalty and attachment to France or a commitment to 'universal' human values, French Zionists developed a variety of arguments intended to illustrate that these ideals were perfectly compatible with support for Zionism and the ethnic understanding of Jewish identity that it entailed.

A Jewish Province of France: Zionism as a Form of 'Regional' Identity

A common theme in Zionist writing in the 1910s and 1920s was the comparison of Jewish particularism with French regionalism: just as one could be Breton and French, some Zionist sympathizers declared, so too could one be both French and ethnically Jewish. We find an early example of this kind of argument in a short story by Charles-Edouard Lévy, who led weekly discussion groups at the Union Scolaire, in the *Echo sioniste* in 1912.[5] Lévy's story centres on two young French Jews, Pierre and Yvonne, who meet on a trip to Brittany and are captivated by the local myths and legends of the region. This fascination ultimately leads them towards a renewed appreciation of their own Jewish heritage. As a result of a Breton tour guide's query as to whether, like Brittany, 'their own regions' preserve a strong sense of local culture, both young people begin to re-evaluate the meaning of their Jewish identity. 'When you questioned me', the young man responds to the local guide after a few days of reflection, 'I was ignorant of the traditions of my ancestors "from the time when we were not yet French". The homage that you do not refuse to druids, sea-devils, and Chouans, I refused to the noblest of my ancestors, under the pretext that their beliefs were no longer

analysis of the principal themes in left-wing French intellectual discourse in the inter-war years, see Prochasson, *Les Intellectuels, le socialisme et la guerre.*

[4] Poppel, *Zionism in Germany, 1897–1933*, 87.
[5] Lévy, 'Du temps qu'on n'était pas encore français', *L'Echo sioniste* (10 Dec. 1912), 245–9.

my own. I took for a religious text that which was, in fact, a question of dignity.'[6] By thinking about his Jewishness as a 'regional' rather than 'religious' affiliation, Pierre suggests that a Jew who feels a strong sense of ethnic attachment to his or her Jewishness is no different from any other French citizen from a province with strong local traditions and history.

We find this equation of Jewishness and regionalism with particular frequency in the discourse of the non-Jewish members of France-Palestine. Justin Godart, for example, expressed his support for the *Revue littéraire juive* by affirming that it would 'provide a window into the French Jewish soul, a French Jewish life impregnated with local traditions and having taken on a territorial flavour'.[7] For Godart and other non-Jews, this line of argument provided a way to express support for Zionism and the ethno-cultural definition of Jewishness it entailed while simultaneously distinguishing themselves from antisemitic spokesmen who might cynically endorse Zionism in the hope that its success would lead to the exodus of Jews from France. This comes across very clearly in another article by Godart explaining the mission of France-Palestine. 'We do not wish', he affirmed, 'should the Zionist movement succeed, to call into question the profound assimilation of French Jews, to doubt their patriotism or weaken it by reproaching them for having two homelands . . . a person can be a French Jew and a Zionist without compromising in the least his scrupulous attachment to France.'[8]

This argument was similar to that made by Louis Brandeis, a judge of German Jewish extraction who became a prominent figure in the American Zionist movement just before the First World War. The Jews' connection to a future Jewish state, Brandeis argued, would be little different from the Irish, Polish, or Italian sense of attachment to their land of origin.[9] In France, however, this argument stood on decidedly tenuous ground. Whereas in the United States these ethnic reference points were all extra-territorial, French Jews' 'region', unlike that of Bretons or Provençals, did not lie inside France, a fact that could easily be invoked by the antisemitic movement to suggest that a Jew was not truly French. As Maurice Liber argued in *L'Univers israélite* in 1926, the highly assimilating thrust of French national culture also made this a rather dubious model of Jewish ethnic survival: within two or three generations, he pointed out, a Lorrain or a Breton no longer thinks of himself as such: 'he is assimilated and his provincialism disappears'.[10] Perhaps

---

[6] Lévy, 'Du temps qu'on n'était pas encore français', 248.

[7] *Revue littéraire juive* (Mar. 1927), 1.

[8] Godart, 'Les Evénements de Palestine', *Palestine* (Sept./Dec. 1929), 66.

[9] Urofsky, *American Zionism*, 130.

[10] Liber made this point in an article criticizing André Spire, who, he contended, was an advocate of this 'regionalist' argument. Spire, however, denied ever expressing this opinion

in response to the rather shaky ground on which this regionalist comparison stood, Zionist supporters often pushed it one step further, suggesting that the presence of both a Jewish state in Palestine and a Jewish ethnicity within France would benefit not only the Jews, but French society as whole.

In an article in *Palestine*, Anatole de Monzie, a socialist minister who was one of the most active non-Jewish members of France-Palestine, praised the spiritual benefits that he imagined the establishment of a Jewish homeland would bring the Jews of the diaspora. 'It is in their own interest for all percep- tive Westerners to be pro-Zionist', he suggested, 'because the Jews with whom we have relations within our own countries would be closer to us, more like us, if their loyalty to their country was complemented by a mystical obedience to the home of their millennial claim.'[11] Here we see that de Monzie, rather than rejecting the assumption of right-wing nationalists— that there is a visceral connection between a people and the land from which they originate—tried to find the Jews a place within this ethnic conception of the nation. By turning the idea of 'double loyalty' around, he suggested that the opportunity to feel the same sense of visceral connection to their history and ancestors as other Frenchmen would in fact enable them to be more genuinely French. Charles-Edouard Lévy made a similar point in his story in *L'Echo sioniste*. While Pierre asserts that pride in one's 'particular' cultural heritage does not make one any less French, Yvonne goes a step further, sug- gesting that this kind of attachment in fact makes one a *better* French citizen. 'While certain people have considered the repudiation of all their family glory as a necessary sacrifice to the nation', she asserts, 'they were wrong. A steadfast attachment to one's ancestral legacy is the surest gauge of one's fidelity to the French heritage.'[12]

Both American and German Zionists formulated versions of this argument. Just as Irish immigrants demonstrated their attachment to the supremely American values of justice and liberty by seeking to encourage them in their land of origin, Brandeis contended, so to would American Jews illustrate their patriotism by fighting for these values in a future Jewish state. The Zionist was a *better* citizen than the assimilationist, certain German Jews argued in a similar vein, because he was closer to the understanding of the 'national sensitivities of the soul of the German Volk'. This idea, Poppel notes, was never articulated by non-Jews and remained hopelessly out of step with the reality of German nationalist ideology. While it was hardly com-

---

and affirmed that, on the contrary, he had often criticized it as 'inexact'. See Judaeus, 'Les Paradoxes de M. Spire', *L'Univers israélite* (31 Dec. 1926), 517–19, and 'Une lettre de M. Spire', *L'Univers israélite* (7 Jan. 1927), 551–4.

[11] De Monzie, 'Réflexions sur le sionisme', *Palestine* (Feb. 1928), 195.

[12] 'Du temps qu'on n'était pas encore français', 248.

monplace in France, the fact that de Monzie, a non-Jew, put forward this line of argument perhaps indicates a greater sympathy among the French towards both Zionism and philosemitism.[13]

Legitimizing Jewish particularism by linking it to French values and culture was especially prevalent in the thought of Pierre Paraf. In his writings and lectures, Paraf often focused on the idea that there was a particular affinity between France and the Jews that should encourage French Jews to affirm their particularity. Responding to a 1926 survey conducted by *Chalom* inviting both Jewish and non-Jewish 'men of letters' to give their impression of the Jewish influence on Western civilization, for example, Paraf wrote enthusiastically about the influence of Judaism on modern French culture and similarities between the French and Jewish spirits. He returned to this idea in a 1930 article for *Menorah*, suggesting that Montaigne owed his spirit of tolerance and internationalism to his partly Jewish origins, and praising Racine for '[singing] the great events of the Jews as if their memory belonged to that of his own people'.[14]

The prominent philosopher André Siegfried made a similar argument at a lecture that he gave in the same year for the Cercle d'Etudes Juives. A shared cult of intelligence, sense of family, and taste for criticism, Siegfried suggested, were all exemplary of the 'essential affinities' between France and the people Israel.[15] This discourse is not that different from that of early Wissenschaft scholars, who drew parallels between the political life of ancient Israel and modern republican ideology, or that of James Darmesteter, for whom the French Revolution represented the fulfilment of the messianic promise. Paraf, however, contrasted his own characterization of Jewish–French compatibility with that of previous generations. The Zionist movement and Jewish cultural renaissance more broadly, he asserted, were:

the inevitable reaction against a period of total assimilation, during which time, in order to better merit the honour of French liberty and equality, the Jews judged it advisable to divorce their ideal from their lived experience, to reduce it to a mere creed.... By contrast, the atmosphere of confidence and friendship that dominates today, the renewed assurance of patriotism that the war bestowed upon the Jewish people, appears to have cured them of their former timidity.[16]

For Paraf, the blossoming of Jewish cultural activity in contemporary French

[13] See Urofsky, *American Zionism*, 126–32; Poppel, *Zionism in Germany*, 122.

[14] 'Nos enquêtes: Réponse de M. Pierre Paraf', *Chalom* (Apr. 1926), 12–13, and 'Israël et la France', *Menorah* (15 Mar. 1930), 89. As noted in *Menorah*, this article was originally published in *Les Cahiers bleus* in February 1930.

[15] Pierre Paraf noted the similarity in their viewpoints in 'Israël dans les démocraties contemporaines', *L'Univers israélite* (23 May 1930), 203.   [16] Paraf, 'Israël et la France', 88.

society was itself evidence of the affinity between France and the Jewish people: it was the very strength of the Jews' attachment to France, rather than a rejection of it, that inspired them to assert their ethnic particularism.

Zionism and Internationalism

Henry Marx, speaking at a meeting of the Association de la Jeunesse Juive in 1919, impressed upon his audience that Zionism should be understood as part of a broader dream rather than as a philanthropic project, to 'reconcile all the interests of all the nations, each with its particular genius in order to further the development of human thought'. Marx invoked the greatness of ancient Jewish civilization, 'sadly forgotten by modern Jews', and suggested that to let the Jews relaunch their 'marvellous civilization in their land of origin' would not only be in their own interests but in the interests of human progress more broadly.[17] This line of argument, presenting Zionism as a 'different' kind of nationalism, characterized by its commitment to pacifism and internationalism, was another central theme in French Zionist discourse in the 1920s.

Most of the leaders of the French Zionist movement were also active in left-wing political and literary circles. Jean-Richard Bloch and Henry Marx were members of the French Communist Party. Léonce Bernheim, Fernand Corcos, and Léon Blum, as well as many of the non-Jewish members of France-Palestine—Paul Painlevé, Albert Thomas, Justin Godart, and Anatole de Monzie—were prominent socialist or radical politicians, many of whom served as government ministers when the Cartel des Gauches (an alliance of radicals and socialists) came to power in 1924.[18] The support of all of these figures for Zionism was part of a larger humanitarian project and must be understood within the context of the strongly cosmopolitan orientation of French left-wing culture in the 1920s.[19]

In his study of left-wing French intellectual culture between 1900 and 1938, Christophe Prochasson distinguishes between activism during the Dreyfus affair and in the aftermath of the First World War. Whereas the Dreyfusard movement defended a certain vision of French republicanism,

[17] The text was printed in *Le Peuple juif* (13 Feb. 1920), 13.
[18] This coalition only lasted until 1926, at which point the moderate leader Raymond Poincaré was re-elected to office.
[19] France-Palestine was in fact the first of a network of analogous organizations, intended to function as a kind of Jewish Society of Nations, that Victor Jacobson helped to create throughout Europe in the mid-1920s: Belgique-Palestine was founded in March 1926, and Italy, Germany, Romania, and Bulgaria followed suit. Jacobson's project to reunite these groups in Geneva in 1927, however, never came to fruition. See Boukara, 'Justin Godart et le sionisme', 200.

he argues, post-war leftist culture in France was distinguished by its internationalism. With the end of the war and the realization of its full horror, liberal intellectuals for the most part abandoned the virulent nationalism of the Union Sacrée and regrouped around internationalist, pacifist platforms.[20] The birth of the Soviet Union also contributed to this internationalist mood. Though many liberal intellectuals became disillusioned with the Soviet Union after the early 1920s and ultimately affiliated with the socialists rather than the Communist Party,[21] the success of the Bolshevik Revolution created great excitement in liberal French circles and, like the Dreyfus affair twenty years earlier, sparked many young intellectuals' involvement with socialist politics.[22]

As was the case in the pre-war years, left-wing French intellectual culture was largely organized around broad-based journals that cut across sectarian lines.[23] These journals were often conceived as international endeavours: the creation of *Clarté* in 1919, published in seven languages, distributed in nine capitals, and organized around the principles of internationalism, pacifism, and justice, was among the first.[24] *Europe*, launched in 1923 as 'a truly independent review, free of all dogmatism, parties, schools of thought, for free spirits of all countries', became one of the most important poles of left-wing French artistic and literary life in the inter-war years.[25]

Zionist journals such as *La Revue juive* and *Palestine* were similarly conceived as Jewish contributions to a larger, universalist project. 'This review will be international', declared Albert Cohen in the first issue of *La Revue juive*, 'because it will teach Jews about themselves [and] provide opportunities for encounters between men of different races and religions.'[26] Justin

[20] Prochasson, *Les Intellectuels, le socialisme et la guerre*, 191–4.

[21] In 1920 the French Socialist Party split into the communist PCF, which was allied with the Soviet Union, and the socialist SFIO, which remained committed to realizing socialist objectives within the structure of French democracy. The majority of French intellectuals who initially joined the PCF had gravitated back to the SFIO by mid-decade. A watershed year came in 1923, when a whole group of prominent figures in the PCF were excluded from the party. These included a number of people active in Jewish circles, including Bernard Lecache, the author of *Jacob*, Henry Torrès, the lawyer who defended Schwartzbard, and Georges Pioch, a non-Jewish Zionist sympathizer who lectured for both the UUJJ and the Association Amicale des Israélites Saloniciens. Torrès and Lecache, as noted in Chapter 4, were among the founders of the Ligue Internationale contre l'Antisémitisme in 1929. Pioch joined the organization in 1930.

[22] Prochasson, *Les Intellectuels, le socialisme et la guerre*, 211. After the initial success of the revolution, Prochasson notes (pp. 248–57), the USSR itself evoked surprisingly little discussion in left-wing journals.   [23] Ibid., ch. 9.   [24] Ibid. 192–7.

[25] While the journal occasionally featured articles by right-wing thinkers (especially in the 1930s), its orientation was overwhelmingly socialist (ibid. 216). For a discussion of the networks of left-wing French literary and political journals created in the 1920s, see especially pp. 216–37.   [26] Cohen, 'Déclaration', 11.

Godart presented *Palestine* in the same light: 'This will be above all, an international review. Jewish life in Palestine and Jewish life the world over will
constantly be presented and analysed in the light of internationalist concerns.'[27] The UUJJ was founded with similarly internationalist and pacifist
goals. Raymond-Raoul Lambert represented the group in 1926 at the
Institute for Intellectual Co-operation, an organization set up by the League
of Nations to encourage young people from different countries to travel and
meet one another,[28] and the group was subsequently designated as a permanent delegate to represent Jewish associations at the Comité d'Entente
des Grandes Associations Internationales.[29]

This emphasis on Zionism as a universal moral good was also an important element in German Zionist discourse in the aftermath of the First World
War. The widely influential philosopher Martin Buber, for example, posited
Zionism as an 'ethical nationalism' as a way of reconciling his commitment
to Jewish nationalism with a sense of scepticism regarding the morality of
the concept of the nation-state.[30] In Germany, however, the liberal heyday of
early Weimar gave way to the growing threat of fascism and mounting antisemitism by the late 1920s, thus rendering this kind of discourse increasingly marginal in terms of German political reality. In France, by contrast,
where the Cartel des Gauches came to power in 1924, left-of-centre politics
continued to exercise a powerful, if intermittent, influence on the political
scene until the defeat of Léon Blum in 1938. This liberal political climate,
accompanied by a sense among contemporaries that antisemitism was on
the decline, helped to legitimize this brand of 'humanitarian Zionism'.

In his classic study *Orientalism*, Edward Said talks about the convergence
between French socialism and colonialism: more than elsewhere in Europe,
he notes, Orientalism was espoused by socialists and liberal republicans and
linked to a universalist, humanist outlook.[31] For progressive French intellectuals and politicians in the 1920s, support for the Zionist movement was
part of this 'humanitarian' colonialism. French Zionists often justified their
support for the movement by suggesting that a future Jewish state in Palestine would act as a positive moral influence in the Middle East. In a 1919 lecture for the Fédération Sioniste de France, Emile Pignot, a non-Jew, invoked
the history of the Jews as a dispersed people who have learned that 'the law of
progress for individuals as for peoples must be built exclusively on the prin-

[27] Godart, 'Le Sens d'une revue française: "Palestine"', *Palestine* (Oct. 1927), 5.
[28] R. R. Lambert, 'La Jeunesse et la coopération intellectuelle', *Chalom* (Mar. 1926), 1–2.
[29] Raymond-Raoul Lambert, 'L'Institut de coopération intellectuelle', *Chalom* (Dec. 1927/
Jan. 1928), 11–13.
[30] See Mendes-Flohr, *Divided Passions*, 168–78.   [31] Said, *Orientalism*, 250–4.

ciple of harmony' to justify his conviction that a future Jewish state would serve as a force of reconciliation and peace.[32] In the opening issue of *Palestine*, Justin Godart explained the *raison d'être* of both the journal and the Zionist movement as a whole in similar terms. Palestine, he explained, was 'a human experiment . . . associated first and foremost with the principle of justice'. Should the Jews' 'national sentiment' become a nationalism associated with religious superstition and political fanaticism, he went on to argue, it would be a major loss for Jews and non-Jews alike. If, by contrast, the Jews avoided these traps, their state would 'have the honour of serving as a role model for Europe'.[33] For Godart, as for Buber, the success of the Zionist experiment depended on the Jews creating a state that maintained its ethical integrity.[34]

Palestine as a Bridge between East and West

One of the most common arguments used to present the Zionist 'mission' in universalist terms was the idea that a Jewish presence in Palestine would form a bridge between East and West.[35] This argument featured prominently in the discussion surrounding the establishment of the Hebrew University of Jerusalem in 1925, which was greeted with an almost messianic fervour among French Zionists and their sympathizers. *Menorah* dedicated an entire issue to the founding of the university and published the thoughts and feelings of numerous Jewish and non-Jewish public figures surrounding the event. These articles emphasize two themes: first, that the university would serve as a spiritual and cultural centre, not just for Jews, but for all humanity; second, that the Jews had a unique and irreplaceable role to play mediating 'between' East and West. Georges Cattaui, whose contribution is entitled 'The Successful Result of Four Thousand Years of History', began by reminding his readers of the important role that Jews and Arabs played during the Middle Ages in transmitting the knowledge of ancient Greece and

[32] Pignot, 'Le Droit des Juifs', published in *Le Peuple juif* (3 Jan. 1919), 3.

[33] Godart, 'Le Sens d'une revue française', 3.

[34] In this context, discussion of 'the Arab problem' was kept to a minimum. French Zionists generally adhered to the official party line, that the establishment of a Jewish national homeland would be in the interests of a local Arab population oppressed by its own elites. De-emphasizing the nationalist aspect of the movement, Catherine Nicault suggests, was also a way for French Zionists to ignore the reality of an Arab–Jewish conflict of interest. See Nicault, 'L'Acculturation des Israélites français au sionisme', 19.

[35] In an article in *Chalom* Meyerkey summarized this argument and noted (approvingly) its prevalence in Zionist discourse of the day: 'Orient et Occident', *Chalom* (Aug. 1927), 22. For a discussion of this Orientalist discourse among French Jews in the 1920s, see Malinovich, '"Orientalism" and the Construction of Jewish Identity in France, 1900–1932'.

Rome to the Western world. After listing all the Jewish thinkers who influenced Western civilization through the ages, Cattaui went on to define what he saw as the particular importance of the Jews' role in the Middle East as 'a living contrast to Oriental sensuality, luxury, and idolatry . . . a vindication of the spirit and the heart'. For Cattaui, it was this special role of the Jewish people, 'who incarnate the link of the flesh that unites Occident and Orient' and 'serve as the intellectual courtesan through which exchanges between Islam and Christianity take place', that legitimated Zionism. Zionism was not merely of interest to the Jews, but rather had a wider humanitarian aim that would enable the Jews to fulfil their divine mission in the region.[36] While Cattaui's analysis clearly reflected a colonialist mindset, he understood the Jews' civilizing mission in the Orient as directly linked to their historic role 'between' East and West. The Jew was not just any European colonizer but rather one with both a visceral and a historical link to the Orient.

In an article in *Palestine*, Jean-Richard Bloch, who actually travelled to Jerusalem for the opening ceremonies, described the Oriental landscape of the university and the Occidental origins of the participants, representatives of 'science and humanism', as a paradox: 'What is this absurd dream, to implant Western science, Western thinking on Mount Scopus?', he asked rhetorically.[37] His response, which drew on the ideas of Martin Buber and the French Jewish Orientalist scholar Sylvain Lévi, was that only the Jews were capable of realizing this 'absurd dream' because they had retained an Oriental soul, while assimilating outwardly to the West.[38] For Bloch, the Jew's Oriental character was expressed in strongly racial terms: he was different from other peoples because he did not live, as they did, in his 'native land' among those who shared his ties of blood.

In Bloch's analysis we see an inversion of antisemitic arguments, which often relied on pointing to the Oriental nature of the Jews to justify their exclusion; while externally adapting to Western culture, the Jews retained their Oriental soul, thus rendering them inevitably and eternally foreign. Bloch, by contrast, evoked the idea of Jews having a distinctive Oriental soul as the source of their contribution to Western civilization: 'Europe offered the Jew liberty, equality, and dignity', he declared, and now was the time to return the favour, to fulfil the Jewish mission of reconciliation between East

[36] *Menorah* (1 May 1925), 126.

[37] Bloch, 'Quel service les Juifs peuvent-ils rendre au monde?', *Palestine* (Dec. 1927), 97–102.

[38] Bloch took Lévi's assertion that science and technology are inextricably linked to a humanist, Western world-view and as such cannot easily be exported to the Orient to suggest that only the Jews were capable of accomplishing this mission.

and West. If the Jew retained his essential nature, Bloch concluded, he would be 'not only a witness to the drama of the modern soul, but a mediator of the European consciousness'.[39] Raymond-Raoul Lambert made a similar argument in a 1928 article for the *Revue littéraire juive,* in which he noted with approval that the non-Jewish philosopher Georges Duhamel had 'dictated to the Jews their mission: to save European culture through the reconciliation of Europe and the Orient'. It was only through 'vital contact' between Orient and Occident, Lambert seconded, that there could be a 'renaissance of the European soul, of which a Mediterranean Judaism will be an influential element'.[40]

French Zionists in the 1920s did not invent this image of the Jew as a mediator between East and West. As early as 1828, Léon Halévy, a Saint-Simonian and the author of the first history of the Jews in the French language, argued that the French Revolution had provided the opportunity for a synthesis between Judaism, the spirit of the Orient, materialism, and industry, and Catholicism, the incarnation of spirituality and intelligence.[41] Similarly, the Wissenschaft scholar Salomon Munk emphasized the influence of medieval Arab Jewish scholars on Greek philosophy in order to illustrate the Jews' historic role as a bridge between East and West.[42] Even as the founders of the Alliance Israélite Universelle distanced themselves from the 'Oriental', Sephardi Jews to whom they intended to bring the benefits of Western civilization, notes historian Michel Abitbol, they too invoked a romantic identification with the 'Orient' to justify their charitable, educational, and cultural activities in the region.[43]

With the development of the French Zionist movement in the 1920s, however, this kind of romantic Orientalist discourse took on a newly concrete and political character. In the statements of Bloch, Cohen, and others, we see a colonialist attitude expressed in more modern terms. While the

[39] 'Quel service les Juifs peuvent-ils rendre?', 102.

[40] Lambert, 'Recherche d'une jeunesse juive de France', *Revue littéraire juive* (July 1928), 601. As noted in the *Revue littéraire juive,* Duhamel's article, entitled 'Enquête sur la culture européenne dans le monde', originally appeared in the Oct./Nov. 1927 issue of *Le Rouge et le noir.*

[41] Halévy's *Résumé de l'histoire des Juifs modernes* (1828) was preceded by his *Résumé de l'histoire des Juifs anciens* (1825). See Simon-Nahum, *La Cité investie,* 35.

[42] Simon-Nahum, *La Cité investie,* 117.

[43] See Abitbol, 'The Encounter between French Jewry and the Jews of North Africa'. In his study of 19th-century French synagogue architecture, Dominique Jarrassé argues that the synagogue itself was often conceptualized as a bridge between Orient and Occident, as a concrete link between the Jews' Eastern roots and their present location in the West. Jarrassé cites, for example, the commentary of the Jewish architect Abraham Hirsch, who wrote of the French synagogue in 1864: 'it served to reconcile the demands of the modern West with a faith that was born in the East'. See Jarrassé, *Une histoire des synagogues françaises,* 214.

means are different, the goal is essentially the same: to use the Jews as a conduit to bring European culture to the Middle East. Now, however, the Jews'
status 'between' Orient and Occident is no longer relegated to the historical,
romantic realm, but rather expressed in a newly racialized language as an
eternal aspect of the Jewish personality justifying Zionist political objectives.

While the Zionist press clearly popularized this notion in the 1920s, this
image of the Jew as a bridge between East and West was not exclusive to
Zionist sympathizers. For example, Sylvain Lévi, the president of the
Alliance Israélite Universelle who so angered André Spire and Chaim Weizmann with his anti-Zionist comments at the Paris Peace Conference, used
similar language to talk about the objectives of the Alliance: it was the students of the Alliance schools, as Orientals, he contended, who were charged
with the mission of constructing a bridge between East and West.[44] For Lévi,
as for the Zionists, this kind of language provided a way to talk about Jewishness in a cultural climate in which group difference—whether expressed
in racial, religious, or national terms—was increasingly taken for granted in
French society as a whole.

As we saw in Chapter 7, the reinvention of the Jew as 'Semitic' or
'Oriental' provoked mixed feelings among French Jews in the 1920s. While
some invoked Jews' 'Oriental' origins as a source of pride and an indicator of
vitality, this kind of discourse also reinforced the idea of the Jew as an eternal
outsider and often provoked strong feelings of alienation and loss. The idea
of the Jew as a link between East and West provided a way for Jews to express
their difference while simultaneously reinforcing the idea that they formed a
vital and necessary element in Western culture. Albert Cohen's euphoric
interpretation of the founding of the Hebrew University of Jerusalem, for
example, was based on the idea of this synthesis, which he had presented as
impossible in *Solal*. Cohen's novel depicts the Jew's territorial displacement,
his transposition from his Oriental home, as a source of alienation and
misery; his Zionist writings, by contrast, present the 'wandering Jew' and
Jewish existence in the diaspora in a positive light. It was the Jews, he declared, who had served as emissaries and united the diverse countries of
Europe. Their very rootlessness made them more universalist than other
peoples, and it was the Jew, as a representative of universalism, who would
unite East and West in Jerusalem: 'The Hebrew University', he declared,
'will be a meeting-place between three continents, a crucible where two conceptions of life will fertilize each other and perhaps give birth to a new
humanity.'[45] By imbuing his Jewishness with a political meaning compatible with the larger ethos of left-wing French culture of the day, Cohen was

---

[44] Chouraqui, *Cent ans d'histoire*, 211.   [45] Cohen, 'Déclaration', 10.

perhaps able to transcend the sense of alienation and 'otherness' that he felt as a Jew on a personal level. Zionism gave him the psychological tools that he needed to transform Jewish distinctiveness from something that tragically set the Jew apart into an essential component of a truly universal society.

In an essay written just before the First World War, 'The Spirit of Judaism and the Orient', Martin Buber similarly linked his support for Zionism to the idea of the Jews as 'mediators' between East and West. For Buber, however, this idea was linked to an anti-colonialist discourse, and in particular the idea that Europe was exercising undue influence on the Asian continent: 'The soul of Asia is being murdered', he concluded, and it was only the Jews who had the potential to keep this destruction at bay.[46] French Zionists, by contrast, often linked the success of the Zionist movement with French concerns about expanding both their political and cultural influence in the Middle East. Here we see the importance of particular national agendas in shaping Zionist discourse and politics. The few colonies that Germany had acquired in the late nineteenth century were lost after its defeat in the First World War. Thus in the Germany of the 1920s colonialism was linked with the authoritarian, militaristic regime brought down by the war and replaced by the Weimar Republic. In France, by contrast, this period marked the heyday of French colonial power and influence, a fact that the left as well as the right integrated into its understanding of national identity.[47] For most liberal French politicians and intellectuals, expanding French power and influence in both Africa and the Middle East became synonymous with the 'universal' goal of spreading the values of liberal humanism around the globe. Within this framework, Zionism became one of the discourses through which liberal politicians and intellectuals justified securing and preserving French power abroad. This idea underlay the creation of the Ligue des Amis Français du Sionisme in 1916, whose members, Catherine Nicault notes, 'saw themselves as champions of the cultural influence that France must legitimately conserve and develop in Palestine'.[48]

By the mid-1920s, a discourse linking Zionism with French national interests had become standard in the Jewish press. 'For our love of Erets Israel', Meyerkey affirmed in *Chalom*, 'we will work for the Jewish renaissance and the expansion of French influence in the Orient.'[49] In his state-

[46] This speech was originally published in 1916 in *The Spirit of Judaism*; it is reprinted in *On Judaism*, 156–78 (quote from p. 177). On German Jewish Orientalism, see the chapter by Mendes-Flohr, '*Fin-de-siècle* Orientalism' in his *Divided Passions*, and Biale, 'Shabataï Tzevi et les séductions de l'orientalisme juif'. Michael Brenner also touches on this theme in *The Renaissance of Jewish Culture in Weimar Germany*.

[47] On the pervasive influence of 'the enterprise of colonialism' on French culture in the inter-war years, see Ezra, *The Colonial Unconscious*.   [48] Nicault, *La France et le sionisme*, 111.

[49] Meyerkey, 'L'Inquiétude dans la renaissance et l'activité juives', *Chalom* (Feb. 1928), 16.

ment in support of the Hebrew University of Jerusalem, Léon Blum noted in a similar vein that the event 'touches doubly my French and Jewish heart'.[50] He first wrote of the Jews' historic mission as 'interpreters' of the Orient for the Occident. Now, he asserted, it was their great privilege to become messengers of 'the gospel that the Occident must bring to the Orient'. Blum went on, however, to express his hope that its founders would allow France, 'the educator and protector of the "peuples renaissants"', to play an important role in this new Jewish university. The new Judea, he concluded, 'will not forget that it was the French Revolution that first broke the Jews' chains and paved the way for their modern awakening'.[51] In Blum's formulation, Frenchmen and Jews would have parallel missions to carry out in the new Jewish homeland. Here we see an updated version of the idea of a linked French–Jewish mission that was such an important aspect of nineteenth-century Franco-Judaism. In the nineteenth century, French Jews equated the essence of Judaism with the ideals of the French Revolution to argue that to be a patriotic Frenchman was compatible with being a good Jew. The Jewish 'mission' was now given a new twist—by being a Zionist one was a good Frenchman, because the Jewish role in the Middle East would be of service to France and to all humanity.[52]

Re-evaluating Nineteenth-Century Franco-Judaism: Between Criticism and Admiration

Whereas André Spire's critique of the assimilatory mission of nineteenth-century French Jews was revolutionary in 1908, by the mid-1920s its basic premise had been integrated into the mainstream of French Jewish thinking. This comes across very clearly in Julien Weill's *La Foi d'Israël* (1926) and *Le Judaïsme* (1931), both written to convey the basic principles of Judaism to the French reading public. In the first chapter of *La Foi d'Israël*, entitled 'La Crise de l'Emancipation et de l'Assimilation', Weill describes the faulty logic by which the first generation of emancipated Jews was forced to redefine Judaism as a 'confession' in order to prove its French patriotism. Seduced by the cult of reason and universalism, he explained, this generation opened

---

[50] *La Revue juive* (Mar. 1925), 227.   [51] Ibid.

[52] French Zionists, Catherine Nicault argues, bolstered the notion that French and Zionist interests were one and the same by deliberately misrepresenting their government's attitudes and actions regarding Jewish nationalism. France-Palestine 'created a myth of a pro-Zionist tradition in French diplomacy', she argues, when in fact the French government's attitude towards the Zionist project—the subject of her 1992 book *La France et le sionisme*—can best be characterized by a combination of incomprehension, indifference, and outright hostility. See Nicault, 'L'Acculturation des Israélites français au sionisme', 20.

FIGURE 8 Léon Blum addressing a Zionist meeting in Paris, *Illustration juive*,
15 September 1922 (p. 14). Blum made his Zionist sympathies known by the
early 1920s. Here he is speaking on the occasion of the ratification of the
Palestinian Mandate by the United Nations in August 1922. The caption reads
'Léon Blum, Parisian deputy, giving his remarkable speech'
Reproduced by permission of the library of the Alliance Israélite Universelle

itself to a rapid process of assimilation that posed a threat to Jewish group
survival. For Weill, the 1905 separation of church and state was a major
turning-point which, in conjunction with the Dreyfus affair, the growth of
the Zionist movement, and finally the trauma of the First World War, forced
Jews to reflect on the significance of their Jewish heritage. This introspection, in turn, led many to renew their commitment to Judaism. Weill took the
variegated nature of modern Jewish identity for granted. While only a small
group of people identified with 'religious Judaism', he says in the introduction to *Le Judaïsme*, which he was invited to write as part of the publisher's
series on different religions, a great many others identified with a 'Judaism
without a label' that could be expressed in a variety of forms; moral, sentimental, or historical.[53]

If Weill's analysis indicates the extent to which a Zionist critique had
been integrated into 'normative' French Judaism by the mid-1920s, it is also

[53] *Le Judaïsme*, 8.

important to note the conciliatory attitude towards figures such as James Darmesteter and Joseph Reinach among Zionist sympathizers during this period. Speaking for the Union des Femmes Juives Françaises pour la Palestine in 1928, for example, Pierre Paraf praised the blossoming of Jewish cultural activity in post-war France. However, he went on to suggest that 'in our excitement for this rediscovered Judaism, we sometimes judge our assimilators . . . the majority of whom conserved a Jewish heart and heightened the prestige of their race . . . too harshly'. It was this first generation of Jews, he reminded his readers, 'that made the Jewish awakening that we celebrate today possible'.[54] For Paraf, the contemporary redefinition of Judaism in ethnic or national terms marked the completion, rather than the rejection, of the process of Jewish integration and acculturation that had begun with the French Revolution.

This perspective was also characteristic of Baruch Hagani. In addition to his writings on Zionism, Hagani published *L'Emancipation des Juifs*, a history of Jewish political emancipation in France, as part of the Rieder series in 1928, as well as numerous essays in the Jewish press on Enlightenment and prominent nineteenth-century figures. In an article on Moses Mendelssohn, for example, Hagani sought to counter the notion that, because Mendelssohn was the author of the ideal of integration and acculturation, contemporary Jews should criticize him for having set in motion the process of assimilation.[55] Rather, Hagani argued, at this point in the Jews' history the integration of Enlightenment ideals into Judaism represented a positive, healthy, and necessary development: 'a culture that turns in on itself and refuses outside influences', he wrote 'becomes sterile, and this was the situation that Jewish culture was in at Mendelssohn's time'.[56] He made a similar point in a 1921 article in *Le Peuple juif*, in which he criticized Zionists who took a negative view of Jewish emancipation as carried out by Napoleon. The process of 'individual' emancipation, Hagani impressed upon his readers, provided the catalyst necessary for the Jews to rise out of the misery of ghetto life to which they were doomed as a persecuted minority. It was the sense of dignity bestowed upon them by their status as equal citizens, in turn, that enabled certain among them to envision an autonomous Jewish state a century later.[57]

[54] Paraf, 'Le Réveil du judaïsme français', *Revue littéraire juive* (July 1928), 583.

[55] 'Moses Mendelssohn', *Menorah* (1 Feb. 1928), 38–40. It is interesting to note that *Menorah* also published a very positive review of Darmesteter's *Les Prophètes d'Israël* when it was republished in 1931: 'Prophetism', the author noted, 'is an eternal teaching, an excellent guide for today's perplexed.' See Henri Sérouya in *Menorah* (Jan./Feb. 1932), 15.

[56] Hagani, 'Moses Mendelssohn', 40.

[57] 'Le Centenaire de Napoléon', *Le Peuple juif* (22 Apr. 1921), 8–9.

While some French Zionists took a more critical stance than Hagani regarding the process of Jewish emancipation, this kind of criticism was often tempered by a conciliatory attitude towards the 'founding fathers' of nineteenth-century French Judaism. A close reading of *Chalom*, the organ of the UUJJ, reveals an interesting variety of attitudes.[58] As we saw in Chapter 5, Pallière and his entourage took the UUJJ in a decisively Zionist direction after 1928, putting the organization in an adversarial position in relation to the French Jewish religious establishment. This polarization was reflected in the pages of *Chalom*, where contributors felt increasingly free to attack the Jewish establishment for perpetuating what they saw as an outdated, assimilationist brand of Judaism. On the occasion of the hundredth anniversary of the death of the Abbé Grégoire, for example, *Chalom* published an article criticizing the mainstream community's hagiographic commemoration of him.[59] French Jews, the article stated, were united in praise of Grégoire as the author of their political emancipation. In fact, the author contended, Grégoire—whose ultimate goal was Jewish conversion to Christianity— should be remembered as an opponent of 'collective Jewish spirituality' who was also responsible for the rapid disintegration of Jewish community in the aftermath of the revolution.[60]

Even among UUJJ spokesmen critical of the Jewish establishment, however, this kind of combative rhetoric was often tempered by a sense of admiration for previous generations of French Jews. Wladimir Rabinovitch, for example, was an outspoken Zionist who responded vociferously to attacks on the UUJJ by the rabbinic leadership. Whereas the rabbis left Jewish youth to fend for itself, he contended in 1930 in *L'Univers israélite*, it was Jewish nationalism that turned the tide and reversed, at least to some degree, what would otherwise have been 'a certain path towards complete disappearance'.[61] In other of his writings, by contrast, Rabinovitch praised the ideals of

[58] While Rabinovitch remained at the UUJJ after the 1928 split, he was much more secular and politically minded than Pallière, and the two men increasingly came into conflict over the direction the organization and its journal should take. While Pallière remained the president of the UUJJ until its demise in the mid-1930s, Rabinovitch replaced him as editor of *Chalom* in 1929. This divergence, Catherine Poujol argues, accounts for the eclectic nature of the journal between 1929 and 1934. Poujol, 'Une exception', 35.

[59] Meir Leviah, 'L'Abbé Grégoire contre la synagogue', *Chalom* (June 1931), 4–7. Abbé Grégoire was the most prominent French proponent of Jewish political emancipation at the time of the revolution. While he defended the rights of Jews as individuals, Grégoire hoped that emancipation would ultimately lead to conversion. On Grégoire, see Sepinwall, *Abbé Grégoire and the French Revolution*. On debates surrounding the emancipation of the Jews, see Hertzberg, *The French Enlightenment and the Jews*, Jay Berkowitz, *The Shaping of Jewish Identity*, and Schecter, *Obstinate Hebrews*.   [60] Leviah, 'L'Abbé Grégoire contre la synagogue'.

[61] Wladimir Rabinovitch, 'L'UUJJ et le Nationalisme', *L'Univers israélite* (29 Aug. 1930), 664.

'the Darmesteters, the Salvadores, the Bernard Lazares', and criticized the leadership for failing to translate them into a commitment to Jewish community. The present generation, he contended, was left with no cultural heritage because 'the chiefs betrayed the troops and did nothing to conserve and awaken the faith of young people'.[62] It was not the ideological thrust of nineteenth-century Franco-Judaism, with its emphasis on the prophets as the bearers of a universal Judaism, to which Rabinovitch objected but rather the failure of the previous generation to translate these ideals into a vibrant modern Jewish community life.

The fact that the Zionism of Rabinovitch, Hagani, Paraf, and others of their generation was bound up with an overt sense of belonging to France as opposed to an ideal of immigration to Palestine undoubtedly played an important role in shaping their attitude towards the heroes of nineteenth-century French Judaism. While they criticized certain of the assumptions of their predecessors—the relegation of Judaism to the private sphere, its definition in purely religious terms—they nonetheless saw themselves as Franco-Judaism's intellectual and moral heirs, charged with the duty of handing on the torch to a new generation.

Reconciling Divergent Perspectives: Between Religion and Ethnicity

While some Zionist advocates in France remained committed to the idea of Zionism as a secular 'replacement' for a religiously based Jewish identity, much more widespread was a discourse emphasizing the spiritual and religious aspects of Zionist ideology and, by extension, the idea that these two visions of Judaism were not in opposition to each other. Similarly, while some religious leaders continued to attack Zionism and the idea of an 'ethnic' identity by arguing (like Théodore Reinach) that any definition of Judaism other than as a religion would call into question the Jews' patriotism, many tried to mesh these changes in Jewish discourse and self-conception with their continuing commitment to the Jewish religion. Two central themes that emerged during this period were, first, the idea that the Jewish 'religion' encompassed an ethnic or national conception of Jewishness and, second, that Zionism would act as an agent of Jewish awakening in the diaspora only if accompanied by a return to religious belief.

Aimé Pallière played a critical role in disseminating his particular brand of religious Zionism among French Jews in the 1920s, and we see his stamp

---

[62] 'Les Bâtisseurs', *Chalom* (15 July 1930), 16–20.

very clearly in the pages of *Chalom* as well as in the numerous other Jewish publications to which he contributed.[63] The notion that relating to Judaism in 'ethnic' or 'national' terms was problematic if it was not accompanied by a renewed sense of religiosity was central to the thinking of Meyerkey, who was a member of the UUJJ's central committee and wrote prolifically for *Chalom*.[64] Nineteenth-century Jews, Pallière, Meyerkey, and others often pointed out, had reduced Judaism to a mere 'confession' in order to align it with Christianity. In fact, however, the Jewish conception of religion was much wider. This idea is expressed very clearly in the UUJJ's educational programme for 1927. 'It is of the utmost importance', the group's education commission reported,

to attract the attention of our members to important religious issues. . . . We should be very careful, however, not to fall back on traditional teachings . . . it is important in particular to insist on the fundamental difference between Judaism and the contemporary formula whereby religion is a domain apart, composed of dogmas and observances that are necessarily associated with faith, whereas Hebraism is itself a life and constitutes a unique and indivisible phenomenon.[65]

Rather than rejecting a religious definition of Judaism, the UUJJ saw itself as redefining the concept of the Jewish religion to include the national and ethnic elements that were integral to it in pre-modern times. Contemporary debates as to whether or not the group was 'religious' in character, Aimé Pallière noted the following year in *Chalom*, would have been nonsensical to Jews in pre-modern society: 'Jewish people, Jewish religion: these elements were inseparable for them . . . the distinction between that which is secular and that which is religious is a foreign import into Judaism.'[66] The novelist Josué Jéhouda, in an interview with Rabinovitch in *Chalom* in 1930, expressed a similar sentiment by distinguishing between 'religion' and 'confession'. When asked, 'Do you think that religion has real significance in contemporary Judaism?', he responded: 'Certainly, but we will never succeed in shrinking Judaism into a confession.' Religion, he went on to explain, in keeping with the mystical orientation that characterized his literature, 'with its rituals and dogmas, is only an external manifestation of a synthetic science that remains hidden to us during an era in which con-

---

[63] On Pallière's influence, see Poujol, *Aimé Pallière*.

[64] Meyerkey, who clearly had a religious bent similar to that of Pallière, sided very strongly with the UUJJ president during the 1928 crisis. See Poujol, 'Une exception', 34.

[65] 'Programme général d'éducation', *Chalom* (1 June 1927), 7. Members of the UUJJ's education commission who were responsible for drafting the document included Guido Bachi, Joseph Castel, Edmond Fleg, Baruch Hagani, Aimé Pallière, Rabbi Stourdzé, and Hillel Zlatopolsky.   [66] Pallière, 'Questions et réponses', *Chalom* (Mar. 1928), 4.

fusion dominates. Our true religion', he asserted, was a much more inclusive concept that was 'the key to all human knowledge'.[67]

Though they often praised Zionism for breathing new life into a stagnant Judaism, many Jewish spokesmen and religious leaders believed that an ethnic or national Jewish identity was meaningless if it was not grounded in religious faith. In a 1918 essay for *Foi et réveil*, for example, Pallière argued that without the participation of religious Jews the new Jerusalem would be missing the most essential ingredient: 'the torch of its ancient faith'.[68] It was for this reason, he impressed upon his readers, that they must participate in the Zionist project. In a series of articles entitled 'Race ou religion' written for *Le Rayon* in 1926, David Berman similarly argued that a racial or ethnic Judaism must not negate religion if it was to maintain its legitimacy. Suppress the tenacity of the Jews' faith, he declared, and they would become a group like any other, destined to disappear 'with the progressive unification of human life'.[69]

In his articles for *Chalom*, Meyerkey spoke from the vantage-point of a leader of the Jewish youth movement of the day. He often defended the UUJJ's open-ended definition of Jewish identity and portrayed the secular aspect of contemporary Jewish youth culture as a healthy adaptation to modern life. In one of a series of articles devoted to issues facing contemporary French Jewry, Meyerkey expressed his support for the development of Jewish culture in a language reminiscent of that of Ahad Ha'am, the father of 'cultural Zionism'. Experience had shown, he argued, that religion as it was presently practised was insufficient to ensure Jewish continuity. André Pallière similarly contended that it was only by immersing themselves in Jewish culture, an endeavour which would be greatly facilitated by the creation of a Jewish centre in Palestine, that Jews would be able to maintain themselves as a distinct community.[70]

Meyerkey, like Ahad Ha'am, envisaged Palestine as a Jewish spiritual centre that would serve as a source of inspiration for those Jews who remained in the diaspora. Importantly, however, whereas Ahad Ha'am imagined a secular Jewish 'culture' replacing 'religion' as the basis of Jewish identity, for Meyerkey cultural activities were not an end in and of themselves, but rather a road back to religious renewal. Like the leaders of Chema Israël, he lamented the loss of religious faith among contemporary Jewish youth. He believed, however, that it was only through developing Jewish

[67] Wladimir Rabinovitch, 'Un quart d'heure avec Josué Jéhouda', *Chalom* (15 Mar. 1930), 12.
[68] 'Jérusalem, un centre spirituel pour l'humanité', *Foi et réveil*, 6 (1918), 27.
[69] *Le Rayon* (15 June 1926), 12.
[70] Meyerkey, 'L'Inquiétude dans la renaissance et l'activité juives', 16.

social and cultural life that faith could be restored. 'Perhaps those who return to Judaism thanks to Zionism and the UUJJ', he reflected, 'will sometimes finish by understanding that faith is the base, the crowning glory of Judaism.'[71] Josué Jéhouda concluded his 1930 interview with *Chalom* in a similar vein: 'Outside religion in a universal sense', he declared, 'there is no such thing as Jewish thought. The genius of the Jewish people is essentially religious.'[72]

Re-evaluating Assimilation

For Jewish communities throughout Europe and the United States in the nineteenth century, assimilation was an essentially positive term that referred to the process of Jewish adaptation and integration into modern society as equals. Certain French Jews, like their German counterparts, began to criticize 'assimilation' with the advent of the Zionist movement, at which point the term came to refer to the complete absorption of the Jews into the surrounding society. Nonetheless, a divergent political and cultural context shaped the way in which French and German Jews developed critiques of assimilation. As Michael Brenner has shown, a common denominator in German Jewish literature in the Weimar years was a negative image of the 'assimilated' German Jew, torn between antisemitism and denial of Jewishness.[73] German Jews had adapted to German cultural and social norms, critics of assimilation argued, but had never truly been accepted as equals by the surrounding society. In France, where Jewish social integration had succeeded to a much greater extent than in Germany, this kind of discourse never became normative. Criticism of the excesses of 'assimilation' was most often tempered by a sense of respect for and gratitude to previous generations, who had paved the way for Jewish integration into French society.

As noted in Chapter 4, David Berman's contributions to *Foi et réveil* in the immediate post-war years focused on the encounter between east and west European Jews on the battle front and the appreciation for divergent models of Jewishness that often grew out of these exchanges. In articles for *Chalom*, *L'Univers israélite*, and *Le Rayon* in the 1920s, Berman became a voice of reconciliation between 'religious' and 'national' Jews. He often tried to stake a middle ground and show the similarities between these two definitions. In

71 Meyerkey, 'L'Inquiétude dans la renaissance et l'activité juives', 16.
72 Rabinovitch, 'Un quart d'heure avec Josué Jéhouda', 12.
73 Brenner, *The Renaissance of Jewish Culture in Weimar Germany*, 131.

an article that appeared in *L'Univers israélite* in 1927, for example, he noted that each of these groups accused the other of assimilation. Zionists contended that religious Jews reduced their Judaism to a mere confession; for religiously minded Jews, by contrast, it was the Zionists' secularism that represented the real 'assimilationist' threat. 'The "Jew on the street" who found himself caught between these two opposing tendencies', Berman lamented, no longer trusted his own judgement: 'Where does assimilation start and where does particularism end? Should we never assert ourselves for fear of being too particularistic, or should we never change for fear of assimilating? Do we stop being men when we live as Jews, and do we stop being Jews when we are preoccupied with being men?'[74]

In fact, Berman proposed, all modern Jews found themselves somewhere on the continuum between assimilation and particularism: whereas religious Jews allowed for 'national, social, and often racial assimilation' while retaining 'the particularism of principles and rites', national Jews 'refuse this national assimilation, but leave the door wide open to intellectual, social, artistic, and worldly assimilation'.[75] A minimum of particularism was as inevitable as a minimum of assimilation, he concluded: 'What makes us all Jews is the *totality* of that which distinguishes us from others.'[76] Many Jewish leaders, both religious and lay, understood this issue in a similar light. Reporting on a 1926 conference held at the UUJJ on the subject 'Will Zionism Resolve the Jewish Question?', for example, *L'Univers israélite* noted that for both Union Libérale rabbi Louis-Germain Lévy and Léonce Bernheim, the president of the short-lived Union Sioniste Française, 'the Zionist movement and assimilation do not necessarily exclude but rather complete one another'.[77]

In a 1931 article for *Chalom* Aimé Pallière sought to rehabilitate the concept of assimilation by distinguishing it from 'de-Judaization'. While the latter represented the negation of one's Jewishness, assimilation, by contrast, was something positive: 'the tendency of the Jewish soul to adapt itself to existing circumstances in order to maintain and save Judaism'.[78] This argument is very similar to that which the Union Libérale (of which Pallière was a leader) used to justify changes to Jewish religious liturgy and ritual. Rather than a sign of the demise of Judaism, change was to be taken as indicative of Judaism's ability to adapt and survive in a new social and cultural context.

[74] Berman, 'Assimilation et particularisme', *L'Univers israélite* (9 Dec. 1927), 357.
[75] Ibid.   [76] Ibid. 358 (original emphasis).
[77] 'Conférence à l'UUJJ', *L'Univers israélite* (5 Nov. 1926), 267.
[78] Pallière, 'Jakin, Boaz et la troisième colonne', *Chalom* (June 1931), 8–10.

Redefining the Essence of Judaism: Jewish Religious Thought in the 1920s

In the post-war years, people writing and lecturing about the Jewish religion emphasized two principal themes: balancing a universalist and particularist understanding of the nature of Judaism and negotiating a definition of Judaism as a rational religion with an emphasis on its spiritual, emotive aspect. While their concerns were different from those of Zionist spokesmen, the basic issues that religious leaders were dealing with were similar. Now that the existence of distinct national or ethnic 'essences' as well as the non-rational aspects of human nature had become widely accepted in French society as a whole, they were faced with the challenge of redefining the 'essence of Judaism' to fit this shifting social and cultural reality.

Between Universalism and Particularism

A discourse emphasizing the universality of Judaism, which was at the core of nineteenth-century Franco-Judaism, remained a guiding principle of Jewish religious thought in the 1920s. At the same time that religious leaders continued to emphasize the idea of Judaism as a universal religion, however, they sought to balance this vision with an ideology emphasizing the value of particularism. For both James Darmesteter and Théodore Reinach, Perrine Simon-Nahum notes, Jewish particularism as exemplified in talmudic law was the result of the Jews' position as an oppressed minority: the true 'essence' of Judaism for these figures lay in its universalist message. In response to Renan's attack on Judaism's exclusivity and dogmatism, for example, Darmesteter argued that this charge was not exclusive to Judaism: in all religious systems, including Christianity, universalist principles such as justice and charity tended to evolve towards sectarianism and dogmatism.[79] In other words, Darmesteter did not defend rabbinic Judaism per se, but rather emphasized 'prophetic', Mosaic Judaism as the unencumbered true essence of the religion. Jewish religious thinkers in the 1920s, by contrast, tended to argue that the particularistic aspects of Judaism were in fact a positive and necessary complement to its universalism.

The reasoning behind Aimé Pallière's decision to remain a Noahide, for example, grew out of his understanding of Judaism as a religion that is both universal and respectful of particularism. Unlike Christianity, he argued, Judaism does not require conversion for salvation, but rather goes beyond the idea of tolerance to embrace 'a sincere respect for all of humanity's reli-

---

[79] Simon-Nahum, *La Cité investie*, 236.

gious forms'.[80] For Pallière, it was this aspect of Judaism that made it the 'true' universal religion: in contrast to Christianity, which holds that all men must believe in its precepts and teachings to be saved, 'Judaism proclaims that men of all races and beliefs will have a place in the world to come if they live a just life'.[81] Pallière's message was very well received within the Jewish community. Speaking at a standing-room-only debate on Pallière's 1926 memoir, *Le Sanctuaire inconnu*, organized by the UUJJ at one of the largest lecture halls in Paris, Meyerkey commented on Pallière's impact on Jewish youth of the day: 'Pallière has never ceased to reveal to them the two aspects of Judaism: its particularism, which justifies their attachment to their own traditions, and its universalism, which . . . has enabled them to think of themselves as citizens of the world.'[82] Meyerkey was joined by rabbis Jules Bauer, Julien Weill, and Louis-Germain Lévy in praising both Pallière's decision to remain a Noahide and his positive influence within the contemporary Jewish community.[83]

In their writings on Jewish prayer, Pallière, Bauer, and Weill all emphasized this idea of Judaism containing a complementary message of universalism and particularism. While the memory of the departure from Egypt exemplified the tribal, ethnic aspect of Judaism, Pallière argued, in prayers such as the Kaddish and the Aleinu this event was given a universal significance because it is linked with a desire for the coming of a messianic age, not only for Jews but for all peoples.[84] The two prayers that precede the Shema, Bauer argued in a similar vein, illustrate the dualistic nature of Judaism. The first has no specifically Jewish content but rather praises God in the name of all humanity, whereas the second speaks specifically to Jews. In this way, 'universalism and particularism, these two inseparable aspects

---

[80] Pallière, 'Le Judaïsme et la pensée contemporaine', *Foi et réveil*, 12 (1920), 133.

[81] Id., 'Le Judaïsme, son évolution, ses caractères distinctifs', *Foi et réveil*, 14 (1921), 1–18.

[82] Meyerkey, '*Le Sanctuaire inconnu* à l'UUJJ', *Le Rayon* (15 Jan. 1927), 5.

[83] Maurice Liber was the only speaker to criticize Pallière's decision to remain a Noahide. For Liber, whose views were seconded by an editorial in *L'Univers israélite* (M. Cohn, 'Le "Sanctuaire inconnu"', *L'Univers israélite* (11 Feb. 1927), 709–13), Noahidism was too vague a concept to serve as a model religion. Numerous Jewish papers featured articles describing the events. See Meyerkey, '*Le Sanctuaire inconnu* à l'UUJJ' and 'Le Sanctuaire inconnu', *Chalom* (15 Feb. 1927), 5–6; and 'Le "Cas Pallière" à la tribune de l'UUJJ', *Menorah* (1 Mar. 1927), 78, summarizing Liber's position. See also Gustave Kahn and André Spire's very favourable reviews of Pallière's memoir: Kahn, 'Le Noachisme', *Menorah* (15 Jan. 1927), 22, and Spire, '*Le Sanctuaire inconnu*', pts 1 and 2, *L'Univers israélite* (12 Aug. 1927, pp. 543–6 and 19 Aug. 1927, pp. 582–3). For more on Pallière's autobiography and reactions to the book among both Christians and Jews, see Poujol, *Aimé Pallière*, 257–70.

[84] Pallière, *La Prière juive*, 26. Pallière elaborated on this argument in 'Le Judaïsme, son évolution, ses caractères distinctifs', 18.

of our religion that mutually illuminate and complete each other, coexist admirably in our liturgy'.[85]

In language that harks back to Louis-Germain Lévy's comments at the Geneva conference in 1905, Weill argued in *La Foi d'Israël* that Judaism's universal message is best conveyed though the practice of its particular rituals and beliefs. A discourse emphasizing Judaism's commonalities with other religions, in particular Christianity, he asserted, responded insufficiently to the need of the present generation to connect with a 'living Judaism' rather than the dry, intellectualized faith developed by nineteenth-century religious thinkers such as Théodore Reinach.[86] Weill further developed this idea in *Le Judaïsme*, in which he described the Jews as a 'minority in service of the majority'. For Weill as for Pallière, Judaism was rooted in the historic and ethnic soil of its origins, and its universal message could only be conveyed to the world if the particular beliefs and practices of the Jewish people were conserved. Universalism and particularism are complementary, he stated, and it was Judaism's particularism that gave life to its universal message.[87]

Creating a 'Spiritual' Judaism

As we saw in Chapter 4, a shifting emphasis on religion as a personal, emotional experience shaped both Jewish and Christian religious discourse in the years before the First World War. This trend was greatly accentuated by the upheaval of war and the devastating toll, both physical and emotional, it took on French society. A sense of spiritual crisis helped to create an audience for books and journals focused on Christian spirituality, and a number of saints' cults created during those years—most importantly, that of Jeanne d'Arc, who was canonized in 1920—were drawing thousands of pilgrims by mid-decade. The Christian mysteries and the lives of the saints were also popularized in the literature, theatre, and cinema of the day.[88] The lessening of the clerical/anti-clerical feud of the nineteenth century played an important role in legitimating this kind of 'spiritual' Catholicism. Religion was no longer seen as a threat to republicanism and, as one contemporary put it, 'the religious idea was integrated into civic life'.[89]

Michael Meyer highlights a similar shift in Jewish religious culture in both Germany and the United States in the post-war years. A comparison of the 1905 and 1922 versions of Leo Baeck's seminal work *The Essence of*

---

[85] Bauer, 'Notre rituel de prières', *Foi et réveil*, 9 (1919), 245.   [86] *La Foi d'Israël*, 18–20.

[87] *Le Judaïsme*, 10–16.   [88] Cholvy, *Histoire religieuse de la France contemporaine*, ii. 324–8.

[89] Quoted ibid. 259. On Catholic religious culture in the 1920s, see also Schloesser, *Jazz Age Catholicism*.

Judaism, he notes, underscores these changes in religious attitudes. The first edition defined Judaism's essence as ethical monotheism and stressed the universal, rational aspects of the religion. The 1922 edition, by contrast, put an emphasis on the 'unfathomability of the divine'.[90] For the younger generation of German rabbis, the rejection of rationalism was often more definitive. Max Weiner, a Berlin rabbi born in 1882, for example, criticized nineteenth-century rationalism as responsible for the decline of modern Jewish religiosity and 'demanded a religious renewal based on the integration of non-rational elements—the feeling of belonging to the Jewish people and the self-consciousness of the particularity of the Jews as a chosen people—into modern Judaism'.[91] By the mid-1920s many Reform rabbis in the United States had similarly come to believe that their movement should respond better to congregants' individual religious needs.[92]

Martin Buber's brand of mystical Judaism played an important role in popularizing this shift in religious discourse in Germany. Deeply influenced by the revival of mystical traditions in the Germany of his day, Buber revolted against the Wissenschaft model of Judaism as a uniquely rational religion and immersed himself in the study of kabbalah and Jewish mysticism. His hasidic tales were enormously popular in the 1920s, in large part because they enabled assimilated Jews to connect with an emotive, mystical brand of Judaism in tune with the broader religious climate of the day.[93] The writings and lectures of Aimé Pallière had a similar impact on French Judaism in the 1920s. Pallière was not an intellectual or cultural figure of Buber's stature, nor was his rejection of nineteenth-century Judaism as radical as Buber's. Nonetheless, in numerous lectures and articles emphasizing mysticism and self-discovery as key elements of the Jewish religious experience, Pallière played an important role in moving French Judaism from the rationalist focus of the nineteenth century. Pallière studied with Elie Benamozegh, the chief rabbi of Livorno, and it was Benamozegh who first introduced him to kabbalah.[94] A fascination with the mystical, irrational aspects of the Jewish

[90] Meyer, *Response to Modernity*, 208.

[91] Brenner, *The Renaissance of Jewish Culture in Weimar Germany*, 45.

[92] Meyer, *Response to Modernity*, 315.

[93] Paul Mendes-Flohr underscores the importance of Buber's hasidic tales *The Story of Rabbi Nachman* (1906) and *Legends of the Ba'al Shem Tov* (1908) in the 'Jewish awakening' of a number of prominent figures in Weimar Germany. See *Divided Passions*, 100. On Buber's impact see also Brenner, *The Renaissance of Jewish Culture in Weimar Germany*. Buber's ideas were one of the main sources of spiritual inspiration for the Weimar youth movements, he notes, which was attracting a third of German Jewish youth by the mid-1920s (p. 47).

[94] Pallière described his encounter with Benamozegh in *Le Sanctuaire inconnu*. It was Benamozegh, André Zaoui notes ('Un grand serviteur de Dieu', 9), who introduced Pallière to kabbalah.

faith remained a key element of Pallière's Judaism throughout his life.[95] Writing about his influence on the Union Libérale, Marcel Greilsammer noted that Pallière's strongly mystical bent balanced the rationalist orientation of Louis-Germain Lévy. One of Pallière's contributions to the Synagogue Libérale de la rue Copernic, for example, was the introduction of a 'meditation hour' between Saturday afternoon services and Havdalah, a ceremony that marks the end of the sabbath.[96]

Pallière talked about the changes that he had helped to bring about in the Union Libérale in an interview for the Orthodox German Jewish newspaper, *Der Israelit*. Unlike its German counterpart, Pallière insisted, French Reform was not a politicized 'scientific' movement at odds with Orthodoxy. Although liberal French Jews had adapted their practices to fit the exigencies of modern life, he explained, they were members of a larger Jewish community organized around the Consistory, in which liberal and traditionalist Jews worked together.[97]

Rabbis Jules Bauer, Julien Weill, and Maurice Liber—the three most important Jewish religious leaders of the day—did not reject the image of Judaism as a rationalist religion worked out over the course of the nineteenth century. In their lectures, sermons, and writings, however, they often expressed a concern with conveying the mystical, emotional side of Jewish religiosity and combating an image of Judaism as a dry, sterile religion that had gained currency in Christian religious thought beginning in the late nineteenth century.[98] Maurice Liber addressed this issue in a 1922 article for *L'Univers israélite* as part of his review of *Le 'Fait religieux' en France*, a book that assessed the impact of the separation of church and state on the Protestant, Catholic, and Jewish communities. In assessing the range of the Jewish community's educational activities, Liber noted, the author correctly

---

[95] Zaoui ('Un grand serviteur de Dieu', 11) notes that Pallière was especially influenced by the concept of *kavanah* (inward intention) as central to one's relationship to religion. This idea was also central to the thinking of German and American religious figures such as Franz Rosenzweig and Abraham Joshua Heschel. See Novak, 'The Quest for the Jewish Jesus', 119.

[96] Greilsammer, 'Aimé Pallière à l'Union Libérale Israélite', 15–22.

[97] The interview, given in conjunction with the translation of *Le Sanctuaire inconnu* into German, was republished in *L'Univers israélite* (6 Jan. 1928), 492.

[98] Meyer discusses the impact of this turn in Christian religious thought on the German Reform movement in the early 20th century. From the 1880s, he notes, prominent German theologians began to contrast Judaism and Christianity in very stark terms: whereas Judaism, to the detriment of genuine spirituality, was concerned exclusively with the law, they argued, Christianity was a 'genuine' religion centred on love and emotion. This idea was developed in particular by Julius Welhausen, one of the most influential German biblical scholars of the late 19th century, and Adolf Harnack, whose 1906 book *The Essence of Christianity* had a major impact on Christian religious thinking of the day. See Meyer, *Response to Modernity*, 202–3.

observed that these were few and far between. Not only did the Jewish community possess little in the way of educational institutions, he concurred with the author, but even these tended to be more philanthropic than religious: 'we are obliged to admit that in almost all of our institutions the spirit of religion is too often replaced by the spirit of charity, which is fundamentally secular in nature'.[99] Liber's concerns must be understood within the context of the wave of Jewish conversions to Catholicism in the immediate post-war years. The predominance of philanthropic institutions within the Jewish community was problematic because he feared that their 'materialistic' orientation would prove insufficient to keep young French Jews, whose search for a spirituality rooted in emotion had been accentuated by the experience of war, to remain within the Jewish fold. It was only in the post-war years, Liber concluded, that the Jewish community had begun to recognize the importance of organs of religious propaganda such as Chema Israël in encouraging the spiritual growth of Judaism.[100] 'Matured by the trials of the war', read the group's first public statement in *L'Univers Israélite*,

we have taken cognizance of the necessity of returning to Judaism, not only to know and admire it, but also to practise it and to adapt our lifestyle to its teachings ... let us unite our efforts to create a generation attached to Judaism ... a generation for which Jewishness will be a living force rather than a mere label, a source of strength rather than pride.[101]

We see a similar concern with the idea of Judaism as a 'living force' in a lecture Liber gave for Chema Israël in 1922 as part of a series entitled 'Initiation au judaïsme', in which he sought to convey to his audience the premodern conception of Jewish community, 'kelal yisra'el', while at the same time avoiding the racial or national understanding of Jewishness associated with Zionism. While Liber referred approvingly to Salomon Reinach's assertion that Judaism was 'the embodiment of morality', he concluded by reminding his audience that 'we should not forget, however, that the spirit animates the body'.[102] Liber's concerns reflect the diminishing importance of *laïcité* as a reference point for French Jews. One of the main concerns of Jewish intellectuals and religious leaders in the nineteenth century had been to link Judaism with secular republican ideals such as justice, equality, and universal human rights. The lessening of the stigma attached to religion in the aftermath of the separation of church and state, however, made this 'secularization' of Judaism less compelling. For Liber and his contemporaries,

---

[99] Review by Ben-Ammi (one of Liber's pen names) of Rébelliau (ed.), *Le 'Fait religieux' en France*: 'Où en est le judaïsme français?', pts 1 and 2, *L'Univers israélite* (7 July 1922, pp. 341–5; 14 July 1922, pp. 365–70).   [100] 'Où en est le judaïsme français?', 368–9.
[101] 'Chema Israël! Appel à la jeunesse israélite', *L'Univers israélite* (28 Nov. 1919), 222–4.
[102] The text was printed in *Paix et droit* (Mar. 1922), 13–15.

the concern was no longer to prove that Judaism was compatible with repub-licanism, but rather to prove that it was as spiritually equipped as Catholi-cism to counter the rootlessness and malaise of modern secular society.

The writings and lectures of both Jules Bauer and Julien Weill were also punctuated by a concern for balancing spirituality and emotion with ration-alism. Speaking at a Chema Israël conference in 1924 on the differences between Jewish and Christian messianism, for instance, Bauer praised the lack of supernatural beliefs in the Jewish conception of the messiah which, he noted approvingly, was 'imprinted with the spirit of reason and wisdom that characterizes Judaism'. In a 1923 article for *Foi et réveil*, by contrast, he responded to those Christian theologians who characterized the religion of the Pharisees as devoid of sentiment and true spirituality. In fact, Bauer assured his readers, the Pharisees' sense of morality was as 'pure, lofty, and generous' as that of the early Christians.[103] For Julien Weill, the superiority of Judaism over Christianity lay in the latter's excessively mystical quality. The concept of the Trinity and the idea of Jesus as the son of God, he argued, obscured the fundamental ethical precepts of religious belief.[104] Like Bauer, however, Weill also addressed contemporary Christian criticisms of Judaism as a 'cold abstraction' by emphasizing the importance of piety and emotion in Jewish religious history, the mysticism of kabbalah, the medieval poetry of Judah Halevi, the hasidic movement. Though he warned of the dangers of relying too heavily on mysticism, Weill concluded that both kabbalah and hasidism were healthy developments that saved Judaism from the excesses of rationalism.[105]

In his numerous writings and lectures, Pallière sought to share this spiritual aspect of Judaism with Jewish youth who, he believed, often turned away from Judaism in the mistaken belief that it could not meet their spirit-ual needs. The testimony of Marcel Greilsammer, who contributed to a posthumous tribute to Pallière, noted the important role that Pallière played in renewing both his own interest in Judaism and that of other Jews of his day: 'He revealed to me', Greilsammer recalled, 'more profoundly than my own family tradition, the profound meaning of our spiritual vocation.'[106] Jenny Schwob, he noted, also attributed her renewed commitment to Judaism to Pallière's influence, as did an 'eminent representative of

---

[103] Bauer, 'La Piété de nos docteurs', *Foi et réveil*, 19 (1923), 97.
[104] Weill, *La Foi d'Israël*, 17.   [105] Ibid. 73.
[106] Greilsammer, 'Aimé Pallière à l'Union Libérale Israélite', 19. Poujol's study, which draws on private correspondence between Pallière and his associates, confirms Greilsammer's insistence on the critical influence that Pallière had on Jewish religious thought in the 1920s.

Sephardi Jewry', whom Greilsammer left unnamed.[107] As Greilsammer's testimony suggests, for many the fact that a Christian's spiritual journey had led him to Judaism was an important factor in convincing them that they should stay within their own religious tradition.

As we saw in Chapter 3, one of the main arguments that the founders of the Union Libérale made in favour of changes in Jewish religious ritual was that many young religiously inclined Jews were turning towards Catholicism, which appeared better suited to their spiritual needs. Only by adapting to modern life, they argued, would Judaism be able to survive. In the 1920s, this theme took on a gendered dimension. Within the pages of *Le Rayon* we often find a similar set of concerns to those expressed by fictional characters such as Noémi or Sarah Lévy, who turned away from male-centred Jewish synagogue ritual at the same time that they valued the role that Judaism played in shaping their inner sense of spirituality. Defending the Union Libérale's sermons in Saturday morning services, *Le Rayon* noted that this innovation was especially important for women, who occupied an important place in the ranks of the Reform movement and were less likely than men to be able to follow a traditional service: 'Our sisters whose inability to read Hebrew separates them even more strongly from the liturgy have the need for personal piety that modern life so rarely provides them with.'[108]

Writing in *Le Rayon* in 1930, Clarisse Eugène-Simon described the group's accomplishments in terms of its success in keeping women within the Jewish fold: 'Among [the Union's] faithful', she stated, 'I know mothers who were tempted to convert both themselves and their children to Christianity. It sufficed to attend one of our services to realize that they would not find anything better in another religion.'[109] In contrast to an organization like Chema Israël that 'preaches to the converted', she concluded, the Union Libérale was committed to reaching out to those on the verge of turning away from Judaism altogether. Reaching out to young Jews who might be tempted to convert to Christianity was of particular importance to Aimé Pallière, who was himself of Christian origin. Though he remained theoretically committed to traditional Judaism, Pallière confessed in a 1924 article in *Le Rayon*, concern about losing Jews—in particular women—both to Christianity and to other spiritual movements of the day had convinced him of the need for the changes instituted by the Union Libérale. The modern reorientation of

---

[107] Ibid. Pallière moved into Jenny Schwob's home after she was widowed, and lived with her from 1933 until her death in 1938. Their relationship, Poujol indicates, was one of 'spiritual companionship' and was almost certainly platonic in nature. *Aimé Pallière*, 274.

[108] 'Le Judaïsme libéral et la tradition', *Le Rayon* (15 June 1927), 4.

[109] 'Les Idées de Louis et Ginette', *Le Rayon* (30 Oct. 1930), 17.

Judaism away from the home and into the synagogue created a great sense of alienation among women, whose religious obligations were traditionally in the home: 'If we could unite all the Jewish women of Paris who are presently frequenting Spiritist, Theosophist, Cosmic, Scientist, Bahai, Spiritualist and Christian churches', he lamented, 'all of the synagogues of the Consistory would not be sufficient to contain them.'[110]

To a certain extent, this shifting emphasis towards personal piety and spirituality within French Judaism can be understood as part of a larger shift in religious culture that affected both Christians and Jews. At the same time, however, this idea, which was of such central importance to Pallière, reflected the extent to which French Jews—and in particular those active in the ranks of the Reform movement—had internalized a Christian understanding of religiosity. Pallière's particular combination of Jewish doctrine and Christian religious sensibility may have appealed to many 'assimilated' French Jews precisely because it enabled them to stay Jewish while adapting to the religious norms of the larger society. Many of the innovations that he suggested—introducing meditation hours at the Union Libérale, organizing a spiritual retreat under the auspices of the UUJJ in 1927—were the same as those that were popular among young Catholics during this period.[111] A central theme in Pallière's writings was the idea, common in Christianity, that the practice of ritual was meaningless if it was not accompanied by 'religious feeling'. Writing in *Le Rayon* in 1921, for example, Pallière remarked that 'it is a great tragedy that true piety is more frequent among Christians than Jews' when in fact 'all of pure Christian piety is also present in Judaism'.[112] As this article suggests, at the same time as Pallière sought to impress upon Jews the richness of their own religious tradition, his concern was not so much to encourage religious observance—which is how religiosity is traditionally defined in Judaism—but rather to bring to light those aspects of Judaism that most resembled a faith-oriented Christian model.

Despite the importance of such a model to the Union Libérale, people involved with the movement also invoked traditional rituals as a necessary conduit towards spiritual renewal. As Michael Meyer has shown in his dis-

[110] 'Simples réflexions sur la "Reforme"', *Le Rayon* (15 Jan. 1924), 4. Pallière's comments, it should be noted, may have rested as much on popular prejudice as on reality. Whereas the evidence in fact suggests that women were more likely to continue practising Judaism than their male counterparts, Hyman, *Gender and Assimilation in Modern Jewish History*, 45, notes that the notion that women bear the primary blame for radical assimilation became a common theme in the Jewish press throughout western Europe and the United States from the late 19th century.

[111] On the religious retreat, see 'Les Dix Commandements du participant à la "Semaine" de la jeunesse juive', *Chalom* (Aug. 1927), 3–4.

[112] 'La Piété juive', *Le Rayon* (15 Oct. 1921), 9–13.

cussion of German and American Reform, the emphasis on spirituality and mysticism in the inter-war years was concurrent with the revival of many practices abandoned by the previous generation, whose principal concern was to adapt Judaism to a rationalist world-view. Traditions such as the wearing of the *talit*, the blowing of the *shofar*, or the construction of a *sukah*, once considered superfluous or antiquated, now began to be revalued as key to both the preservation of Jewish community and the promotion of genuine religiosity.[113] In France, where the Reform movement was only created in 1907, this shift took place within a much shorter time-frame. A 1924 article in *Le Rayon*, for example, lamented the abandonment of rituals welcoming fiancées into the synagogue and presenting newborn children to the congregation: 'these touching ceremonies', the paper noted, 'give the Jewish religion a familial quality that other religions rightly envy'. 'Our desire', the author concluded, 'is to resuscitate this community life as much as possible by reacquainting ourselves with these customs and transforming them.'[114] Here we see an attitude towards religious ritual similar to that of certain elements within the Zionist movement. As Shlomo Avineri notes in an essay on Zionism and Jewish religious tradition, labour Zionists in particular did not reject Jewish religious ritual so much as they sought to transfer its value to support Jewish community life. Holidays such as Passover, Hanukah, and even the sabbath were no less important for socialist kibbutzim than for their Orthodox compatriots, but these holidays were interpreted in particular ways: Hanukah was a triumph in a nationalist Jewish war; Passover became both a spring agricultural festival and a celebration of liberation.[115]

For the Union Libérale, it was the ideal of awakening one's inner spirituality that the practice of traditional Jewish religious rituals would ultimately accomplish. Often, however, this took the form of emphasizing the importance of the family-based, communal aspect of Judaism. At a sermon for the group's monthly youth service in 1925, for example, Louis-Germain Lévy told the story of a young boy from an assimilated family who, having spent Passover with his pious grandfather, found his soul awakened to the pleasures of Jewish ritual and family life. Lévy concluded with the hope that his young audience would have a similar experience at their own seders. The Union Libérale, like Chema Israël, organized seders for members who did not have a family group with which to celebrate. This practice, *Le Rayon* asserted, was intended to honour the familial aspect of Judaism, which should occupy as important a place in Jewish life as public rituals.[116]

[113] See Meyer, *Response to Modernity*, chs 5 and 8.
[114] 'La Vie de la communauté', *Le Rayon* (15 May 1924), 5.
[115] Avineri, 'Zionism and Jewish Religious Tradition', 6.
[116] 'La Vie de la communauté', 6.

Reflecting on Martin Buber's impact on contemporary Jewish thinking, Julien Weill acknowledged both the influence and the limits of the German philosopher's ideas in France. In contrast to Germany, where Buber's brand of 'mysticism of race and blood' had obtained a cult-like following, he explained, in France these ideas formed but one component of a multi-faceted Judaism: 'While it may not be the dominant influence', Weill concluded in his own discussion of Judaism, 'Jewish blood inspired at least to some degree the Jewish outlook and sensibilities.'[117] At the same time as Weill was attracted to certain aspects of Buber's thinking, he also distanced himself and French Judaism from it, stating unequivocally: 'this thinker belongs to German Judaism'.[118] Weill's comment reveals an important difference between French and German sensibilities. German Jews, living in a nation with a highly racialized understanding of national identity, adopted a similar understanding of their own sense of connection to Judaism. In France, by contrast, where nationalism was defined more in cultural terms, Buber's highly racialized discourse, with its essentialist emphasis on Jewish difference, remained a distinctively foreign import.

Weill's comments highlight both changes and continuities within Franco-Judaism in the 1920s. While French Jews may have experienced Judaism as more than a 'confession' at the turn of the century, by the early 1930s they had developed a language with which to express the complexity of their identity. While by no means universally accepted, an ethno-cultural understanding of Judaism—whether expressed within the framework of Zionism or within a religious discourse emphasizing the value of Jewish particularism—had come to exercise an important influence in France by 1932. Importantly, however, this interest in Jewish particularism was not accompanied, for the most part, by an essentialized understanding of Judaism as an all-encompassing 'racial' identity. As they had in past generations, French Jews continued to express their particularism through the language of universalism and a sense of belonging and attachment to France.

---

[117] Weill, *Le Judaïsme*, 184–5. [118] Ibid.

Conclusion

THIS STUDY has described a process of Jewish self-questioning and cultural activity in France that began with the Dreyfus affair and reached its peak in the late 1920s. In contrast with Germany, where the Nazi rise to power marked a clear moment of closure for the Jewish cultural renaissance of the Weimar era, the trends and activities that I have described in France did not end abruptly in 1933. And yet by the mid-1930s, important changes, both in France and on the international stage, changed the priorities, concerns, and activities of French Jews. The Nazi rise to power had a profound, if initially indirect, impact in France. Whereas the problem of antisemitism remained a relatively minor issue for French Jews in the 1920s, in the 1930s it necessarily became a central concern. The advent of a virulently antisemitic dictatorship that enacted discriminatory legislation against Jews in western Europe sent shock waves through the French Jewish population. The fact that an antisemitic government had been elected to power in a modern democratic nation with a highly acculturated Jewish population belied the assumption, dominant in France in the 1920s, that antisemitism was atavistic and in the process of disappearing with the progress of democracy. Furthermore, in contrast to the 1920s, antisemitism was also on the rise in France in the 1930s: 'Economic depression, mass migration, the emergence of the Popular Front, and the threat of war', Paula Hyman notes, 'combined to fuel antisemitic sentiment that was then widely disseminated by the press and popular literature.'[1] Antisemitic press organs proliferated in the 1930s, reaching a circulation in the millions by the end of the decade. The economic depression also played a critical role in increasing hostility towards immigrants. Action Française regularly sent hooligans into immigrant neighbourhoods, and a number of other right-wing political leagues had taken a decided turn towards antisemitism by the mid-1930s.[2]

---

[1] Hyman, *The Jews of Modern France*, 145.

[2] Ibid. 147. The extent and nature of antisemitism in France in the 1930s has been an issue of debate among scholars. While some emphasize its pervasiveness as paving the way for Vichy's anti-Jewish legislation, others analyse manifestations of antisemitism in the 1930s primarily as part of a larger and ultimately more deep-seated xenophobia rampant in France during this period. For the former position, see notably Schor, *L'Antisémitisme en France pendant les*

Both the economic depression and the increase in antisemitism dealt a severe blow to many of the organizations and activities that were at the centre of the Jewish cultural renaissance of the 1920s. *Palestine* and the *Revue littéraire juive* ceased publication in 1931. *Menorah*'s last issue appeared in 1933, the same year as the final book in Rieder's Judaism series. Both Chema Israël and the UUJJ had ceased to exist by 1935. Their demise was due to a variety of factors, one of the primary ones, to be sure, being economic. Even more importantly, however, the mood of crisis of the 1930s exacerbated many of the tensions and differences within them. While Zionist, religious, politically active, and spiritually oriented Jews could coexist within an organization such as the UUJJ in the 1920s, these kinds of differences became much more problematic once the need to respond to the antisemitic crisis had taken centre stage.

Writing in 1950, Wladimir Rabinovitch recalled a major disagreement between himself and Pallière that led him to resign from the UUJJ. Observing the rise of antisemitism both in Nazi Germany and in France, Rabinovitch became much more political in terms of his personal orientation and the direction in which he wanted to take the group. He expressed these concerns in a 1934 article for *Chalom*: 'an extremely violent text', he recalled, in which he expressed his conviction that 'discussion was pathetic if it was not transformed into action'.[3] In his response the following week, Pallière expressed his disapproval of the virulently secular tone of the article, and in the central committee meeting that followed Rabinovitch resigned from the organization. He later regretted his decision. Pallière's attitude was conciliatory, he recalled, and he did everything possible to keep him in the group. But it was 1934 and 'we all had our teeth on edge. The great shadow of our fate was slowly advancing.'[4] For Rabinovitch, as for many of his fellow Jews, by the mid-1930s the concerns that had permeated the UUJJ and Jewish youth culture more broadly—who was a Jew, how a more vibrant Jewish cultural life could be built, how to respond to the spiritual needs of the younger

années trente; Marrus and Paxton, *Vichy France and the Jews*; Birnbaum, *Anti-Semitism in France*; and Sternhell, *Neither Right Nor Left*. On the second point of view see Millman, *La Question juive entre les deux guerres*, and Weber, *The Hollow Years*. Caron summarizes this debate in her article 'The Anti-Semitic Revival in France in the 1930s', which argues that antisemitic campaigns in this period were motivated by middle-class fear of competition from German Jewish refugees. She develops this argument in *Uneasy Asylum*.

[3] Rabi, 'Aimé Pallière et notre futile jeunesse', 30–1.

[4] Ibid. 31. The early 1930s also marked the waning of Pallière's involvement in and influence on French Judaism. While he remained close to the Jewish community and played a vital role in helping to ensure Jewish religious services could be held during the Occupation, Pallière began a slow return towards Catholicism in 1933, and his intellectual contribution to Judaism subsequently tapered off. See Poujol, *Aimé Pallière*, 273–83.

generation—gave way to a concern with responding to the antisemitic crisis at hand. Whereas in the 1920s 'culture' took precedence over 'politics', now the reverse was the case. The groups that galvanized Jewish activism in the 1930s were the Ligue Internationale contre l'Antisémitisme and the political Zionist movement, which gained more support within the established Jewish community in the 1930s. Whereas French Zionist supporters in the 1920s had focused for the most part on the movement's cultural programme, by the mid-1930s the rise of fascism brought the movement's potential for resettling masses of persecuted Jews from central and eastern Europe to the fore.[5]

This heightened antisemitism also signalled a shift of theme and focus for Jewish literature. After 1933, Isabelle Ebert notes, Jewish writers were drawn more to essays and journalism than fiction,[6] and the kind of 'semitism' that had come into vogue a decade earlier became much more problematic. As we have seen, some objected to essentialist portrayals of Jewish difference in the 1920s because they felt that they were too close to antisemitic perspectives. In an atmosphere in which there was a general consensus that antisemitism was on the decline, however, these fears remained largely abstract and theoretical. With the rise of Nazi Germany and the increase in antisemitism in France they became much more concrete. As anti-Jewish discourse—under the influence of propaganda from Nazi Germany—became more racialized, Jewish literature took on a new tone: if there was one dominant attitude expressed in Jewish writing in the 1930s, Ebert concludes, 'it seems to have been that Jews should make themselves as inconspicuous as possible'.[7] The era ushered in, in the aftermath of the Dreyfus affair and the First World War, in which Jews had felt free to speculate on and emphasize their difference in the public sphere, had drawn, at least temporarily, to a close.

While these changes in the French social and cultural landscape played an important role in the demise of many of the organizations and publications that flourished in the 1920s, the question remains as to the viability of the Jewish culture that was created during those years. In a 1929 article for *Chalom*, Jaime Azancot predicted that the heightened interest in Judaism and the enlivened Jewish public sphere of the 1920s would not be substantive enough to transmit a Jewish heritage to the next generation.[8] It is of course difficult to know whether his predictions would have been borne out had the international political and economic scene remained stable. The

---

[5] Hyman, *From Dreyfus to Vichy*, 172.
[6] Ebert, 'The Jewish Writer in France from the Dreyfus Affair to 1939', 256.
[7] Ibid.   [8] Azancot, 'Le Judaïsme de demain', *Chalom* (1 Mar. 1929), 18–19.

evidence suggests that much of the Jewish activity that took place during this period was essentially a one-generation phenomenon. This was especially true of the involvement of intellectuals whose process of self-questioning began during or in the aftermath of the Dreyfus affair. Initially pushed towards a sense of reconnection with the Jewish people by their confrontation with antisemitism, their quest to define a modern Jewish identity grew more out of a personal need for soul-searching than a concern about Jewish continuity. Most of the intellectuals active in Zionist and Jewish literary circles during this period were strongly identified with French left-wing culture, and the new openness in this milieu towards the idea of ethnic and cultural difference encouraged them to affirm their Jewish identity. It is important to remember, however, that these intellectuals continued to translate their sense of Jewish belonging through the universalist values of the French left. While they defined their Judaism in terms different from those of their nineteenth-century predecessors, they remained firmly attached to the ideals of French republicanism and a French–Jewish synthesis.

One can also question the extent to which this ethno-cultural definition of Jewishness penetrated French culture and consciousness. While the idea that an ethno-cultural or even 'racial' definition of Jewishness was compatible with acceptance of the Jews as fully fledged members of the French nation gained support in these years, it nonetheless remained controversial and, for many, difficult to fully comprehend. Catherine Fhima argues, for example, that while French literary journals in the 1920s took note of the 'renaissance juif', with few exceptions they did little more than that: novels on Jewish themes were more often than not presented in brief, and the phenomenon of the Jewish literary renaissance did not form the object of in-depth analytical essays. This 'relative silence', Fhima suggests, stemmed in part from the difficulty that the editors and contributors in these journals had in making sense of Jewish identity outside a religious context. While the 'Juif nouveau' had become emblematic in the Jewish associational and literary worlds of the 1920s, the notion of a fully modern, fully French 'ethnic Jew' remained difficult to make sense of in the decidedly secular world of French left-wing intellectual culture.[9]

While the idea of an ethno-cultural Jewish identity generated a good deal of excitement in the 1920s, a means of perpetuating a non-religious Jewishness in real practical terms was never really articulated. Those for whom generational transmission was important remained, for the most part, convinced of the centrality of religious practice in ensuring Jewish continuity.

---

[9] Fhima, 'Au cœur de la "renaissance juive"', 6.

While this was obviously the case for rabbis such as Maurice Liber or Julien Weill, it was also true of communal activists such as Meyerkey, who believed that even if Jewishness should be seen through a wider lens than simply 'religion', it was nevertheless only through religious practice that French Judaism would survive. The success of these leaders in winning over Jewish youth was limited. Some young French Jews, to be sure, were drawn in by the religious revival of the era. This remained a minority phenomenon, however: most were influenced by the dominantly secular mood that characterized French and, in particular, Parisian society of the day.

Significantly, however, the impact of second-generation French Jews was only beginning to be felt when the crises of the 1930s began. While the sons and daughters of immigrants were in the process of secularization and integration into mainstream French culture and society during this period, many among them were simultaneously creating new social spaces in which to be ethnically Jewish. The progressive influence of the Zionist movement on French Jewish life was critical in this respect. Cultural Zionism, which became increasingly acceptable in France in the 1920s, provided both an institutional structure and an ideological justification for Jewish communal survival that had not been available to previous generations. While some of the groups and publications inspired by this ideology had faded out by the mid-1930s, others, such as the Eclaireurs and the Maccabi club, continued to thrive.

Reflecting on the legacy of the Eclaireurs movement of the 1920s and 1930s, Alain Michel notes that many French Jewish communal leaders of the post-war years were former Scouts, and that the pluralist ideology of the Jewish Scout movement, with its insistence on welcoming all those who defined themselves as Jews irrespective of their religious or political orientation, became a founding principle of post-war Jewish associational life.[10] Catherine Poujol similarly insists on the intellectual and cultural legacy of the UUJJ. While the Parisian section of the organization was reduced to a core group of twenty members after 1928, she notes, a good number of Jewish communal leaders of the 1930s and tragic 1940s were a part of this group. Through their participation in the UUJJ, she notes, many of these young people, for the most part born into the Parisian Jewish bourgeoisie, 'discovered that they were Jews, rather than simply Israelites', and forged a self-consciously ethnic brand of Jewishness very different from that of their parents' generation.[11]

[10] Michel's article 'Qu'est-ce qu'un Scout juif?' is part of an *Archives juives* issue devoted to the theme of the transmission of Jewish identity in post-emancipation France (*Archives juives*, 35/2 (2002)). [11] Poujol, 'Aimé Pallière', ii. 532.

The 1920s were a unique period in French Jewish history in a number of ways. It was during this period that the idea of ethnicity was first articulated in France, and this posed a new set of challenges and possibilities for French Jews. Rather than denying their particularism or asserting it in a schematic way, Jews felt freer during these years than ever before both to explore their difference from a wide variety of perspectives and to create new organizations and institutions that would enable them to do so. This sense of freedom, however, was dependent on an overriding feeling that antisemitism was on the decline. Once the political and social climate shifted, so too, inevitably, did the cultural climate within the French Jewish community.

With the end of the war and the Vichy era of Jewish persecution, however, issues of Jewish identity and self-definition that had occupied religious and communal leaders in the 1920s once again became relevant. In the 1950s and 1960s, the Jewish community was transformed by a myriad of new developments, including French Jews' own recent history of persecution, the creation of the state of Israel, and the arrival of thousands of new immigrants from North Africa. All of these developments further complicated both the ideology of assimilation and a narrowly religious understanding of Jewish identity, and encouraged French Jews to build on the shifts in communal self-understanding and self-perception that began in the early twentieth century.[12]

---

[12] On continuities between French Jewish identity in the 1950s and the pre-war years, see Mandel, *In the Aftermath of Genocide*.

APPENDIX I

Books, Plays, and Films on Jewish Themes Debated at the Club du Faubourg 1924–1929

Dates refer to the year of discussion rather than that of publication

1924 Josué Jéhouda, *Le Royaume de justice*

1925 Pierre Benoît, *Le Puits de Jacob*

Raymond Geiger, *Nouvelles histoires juives*

Jacob Lévy, *Les Pollaks*

Alfred Savoir and Fernand Nozière, *Le Baptême* (play; on the occasion of its restaging)

La Terre promise (a film produced by Keren Kayemet that played in cities throughout France)

1926 Jean Izoulet, *Paris: Capitale des religions ou la mission d'Israël*

1927 André Billy and Moïse Twersky, *Le Fléau du savoir*

Elian Finbert, *Sous le règne de la licorne et du lion*

Edmond Fleg, *L'Enfant prophète*

Josué Jéhouda and Panaït Istrati, *La Famille Perlmutter*

Joseph Kessel, *Les Cœurs purs*

Bernard Lecache, *Quand Israël meurt*

Jacob Lévy, *Les Doubles-Juifs*

Pierre Samuël, *Mon rabbin chez les riches*

1928 Henry Torrès, *Le Procès des pogromes*

1929 Maurice Donnay, *Le Retour de Jérusalem* (play)

Sarah Lévy, *O mon goye!*

Géo London, *Lévy-Pendules*

1929   René Schwob, *Moi Juif, livre posthume* (discussed in conjunction with Savoir and Nozière's *Le Baptême*)

Isaac Kadmi-Cohen, *Nomades*

Suzanne Roukhomovsky, *Gastronomie juive*

Le Chanteur de jazz (*The Jazz Singer*, American film)

APPENDIX II

Titles in the Rieder Series

'Œuvres'

General Editor: Edmond Fleg

1922 Blumenfeld, Lupus (ed.), *Anthologie des conteurs yiddish*

1925 Sholem Aleykhem [Sholem Aleichem], *L'Histoire de Tévié*, translated into Alsatian Judaeo-French by Edmond Fleg

Siméon bén Yohay (attrib.), *Le Livre du Zohar*, translated from the Chaldaic by Jean de Pauly

Edmond Fleg, *Le Juif du Pape*

1926 Heinrich Heine, *Ecrits juifs*, translated with an introduction and notes by Louis Laloy

Aimé Pallière, *Le Sanctuaire inconnu: Ma 'conversion' au Judaïsme*

1927 An-Ski [S. Ansky], *Le Dibbouk: A Dramatic Legend in 3 Acts*, adapted into French by Marie-Thérèse Koerner

Léon Berman (ed.), *Contes du Talmud*, chosen and translated from Hebrew [by Léon Berman]

1928 Bernard Lazare, *Le Fumier de Job: Fragments inédits précédés du portrait de Bernard Lazare, par Charles Péguy*

Israel Zangwill, *Comédies du ghetto*, translated by Mme Marcel Girette

1929 Stefan Zweig, *Jérémie*, translated by Louis-Charles Baudouin

1930 Maimonides, *Le Guide des égarés*, translated by Salomon Munk

Léon de Modène, *Cérémonies et coutumes qui s'observent aujourd'huy parmy les Juifs*, translated by Richard Simon (priest of Bonneville) with commentary by Edmond Fleg

Israel Zangwill, *Nouvelles comédies du ghetto*, translated by Mme Marcel Girette

1931 Theodor Herzl, *Terre ancienne, terre nouvelle*, translated by L. Delau and J. Thursz

1932 Edmond Fleg, *Ma Palestine*

Judah Halevi, *Le Livre du Kuzari*, translated with a foreword by Moïse Ventura

Ludwig Lewisohn, *Les Derniers Jours de Shylock*, translated from the English, with an introduction, by Maxime Piha; original illustrations by Arthur Szyk

1933 Simon Debré, *L'Humour judéo-alsacien: Expressions humoristiques judéo-alsaciennes*

Auguste Hollard, *Le Dieu d'Israël*, with a preface by Adolphe Lods

'Etudes'

General Editor: Paul-Louis Couchoud

1925 Isaac Abrahams, *Valeurs permanentes du Judaisme*, translated by Germaine Constantin-Weyer

Josué Jéhouda, *La Terre promise*

1926 Uriel Acosta, *Une vie humaine*, translated with a study of the author by Abraham Beer Duff and Pierre Kaan

Israel Zangwill, *La Voix de Jérusalem*, translated by Andrée Jouve

1927 Mayer Abraham Halévy, *Moïse dans l'histoire et dans la légende*

1928 Elie Eberlin, *Les Juifs d'aujourd'hui*

Baruch Hagani, *L'Emancipation des Juifs*, with a preface by Charles Guignebert

1929 *Le Poème de Job*, new translation, introduction, and notes by Paul Bertie

Emile Vandervelde, *Le Pays d'Israël: Un marxiste en Palestine*, followed by

Jeanne-Emile Vandervelde, *Les Œuvres d'assistance en Palestine juive*

1930 A. Audin, *La Légende des origines de l'humanité*, preceded by the first eleven chapters of Genesis, with an introduction, translation, and commentary by Paul Bertie

Pascale Saisset, *Heures juives au Maroc*

1931 James Darmesteter, *Les Prophètes d'Israël*, with a preface by Salomon Reinach

Hans Kohn, *L'Humanisme juif: Quinze essais sur le Juif, le monde et Dieu*

APPENDIX III

An Overview of Fiction on Jewish Themes 1900–1940

LÉON BERMAN (ed.), *Contes du Talmud* (Paris: Rieder, 1927).

HENRI BERNSTEIN, *Israël* (Paris: Fayard, 1908).

ANDRÉ BILLY and MOÏSE TWERSKY, *L'Epopée de Ménaché Foïgel*, 3 vols (Paris: Plon); vol. i: *Le Fléau du savoir* (1927); vol ii: *Comme Dieu en France* (1928); vol. iii: *Le Lion, l'ours et le serpent* (1928).

JEAN-RICHARD BLOCH, *...et Cie* (Paris: Gallimard, 1918).

—— *Lévy: Premier livre de contes* (Paris: Gallimard, 1912).

LUPUS BLUMENFELD (ed.), *Anthologie des conteurs yiddish* (Paris: Rieder, 1922).

EDMOND CAHEN, *Le Juif et l'Auvergnat* (Paris: Fasquelle, 1932).

—— *Juif, non!... Israélite* (Paris: Librairie de France, 1930).

—— *Léon-des-Landes* (Paris: Fasquelle, 1934).

ALBERT COHEN, *Paroles juives* (Geneva: Kundig & Crès, 1921).

—— *Solal* (Paris: Gallimard, 1930).

PIERRE CRÉANGE, *La Paria au manteau de soleil*, illustrated by Max Nordau (Paris: Albert Messein, 1928).

—— *Vers les pays qui ne sont pas... poèmes* (Paris: Albert Messein, 1932).

BENJAMIN CRÉMIEUX, *Le Premier de la classe* (Paris: Grasset, 1920).

MAURICE DONNAY, *Le Retour de Jérusalem* (Paris: E. Fasquelle, 1904).

ELIAN FINBERT, *Le Batelier du Nil* (Paris: Ollendorf, 1901).

—— *Le Destin difficile* (Paris: Fasquelle, 1932).

—— *Le Fou de Dieu* (Paris: Fasquelle, 1932).

—— *Sous le règne de la licorne et du lion* (Paris: Monde Moderne, 1925).

EDMOND FLEG, *Anthologie juive* (Paris: Editions Georges Crès, 1923).

—— *La Bête* (Paris: Rey, 1910).

—— *Les Dieudieux: Moralité en trois actes et sept tableaux* (Paris: Société Générale d'Imprimerie et d'Edition, 1931).

—— *Ecoute Israël* (Paris: Georges Crès, 1921).

—— *L'Enfant prophète* (Paris: Gallimard, 1926).

EDMOND FLEG, *Jésus raconté par le Juif errant* (Paris: Gallimard, 1933).

—— *Le Juif du Pape* (Paris: Rieder, 1925).

—— *Le Marchand de Paris* (Paris: Comédie-Française, 1929).

—— *Moïse* (Paris: Gallimard, 1928).

—— *Le Mur des Pleurs: Poème* (Paris: C. Bloch, 1919).

—— *Le Psaume de la terre promise* (Geneva: Kundig, 1919).

—— *Salomon* (Paris: Gallimard, 1930).

HENRI FRANCK, *La Danse devant l'arche*, preface by Anna de Noailles (Paris: Gallimard, 1912).

RAYMOND GEIGER, *Histoires juives* (Paris: Gallimard, 1924).

—— *Nouvelles histoires juives* (Paris: Gallimard, 1925).

—— *Ténèbres* (Paris: Marcel Lesage, 1925).

MYRIAM HARRY, *La Conquête de Jérusalem: Roman* (Paris: C. Lévy, 1903).

—— *La Jérusalem retrouvée* (Paris: Flammarion, 1930).

—— *La Nuit de Jérusalem* (Paris: Flammarion, 1928).

—— *La Petite Fille de Jérusalem* (Paris: A. Fayard, 1914).

—— *Sion à Paris* (Paris: A. Fayard, 1919).

HENRI HERTZ, *Tragédie des temps volages: Contes et poèmes, 1906–1954* (Paris: Seghers, 1955).

LILY JEAN-JAVAL, *L'Inquiète* (Paris: Plon, 1927).

—— *Noémi: Roman d'une jeune fille juive en Pays Basque* (Paris: Plon, 1925).

—— *Nuages* (Paris: Dordon, 1933).

JOSUÉ JÉHOUDA, *Le Royaume de justice: Roman juif*, preface by André Spire (Paris: Editions du Monde Nouveau, 1923).

—— *La Tragédie d'Israël*, 2 vols (Paris: Grasset); vol. i: *De père en fils* (1927), vol. ii: *Miriam* (1928).

—— and Panaït Istrati, *La Famille Perlmutter* (Paris: Gallimard, 1927).

GUSTAVE KAHN, *Contes juifs* (Paris: Fasquelle, 1926).

—— *Images bibliques: Poèmes* (Paris: Snell, 1929).

—— *Terre d'Israël: Contes juifs* (Paris: Fasquelle, 1933).

—— *Vieil Orient, Orient neuf* (Paris: Fasquelle, 1928).

JOSEPH KESSEL, *Les Cœurs purs* (Paris: Gallimard, 1927).

—— *Nouveaux contes* (Paris: Editions des Cahiers Libres, 1928).

—— and Hélène Iswolsky, *Les Rois aveugles* (Paris: Editions de France, 1925).

KISLEV, *Contes de Hanouka* (Paris: Durlacher, 1922).

JACQUES DE LACRETELLE, *Le Retour de Silbermann* (Paris: Gallimard, 1930).

—— *Silbermann* (Paris: Gallimard, 1922).

BERNARD LECACHE, *Jacob* (Paris: Gallimard, 1925).

JACOB LÉVY, *Les Juifs d'aujourd'hui*, 3 vols (Paris: Ferenczi); vol. i: *Les Pollaks* (1925); vol. ii: *Les Demi-Juifs* (1926); vol. iii: *Les Doubles-Juifs* (1927); published under the individual volume titles, together with *Les Chrétiens* (1928), in 1 vol. (Paris: Les Belles Lettres, 1999).

SARAH LÉVY, *Ma Chère France* (Paris: Flammarion, 1930).

—— *O mon goye!* (Paris: Flammarion, 1929).

GABRIELLE LIPMAN-MOYSE, *Les Sanédrin* (Poligny: A. Jacquin, 1910).

GÉO LONDON, *Lévy-Pendules* (Paris: Librairie des Champs-Elysées, 1929).

ARMAND LUNEL, *Esther de Carpentras* (Paris: Gallimard, 1926).

—— *L'Imagerie du cordier* (Paris: Gallimard, 1924).

—— *Jérusalem à Carpentras* (Paris: Gallimard, 1937).

—— *Nicolo-Peccavi, ou l'affaire Dreyfus à Carpentras* (Paris: Gallimard, 1926).

DARIUS MILHAUD, *Poèmes juifs* (Paris: Eschig, 1916).

A. H. NAVON, *Joseph Pérez: Juif du ghetto* (Paris: Calmann-Lévy, 1925).

IRÈNE NÉMIROVSKY, *Le Bal* (Paris: Grasset, 1930).

—— *David Golder* (Paris: Grasset, 1929).

—— *Pion sur l'échiquier* (Paris: Albin Michel, 1934).

—— *Le Vin de solitude* (Paris: Albin Michel, 1935).

LÉO POLDÈS, *L'Eternel ghetto* (Paris: Editions Radot, 1928).

FRANÇOIS PORCHÉ, *La Race errante* (Paris: Editions de l'Illustration, 1932).

MARCEL PROUST, *A la recherche du temps perdu*, 7 vols (Paris: Gallimard, 1913–27).

ELISSA RHAÏS, *Le Café-chantant. Kereb. Noblesse arabe* (Paris: Plon-Nourrit, 1920).

—— *La Convertie* (Paris: Flammarion, 1930).

—— *La Fille de pachas: Roman* (Paris: Plon-Nourrit, 1922).

—— *Les Juifs, ou la fille d'Eléazer* (Paris: Flammarion, 1922).

—— *Saâda la Marocaine* (Paris: Plon-Nourrit, 1919).

ROMAIN ROLLAND, *Jean Christophe* (Paris: Ollendorf, 1908–14).

RYVEL, *L'Enfant de l'oukala et autres contes de la Hara*, preface by Pierre Hubic (Tunis: La Kahena, 1931).

——J. VEHEL, and V. DANON, *La Hara conte: Folklore judéo-tunisien* (Paris: Ivrit, 1929).

PIERRE PAMUËL, *Mon rabbin chez les riches* (Paris: Ferenczi, 1926).

ALFRED SAVOIR and FERNAND NOZIÈRE, *Le Baptême* (Paris: Librairie Théâtrale, 1908).

IDA SÉE, *De ghetto à l'université: Roman* (Paris: R. Chiberre, 1923).

—— *Enfants de la balle* (Paris: Eugène Figuière, 1913).

IDA SÉE, *Les Exclus* (Paris: Eugène Figuière, 1929).

ANDRÉ SPIRE, *Refuges* (Paris: Editions de la Belle Page, 1926).

—— *Samaël* (Paris: Georges Crès, 1921).

—— *Le Secret* (Paris: Gallimard, 1919).

—— *Versets; Et vous riez; Poèmes juifs* (Paris: Société du Mercure de France, 1908; enlarged edn, Geneva: Kundig, 1919).

JEAN THARAUD and JÉRÔME THARAUD, *L'Ombre de la croix* (Paris: Plon-Nourrit, 1917).

—— *La Rose de Saron* (Paris: Plon-Nourrit, 1927).

—— *Un royaume de dieu* (Paris: Plon-Nourrit, 1920).

ARTHUR WEILL, *Contes et Légendes d'Israël*, illustrated by Kuhn-Regnier (Paris: Fernand Nathan, 1928).

Bibliography

Contemporary Periodicals

L'Appui français (1930–2)

Archives israélites (1840–1935)

Bené-Mizrah (1930–1)

Les Cahiers de la Quinzaine (1900–14)

Chalom (1924–35)

Clarté (1919–28)

Connaître: Revue mensuelle juive, sioniste, littéraire et philosophe (1924–30)

L'Echo sioniste (1899–1905 and 1912–14); reappeared in 1916 as *Le Peuple juif* (1916–21); returned briefly to original title in 1921; renamed *La Nouvelle Aurore* (1922–6)

L'Effort libre (1910–19)

L'Emancipation juive (January–December 1916)

Europe (1923–39)

Les Flambeaux (1926)

Foi et réveil (1913–38)

La Jeunesse juive (1926–9)

Menorah (= *L'Illustration juive*) (1922–33)

Le Mercure de France (1890–)

Le Mouvement socialiste (1899–1914)

Notre temps (1927–40)

La Nouvelle Aurore, see *L'Echo sioniste*

Pages libres (1901–9); from October 1909 to 1940 part of *La Grande Revue*

Paix et droit (1921–39)

La Palestine nouvelle (1918–19)

Palestine: La Nouvelle Revue juive (1927–31)

Le Peuple juif, see *L'Echo sioniste*

La Phalange (1906–39)

Les Pionniers (1912–14)

Le Rayon (1912–39)

Le Réveil israélite (1919–20)

La Revue blanche (1891–1903)

Revue des études juives (1881–)

La Revue israélite (1923–4)

La Revue juive (1925)

Revue littéraire juive (1927–31)

La Terre retrouvée (1928–40)

La Tribune juive (1919–39)

L'Union scolaire (1900–34)

L' Univers israélite (1844–1939)

Le Volontaire juif (1931–5)

Other Sources

ABECASSIS, JACK, *Albert Cohen: Dissonant Voices* (Baltimore: Johns Hopkins University Press, 2004).

ABITBOL, MICHEL, *Les Deux Terres promises: Les Juifs de France et le sionisme, 1897–1945* (Paris: O. Orban, 1989).

——'The Encounter between French Jewry and the Jews of North Africa: Analysis of a Discourse', in Frances Malino and Bernard Wasserstein (eds), *The Jews in Modern France* (Hanover: University Press of New England, 1985).

ABRAHAM, PIERRE [pseud. of Pierre Bloch], *Les Trois Frères* (Paris: Editeurs Français Réunis, 1971).

AGATHON [pseud. of Henri Massis and Alfred de Tarde], *L'Esprit de la nouvelle Sorbonne: La Crise de la culture classique, la crise du français* (Paris: Mercure de France, 1911).

——*Les Jeunes Gens d'aujourd'hui* (Paris: Plon-Nourrit, 1913).

ALBERT, PHYLLIS COHEN, 'Ethnicity and Jewish Solidarity in Nineteenth-Century France', in Jehuda Reinharz and Daniel Swetschinski (eds), *Mystics, Philosophers, and Politicians: Essays in Jewish Intellectual History in Honor of Alexander Altman* (Durham: University of North Carolina Press, 1982).

——'Israelite and Jew: How Did Nineteenth-Century French Jews Understand Assimilation?', in Jonathan Frankel and Steven J. Zipperstein (eds), *Assimilation and Community: The Jews in Nineteenth-Century Europe* (Cambridge: Cambridge University Press, 1992).

——'Les Juifs de France et l'idée de restauration nationale', *Les Nouveaux Cahiers*, 112 (Spring 1993), 27–32.

——*The Modernization of French Jewry: Consistory and Community in the Nineteenth Century* (Waltham, Mass.: Brandeis University Press, 1977).

ALBERTINI, J., 'Jean-Richard Bloch: De l'affaire Dreyfus à la *Nuit kurde*', in Geraldi Leroy (ed.), *Les Ecrivains et l'affaire Dreyfus, actes du colloque organisé par le Centre C. Péguy et l'Université d'Orléans* (Paris: Presses Universitaires de France, 1983).

ALGAZI, LÉON, 'Un entretien avec Edmond Fleg', *Revue de la pensée juive*, 8 (July 1951), 105–11.

L'Almanach juif (Paris: La Nouvelle Génération for La Colonie Scolaire, 1931).

ARON, ROBERT, 'Visite chez Benamozegh', *Revue de la pensée juive*, 8 (Jan. 1951), 38–40.

ASCH, SCHOLEM, *La Chaise électrique*, trans. Alzir Hella and Isa Altkaufer, preface by Stefan Zweig (Paris: Stock, 1931).

——*Le Juif aux psaumes*, trans. Juliette Pary and J. Pougatz (Paris: Flammarion, 1939).

——*Pétersbourg*, trans. Alexandre Vialatte, preface by Stefan Zweig (Paris: Grasset, 1933).

AVINERI, SHLOMO, 'Zionism and Jewish Religious Tradition', in Shmuel Almog, Jehuda Reinharz, and Anita Schapira (eds), *Zionism and Religion* (Hanover: University Press of New England, 1998).

BALIBAR, ETIENNE, 'Racism and Nationalism', in Etienne Balibar and Immanuel Wallerstein (eds), *Race, Nation, Class: Ambiguous Identities* (London: Verso, 1991).

BANDONE, ELLEN, 'Ethnicity, Folklore and Local Identity in Rural Brittany', *Journal of American Folklore*, 100/96 (Apr. 1987), 161–90.

BARRÈS, MAURICE, *L'Angoisse de Pascal* (Paris: Les Bibliophiles Fantaisistes, Dorbon, 1910).

——*La Culte du moi: Examen de trois idéologies* (Paris: Perrin, 1892).

——*Les Déracinés* (Paris: E. Pasquelle, 1897).

——*Les Diverses Familles spirituelles de la France* (Paris: Emile-Paul Frères Editeurs, 1917).

BARROT, OLIVIER, and PASCAL ORY, *La Revue blanche* (Paris: C. Bourgeois, 1989).

BASCH, FRANÇOISE, *Victor Basch: De l'affaire Dreyfus au crime de la Milice* (Paris: Librairie Plon, 1994).

——Lilliane Crips, and Pascale Gruson (eds), *Victor Basch: Un intellectuel cosmopolite, 1863–1944* (Paris: Berg International Editors, 2000).

BAUER, JULES, *L'Ecole rabbinique de France (1830–1930)* (Paris: Presses Universitaires de France, 1930).

——*Notre livre de prières* (Paris: Durlacher, 1921).

——*Prières à l'usage de l'enfance* (Paris: Durlacher, 1928).

BENAIN, ALINE, and AUDREY KICHELEWESKI, 'Parizer Haynt et Naïe Presse, les itinéraires paradoxaux de deux quotidiens parisiens en langue yiddish', *Archives juives*, 36/2 (2003), 52–69.

BENBASSA, ESTHER, 'L'Alliance Israélite Universelle et le sionisme', *Archives juives*, 30/2 (1997), 38–48.

BENGUIGUI, IDA, 'L'Immigration juive à Paris entre les deux guerres', Diplôme d'Etudes Supérieures (Paris: Faculté des Lettres et Sciences Humaines, 1965).

BENOIT, PIERRE, *Le Puits de Jacob* (Paris: Albin Michel, 1925).

BENVENISTE, ANNIE, *Le Bosphore à la Roquette: La Communauté judéo-espagnole à Paris, 1914–1940* (Paris: L'Harmattan, 1989).

BERG, ROGER, 'Traducteur parce qu'anthologiste', *Revue de la pensée juive*, 2 (Jan. 1950), 37–9.

BERKOWITZ, JAY R., 'Ritual and Emancipation: A Reassessment of Cultural Modernization in France', *Historical Reflections/Réflexions historiques*, 32/1 (2006), 9–38.

——*The Shaping of Jewish Identity in Nineteenth-Century France* (Detroit: Wayne University Press, 1989).

BERKOWITZ, MICHAEL, *The Reception of Zionism in Western Europe and the United States, 1914–1933* (Cambridge: Cambridge University Press, 1996).

BERMAN, LÉON (ed.), *Contes du Talmud* (Paris: Rieder, 1927).

BERNSTEIN, HENRI, *Israël* (Paris: Fayard, 1908).

BIALE, DAVID, 'Shabataï Tzevi et les séductions de l'orientalisme juif', *Cahiers du judaïsme*, 2 (Summer 1998), 13–22.

BIELINKY, JACQUES, *Journal 1940–1942: Un journaliste juif à Paris sous l'Occupation*, ed. Renée Poznanski (Paris: Cerf, 1992).

BILLY, ANDRÉ, and MOÏSE TWERSKY, *L'Epopée de Ménaché Foïgel*, 3 vols (Paris: Plon); vol. i: *Le Fléau du savoir* (1927); vol. ii: *Comme Dieu en France* (1928); vol. iii: *Le Lion, l'ours et le serpent* (1928).

BIRNBAUM, PIERRE, *Anti-Semitism in France: A Political History from Léon Blum to the Present* (Oxford: Blackwell, 1992).

——'La Citoyenneté en péril: Les Juifs entre intégration et résistance', in id. (ed.), *La France de l'affaire Dreyfus* (Paris: Gallimard, 1994).

——*The Jews of the Republic: A Political History of State Jews in France from Gambetta to Vichy*, trans. Jane Marie Todd (Stanford: Stanford University Press, 1996).

——(ed.), *Histoire politique des Juifs de France* (Paris: Presses de la Fondation Nationale Scientifique, 1990).

BITTON, MICHÈLE, *Présences féminines juives en France, XIXe–XXe siècles: Cent itinéraires* (Paris: Editions 2M, 2002).

BLOCH, JEAN-RICHARD, *...et Cie*, 19th edn, published as *Et Compagnie* (Paris: Gallimard, 1947).

——*Lévy: Premier livre de contes* (Paris: Gallimard, 1912).

BLOT, JEAN, *Albert Cohen* (Paris: Ballard, 1986).

BLUM, LÉON, *Œuvres*, vol. ii, ed. Louis Faucon (Paris: Albin Michel, 1962).

——*Souvenirs sur l'affaire* (Paris: Gallimard, 1935).

BLUMENFELD, LUPUS (ed.), *Anthologie des conteurs yiddish* (Paris: Rieder, 1922).

BONARDI, PIERRE, *Le Retour à Jérusalem*, with 64 original illustrations by Feder (Paris: André Depluch, 1927).

BONSIRVEN, JOSEPH, *Sur les ruines du Temple* (Paris: Grasset, 1928).

BOUKARA, PHILIPPE, 'Justin Godart et le sionisme: Autour du *France-Palestine*', in Annette Wieviorka (ed.), *Justin Godart: Un homme dans son siècle (1871–1956)* (Paris: Editions CNRS, 2004).

BRANDON-SALVADORE, MARGUERITE, *A travers les moissons* (Paris: Félix Alcan, 1903).

BREDIN, JEAN-DENIS, *The Affair: The Case of Alfred Dreyfus* (New York: George Braziller, 1986).

——*Bernard Lazare: De l'anarchiste au prophète* (Paris: Editions de Fallois, 1992).

BRENNER, MICHAEL, *The Renaissance of Jewish Culture in Weimar Germany* (New Haven: Yale University Press, 1996).

BRUBAKER, ROGERS, *Citizenship and Nationhood in France and Germany* (Cambridge, Mass.: Harvard University Press, 1992).

BUBER, MARTIN, *On Judaism*, trans. Nahum Glatzer, ed. Eva Jospe (New York: Schocken Books, 1967).

BURNS, MICHAEL, *Dreyfus: A Family Affair, 1789–1985* (New York: Harper-Collins, 1991).

CACÉRÈS, BENIGNO, *Histoire de l'éducation populaire* (Paris: Editions du Seuil, 1964).

CAHEN, EDMOND, *Juif, non!... Israélite* (Paris: Librairie de France, 1930).

CARON, VICKI, 'The Anti-Semitic Revival in France in the 1930s: The Socio-economic Dimension Reconsidered', *Journal of Modern History*, 70/1 (Mar. 1998), 24–73.

——'French Jewish Assimilation Reassessed: A Review of the Recent Literature', *Judaism*, 42/2 (1993), 134–59.

——*Uneasy Asylum: France and the Refugee Crisis, 1933–1942* (Stanford: Stanford University Press, 1994).

CHEYETTE, BRYAN, *The Construction of the 'Jew' in English Literature and Society, 1875–1945* (Cambridge: Cambridge University Press, 1993).

CHOLVY, GÉRARD, *Histoire religieuse de la France contemporaine*, 2 vols (Toulouse: Privat, 1985–8).

——(ed.), *Mouvements de jeunesse chrétiens et juifs: Sociabilité juvénile dans un cadre européen, 1799–1968* (Paris: Gérard, 1985).

CHOURAQUI, ANDRÉ, *Cent ans d'histoire: L'Alliance Israélite Universelle et la renaissance juive contemporaine (1860–1960)* (Paris: Presses Universitaires de France, 1965).

COHEN, ALBERT, *Paroles juives* (Geneva: Kundig & Crès, 1921).

COHEN, ALBERT, *Solal* (1930); repr. in id., *Œuvres* (Paris: Gallimard, Bibliothèque de la Pléiade, 1986).

COHEN, DAVID, *La Promotion des Juifs en France à l'époque du second empire (1852–1870)*, 2 vols (Aix-en-Provence: University of Provence, 1980).

COHEN, RICHARD I., 'Nostalgia and "Return to the Ghetto": A Cultural Phenomenon in Western and Central Europe', in Jonathan Frankel and Steven J. Zipperstein (eds), *Assimilation and Community: The Jews in Nineteenth-Century Europe* (Cambridge: Cambridge University Press, 1992).

COHEN YOLANDE, *Les Jeunes, le socialisme et la guerre: Histoire des mouvements de jeunesse en France* (Paris: Editions d'Harmattan, 1989).

COMTE, MADELEINE, 'De la conversion à la rencontre: Les Religieuses de Notre-Dame-de-Sion (1843–1986)', *Archives juives*, 35 /1 (2002), 102–19.

CORCOS, FERNAND, *Le Sionisme au travail*, 2 vols; vol. i: *La Terre promise* (Paris: Rieder, 1923); vol. ii: *A Travers la Palestine juive* (Paris: Jouve, 1925).

COUTROT, ALINE, *Les Forces religieuses dans la société française* (Paris: Armand Colin, 1965).

——'Le Mouvement de jeunesse: Un phénomène au singulier?', in Gérard Cholvy (ed.), *Mouvements de jeunesse chrétiens et juifs: Sociabilité juvénile dans un cadre européen, 1799–1968* (Paris: Gérard, 1985).

CRÉANGE, PIERRE, *Epîtres aux Juifs* (Paris: Albert Messein, 1937).

——*La Paria au manteau du soleil*, illustrated by Maxa Nordau (Paris: Albert Messein, 1928).

——*Vers les pays qui ne sont pas... poèmes* (Paris: Albert Messein, 1932).

CRÉMIEUX, BENJAMIN, 'La Littérature juive française', *La Revue juive de Genève*, 45 (Feb. 1937), 196–200.

DANIÉLOU, JEAN, 'Edmond Fleg et le christianisme', *Revue de la pensée juive*, 2 (Jan. 1950), 43–6.

DARMESTETER, JAMES, *Les Prophètes d'Israël* (Paris: Calmann-Lévy, 1891).

DELMAIRE, DANIELLE, 'Mouvements de jeunesse juifs en France, 1919–1939', in Gérard Cholvy (ed.), *Mouvements de jeunesse chrétiens et juifs: Sociabilité juvénile dans un cadre européen, 1799–1968* (Paris: Cerf, 1985).

DELMAIRE, JEAN-MARIE, 'La France à Bâle: Les Délégués français au premier congrès sioniste', *Archives juives*, 30/2 (1997), 4–21.

DONNAY, MAURICE, *Le Retour de Jérusalem* (Paris: E. Fasquelle, 1904); repr. in *La Petite Illustration* (9 Jan. 1929), 1–38.

'Dossier Albert Cohen', special issue of *Magazine littéraire*, 147 (Apr. 1979).

EBERT, ISABELLE, 'The Jewish Writer in France from the Dreyfus Affair to 1939', Ph.D. diss. (University of Southern California, 1980).

ELADAN, JACQUES, *Poètes juifs de langue française* (Paris: Noël Bladin, 1992).

EZRA, ELIZABETH, *The Colonial Unconscious: Race and Culture in Interwar France* (Ithaca: Cornell University Press, 2000).

FEIGELSON, RALPH, *Ecrivains juifs de langue française* (Paris: Jean Grassin, 1960).

FHIMA, CATHERINE, 'Au cœur de la "renaissance juive" des années 1920: Littérature et judéité', *Archives juives*, 39/1 (2006), 29–45.

——'Aux sources d'un renouveau identitaire juif en France: André Spire et Edmond Fleg', *Cahiers Georges Sorel*, 13 (1995), 171–89.

——'Les Ecrivains juifs français et le sionisme (1897–1930)', *Archives juives*, 30/2 (1997), 49–70.

——'Jean-Richard Bloch et la renaissance culturelle juive en France (1910–1930)', in Katalin Halász and István Csüry (eds), *Destins du siècle: Jean-Richard Bloch et Roger Martin du Gard. Mélanges offerts au professeur Tivadar Gorilovics*, Studia Romanica de Debrecen, Series Litteraria, fasc. XXIII (Dec. 2003), 37–49.

——and CATHERINE NICAULT, 'Victor Basch et la judéité', in Françoise Basch, Liliane Crips, and Pascale Gruson (eds), *Victor Basch: Un intellectuel cosmopolite, 1863–1944* (Paris: Berg International Editors, 2000).

FINBERT, ELIAN, *Sous le règne de la licorne et du lion* (Paris: Monde Moderne, 1925).

FINE, DAVID MARTIN, 'In the Beginning: American-Jewish fiction, 1880–1930', in Lewis Fried (ed.), *Handbook of American Jewish Literature* (New York: Greenwood Press, 1988).

FISCHER, JOSEPH, 'Aimé Pallière et le Keren Kayemet Leyisrael', *Revue de la pensée juive*, 8 (July 1951), 32–7.

FLEG, EDMOND, *Anthologie juive* (Paris: Georges Crès, 1923).

——*Correspondance d'Edmond Fleg pendant l'affaire Dreyfus*, ed. André Elbaz (Paris: A. G. Nizet, 1976).

——*Ecoute Israël* (Paris: Georges Crès, 1921; enlarged edn, Paris: Flammarion, 1954).

——*L'Enfant prophète* (Paris: Gallimard, 1926).

——*Jésus raconté par le Juif errant* (Paris: Gallimard, 1933).

——*Le Juif du Pape* (Paris: Rieder, 1925).

——*Ma Palestine*, 'Judaïsme' (Paris: Rieder, 1932).

——*Pourquoi je suis Juif* (Paris: Editions de France, 1928); English edn: *Why I Am a Jew*, trans. Louise Waterman Wise, foreword by Stephen S. Wise (New York: Bloch, 1929).

FORD, CAROLINE, *Creating the Nation in Provincial France: Religion and Political Identity in Brittany* (Princeton: Princeton University Press, 1993).

FRANCK, HENRI, *La Danse devant l'arche*, preface by Anna de Noailles (Paris: Gallimard, 1912).

FRANCK, HENRI, *Lettres à quelques amis*, ed. André Spire (Paris: Grasset, 1926).

FRANKEL, JONATHAN, 'The Paradoxical Politics of Marginality: Thoughts on the Jewish Situation During the Years 1914–21', *Studies in Contemporary Jewry*, 4 (1988), 3–21.

FRIEDEN, KEN, *Classic Yiddish Fiction: Abramovitsh, Sholem Aleichem, and Peretz* (New York: State University of New York Press, 1995).

FUMET, STANISLAS, 'Réflexions sur "Pourquoi je suis Juif"', *Revue de la pensée juive*, 2 (Jan. 1950), 47–53.

GAMZON, ROBERT, 'Edmond Fleg et les Eclaireurs Israélites de France', *Revue de la pensée juive*, 2 (Jan. 1950), 18–21.

GARTNER, LLOYD, *History of the Jews in Modern Times* (Oxford: Oxford University Press, 2001).

GEIGER, RAYMOND, *Histoires juives* (Paris: Gallimard, 1924).

——*Nouvelles histoires juives* (Paris: Gallimard, 1925).

GILLE, ELISABETH, *Le Mirador: Mémoires rêvés* (Paris: Presses de la Renaissance, 1992; 2nd edn, Paris: Stock, 2000).

GILMAN, SANDER, *Jewish Self-Hatred* (Baltimore: Johns Hopkins University Press, 1986).

GODART, JUSTIN, *France-Palestine* (Paris: Le Monde Nouveau, 1926).

GOUBLET, JULIETTE, *Léo Poldès, le Faubourg* (Aurillac: Editions du Centre, 1965).

GOURFINKEL, NINA, *Aux prises avec mon temps*, 2 vols (Paris: Seuil, 1953); vol. i: *Naissance d'un monde*; vol. ii: *L'Autre Patrie*.

GRAETZ, MICHAEL, *The Jews in Nineteenth-Century France: From the French Revolution to the Alliance Israelite Universelle*, trans. Jane Marie Todd (Stanford: Stanford University Press, 1996).

GREEN, NANCY, *The Pletzl of Paris* (New York: Holmes & Meyer, 1986).

GREILSAMMER, ILAN, *Blum* (Paris: Flammarion, 1996).

GREILSAMMER, MARCEL, 'Aimé Pallière à l'Union Libérale Israélite', *Revue de la pensée juive*, 8 (July 1951), 15–22.

GROGIN, ROBERT C., *The Bergsonian Controversy in France, 1900–1914* (Calgary: University of Calgary Press, 1988).

GRUSON, PASCALE, 'La Carrière universitaire de Victor Basch', in Françoise Basch, Liliane Crips, and Pascale Gruson (eds), *Victor Basch: Un intellectuel cosmopolite, 1863–1944* (Paris: Berg International Editors, 2000).

GUGELOT, FRÉDÉRIC, *La Conversion des intellectuels au catholicisme en France, 1885–1935* (Paris: Editions CNRS, 1998).

——'De Ratisbonne à Lustiger: Les Convertis à l'époque contemporaine', *Archives juives*, 35/1 (2002), 8–26.

GUY-GRAND, GEORGES (ed.), *La Renaissance religieuse* (Paris: Librairie Félix Alcan, 1928).

HAGANI, BARUCH, 'André Spire et l'action juive', in *Hommage à André Spire* (Paris: Librairie Lipschutz, 1939).

——*L'Emancipation des Juifs*, preface by Charles Guignebert (Paris: Rieder, 1928).

HALÉVY, DANIEL, 'Voici quelques quarante ans', in *Hommage à André Spire* (Paris: Librairie Lipschutz, 1939).

HAMMEL, FRÉDÉRIC, *Souviens-toi d'Amalek: Témoignage sur la lutte des Juifs en France (1938–1944)* (Paris: CLKH, 1982).

HARRY, MYRIAM, *Les Amants de Sion* (Paris: A. Fayard, 1923).

HAUS, BRIGITTE, 'Les Artistes juifs de l'Ecole de Paris où la conquête de la liberté', *Archives juives*, 31/2 (1998), 42–60.

HAUS, JEFFREY, 'The Practical Dimensions of Ideology: French Judaism, Jewish Education and State in the Nineteenth Century', Ph.D. diss. (Waltham, Mass.: Brandeis University, 1997).

HERTZBERG, ARTHUR, *The French Enlightenment and the Jews* (New York: Columbia University Press, 1976).

HOFFMAN, ROBERT, *More Than a Trial: The Struggle over Captain Dreyfus* (New York: The Free Press, 1980).

HOMBERGER, ERIC, 'Some Uses for Jewish Ambivalence: Abraham Cahan and Michael Gold', in Bryan Cheyette (ed.), *Between 'Race' and Culture: Representations of 'the Jew' in English and American Literature* (Stanford: Stanford University Press, 1996).

'Hommage à Aimé Pallière', special issue of *Revue de la pensée juive*, 8 (July 1951).

'Hommage à Edmond Fleg', special issue of *Revue de la pensée juive*, 2 (Jan. 1950).

HYMAN, PAULA, *The Emancipation of the Jews of Alsace: Acculturation and Tradition in the Nineteenth Century* (New Haven: Yale University Press, 1991).

——*From Dreyfus to Vichy: The Remaking of French Jewry, 1906–1939* (New York: Columbia University Press, 1979).

——*Gender and Assimilation in Modern Jewish History* (Seattle: University of Washington Press, 1995).

——*The Jews of Modern France* (Berkeley: University of California Press, 1998).

——'Joseph Salvador: Proto-Zionist or Apologist for Assimilation?', *Jewish Social Studies*, 34/1 (1972), 1–22.

ISAAC, JULES, *Expériences de ma vie* (Paris: Calmann-Lévy, 1959).

IZOULET, JEAN, *Paris: Capitale des religions ou la mission d'Israël* (Paris: Albin Michel, 1926).

JARRASSÉ, DOMINIQUE, 'L'Eveil d'une critique d'art juive et le recours au "principe ethnique" dans une définition de l'"art juif"', *Archives juives*, 39/1 (2006), 63–75.

——*Une histoire des synagogues françaises: Entre Occident et Orient* (Paris: Hebraica, 1997).

JEAN-JAVAL, LILY, *L'Inquiète* (Paris: Plon, 1927).

——*Noémi: Roman d'une jeune fille juive en Pays Basque* (Paris: Plon, 1925).

JÉHOUDA, JOSUÉ, *Le Royaume de justice: Roman juif*, preface by André Spire (Paris: Editions du Monde Nouveau, 1923).

——*La Terre promise* (Paris: Rieder, 1925).

——*La Tragédie d'Israël*, 2 vols (Paris: Grasset); vol. i: *De père en fils* (1927); vol. ii: *Miriam* (1928).

——and Panaït Istrati, *La Famille Perlmutter* (Paris: Gallimard, 1927).

JESSULA, GEORGES, 'Armand Lunel: Homme de lettres', *Archives juives*, 39/1 (2006), 140–2.

JICK, LEON, *The Americanization of the Synagogue, 1820–1870* (Hanover: published for Brandeis University Press by the University Press of New England, 1976).

JOB, FRANÇOISE, 'Gédéon Geismar: Géneral de brigade', *Archives juives*, 39/1 (2006), 137–9.

JOSELIT, JENNA WEISSMAN, 'Against Ghettoism: A History of the Intercollegiate Menorah Association, 1906–1930', *American Jewish Archives Journal*, 30/2 (Nov. 1978), 133–54.

KADMI-COHEN, ISAAC, *Nomades: Essai sur l'âme juive*, preface by A. de Monzie (Paris: F. Alcan, 1929).

KAHN, GUSTAVE, *Contes juifs* (Paris: Fasquelle, 1926).

KASPI, ANDRÉ, *Les Juifs pendant l'Occupation* (Paris: Seuil, 1991).

KAUFMAN, DAVID, *Shul with a Pool: The Synagogue Center in American Jewish History* (Hanover: University Press of New England, 1999).

KESSEL, JOSEPH, *Les Cœurs purs* (Paris: Gallimard, 1927).

——*Terre d'amour* (Paris: Flammarion, 1927).

KISLEV [pseud. of Fernand Lévy-Wogue], *Contes de Hanouka* (Paris: Durlacher, 1922).

KOHN, HANS, *L'Humanisme juif: Quinze essais sur le Juif, le monde et Dieu* (Paris: Rieder, 1931).

KORELITZ, SETH, 'The Menorah Idea: From Religion to Culture, from Race to Ethnicity', *American Jewish History*, 85/1 (Mar. 1997), 75–100.

KSIAZENICER, CAROLE, and RACHEL ERTEL, *Une maisonnette au bord de la Vistule, et autres nouvelles du monde yiddish* (Paris: Albin Michel, 1989).

LACRETELLE, JACQUES DE, *Silbermann* (Paris: Gallimard, 1922).

LALOUM, JEAN, 'Les Juifs d'Afrique du Nord au Pletzl? Un présence méconnue et des épreuves oubliées (1920–1945)', *Archives juives*, 38/2 (2006), 47–83.

LANDAU, PHILIPPE, *Les Juifs de France et la Grande Guerre: Un patriotisme républicain 1914–1941* (Paris: Editions CNRS, 1999).

——*L'Opinion juive et l'affaire Dreyfus* (Paris: Albin Michel, 1995).

LANDEAU, L., 'Jules Isaac', in A. Chouraqui (ed.), *Contributions à l'histoire juive contemporaine*, vol. ii (Brussels: Editions de l'Institut de Sociologie de l'Université Libre de Bruxelles, 1965).

LE GOFF, JACQUES, and RENÉ RÉMOND (eds), *Histoire de la France religieuse*, 4 vols (Paris: Seuil, 1992).

LEBOVICS, HERMAN, *True France: The Wars Over Cultural Identity, 1900–1945* (Ithaca: Cornell University Press, 1992).

LECACHE, BERNARD, *Au pays des pogroms: Quand Israël meurt* (Paris: Progrès Civiques 1927)

——*Jacob* (Paris: Gallimard, 1925).

——*Les Porteurs de croix: Palestine 1929* (Paris: Edition des Portiques 1930).

——*Les Ressuscités* (Paris: Editions du Carrefour, 1934).

LEFF, LISA MOSES, *Sacred Bonds of Solidarity: The Rise of Jewish Internationalism in Nineteenth-Century France* (Stanford: Stanford University Press, 2006).

——'Self-Definition and Self-Defense: Jewish Racial Identity in Nineteenth-Century France', *Jewish History*, 19/1 (2005), 7–28.

LEHRMANN, CHARLES, *The Jewish Element in French Literature*, trans. George Klin (Madison, NJ: Fairleigh Dickinson University Press, 1971).

LEROY, GERALDI (ed.), *Les Ecrivains et l'affaire Dreyfus, actes du colloque organisé par le Centre C. Péguy et L'Université d'Orléans* (Paris: Presses Universitaires de France, 1983).

'Les Juifs et l'affaire Dreyfus', special issue of *Archives juives*, 27/1 (1994).

LEVENE, MARK, *War, Jews, and the New Europe: The Diplomacy of Lucien Wolf, 1914–1919* (Oxford: Oxford University Press, 1992).

LEVIGNE-NICAULT, CATHERINE, 'Le Mouvement sioniste en France des environs de 1880 à 1921', *Le Monde juif* (Apr.–May 1978), 137–53.

LÉVY, JACOB [pseud. of Gaston Edinger], *Les Juifs d'aujourd'hui*, 3 vols (Paris: Ferenczi); vol. i: *Les Pollaks* (1925); vol. ii: *Les Demi-Juifs* (1926); vol. iii: *Les Doubles-Juifs* (1927); published under the individual volume titles, together with *Les Chrétiens* (1928), in 1 vol. (Paris: Les Belles Lettres, 1999).

LÉVY, LOUIS-GERMAIN, *Une religion rationnelle et laïque: La Religion du vingtième siècle* (Dijon: Barbier Marilier, 1904; repr. Paris: E. Nourry, 1908).

LÉVY, SARAH, *O mon goye!* (Paris: Flammarion, 1929).

LEWISOHN, LUDWIG, *The Island Within* (New York: Harper & Bros, 1928).

LEYMARIE, MICHEL, 'Les Frères Tharaud: De l'ambiguïté du "filon juif" dans les années 1920', *Archives juives*, 39/1 (2006), 89–109.

LIPMAN-MOYSE, GABRIELLE, *Les Sanédrin* (Poligny: A. Jacquin, 1910).

LONDON, GÉO, *Lévy-Pendules* (Paris: Librairie des Champs-Elysées, 1929).

LOYRETTE, HENRI (ed.), *La Famille Halévy* (Paris: Librairie Arthème Fayard, 1996).

LUNEL, ARMAND, 'André Spire et notre génération', in *Hommage à André Spire* (Paris: Librairie Lipschutz, 1939).

——*Esther de Carpentras* (Paris: Gallimard, 1926).

——*L'Imagerie du cordier* (Paris: Gallimard, 1924).

——*Nicolo-Peccavi, ou l'affaire Dreyfus à Carpentras* (Paris: Gallimard, 1926).

MALINOVICH, NADIA, 'Between Universalism and Particularism: Redefining Jewish Identity in France, 1900–1932', *Historical Reflections/Réflexions historiques*, 32/2 (Spring 2006), 143–63.

——'"Orientalism" and the Construction of Jewish Identity in France, 1900–1932', *Jewish Culture and History*, 2/1 (Summer 1999), 1–25.

——'Race and the Construction of Jewish Identity in French and American Jewish Fiction of the 1920s', *Jewish History*, 19/1 (2005), 29–48.

——review of Gilbert Michlin, *Of No Interest to the Nation: A Jewish Family in France, 1925–1945*, H-France, 5/23 (July 2005), <www.h-france.net>.

——'Une expression du "Réveil juif" des années vingt: La Revue *Menorah* (1922–1933)', *Archives juives*, 37/1 (2004), 86–96.

MANDEL, ARNOLD, *Les Temps incertains* (Paris: Calmann-Lévy, 1950).

MANDEL, MAUD S., *In the Aftermath of Genocide: Armenians and Jews in Twentieth-Century France* (Chapel Hill, NC: Duke University Press, 2003).

MARRUS, MICHAEL, *The Politics of Assimilation: A Study of the French Jewish Community at the Time of the Dreyfus Affair* (Oxford: Clarendon Press, 1971).

——and Robert O. Paxton, *Vichy France and the Jews* (Stanford: Stanford University Press, 1995).

MARX, HENRY, *La Gloire intérieure* (Paris: Bernard Grasset, 1913).

MAYEUR, JEAN-MARIE, and MADELEINE REBÉRIOUX, *The Third Republic: From its Origins to the Great War, 1870–1914*, trans. J. R. Foster (Cambridge: Cambridge University Press, 1984).

MENDES-FLOHR, PAUL, *Divided Passions: Jewish Intellectuals and the Experience of Modernity* (Detroit: Wayne State University Press, 1991).

MERCER, LUCIEN, *Les Universités populaires: 1899–1914* (Paris: Editions Ouvrières, 1986).

MEYER, MICHAEL, *Response to Modernity: A History of the Reform Movement in Judaism* (New York: Oxford University Press, 1988).

MEYER-PLANTUREUX, CHANTAL, *Les Enfants de Shylock, ou l'antisémitisme sur scène* (Brussels: Editions Complexes, 2005).

——'Du Baron de Horn à Ezéchiel ou la "question juive" à la Comédie-Française dans les années vingt', *Archives juives*, 39/1 (2006), 76–88.

MICHEL, ALAIN, *Juifs, Français et Scouts: L'Histoire des E.I. de 1923 aux années 1990* (Jerusalem: Editions Elkana, 2003).

——'Qu'est-ce qu'un Scout juif?' L'Education juive chez les Eclaireurs Israélites de France de 1923 au début des années 1950', *Archives juives*, 35/2 (2002), 77–101.

MICHLIN, GILBERT, *Of No Interest to the Nation: A Jewish Family in France, 1925–1945* (Detroit: Wayne State University Press, 2004).

MILLMAN, RICHARD, *La Question juive entre les deux guerres: Ligues de droite et antisémitisme en France* (Paris: Armand Colin, 1992).

MOYSE, GABRIELLE, *Le Féminisme dans la Bible hébraïque* (Versailles: Lostanges-Meyssac, 1934).

——*Héroïnes bibliques, reines, prophétesses, guerrières* (Geneva: Editions Antar, 1917).

NAVON, A. H., *Joseph Pérez: Juif du ghetto* (Paris: Calmann-Lévy, 1925).

NÉMIROVSKY, IRÈNE, *David Golder* (Paris: Grasset, 1929).

——*Suite française*, preface by Myriam Anissimov (Paris: Firmin-Didot, 2004).

NICAULT, CATHERINE, 'L'Acculturation des Israélites français au sionisme après la Grand Guerre', *Archives juives*, 39/1 (2006), 9–28.

——*La France et le sionisme, 1897–1945: Une rencontre manquée?* (Paris: Calmann-Lévy, 1992).

——'L'Israélitisme au tournant du siècle: Remise en cause ou réaffirmation?', in Marie-Anne Matard-Bonucci (ed.), *Antisémythes: L'Image des Juifs entre culture et politique (1848–1939)* (Paris: Editions Nouveau Monde, 2003).

——'Yvonne Netter, avocate, militante féministe et sioniste', *Archives juives*, 30/1 (1997), 116–20.

NOVAK, DAVID, 'The Quest for the Jewish Jesus', *Modern Judaism*, 8/2 (1988), 119–38.

ORIOL, PHILIPPE, *Bernard Lazare* (Paris: Stock, 2003).

——(ed.) *Bernard Lazare: Anarchiste et nationaliste juif* (Paris: Honoré Champion, 1999).

ORY, P., and JEAN-FRANÇOIS SIRINELLI, *Les Intellectuels en France, de l'affaire Dreyfus à nos jours* (Paris: A. Collin, 1992).

PALLIÈRE, AIMÉ, *La Prière juive* (Paris: Cahiers de la 'Voix d'Israël', n.d.).

——*Le Sanctuaire inconnu: Ma 'conversion' au judaïsme*, foreword by Edmond Fleg (Paris: Rieder, 1926); English edn: *The Unknown Sanctuary: A Pilgrimage from Rome to Israel*, trans. Louise Waterman Wise (New York: Bloch, 1929).

PARAF, PIERRE, *Quand Israël aima* (Paris: La Renaissance du Livre, 1929).

——*Sous la terre de France* (Paris: Payot, 1917).

PASQUINI, PIERRE, 'Le Félibrige et ses traditions', *Ethnologie française*, 18/3 (1988), 257–66.

PÉGUY, CHARLES, *Notre jeunesse* (Paris: Ollendorff, 1910).

PERETZ, I. L., *Bontché le silencieux et autres contes juifs*, trans. Charles Boltz, preface by Pierre Mille (Paris: Mercure de France, 1914).

PIERRARD, PIERRE, *Juifs et catholiques français, de Drumont à Jules Isaac, 1886–1945* (Paris: Fayard, 1970).

POLDÈS, LÉO, *L'Eternel ghetto* (Paris: Editions Radot, 1928).

POLIAKOV, LÉON, *Histoire de l'antisémitisme*, vol. iv: *L'Europe suicidaire* (Paris: Calmann-Lévy, 1977).

POPPEL, STEPHEN, *Zionism in Germany 1897–1933: The Shaping of a Jewish Identity* (Philadelphia: Jewish Publication Society of America, 1977).

POUGATCH, ISAAC, *Un bâtisseur: Robert Gamzon, dit 'Castor Soucieux' 1905–1961* (Paris, Service Technique pour l'Education, 1971).

POUJOL, CATHERINE, *Aimé Pallière (1868–1949): Itinéraire d'un chrétien dans le judaïsme* (Paris: Desclée de Brouwer, 2003).

——'Aimé Pallière (1868–1949): Itinéraire d'un chrétien dans le judaïsme', Ph.D. diss., 3 vols (Paris: University of Paris I, 2002).

——'Autour du "cas" Pallière: Débats sur la conversion entre Juifs orthodoxes et libéraux', *Archives juives*, 35/1 (2002), 60–76.

——'Une exception dans la presse des mouvements de jeunesse: *Chalom* (1925–1935), véritable mensuel d'information', *Archives juives*, 36/1 (2003), 25–39.

PRAJS, LAZARE, *Péguy et Israël* (Paris: A. G. Nizet, 1970).

PROCHASSON, CHRISTOPHE, *Les Intellectuels, le socialisme et la guerre, 1900–1938* (Paris: Editions du Seuil, 1993).

PSICHARI, HENRIETTE, *Les Convertis de la belle époque* (Paris: Editions Rationalistes, 1972).

RABI [pseud. of Wladimir Rabinovitch], 'Aimé Pallière et notre futile jeunesse', *Revue de la pensée juive*, 8 (July 1951), 28–31.

——*Anatomie du judaïsme français* (Paris: Editions du Minuit, 1962).

——'André Spire', *Revue de la pensée juive*, 5 (1950), 22–41.

RÉBELLIAU, ALFRED (ed.), *Le 'Fait religieux' en France: Documents sur les églises* (Paris: Correspondances de l'Union Pour la Vérité, 1922).

REBSTOCK, ROGER, 'Aimé Pallière tel que je l'ai connu', *Revue de la pensée juive*, 8 (Jan. 1951), 22–7.

REECE, JACK, *Bretons against France: Ethnic Minority Nationalism in 20th-Century Brittany* (Chapel Hill: University of North Carolina Press, 1971).

REINACH, THÉODORE, *Histoire des Israélites depuis la ruine de leur indépendance nationale jusqu'à nos jours* (1885; 2nd edn, Paris: Hachette, 1901).

RHAÏS, ELISSA [pseud. of Rosine Boumedine], *Saâda la Marocaine* (Paris: Plon-Nourrit, 1919).

RODITI, E., 'Les Peintres russes de Montparnasse', in *Kikoïne* (Paris: Piazza, 1973).

RODRIGUE, ARON, 'Rearticulations of French Jewish Identities after the Dreyfus Affair', *Jewish Social Studies*, 2/3 (Spring/Summer 1996), 1–24.

ROLLAND, ROMAIN, *Jean Christophe* (Paris: Ollendorf, 1908–14).

ROUKHOMOVSKY, SUZANNE, *Gastronomie juive: Cuisine et pâtisserie de Russie, d'Alsace, de Roumanie et d'Orient* (Paris: Flammarion, 1929).

——*Palestine dernière heure* (Paris: Librairie Lipschutz, 1933).

RYVEL [pseud. of Raphaël Lévy], *L'Enfant de l'oukala et autres contes de la Hara*, preface by Pierre Hubic (Tunis: La Kahena, 1931).

——J. VEHEL, and V. DANON, *La Hara conte: Folklore judéo-tunisien* (Paris: Ivrit, 1929).

SAID, EDWARD, *Orientalism* (New York: Vintage Books, 1979).

SAMUËL, PIERRE, *Mon rabbin chez les riches* (Paris: Ferenczi, 1926).

SARNA, JONATHAN, *A Great Awakening: The Transformation that Shaped Twentieth-Century American Judaism and its Implications for Today*, CIJE Essay Series (New York: Council for Initiatives in Jewish Education, 1995).

——*JPS: The Americanization of Jewish Culture, 1888–1988* (Philadelphia: Jewish Publication Society of America, 1989).

SAVOIR, ALFRED, and FERNAND NOZIÈRE, *Le Baptême* (Paris: Librairie Théâtrale, 1908).

SCHECTER, RONALD, *Obstinate Hebrews: Representations of Jews in France, 1715–1815* (Berkeley: University of California Press, 2003).

SCHLOESSER, STEPHEN, *Jazz Age Catholicism: Mystic Modernism in Postwar Paris, 1919–1933* (Toronto: University of Toronto Press, 2005).

SCHOR, RALPH, *L'Antisémitisme en France pendant les années trente: Prélude à Vichy* (Brussels: Editions Complexe, 1992).

SCHWARTZ, SHULY, *The Emergence of Jewish Scholarship in America* (Cincinnati: Hebrew Union College Press, 1991).

SCHWARZFUCHS, SIMON, 'Les Débuts de la science du judaïsme en France', *Pardes*, 19–20 (1994), 204–15.

SCHWOB, RENÉ, *Moi Juif, livre posthume* (Paris: Les Petits Fils de Plon et Nourrit, 1928).

SEPINWALL, ALYSSA, *Abbé Grégoire and the French Revolution: The Making of Modern Universalism* (Berkeley: University of California Press, 2005).

SHTERNSHIS, ANNA, 'Jewish Theatrical Trials in the Soviet Union (1917–1941)', unpublished paper presented at the Association for Jewish Studies Conference (1999).

SHURKIN, MICHAEL R., 'Consistories and Contradictions: From the Old to the New Regime', *Historical Reflections/Réflexions historiques*, 32/1 (2006), 65–82.

SILVER, K. E., and R. GOLAN (eds), *The Circle of Montparnasse: Jewish Artists in Paris, 1905–1945* (New York: The Jewish Museum, 1985).

SILVERA, ALAIN, *Daniel Halévy and his Times* (Ithaca: Cornell University Press, 1966).

SILVERSTEIN, ALAN, *Alternatives to Assimilation: The Response of Reform Judaism to American Culture, 1840–1930* (Waltham, Mass.: Brandeis University Press, 1994).

SIMON-NAHUM, PERRINE, *La Cité investie: La 'Science du judaïsme' française et la République* (Paris: Cerf, 1991).

SOWERINE, CHARLES, France Since 1870: Culture, Politics and Society (New York: Palgrave, 2001).

——and CLAUDE MAIGNIEN, *Madeleine Pelletier: Une féministe dans l'arène politique* (Paris: Editions Ouvrières, 1992).

SPIRE, ANDRÉ, *Poèmes juifs* (Paris: Albin Michel, 1959); 1st published as *Versets; Et vous riez; Poèmes juifs* (Paris: Société du Mercure de France, 1908; enlarged edn, Geneva: Kundig, 1919).

——'Les Problèmes juifs dans la littérature', in Georges Guy-Grand (ed.), *La Renaissance religieuse* (Paris: Librairie Félix Alcan, 1928).

——*Quelques Juifs et Demi-Juifs*, 2 vols (Paris: Bernard Grasset, 1928): vol. i: *Quelques Juifs* (1st published Paris: Société du Mercure de France, 1913); vol. ii: *Quelques Juifs et Demi-Juifs.*

——*Souvenirs à bâtons rompus* (Paris: A. Michel, 1962).

STERNHELL, ZE'EV, *Maurice Barrès et le nationalisme français* (Paris: Presses de la Fondation Nationale Scientifique, 1972).

——*Neither Right Nor Left: Fascist Ideology in France* (Berkeley: University of California Press, 1986).

——'The Roots of Popular Antisemitism in the Third Republic', in Frances Malino and Bernard Wasserstein (eds), *The Jews in Modern France* (Hanover: University Press of New England, 1985).

STOCK, PHYLLIS, 'Students versus the University in Pre-World War I Paris', *French Historical Studies*, 7/1 (1971), 93–110.

STRAUSS, LAUREN B., 'Staying Afloat in the Melting Pot: Constructing an American Jewish Identity in the *Menorah Journal* of the 1920s', *American Jewish History*, 84/4 (1996), 315–31.

STRENSKI, IVAN, *Durkheim and the Jews of France* (Chicago: University of Chicago Press, 1997).

SZAJKOWSKI, ZOSA, *Jewish Education in France, 1789–1939*, Jewish Social Studies monograph series 2 (New York: Columbia University Press, 1980).

TCHERNOFF, JEHOUDA, *Dans le creuset des civilisations*, 4 vols (Paris: Rieder, 1936–8); vol. i: *De Nijni-Novgorod à Paris*; vol. ii: *Le Destin d'un émigré*; vol. iii:

De l'affaire Dreyfus au dimanche rouge à Saint-Pétersbourg; vol. iv: *Des prodromes du bolchévisme à une société des nations.*

THARAUD, JEAN, and JÉRÔME THARAUD, *L'Année prochaine à Jérusalem* (Paris: Plon-Nourrit, 1924).

——*L'Ombre de la croix* (Paris: Plon-Nourrit, 1917).

——*La Palestine* (Paris: Editions Alpina, 1930).

——*Petite histoire des Juifs* (Paris: Plon-Nourrit, 1927).

——*Quand Israël est roi* (Paris: Plon-Nourrit, 1924).

——*La Rose de Saron* (Paris: Plon-Nourrit, 1927).

——*Un royaume de Dieu* (Paris: Plon-Nourrit, 1920).

THIESSE, ANNE-MARIE, 'Le Mouvement littéraire régionaliste, 1900–1945', *Ethnologie française*, 18/3 (1988), 220–32.

TORRÈS, HENRY, *Le Procès des pogromes* (Paris: Editions de France, 1928).

TOURNY, O., 'Léon Algazi', *Archives juives*, 30/1 (1997), 103–5.

TREBITSCH, MICHEL, 'Les Intellectuels juifs en France dans les années vingt', *Combat pour la Diaspora*, 3 (1987), 43–57.

TWERSKY, MOÏSE, and PIERRE GUÉDY, *Israël à New York* (Paris: Les Œuvres Représentatives, 1931).

UDELSON, JOSEPH H., *Dreamer of the Ghetto: The Life and Works of Israel Zangwill* (Tuscaloosa: University of Alabama Press, 1990).

Université Populaire Juive, *Compte rendu annuel et statuts* (Paris: N. L. Danzig, 1904).

UROFSKY, MELVIN, *American Zionism from Herzl to the Holocaust* (New York: Doubleday, 1976).

VALBERT, GÉRARD, *Albert Cohen, le seigneur* (Paris: B. Grasset, 1990).

WEBER, EUGENE, *France: Fin de siècle* (Cambridge, Mass.: Harvard University Press, 1986).

——*The Hollow Years: France in the 1930s* (New York: Norton, 1994).

WEILL, JULIEN, *La Foi d'Israël: Essai sur la doctrine du judaïsme* (Paris: Presses Universitaires de France, 1926).

——*Le Judaïsme* (Paris: Librairie Félix Alcan, 1931).

——*Zadoc Kahn* (Paris: Félix Alcan, 1912).

WIGODER, GEOFFREY, *Dictionary of Jewish Biography* (Jerusalem: Jerusalem Publishing Company, 1991).

WILSON, NELLY, *Bernard Lazare: Antisemitism in France and the Problem of Jewish Identity in Late Nineteenth-Century France* (Cambridge: Cambridge University Press, 1978).

WILSON, STEPHEN, *Ideology and Experience: Antisemitism in France at the Time of the Dreyfus Affair* (Rutherford, NJ: Fairleigh Dickinson University Press, 1982).

WINOCK, MICHAEL, *La France et les Juifs, de 1789 à nos jours* (Paris: Seuil, 2004).

WISTRICH, ROBERT, *Between Redemption and Perdition: Modern Antisemitism and Jewish Identity* (London: Routledge, 1990).

WRIGHT, GORDON, *France in Modern Times: 1760 to the Present*, 4th edn (New York: W. W. Norton, 1987).

ZANGWILL, ISRAEL, *Dreamers of the Ghetto* (New York: Harper & Bros., 1898).

ZAOUI, ANDRÉ, 'Un grand serviteur de Dieu', *Revue de la pensée juive*, 8 (July 1951), 3–14.

Index

*In alphabetizing the names of French publications and institutions the
initial definite article has been ignored.*

Printed and bound by CPI Group (UK) Ltd, Croydon, CR0 4YY

13/04/2025

14656576-0005